International Business and Government Relations in the 21st Century

This book offers an outlook on relations between national governments and multinational companies that provides broad coverage of the key issues likely to determine that relationship in the new century. From the perspective of the company decision maker concerned with national regulation and incentive policies, to the host government policymaker in an emerging market, to the home government policymaker in a Triad country, each dimension is considered and analyzed in light of the others. As well, additional stakeholders such as labor groups, shareholders, non-governmental organizations, local governments, and regional organizations are discussed and their impacts on the relationship are evaluated.

ROBERT GROSSE is Professor of International Business and Director of CIBER at Thunderbird, The Garvin School of International Management.

International Business and Government Relations in the 21st Century

EDITED BY ROBERT GROSSE

CAMBRIDGE
UNIVERSITY PRESS

CAMBRIDGE UNIVERSITY PRESS
Cambridge, New York, Melbourne, Madrid, Cape Town, Singapore, São Paulo

CAMBRIDGE UNIVERSITY PRESS
The Edinburgh Building, Cambridge CB2 2RU, UK

Published in the United States of America by Cambridge University Press, New York

www.cambridge.org
Information on this title: www.cambridge.org/9780521850025

First published 2005

Printed in the United Kingdom at the University Press, Cambridge

A catalogue record for this book is available from the British Library

ISBN-13 978-0-521-85002-5 hardback
ISBN-10 0-521-85002-9 hardback

Contents

List of figures   page viii

List of tables   ix

List of contributors   xi

Acknowledgments   xii

Introduction
Robert Grosse   1

Part I: History and theories of analysis of international
business–government relations   23

1   Early US business-school literature (1960–1975) on
    international business–government relations:
    its twenty-first-century relevance
    Jean Boddewyn   25

2   Institutional reform, foreign direct investment,
    and European transition economies
    John Dunning   49

3   Corporate governance in the global economy:
    international convergence or continuing diversity?
    Lee E. Preston   79

4   Revisiting rival states: beyond the triangle?
    John Stopford   103

Part II: The shifting international business–government
partnership   117

5   Foreign direct investment and government policy
    in Central and Eastern Europe
    Klaus E. Meyer and Camilla Jensen   119

6 Global warming and climate change: new issues
   for business strategy, government policy, and research
   on business–government relations
   Thomas L. Brewer   147

7 Business–government relations in the cultural industry:
   the evolution of the government's role in Korea
   Dong-Sung Cho and Wijin Park   171

8 Multinational enterprise, public authority, and public
   responsibility: the case of Talisman Energy and
   human rights in Sudan
   Stephen J. Kobrin   191

9 Direct private foreign investment in developing
   countries – the judo trick
   Paul Streeten   217

Part III: Bargaining theory and the obsolescing bargain   249

10 From the obsolescing bargain to the political
    bargaining model
    *Lorraine Eden, Stefanie Lenway, and Douglas
    A. Schuler*   251

11 The bargaining view of government–business
    relations
    Robert Grosse   273

12 Shifts of Chinese government policies on inbound
    foreign direct investment
    Yadong Luo   291

13 Has the obsolescing bargain obsolesced? Negotiating
    with foreign investors
    Alvin G. Wint   315

**Part IV: Host and home government views of international
business   339**

14 Global regulatory convergence: the case of intellectual
    property rights
    Ravi Ramamurti   341

15 Regional multinationals and government policy:
the end of global strategy and multilateralism
Alan M. Rugman   361

16 How will third world countries welcome foreign
direct investment in the twenty-first century?
Stefan H. Robock   381

17 Assessing government policies for business
competitiveness in emerging market economies: an
institutional approach
Dennis A. Rondinelli   395

18 Protecting foreign investors in the developing world:
a shift in US policy in the 1990s?
Louis T. Wells   421

Conclusions
Robert Grosse   463

References   475

Select bibliography of J. N. Behrman's works   507

Index   511

Figures

2.1 Host country determinants of FDI   *page* 54
2.2 Push and pull factors and institutional measures
    attracting FDI   56
2.3 Assessing the features and impact of FDI: a flow chart   58
3.1 Conventional corporate governance model   85
3.2 An expanded view of corporate governance   87
5.1 A process perspective on privatization acquisitions   132
6.1 Trends and projections of global warming   159
7.1 The firm in society – general framework   174
7.2 The firm in Korean society   174
7.3 A framework for analyzing business–government
    relations   180
7.4 A historic review of business–government relations:
    a global picture   181
7.5 Empirical test of the evolution of overall industrial
    policies in Korea   182
7.6 Evolution of the Korean government's role in the
    cultural industry   187
7.7 Market share of Korean movies   189
11.1 Host government–foreign MNE relations   277
11.2 The bargaining relationship between MNE and
     host government   281
14.1 Levels of MNC–government relations   344
17.1 Institutional attributes of market economies   402

Tables

2.1	Indicator's scores for selected institution-related variables in the EIU Business Ranking Model (i) 1998–2002 (ii) 2003–2007	*page* 68
2.2	Business environment scores for transition economies (TEs), India, and China (i) 1998–2002 (ii) 2003–2007	71
2.3	Business environment rankings (BER), FDI per capita, and GDP per capita for ten transition economies (i) 1998–2002 (ii) 2003–2007	74
Appendix 2.1	Business environment rankings for ten transition economies for (i) 1998–2002 and (ii) 2003–2007	77
3.1	Comparison of systems of corporate governance	91
3.2	Factors contributing to convergence/divergence	95
5.1	FDI and institutional development, 2001	124
5.2	Investment rules and legislation in individual CEE countries	126
5.3	Overview of regular incentive schemes offered in Eastern Europe	139
6.1	Sources of carbon dioxide emissions	160
6.2	Economic and insured losses from natural catastrophes	161
7.1	Multivariate test results	185
7.2	Univariate test results	185
7.3	Multiple comparisons	186
10.1	From an obsolescing bargain to a political bargaining model of MNE–state relations	270
13.1	Investment disputes registered with ICSID: 1966–2003	320
13.2	Sectors represented among completed and pending ICSID cases (%)	322
15.1	Intra-regional trade in the Triad, 1980–2000	368
15.2	The top twenty-five home region-based companies	371

15.3   Classification of the top 500 MNEs   373
15.4   US consumption of petroleum, by country of origin, 2001   375
15.5   US petroleum imports   376
17.1   Institutional framework for assessing country
         business climate   418
17.2   TNC country selection matrix   419

Contributors

Jean Boddewyn, Baruch College (CUNY)

Thomas L. Brewer, Georgetown University

Dong-Sung Cho, Seoul National University

John Dunning, Rutgers/Reading University

Lorraine Eden, Texas A&M University

Robert Grosse, Thunderbird, The Garvin School of International Management

Camilla Jensen, Copenhagen Business School

Stephen J. Kobrin, Wharton School, University of Pennsylvania

Stefanie Lenway, University of Minnesota

Yadong Luo, University of Miami

Klaus Meyer, Copenhagen Business School

Wijin Park, Director, Ministry of Culture, South Korea

Lee E. Preston, University of Maryland

Ravi Ramamurti, Northeastern University

Stefan H. Robock, Columbia University

Dennis A. Rondinelli, University of North Carolina

Alan M. Rugman, Indiana University

Douglas A. Schuler, Rice University

John Stopford, London Business School

Paul Streeten, American University

Louis T. Wells, Harvard Business School

Alvin G. Wint, University of the West Indies

Acknowledgments

This book was written in honor of Jack N. Behrman, long-time Professor of International Business at the University of North Carolina and pioneer in the field of international business. His writings on international business–government relations began in the 1950s, and he focused more on this issue than any of the other leaders of the field at that time. His insights into problems such as international licensing of technology, multinational firms and the balance of payments, multilateral regulation of multinational firms, multinationals and US interests, and the large theme of the legitimacy of the multinational enterprise have identified central problems and possible solutions in government–business relations that remain valuable in the debates today.

The book was an attempt to bring together many of the leaders in thinking about international business–government relations from the past forty years, and to explore the direction of these relations in the new century. Authors were asked to prepare papers that would look conceptually at what they considered to be major issues today, and to analyze them in a forward-looking manner such that their conclusions might provide guidance to managers and policymakers in the new century. The papers were presented in a conference at Thunderbird in Arizona on January 5, 2004. Although two of the authors were unable to attend, the rest spent a day of debate and reflection on issues ranging from the obsolescing bargain to the problems of firms dealing with multiple jurisdictions and pressure groups with different agendas. What emerged was a consensus that the subject is alive and well in the academic arena – and a hope that new decision makers might be able to learn from and avoid some of the mistakes of their predecessors, about whom we have written in the past.

We would like to thank Jack N. Behrman for his contributions to the field of international business, and especially his contributions to the understanding of international business–government relations. His participation in the conference at which these papers were presented added a very valuable dimension to the discussions, and it was a wonderful opportunity for colleagues to share our appreciation with him. To illustrate the scope of his contributions, a separate listing of selected publications of Jack N. Behrman on government–business relations is included in the reference section of this book.

The editor would also like to thank several people at Thunderbird who helped in making the conference and the book a success. Tania Marcinkowski and Marie Gant, CIBER Assistant Directors, both made great efforts in putting together the conference, interacting with the authors, tracking down both logistical details as well as bibliographic ones, and adding their suggestions to improve the whole process. Graduate assistants Tamara Bennett, Eric Grimmer, Yanfang Lei, and Santiago Martello provided excellent research assistance. And Thunderbird, The Garvin School of International Management, provided major financial support for the whole project.

Introduction

ROBERT GROSSE

T HIS book takes some initial steps into the twenty-first-century discussion of relations between national governments and multinational firms. This is the issue that defines international business (IB), since business that crosses national boundaries must necessarily deal with at least two national governments. As a result of the necessary interactions, there may be conflict or congruence between two governments' policies or between governments and multinational firms. Differences in policies or interests can often require mediation of some sort, resulting in the establishment of new rules on the relations of companies with home and host governments. Even if policies are mutually supportive between home and host governments, disagreements may arise over the distribution of benefits from company activities such as foreign direct investment (FDI), and thus produce conflicts that must be resolved.

Much of the recent literature on *international* business–government relations has emphasized the more cooperative, accommodative relationship that has arisen between governments that want to pursue economic growth and development, and companies that want access to markets or to production inputs. This is quite a shift from the situation during the 1960s through the 1980s, when many governments were reluctant to permit entry of foreign firms or imposed major constraints on their operations. Even so, this new more welcoming attitude is not the only feature of the relationship that matters today. For example, the issue of environmental protection is one increasingly important element in present and future relations that has potential for very serious conflict between companies and governments. Also, national governments are increasingly facing regulatory competition from local governments and from transnational organizations such as the European Union and the Free Trade Area of the Americas (FTAA). This fact means that national governments have to deal with these additional regulatory stakeholders at the same time as they deal directly with the companies.

The range of cooperative and conflictive relations between governments and multinational enterprises (MNEs) covers quite a wide scope. Some of the more conflictive issues in recent years include situations where national governments want:

- to achieve economic growth, but they are not as positive about foreign (firms') ownership of parts of the local economy;
- development of technology and skills, but not necessarily dependence on foreign provision of these key underpinnings of competitiveness;
- economic development, but without the environmental damage or social conflict that foreign (and local) firms might cause;
- the opportunity for local citizens to enjoy products and services from around the world, but still to maintain a national or local culture and values;
- their sovereignty to pursue national interests, when the increasingly global economy often forces supra-national goals on them.

These are not simple problems to resolve, and they will remain as part of the constellation of concerns between governments and international firms in the years ahead. Our interest is to illuminate the main facets of government–international business relations in the early twenty-first century, and to help government policymakers and company managers improve their ability to make decisions in this context.

Conceptual bases

A number of writers in recent years have offered conceptual tools to help understand the relationships between companies and governments. The authors in this volume have been the leaders in exploring the relations between *international* firms and national governments. In addition, very useful insights have been developed by authors in a variety of social science disciplines. For example, the literature broadly called Institutional Theory has developed in political science, sociology, anthropology, and economics. Each discipline shines a somewhat different light on relations between firms and governments, again mainly with a focus on domestic firms and governments.

One line of institutional theory has its roots in sociology, emphasizing the behavior of the firm as mirroring societal norms and traditions. This view of the firm as part of a broader institutional context (Oliver, 1991;

Powell and DiMaggio, 1991) emphasizes the limits of rational maximizing behavior in the light of pressures from other institutional participants.[1] This perspective opens the analysis to consider organizational behaviors (e.g., follow-the-leader behavior between firms; cultural differences between MNEs deriving from differences among their societies of origin) from a sociological point of view. This line of reasoning has not been applied to the issue of the relation of multinational firms with national governments, though it certainly has been used in analyzing the multinational firm more broadly (e.g., Westney, 1993).

A second line of institutional theory comes from economics. The New Institutional Economics, particularly as framed by Oliver Williamson (1975), opens the way to examine transaction costs as a central element in economic organization. Williamson identified three types of transaction cost problems – information impactedness, bounded rationality, and opportunistic behavior. To deal with each of these problems, firms are organized to internalize the costs (and benefits) of information-sharing; firms pool risk for individuals who are limited by imperfect knowledge of the alternatives available to pursue; and firms constrain individuals to pursue goals that support the whole organization's purpose rather than goals that may reduce overall welfare by raising costs to others while the individual benefits.

At the international level, these transactions costs have been explored by a number of international business authors, including Rugman (1981), Teece (1981, 1993), and Hennart (1982). Rugman and Hennart, among others, have focused on the internalization of external activities by multinational firms as the linchpin of their reasoning. In none of these cases are government–business relations a central concern, though Dunning (who also emphasizes internalization in his theorizing) has pursued specifically the international business–government relationship in his extension of his eclectic model (Dunning, 1997).

---

[1] "This perspective emphasizes the ways in which action is structured and order made possible by shared systems of rules that both constrain the inclination and capacity of actors to optimize as well as privilege some groups whose interests are secured by prevailing rewards and sanctions" (Powell and DiMaggio, 1991, p. 11).

A third line of institutional theory comes from political science (March and Olsen, 1984) and emphasizes the hierarchy of relationships from governments to companies to individuals. This point of view opens the analysis to consider such things as the bargaining relationship between governments and companies, and the need for the firm to respond to demands of pro-labor and pro-environment groups, among others.

The political-science-based view of Hall and Soskice (2001) has received extensive comments in the past few years. They argue that capitalist economies are quite varied in their institutions and their relationships between firms and between firms and governments. They trace two major categories of countries, following either the US–UK model (liberal), or the German–Nordic model (coordinated). Countries in the former category tend to use markets (contracts) to resolve such issues as wages, forms of collaboration between companies, and corporate governance issues. These countries tend to have weak collaborations between companies and with government. Countries in the latter category (coordinated) tend to use inter-group cooperation between firms and between companies and employees to resolve those same issues. These latter countries tend to have much stronger forms of collaboration between companies (e.g., *keiretsu* or similar groupings) and with government (e.g., greater amount of shared economic planning).

Hall and Soskice then argue that the institutions that characterize each set of countries have pervasive differences that tend to support firms that operate in ways that are consistent with those institutions. Inter-firm collaboration is much more acceptable in coordinated economies; while such collaboration is frequently subject to anti-trust policy in the liberal economies. At the level of international business, their argument could be extended to treatment of foreign multinational firms, possibly reasoning that firms from other similar (liberal or coordinated) countries would have greater success in dealing with the government of the host country. Their argument could be extended to explore the kinds of incentive policy and tax treatment that could be expected in different countries. In sum, the perspective offers the potential for exploration at the international level, but it has not yet been pursued in that context.

The present volume offers a variety of conceptual perspectives on the relations between national governments and multinational firms, without any one being central to all of the analyses. Several of the chapters do use a bargaining model of these relations, based on Vernon's obsolescing bargain, or Stopford and Strange's tripartite relationship, or Behrman and Grosse's three-dimensional bargaining model. The bargaining models are not overarching views of the corporation or of the organization of economic activity, but rather they are tools to help understand the specific context of dealings between national governments and international firms. Each of these bargaining approaches is discussed below, along with the other conceptual approaches that are used to describe and understand the relationship between MNEs and governments.

Approaches to these relations in the chapters below come from the academic areas of business strategy, organizational theory, economics, and international business – and each develops conceptual views of the government–business relationship, rather than testing hypotheses through the use of new empirical evidence. The full set of analyses then are useful in looking at international business–government relations, by offering a multifaceted understanding of how each side can or should deal more successfully with the other.

An overview of the analyses

The book is divided into four parts:
1. History and theories of analysis of international business–government relations
2. The shifting international business–government partnership
3. Bargaining theory and the obsolescing bargain
4. Host and home government views of international business

The first takes a purely conceptual approach, looking at the last four decades of research on the subject and reviewing the perspectives that have been brought to bear on the international business–government relationship. The second part takes up the current context in which relations between firms and governments have become more positive, with each side looking for ways to work successfully with the other, rather than being antagonistic. The third part looks at a number of aspects of the bargaining view of IB/government relations, originating from Vernon's (1971) idea of an obsolescing bargain, and proceeding on to present patterns. The final part looks at the government view, both home and host.

Part I: History and theories of analysis of international business–government relations

The first chapter lays out an initial overview of theoretical perspectives on government–business relations (from authors such as Hymer, Behrman, Fayerweather, and Vernon). The second looks at the changing relationship in transition economies, based on an institutional theory framework and specifically looking at direct investment decisions. The third takes a broader stakeholder point of view and considers the question of corporate governance. The fourth brings the earlier Stopford and Strange perspective forward into twenty-first-century relations.

Jean Boddewyn's study reflects on the contributions of Behrman, Fayerweather, and Robinson to the understanding of government–international business relations in the 1950s and 1960s. They wrote numerous analyses of the impact of governments on company activities and decisions, of the risks to companies in dealing with (foreign) governments, and of the interactions between multinational companies and governments. In that period the relations tended to be relatively conflictive, in the sense that governments and companies tended to view their interests as different. Their interactions could have qualified as either accommodating or protective, but seldom collaborative. Boddewyn traces the intellectual tradition established by these early leaders in the field, and shows how their work led to subsequent analyses such as the Stopford and Strange view that appears later in this section.

Boddewyn points out that none of the early writers developed an overarching theory of international business–government relations, but that Fayerweather came closest to doing so. According to Fayerweather,

The two processes of "resource transmission" and "relations with host societies" are "interconnected" and constitute "the distinctive aspects of an international business as distinguished from a domestic one." They result, on the one hand, in "mutually beneficial, constructive activities for both the multinational firm and the interests of the affected nations" and, on the other hand, in "elements of conflict related to the confrontation of the interests of the firm with different national interests and nationalistic attitudes." These transmissions, relations and conflicts in individual foreign countries lead toward "a fragmented, diversified pattern of policies and activities [that] weakens the effectiveness of the multi-national corporation whose unique potentials vis-à-vis local national firms lie largely in its unified, global capabilities. The achievement of balance between fragmentation and unification therefore composes the final element in the conceptual framework." (1969, p. 12)

Boddewyn concludes that the groundwork had been laid in the 1960s and early 1970s for the understanding that we have today of the multi-faceted relationships between international companies and home/host governments.

The chapter by John Dunning presents a view of the importance of government in the process of foreign direct investment (FDI), and the institutional (government-related) factors that encourage or discourage FDI. This view is then explored with empirical evidence as presented in several recent studies by other authors, and applied specifically to policies and practices in the formerly communist countries of Central and Eastern Europe. Dunning's interest is to evaluate the importance of institutions and of institutional reforms in attracting direct investment. His conceptual base is founded on institutional theory, as proposed by North (1990), in the context of a set of countries where major institutional change took place during the 1990s, namely the "transition economies." The key questions are whether and how institutions affect FDI. Dunning concludes that more transparent institutions and policy liberalization lead to increased FDI.

Lee Preston next takes on the question of *legitimacy* of the international firm from the perspective of host societies. His concern is with the ability of firms to achieve sufficient acceptance by governments so that they can pursue their corporate goals in harmony with societal goals. He says that "the issues involved can be best understood as aspects of *corporate governance*, which includes both the pattern of enterprise ownership (including state ownership) and the ways in which ownership, regulation, and other bases of control are utilized to legitimate the corporation as an institution and direct/restrict its activities."

Preston reviews a number of analyses of corporate governance, toward the goal of identifying trends of convergence among countries. He believes that the German model, with a managerial board and a separate oversight board, is the model around which governance rules are coalescing.[2] If this is true, then governments need to establish

---

[2] There is certainly not a consensus of opinion on this issue. A number of authors argue that convergence is not occurring, while others maintain that convergence is occurring on the US model (e.g., Sundaram et al., 2000).

policies that foster constructive collaboration between corporations and the various relevant stakeholders with whom they interact.

John Stopford's chapter revises his earlier analysis of the triangular relationship among international companies and governments (i.e., between company and government, between two companies, and between two governments) (Stopford and Strange, 1992). He argues that the end of the Cold War changed the global political structure, and the internet age changed the global economic structure, such that a new triangle of interactions is needed to think about government–business relations. Stopford's new triangle includes: (1) the balance of power between States, but particularly between any other State and the one remaining superpower, the USA; (2) the balance of power between markets and States; and (3) the balance of power between individuals and States.

This new set of dimensions reflects the changed reality of the twenty-first century, and puts government–business relations into a context in which both sides are embedded in webs of stakeholders – the firms with strategic alliance partners, among other stakeholders, and the governments in regional blocs as well as with sub-national jurisdictions and pressure groups. Decision making by both national governments and multinational companies now must take into account these added complexities to pursue their goals. For example, companies face "reputational risk" in that their activities in one country (e.g., manufacturing there and causing pollution or allowing substandard working conditions) may be used by pressure groups in another country to try to influence company behavior and/or government regulation. The terms of reference have expanded in a world that is more and more integrated, and decreasingly divided.

Part II: *the shifting international business–government partnership*

This part presents a series of analyses of particular industries and countries, in each instance focusing on the evolving relationship of host countries with foreign multinationals, as political conditions, technology, and competitive conditions change over time. While the general trend toward less confrontational relations is evident in the 1990s, more recently government policies and company positions have moved from accommodation to conflict and back as conditions have changed.

Klaus Meyer and Camilla Jensen explore how the efforts of governments in the formerly communist countries of Central and Eastern Europe to deal with the problems of economic development have led to greater or lesser success. They compare country experiences in three categories of transition from command to market economy, and they demonstrate how greater direct investment flows have occurred under conditions of greater liberalization. They also compare company experiences with acquisitions versus greenfield investments, showing that greenfield investments tend to have greater bargaining power relative to the host government than do acquisitions of existing firms, especially acquisitions of state-owned firms.

For FDI that takes place through *acquisition*, the foreign firm's key concerns have related to bargaining with government authorities and their ability to restructure formerly state-owned enterprises to reduce inefficiencies. Over time, foreign investors increasingly are acquiring private firms, thus reducing the intensity of their interaction with the authorities.[3] Foreign investors pursuing *greenfield* entry have more degrees of freedom with respect to their intra-country location choices. This gives them greater bargaining power vis-à-vis localities (states, counties, cities, etc.), and the opportunity to take advantage of special incentives in Special Economic Zones and industrial parks.

Thomas Brewer focuses on the problem of global warming, an issue that is increasingly salient in government–MNE relations. Global warming is responsible for a variety of changes in the economic and political environment of firms. His study focuses not only on the relationship between host governments and foreign multinationals, but more generally on the issues of business–government relations that have ensued from it.

For instance, the European Union has created an Emissions Trading Scheme that imposes greenhouse gas emission targets on more than 10,000 individual establishments throughout the EU and establishes a system for trading emission allowances. Other issues of business–government relations involve regulations on auto emissions, which require auto and energy firms' responses, subsidies for use of renewable energy sources and the development of alternative-fuel vehicles, and

---

[3] Even so, when buying a recently privatized firm, direct investors may face very significant restructuring needs, to shed the legacy of a firm once run as a socialist enterprise.

carbon taxes. One of the striking features of the emerging regulatory regimes for the mitigation of climate change is the extent to which the US national government has been isolated from developments in the rest of the world, and the extent to which many US-based firms have lagged behind their industry rivals in responding to these new issues.

The chapter by Dong-Sung Cho and Wijin Park looks at the relationship between the national government and foreign film producers (e.g., Warner Brothers, Fox, Paramount) in Korea. This analysis is much in the spirit of the stakeholder analysis of Preston and the three-dimensional model of Stopford, in that Cho and Park show that the dealings between the foreign movie companies and the Korean government during 1959 to 2002 reflect the interests and bargaining power of the government and companies, plus the interaction of each of them with the local Korean film producers. That is, the relationship is tripartite, grouping local competitors, foreign competitors, and the government in the bargaining context.

Cho and Park suggest a four-way range in which governments play a role in regulating/subsidizing company activities. Their categories – laissez-faire, mercantilism, constitutionalism, and paternalism – show that Korean government policy toward business overall has followed a sequence through these four archetypes in the past half-century. A government will take one of these four positions, depending on domestic political and social conditions. The impact on foreign companies will consequently be more restrictive (especially under the paternalist type of policy regime) or more accommodating (especially under a mercantilist system). They illustrate these relations with the case of the movie industry in Korea, in which the government's role since 1945 has moved through the sequence of laissez-faire, constitutionalist, and, most recently, paternalist.

This analysis is somewhat unique in its focus on a "cultural industry," namely film production and distribution. This kind of industry is one that anti-globalization partisans have raised as examples that should be protected from foreign firms and products to maintain national (or ethnic) cultures. The trade-off between protecting domestic firms versus allowing domestic consumers access to globally accepted products/services is striking. And the evolution of the Korean government's policy in the movie industry shows the influences of industry competitors, domestic pressure groups, and also external factors such as the government's need to impress the outside world at the time of the 1988 Seoul Olympics. Cho and Park conclude that international firms need to understand the full context in which the government and its policies operate in order to establish successful bargaining strategies for dealing with the government.

Stephen J. Kobrin uses the example of a legal case involving a Canadian company's subsidiary in the Sudan to illuminate the issue of multinational corporation responsibility for human rights. This case is significant because it involves a company from one country (Canada) being accused in the court of a second country (USA) of involvement in acts undertaken by the government of a third country (Sudan). It illustrates the reality that multinational firms are today being held accountable for social responsibility worldwide, whether or not a local government chooses or is able to enforce that responsibility.

The case of Talisman company presents a situation in which the company is sued by a non-government organization (NGO) in a US court, seeking damages for the firm's subsidiary's failure to intervene in the Sudan to stop human rights abuses by the government of that country. In simplest terms, Talisman's operation of oil production in the Sudan generated massive income for the government, which used that income to pursue a civil war and grave human rights violations against non-Muslim inhabitants of the southern part of the country. Talisman was charged with being complicit in perpetrating the violations. This is far removed from traditional host-government–MNE interactions, and in fact it shows how law and responsibility of MNEs are evolving toward global norms today. Kobrin's analysis provides a broad perspective on this problem.

Kobrin's chapter raises new issues, much as the company has in the legal case. The issues fall under the broad rubric of corporate legitimacy, as raised earlier by Preston and indirectly by Brewer. The MNE, whether it chooses or not, is acting as one of the direct participants in international relations, and it must take on the challenges and responsibilities of acting in that sphere in the twenty-first century.

Paul Streeten takes a broad view of direct investment in emerging markets, and looks for ways for governments to channel MNEs in directions desired for public policy. He calls for two new forms of partnership. First, he argues in favor of a new emphasis on public–private alliances, especially between host country governments in emerging markets and foreign MNEs. He reasons that a form of collaboration in which each partner owns about half of such a venture, particularly in agricultural businesses, would foster increased FDI due to greater credibility of the investment rules, and would push for greater transfer of skills and knowledge in this resource sector. The reasons for failure of such policies in the past are largely related to governments' lack of trust in MNEs, and their consequent unwillingness to work collaboratively with them.

Second, Streeten also argues for the promotion of alliances between the formal and informal sectors in emerging markets, in the form of large-scale foreign firms working in alliance with informal and/or small local firms as suppliers of various inputs. This would enable the host country firms to perform a "judo trick" in enticing the large foreign firms to utilize small, flexible, local, formal, or informal firms in a kind of outsourcing that would help transfer knowledge, skills, and financial benefits to the locals. Emerging market governments thus can foster the use of MNEs' own activities and motivations as leverage to direct the companies in desired directions. When the government–business relationship is seen as a partnership, this judo trick is a natural outcome.

Part III: *bargaining theory and the obsolescing bargain*

The most widely studied view of bargaining between multinational firms and national governments remains Vernon's obsolescing bargain concept. Vernon used the term "obsolescing bargain" to refer to the situation in emerging markets when a foreign MNE would enter and set up local operations. The logic is that, before entry, the firm has very strong bargaining power, because the government wants what the firm can offer (e.g., jobs and income, exports, technology transfer), while the firm has little or nothing at risk. Once the firm agrees to invest and sets up a facility, then it has assets that can be held hostage by the host government, so that the bargaining power shifts toward the government, while the bargaining position of the company obsolesces. Numerous studies have investigated the ways in which government–MNE bargains have evolved, in light of Vernon's idea. In this section, the first two papers present conceptual updates on the bargaining model, and the last two papers use empirical evidence to support the view that there is continued value in applying a bargaining view to understand government–business relations.

The chapter by Lorraine Eden, Stefanie Lenway, and Doug Schuler argues that Vernon's idea needs updating, and they present a "political bargaining model" of government–business relations. Their model emphasizes the time dimension and the iterative nature of the bargaining relationship, stressing political as well as economic aspects. They recognize that today the relationship is far more collaborative and less restrictive than at the time of Vernon's writing, so their political bargaining model does not lead to obsolescence of the company's bargaining position. But they conclude that Vernon's essential insight – "that bargaining processes and outcomes depend on the parties' goals, resources, and constraints" – remains accurate, and they proceed to build their model on that foundation. Hence, Eden, Lenway, and Schuler's model asserts that:

MNEs and nation-states engage in political bargaining over a government policy that affects either the MNE directly or the industry of which it is a part. In the negotiations (which can include lobbying), the MNE seeks legitimacy and higher economic profits, and offers, in return for more favorable policies, improved access to the MNE's own non-location-bound resources (FSAs). The host government, as part of the policy negotiations, offers the MNE improved access to its location-bound resources (CSAs). The valuation each party places on the other's resources determines its potential bargaining power.

They cite a range of empirical studies that have tested the bargaining model, and conclude that the conditions present today fit into their model much better than into Vernon's original model, which implied greater conflict in the relationship.

Robert Grosse follows with a parallel effort to build a model of the bargaining relationship to reflect the twenty-first-century conditions. He builds on a framework by Behrman and Grosse (1990), which identifies a three-dimensional relationship between governments and MNEs. Bargaining strength can be evaluated based on the relative resources held by each party; on what is at stake for each of them in the given bargaining context; and on how similar their interests are. The framework is expanded to account for changing contextual conditions over time, principally changing macroeconomic conditions (booms and recessions) and changing competitive conditions (e.g., introduction of new technologies).

Grosse uses examples of host government–MNE relations that developed in three cases – banking in the US and in Mexico during the 1980s and 1990s; oil in Ecuador during 1995 to 2003; and computers in

Brazil during 1978 to 1995. In all three situations the bargaining positions changed, due largely to macroeconomic conditions in the particular country. A major recession or financial crisis led to greatly increased bargaining power for the companies in that situation, though company interest in the given country often declined significantly during the time of the crisis. Thus, a bargaining model of government–business relations must offer some mechanism for bringing in the dynamic features of the macroeconomy in order to offer lessons useful in either company strategy or government policy. Grosse proposes a two-stage model to evaluate the bargaining situation, beginning with the macroeconomic environment and then moving onto the second step of comparing bargaining resources, stakes, and interests between company and government.

Grosse's view is quite consistent with that of Eden, Lenway, and Schuler, with the difference that Grosse focuses on the dynamics that routinely change the bargaining capabilities of the firm or the government, while those authors focus on showing why the bargaining position of the company does not necessarily obsolesce. These two initial essays in this part then lead to two more detailed empirical examinations of the bargaining between host governments in China and Jamaica and foreign multinational firms in those countries.

Yadong Luo examines the shifting bargaining relationship between China's government and foreign multinationals. He makes the case that China's policy has been changed unilaterally since its opening to FDI in 1979. The altered conditions include policies that shift from:
1. entry intervention to operational interference;
2. separation from domestic policies to convergence with domestic policies;
3. overt control to covert intervention;
4. regulatory homogeneity to regulatory heterogeneity;
5. policy rigidity to treatment elasticity.

Luo's chapter examines each of these government policy changes in some detail, suggesting why the changes have occurred and recommending strategy responses for companies. It traces the recent history of China's economic development and thus shows why a more collaborative environment now exists between foreign firms and the Chinese government. The picture painted by Luo puts distinct changes into a coherent whole, in which Chinese policy is placing foreign enterprises on an increasingly similar footing with domestic private enterprises. However, his report that regulation has in a number of cases become less transparent and more "covert" casts some doubt on the view that China's government really is moving toward a Western Europe or North American level of policy openness.

Alvin Wint pursues a similar tracing of the bargaining relationship between foreign multinationals and the national government of another emerging market, Jamaica. He poses the initial question of whether or not the post-Cold War conditions that have led to greater cooperation between governments and foreign companies have made the obsolescing bargain model itself obsolescent. He then draws on a progression of bargaining situations between Jamaica's government and foreign multinationals in the 1960s, 1980s, and early 2000s. The results of this historical progression do show a greater degree of government–company cooperation, but also a continuing need to consider the bargaining goals and power of the two sides in order to understand regulation that occurs.

Wint's three cases are: (1) tax arrangements between the Jamaican government and foreign aluminum companies in the 1960s; (2) a telecommunications agreement with Cable & Wireless at the time of privatization of the Jamaican telephone system in 1988; and (3) rules on electric power provision at the time of privatization of the Jamaican electricity system in 2001. He shows the progression of the bargaining relationship in the bauxite/aluminum sector, in which company bargaining power did obsolesce in the 1970s. The telecom agreement in which Cable & Wireless became the sole operator of Jamaica's privatized telephone system led to monopoly power and practices by the company. This situation was altered after a long legal process that ultimately opened up the system to competition, for internet service as well as various forms of telephony. The bargain clearly obsolesced – but the reasons were more similar to the reasons for deregulating telecommunications around the world than to the specific situation of this company in Jamaica. And finally, the privatization of the electric power company, Jamaica Public Service, had progressed only to the point of the initial bargain between Jamaica's government and the Mirant company (Southern Electric), so that an evaluation of obsolescence was not yet possible.

Wint's key point in reviewing these three bargains is that some industries will continue to present characteristics similar to those of the extractive industries that were so clearly subject to obsolescing bargains in the 1960s and 1970s. The infrastructure sectors such as telecommunications and electric power provision are two of these. The more recent history of the telecom industry in Jamaica shows a weakened company position after the initial entry bargain, but the reasons for this shift in bargaining power have more to do with competition and technology change than with the hostage effect of fixed investment in the host country. Wint argues that the key element of the obsolescing bargain is the transactional relationship between company and government. When the transaction conditions change, both sides need to be willing to alter the agreement, just as with alliances between companies. Viewed in this way, the obsolescing bargain model has plenty of life left in it.

Part IV: host and home government views of international business

This final part emphasizes both home and host perspectives on government–MNE relations in emerging markets.

Ravi Ramamurti uses the example of Pfizer's efforts to generate a global agreement on intellectual property protection in the pharmaceuticals industry to show how some issues have produced a globalization of policy toward (multinational) firms. In this instance, he notes that the conditions for this shift of policymaking venue, from national governments to the World Trade Organization's TRIPS (trade-related intellectual property) level, were highly specific to the industry, the company, and the times. Even so, the result is a model that may well spread to other sectors as a part of globalization. Ramamurti explores the process through which a US-based MNE, Pfizer, was able to put together a sufficient alliance among companies and national governments that an accord was reached to help protect the drug companies' proprietary pharmaceuticals.

Alan Rugman extends his earlier argument about the regional[4] nature of MNEs, in which he asserts that they are not global but rather almost all focused on their home region of the Triad (European Union, North America, and Asia). He offers a counterpoint to Ramamurti's

---

[4] "Regional" in this context means multicountry in a geographic region of the world. The Triad regions include: the European Union, North America, and Japan plus a handful of Asian Tigers.

study of global regulatory harmonization, by showing how regional government policies are rapidly coming to the fore in regulation of MNEs as well as in other applications. The European Union has created a monetary union and is in the process of establishing a regional constitution. The North American Free Trade Area is in the process of expanding to include all of the Americas, enlarging that Triad region and establishing regional policies that relate to MNE activities there. Asian countries are formalizing shared policies toward business through multiple associations including ASEAN (Association of South East Asian Nations) and APEC (Asia-Pacific Economic Cooperation). In sum, the regionalization of government policy toward multinationals is becoming part of the context in which these firms operate today. Rugman's chapter discusses the reasons why and ways in which national governments can be expected to pursue regional policy harmonization to support their regional economic blocs.

Of course, not all policies are becoming regionalized. In fact, local jurisdiction policies (in individual cities and individual provinces or states within a country) are also recognized as a key part of the government–business interaction in many countries. Still, Rugman demonstrates that a large body of policy relevant to MNEs is taking shape at the regional level, so that MNEs need to take this new level of government relations into account in their strategies.

Stefan Robock writes that emerging market governments, from the less developed Latin American and Asian countries to the transition economies of Central and Eastern Europe, have become more pragmatic and less ideological in their dealings with foreign MNEs since the era of confrontation in the 1970s. He draws on his experience as an advisor (frequently through the United Nations) to a number of national governments in those regions. Robock's central conclusion is that the more collaborative relations between these emerging market host governments and the foreign MNEs from the Triad countries are a reality, and that firms can build their strategies and government–relations policies on that basis. For example, there is no longer need to worry about expropriation of affiliates, but there are still areas of conflict between host governments and foreign firms that must be managed.

Robock identifies a handful of government characteristics that need to be dealt with by MNEs operating in emerging markets in the early 2000s. These characteristics include: ideologies and nationalism, concern for national security, development strategies, negotiation muscle and experience, incentive policies, controls on (foreign) firms, and the degree of pragmatism. He uses examples of each of these characteristics to demonstrate how the government–business relationship in emerging markets has evolved in recent years. While the general tendency of these relations is positive and trending toward more collaborative interactions, there still remain some serious concerns. According to Robock: "probably the major uncertainty in international and host country relations is the anti-globalization movement and the international disagreements in the area of international trade." Some differences are seen as intractable, remaining without solution and requiring repeated renegotiation.

Dennis Rondinelli argues that foreign MNEs need to use an institutional approach to evaluate the attractiveness of emerging markets for direct investments or other international business operations, expanding on the views of several others in this volume. He does not directly take the government's point of view, but rather approaches the question from the perspective that the firms need to evaluate a country's institutions in making commitments of capital and knowledge, and thus governments need to offer an environment that is sufficiently attractive to firms to entice them to provide these flows of capital and knowledge.

Rondinelli's ultimate step in the evaluation of government institutional characteristics is to provide a matrix of features and rankings, similar to country risk ratings that are offered by various organizations (e.g., Political Risk Services; Euromoney). The specifics of his matrix may be subject to debate, but the basic idea of trying to evaluate institutional strengths and weaknesses as they may affect company activities is certainly useful. This perspective offers one more tool for thinking about the government–business relationship, particularly in emerging markets.

Louis Wells examines the position of the home government of investors, focusing on the issue of how home governments offer protection to their MNEs for their activities in emerging markets. He traces the history of US support or lack of support for its firms' activities in emerging markets since the Second World War. The initial period reflected Cold War realities, when US firms rarely received support when their assets were taken (expropriated) by emerging market governments. This, even though the United States had tools that could force compensation "or else." The "or else" included loss of US foreign aid and other support.

Since then, US policy has shifted largely from State Department resistance to helping US investors to Commerce Department-led support for US firms in their dealings with emerging market governments. The new model reflects the lack of ideological enemies such as existed during the Cold War period. Wells sees the new support as threatened, if the war on terrorism leads to new concerns about angering countries that are viewed as critical in the fight against this new threat to global stability.

Conclusions

The set of studies in this volume offer a comprehensive view of international business–government relations moving into the early twenty-first century. It cannot be said that there is a convergence within these views of the relationship, but the models and perspectives presented here do offer a wealth of understanding of this phenomenon that will serve policymakers and company decision makers well.

The studies presented here do not pretend to offer a conclusive view of international business–government relationships, given the multidimensional reality of such dealings and the many levels of investigation that are possible to use in studying these phenomena. Also, the studies in most cases focus on dealings between governments in emerging markets and companies from the US, Western Europe, and Japan. There is plenty of room for further analysis from different perspectives and with greater emphasis on the current geographic focus of MNE activities, which clearly is in the Triad countries (e.g., Rugman, 2004).

PART I

History and theories of analysis of international business–government relations

1 Early US business-school literature (1960–1975) on international business–government relations: its twenty-first-century relevance

JEAN BODDEWYN

R OBERT M ERTON once remarked that "[the sociologist] has ample reasons to study the works of Weber, Durkheim and Simmel and, for that matter, to turn back occasionally to the works of a Hobbes, Rousseau, Condorcet or Saint Simon ... Previously unretrieved information is still there to be usefully employed as new points of departure" (1967, pp. 34 and 37).

His exhortation certainly applies to international business–government relations (IBGR), but who still reads Jack Behrman, Richard D. Robinson, and John Fayerweather who wrote expertly and at length on this topic? For that matter, who has even heard of them among the younger generation of IBGR scholars? The late Raymond Vernon and Charles Kindleberger (partly on account of Hymer's thesis) have fared better in this regard, but why has this happened?

One could speculate that the relevant and cumulative knowledge of the past (here defined as 1960 to 1975) has been substantially incorporated in subsequent formulations, so that the above authors need no longer be read and cited since many textbooks on international business, marketing, finance, management, and strategy now include sections and even chapters on the structures and roles of governments as well as on negotiating with them.

Besides, the search for relevance in teaching and research has dictated a focus on current phenomena, institutions, and developments – such as globalization, the North American Free Trade Association (NAFTA), and the World Trade Organization (WTO) – which far surpass in size and scope those analyzed by scholars of the 1960s and 1970s. Multinational enterprises (MNEs) were duly examined by them, but the multinationals of their times had not yet achieved the reach, impact, and organizational complexity of current ones. So what is still relevant in these pioneering authors as we move into the twenty-first century?

The scope of this analysis

I will focus on four early contributors, besides Jack Behrman for whom this *Festschrift* was composed: Raymond Vernon (Harvard), Charles Kindleberger (MIT), Franklin Root (Wharton), and John Fayerweather (NYU) who were all affiliated with US business schools. My justification for this limited scope is that they contributed most of the IBGR terminology and conceptualization which have remained in use to this day – particularly, the MNE as a new institution, political vulnerability and risk, the obsolescing bargain, the investment climate, legitimacy, confrontation and accommodation, and the resolution of conflicts between national and corporate interests.

Most research then centered on public policies toward inward and outward foreign direct investments (FDI) and the latter's impacts on balances of payments and other economic targets, but not on international business–government relations (IBGR). My five authors borrowed issues, facts, and ideas from scores of economists and public-policymakers in the United States, Canada, the United Kingdom, Australia, France, and various developing countries.[1] Their unique contributions lie in: (1) focusing on MNE–government relationships in the context of the emergence of the multinational enterprises as a new institution and of the novel responses they required of national governments, and (2) crystallizing new concepts and partial theories that have anchored the study of international business–government relations ever since.

---

[1] John Dunning, who contributed significantly to the study of foreign production after 1958, drew my attention to US and foreign scholars whose analyses were frequently used by the five authors highlighted in this chapter. Safarian studied the impact of foreign ownership in Canadian industry (1966) and Brash did the same for Australia (also in 1966); Litvak and Maule analyzed the experience of host countries (1970); Mikesell studied US investments abroad (1962), and Servan-Schreiber's *The American Challenge* (1968) stirred controversies about the invasion of Europe by US MNEs. Many more names could be cited – Hufbauer and Adler, Gilpin and Lall, among others – as well as various publications of the National Industrial Conference Board. John Dunning edited a book titled *The Multinational Enterprise* (1971) which included a chapter by Jack Behrman.

Most of these conceptual and theoretical developments took place between 1960 and 1975 – a period which sits roughly between David Lilienthal's 1960 proclamation of the advent of "the multinational corporation" and the 1975 Praeger publication of the proceedings of the first conference centered on IBGR: P. M. Boarman and Hans Schollhammer's edited work *Multinational Corporations and Governments*. The concluding section of this chapter refers to some contemporary and later authors that deserve further attention. I will now characterize and outline these five pioneers' approaches and contributions.

Their days and their ways

In the *first* place, they conducted their research, issued diagnostics, and advanced remedies in a period which Fayerweather labeled "an era of confrontation" between governments and MNEs. The Suez Canal had been expropriated in 1963 after an abortive war, and multiple confiscations had taken place in Latin America (including Cuba after 1959) and Africa. Toward the end of this era, there were the 1971 Chilean expropriations (including the fateful one of International Telephone and Telegraph) and the war-related engagements between OPEC and major foreign oil companies in 1973. The Japanese had already developed their cautious if not hostile engagement with foreign investors, which would last to these days and inspire other governments (e.g., those in South Korea and Malaysia).

Second, they argued that governments do matter, that we must understand why and how, and that the problems of negotiating with them face all international traders and investors to some extent. This may sound obvious but it had to be proven then, and there are still many studies of MNEs today that rely on organizational economics (transaction-costs and agency theories, the resource-based view, etc.) and its extreme focus on economic markets, as if nonmarket actors – particularly governments – did not exist or matter. Recent references to "stateless corporations" in the case of virtual companies foster the notion that governments have become less important, while new conceptualizations of the firm – domestic and international – in terms of "knowledge" reveal the continuous tendency to search for universal and location-free interpretations.

Third, several of these pioneers had served in government positions in the Second World War or thereafter, and this experience imparted relevance to their writings. They did not have to rely exclusively on secondary sources to enumerate the benefits and problems associated with the General Agreement on Tariffs and Trade (GATT), the Marshall Plan, the Organization for Economic Cooperation and Development (OECD), the Alliance for Progress, the United Nations' (UN) attempts at codes of conduct for multinationals, and other major institutional developments. Today, such experienced voices are largely missing about how governmental organizations work, succeed, and fail.

Fourth, their defenses and criticisms of governments and multinationals were often founded on having advised one or both sides. They testified before Congress, wrote position papers, and inveighed all over the place. Richard Robinson, Ray Vernon, and Charles Kindleberger were particularly vocal, but Jack Behrman went as far as practically resigning from his position as Assistant Secretary of Commerce when President Kennedy imposed voluntary capital restraints on US FDI, which Jack thought to be misguided and ultimately ineffective.

Fifth, they relied mostly on personal interviews with hundreds of companies at home and abroad. This methodological approach was usually facilitated by their degrees from, and appointments in, prestigious schools (Harvard, MIT, Princeton, Columbia, Yale, etc.), which opened many doors to their inquiries, while funding was relatively ample then (e.g., from the Ford Foundation). Good secondary data were largely missing at the time, and some of our authors (e.g., Ray Vernon) remained skeptical about the relevance and validity of most mail surveys to study important issues. Jack Behrman generated the first balance-of-payments data on licensing and other intellectual-property flows among developed countries. Many of them wrote cases based on their own field research, which provided elements for the emergence of a broader conceptualization of international business and its management, as was done by John Fayerweather (see below).

Sixth, they were extremely well read – keeping in mind that publications were less abundant then. They knew each other's works and drew facts and ideas from them, even though they did not try to develop a theory of IBGR. They quoted the then young John Dunning (on US investment in the UK), Franklin Root (on political risk), Yair Aharoni (on the foreign direct investment decision process) and John Stopford (on the organizational structures of MNEs).

John Fayerweather was probably the most informed of them all since he read practically everything related to international business on account of his editing the quarterly publication, *The International*

Executive, which included reviews and an extensive bibliography. (For excerpts, see his self-published compilation of selected reviews, *International Business Policy and Administration* [1976], which included a section on "International business–government affairs" and one on "Relations with host societies.")

Seventh, most of them were economists, and their first appointments and writings were based on that discipline, *which provided the basis for their analyses*. However, John Fayerweather was an engineer who got a DCS degree from Harvard when a business education was rare, while Richard Robinson had a PhD in management, economic development and international politics, which informed his scholarship and views.

Eighth, they all wrote books to express their findings and thoughts. Apart from the *Harvard Business Review*, there were no major business and international-business journals in which to publish about IBGR until the middle of this period: *Management International Review* dates from 1960, the *Columbia Journal of World Business* started in 1965 and the *Journal of International Business Studies* appeared in 1969 (Ashok Kapoor's article on negotiating with the Indian government was the leading article in its inaugural issue – he was, like Robert Grosse, a doctoral student of Jack Behrman). Thus, Robinson's 1964 book *International Business Policy* acknowledged partial publication in then popular university-based journals such as the *Boston University Business Review* and the *Oregon Business Review*.

Who remembers that Howard Perlmutter's first version of his famous ethnocentric–polycentric–geocentric distinction appeared in the then influential *Quarterly Journal of AIESEC International* in 1967? Also very receptive to IB research and thinking were *MSU Business Topics*, *Worldwide P&I Planning*, *Business International* (Elliott Haynes), *The McKinsey Quarterly*, and the publishing arm (AMACOM) of the American Management Association.

Ninth, the books they wrote were aimed more at the general reader than at business-school faculty audiences, and their textbooks fitted mostly case-oriented schools. Gordon and Howell's 1959 study *Higher Education for Business* made no mention of international business, and political science and political economy never became significant parts of business doctoral programs. Compared to other functional areas, international-management (IM) courses took a while to emerge, and they have not achieved any standardization of contents to this day – as has been the case with international business, economics and marketing

texts – so that IBGR has received varying degrees of attention, elaboration, and sophistication in IM courses and textbooks.

The remainders of their days

Any selection of their non-obsolescent ideas is bound to be subjective in
the light of one's research interests and connections. I was hired by
John Fayerweather at New York University after writing my dissertation on business political behavior at the University of Washington's
business school where "business and its environment" was a thriving
area. I worked with him at NYU from 1964 to 1973, and he was my
"mentor" – if this expression had been current then and if this modest
man had accepted such an accolade. So, here are my views.

The rise of the MNE in relation to governments

We take the MNE for granted, but it was a striking novelty for them.
Several traced their emergence or "rise" to the late 1950s and early 1960s,
so that they were "present at the occasion." Jack Behrman, in particular,
wrote volumes about this new phenomenon, but they all used their field
interviews and secondary data to examine the contours, innards, and
avatars of this novel elephant. They wrote extensively about the differences between the "multinational enterprise," passive "foreign portfolio
investment" and the "international holding company" that usually controlled active but uncoordinated foreign operations designed to serve
local markets – particularly, in manufacturing. They also analyzed
extractive industries but shied away from services. A late definition by
Jack Behrman captures the nature of the new MNE phenomenon:

> The purpose of the ME [multinational enterprise] is to serve the world market
> by investing wherever in the world it can [in order] to achieve the most efficient
> (i.e., least cost) operation. Thus the ME is integrating affiliates both horizontally
> and vertically (rationalizing its operations) to reduce costs, diversify product
> lines, and gain as much of the market for its products as possible. (1974, p. 6)

Not bad for a thirty-year-old definition, but that is the point – namely,
that these researchers had succeeded in differentiating the new player in
international markets. But why did they devote so much effort to its
definition and analysis? This is where international business–government
relations enters the picture.

On the one hand, *they were afraid that governments at home and abroad would keep applying or devising inappropriate policies and regulations because they did not understand the new MNE's objectives and needs* – particularly, regarding the necessary centralization and coordination of its far-flung but now interconnected subsidiaries and home-country operations. Therefore, the nature, structure, and functioning of the MNE had to be explained in great detail – just as Chris Bartlett and Sumantra Ghoshal did when they defined their new "transnationals." In particular, Jack Behrman discussed this issue in his 1971 book *US International Business and Governments*.

On the other hand, these early students realized that, wittingly or not, *the new MNE would generate conflicts with home and host governments*. Richard Robinson unveiled this threat in his 1964 book, *International Business Policy*, which a business executive called "subversive." Robinson argued that most MNE projects did not take national interests sufficiently into consideration and were therefore vulnerable to nationalization and expropriation in less-developed countries and to severe restrictions on their operations in developed ones (see below). Jack Behrman gave an apt interpretation of this permanent "love–hate" relationship which he linked to "legitimacy" – a new IBGR concept then:

The multinational enterprise is in a quite different position as to both legitimacy and responsibility. It derives its legitimacy from no single government but from a [legal] convention that provides that one government shall give to foreign enterprises the same "national treatment" it extends to domestic enterprises. But this legitimacy is extended *only* to the affiliate – *not* to the parent company itself, nor to its decisions. In addition, the idea that "responsible action" provides legitimacy and that the parent company can gain legitimacy by being a "good corporate citizen" is not parallel to the same concepts within an economy. The group or entity to which the foreign-owned affiliate is ultimately responsible is *not* a person within the host country, but an artificial person in the form of a foreign corporation. The multinational enterprise, therefore, raises anew the old problems of the legitimacy of economic power and its responsible use, but this time in a more complex setting – one of nation-states that are being pulled both toward internationalism and away from it by recurrent nationalism (1970, p. 5).

Many things have changed since their definitions were written. Thus, "globalization" has been proclaimed, denied, and attacked intellectually, morally, and physically – and so has "the end of the nation-state." A communication and logistics revolution has taken place, together with the internet and global outsourcing. Tax and corporate havens as well as international strategic alliances, mergers, and acquisitions have multiplied in number and sophistication, and the roles and relationships of subsidiaries vis-à-vis headquarters and each other have significantly changed and become more complex.

Yet, IBGR scholars of today can still learn a lot about the nature of the multinational enterprise and its inevitable confrontations with governments by reading these early authors whose profound understanding of this momentous development remains unsurpassed today when the MNE is taken for granted and much research attention has shifted to "global," "transnational," "metanational," and "stateless" variations.

Political vulnerability and risk

Any economic historian could tell us that risk has always existed in business–government relations, that it takes varying forms from country to country, and that crossing borders magnifies this risk when two or more governments are involved. What our pioneers did was to articulate this risk in its modern forms in the context of newly independent political regimes in scores of former colonies and of the postwar predilection of governments in many developed and developing countries for planning their economy. Both developments brought up the issue of how multinationals would cope with "national interests" in the light of their own "corporate interests."

Political vulnerability
Richard Robinson offered in his 1964 book an extensive analysis of this topic that has remained unmatched to this day in terms of the multiple criteria he developed regarding the accommodation of national interests by MNEs. They ranged from macro impacts on a country's net national value added to the size of a foreign investment in relation to the total economy of the host society, and they included his then famous list of twelve criteria of "product vulnerability" – starting with: "Is the product ever the subject of important political debates in relation to adequacy of supply [e.g., gasoline]?" His conclusions were very categorical:

[If] management cannot justify a project and its participation in it in terms of all [of these] criteria, then it should restructure that project in respect to employment of resources, ownership, control, management, profits and fees, or personnel. If the project still does not measure up, the firm should refrain from involvement. (1964, p. 144)

Some readers may object to these generalizations on the ground that a large percentage of international investment – in the traditional financial sense – would be ruled out. That is precisely the point. It is the author's conclusion that the choice of projects by Western business in general and the manner in which business relates itself to many of these projects (ownership, control, management, personnel) threatens to set up a massive conflict of interest between the developed industrial states of the West and nonindustrial societies of the non-West. (1964, p. 145)

His prediction was on target since nationalizations and expropriations kept multiplying, but it became less relevant after the "era of confrontation" ended in the 1970s and as governments came to recognize that national interests had to include a recognition of the benefits of internationalism and of their bearers, the MNEs. This issue is still alive today in the new context of "globalization and its discontents."

Political risks

Robinson's political-vulnerability criteria were absolute and relatively quantifiable but "political risk" put probability into the picture. Franklin Root pointed out that the most critical features of the future "investment climate" (a new concept then) are political in nature but these climates will change. Hence, "because the future is uncertain, management's assessment of prospective political behavior in the host country can be expressed at most in probabilistic terms" (1987, pp. 126, 129 – based on his 1968 *MSU Business Topics* article on political risks [pp. 73–80]). Root also introduced the felicitous combination of "market opportunities and political risks" that provided the basis for many studies of business political behavior because international firms can also exploit situations of "political opportunities and market threats" and other permutations.

Ever since, a sizeable academic literature (e.g., by Stephen Kobrin and Stefan Robock)[2] and a consulting industry (e.g., F.T. Haner's

---

[2] S.H. Robock's "Political Risk: Identification and Assessment" was published in 1971 in the *Columbia Journal of World Business* (July–August, pp. 6–20). He and Kenneth Simmonds published the first international-management textbook to incorporate a large section on IBGR and to go

BERI and Business International) have analyzed political risks in terms of: (1) whether they center on ownership or operations; (2) whether firm-specific political risks are more relevant than general ones applying to either the entire economy or exclusively to foreign direct investments; and (3) what indices of political instability are most useful. These issues would not be as intelligently debated today if our early writers had not put them firmly on the agenda of IBGR researchers.

The obsolescing bargain

Raymond Vernon never claimed full credit for coining this long-lasting concept and theory whose antecedents can be found in earlier writings by Robinson, Fayerweather, Behrman, and others, but he added it to the IBGR lexicon by clearly articulating the following arguments.[3]

Without fundamentally altering their economic system (as in Cuba in 1960), host governments have continued to nationalize and expropriate *selected* foreign-owned enterprises while leaving others alone. This has been possible because, from the moment an investment is made, the foreign investor's bargaining position begins to deteriorate on account of his investment's sunk costs which cannot be readily recovered. Besides, the locals eventually learn the relevant technologies and how to manage the projects, while the foreign investor cannot always guarantee access to foreign markets for his products. Moreover, changes in the international markets for capital, technology, and management services have increased the options of host countries in some industries (e.g., oil) and have allowed them to bargain earlier and harder with their ensconced and trapped foreign investors. As the bases for the original bargain erode, these investors are likely to face increasing pressures from the host government for a renegotiation or renunciation of the "bargain's" terms, all the way to nationalizations and expropriations. In Oliver Williamson's future terms, international "transaction-specific" investments were very vulnerable.

through several editions: *International Business and Multinational Enterprise.*
[3] Vernon (1971) has a section (pp. 46–53) entitled "The Obsolescing Bargain" (a topic not listed in its Index!) but a more explicit discussion can be found in Vernon (1980), pp. 281–286. This chapter also applies the obsolescing-bargain model to manufacturing and to developed countries, thereby reaching beyond his original focus on extractive industries in developing countries. See also Vernon (1968).

The implications of this new situation were that: (1) foreign investors would have to expect frequent renegotiations, even with friendly governments; (2) their control of foreign subsidiaries would be impeded by requirements for joint ventures, management contracts, import and export quotas, and co-production agreements; and (3) these firms could retain ownership, control, and large profits only if they could renew their competitive advantages (e.g., with new technologies and products, access to larger markets, and the value of their brands).

Another contribution of Vernon's argument was that it made the behaviors of host governments appear *rational* – instead of interpreting them in terms of irrational nationalistic impulses or the greed-based caprices of political leaders in underdeveloped countries. The obsolescing-bargain model has been extensively tested as well as extended by a variety of researchers, including Louis T. Wells, Jr., and Stephen Kobrin, and it promises to remain a key concept in the understanding and treatment of international business–government relations.

Sovereignty at bay

This much quoted title of Ray Vernon's major work is an opaque one never explicitly defined in his book subtitled *The Multinational Spread of US Enterprises* (1971) in order to make the point that, despite the above difficulties, the overall position of MNEs in the world economy, including the developing countries, had kept growing in the postwar period. Yet, his *opus magnum* remains eminently readable because Ray was a superb author "writing with his accustomed verve and lucidity," as the book's blurb said.[4] His message was not fundamentally different from that of Jack Behrman whose research was supported by Ray's project, but it was couched in more "reasonable" terms – full of "on the one hand and the other," "it is fair to conclude," "if we use different assumptions" (e.g., that multinationals did not exist) and plain "we don't know."

What did "sovereignty at bay" mean? The opening line (p. 3) is: "Suddenly, it seems, the sovereign states are feeling naked [vis-à-vis multinationals]." The key word here is "seems" because Vernon keeps

---

[4] Vernon's book was based on the rich data provided by Harvard's Multinational Enterprise Project that started in 1965, focused on 187 US films and drew from a huge variety of primary and secondary sources.

returning to the importance of *perceptions* by host governments, local elites, and intelligentsias:

As long as governments feel that they need those resources of foreign subsidiaries, they are likely to be vulnerable. And being vulnerable, they will continue experiencing the discomfiture that foreign-owned enterprises have so commonly produced. (p. 247)

The crux is to be found in the inherent nature of the multinational enterprise, as the leaders in the host countries see it. These enterprises draw their special strengths from the ability and opportunity to think in terms that extend beyond any single country and to use resources that are located in more than one jurisdiction. These characteristics are seen as posing a threat for government leaders bent on control, for local businessmen who aspire to compete, and for intellectuals who are hoping to challenge the status quo. (p. 265)

Now, it is governments that are feeling vulnerable – a situation generating *tensions* (a favorite concept of Behrman and Vernon) that will endure as long as these perceptions last, so that satisfying national interests will not suffice:

The question of whether US-controlled enterprises have generated tension [in host countries] ... is not to be confused with the question of whether they contributed to the welfare of those countries, however "welfare" may be defined. Tension, it should hardly be necessary to point out, is just as commonly associated with constructive forces as with those that make a negative contribution. (p. 25)

Forever the skeptic, Ray Vernon was implicitly challenging Richard Robinson's strongly held view that MNEs had to satisfy all national interests. Assume that these firms have complied with all major government requests to improve their behaviors (e.g., regarding balance-of-payments effects, transfer pricing and fair conduct):

Would these measures be enough to eliminate the problems generated by multinational enterprises, as seen by those they confront? The answer is clearly no. The capability of multinational enterprises to exercise flexibility and choice would still seem oppressive in the eyes of many that had to deal with them. (pp. 231–232).

In other words, *sovereignty is at bay because MNEs seem to have more options than home and host governments – and this situation is likely to persist.* Vernon made few explicit recommendations regarding international business–government relations, apart from reporting that his respondents thought that pitching one government against another created too much ill will and retaliation (p. 262).

Although Vernon remains vulnerable to being misquoted about the meaning of "sovereignty at bay" – particularly, that governments had lost control over MNEs and would "fade away" – it remains a critical reading because of its informed and balanced analysis of "thrusts" and "responses" on the part of MNEs and governments.[5]

Kindleberger on governments

Kindleberger was an economist rooted in the study of economic development, including its historical and political aspects. He claimed at the outset of his 1969 book *American Business Abroad* that it "is heavily weighted on the economics of the question" and will "only note when political issues of power, prestige, independence, neocolonial status, domination, and the like are brought into the debate" (p. vi). That was quite some "note" because he inveighed repeatedly against "sentiments."

While other early authors had identified national and corporate interests and weighed their merits and possible reconciliation, Kindleberger challenged them head on by arguing that one cannot conclude anything about the desirability of the MNE which can be simultaneously a monopolist through foreign takeovers, a perfector of markets' efficiency through competition, and a creator of imperfect markets for goods and factors of production – the latter, his memorable translation of Stephen Hymer's 1960 dissertation argument:

[In] a world of perfect competition for goods and factors, direct investment cannot exist. In these conditions, domestic firms would have an advantage over foreign firms in the proximity of their operations to their decision-making centers, so that no firm could survive in foreign operations. For direct investment to thrive there must be some imperfection in markets for goods or factors, including among the latter technology, or some interference in competition by government or by firms, which separates markets. (Kindleberger, 1969, p. 13)

---

[5] In his last book, Vernon (1998) tried to dispel the notion that nation-states and MNEs were destined to become obsolete.

In facing this conundrum, governments usually have no inkling of what they are doing or should be doing. The following quote illustrates Kindleberger's marvelous (at times, self-deprecatory) wit, which even surpasses Ray Vernon's dry humor:

> Anyone like me who argues that governments are composed of intelligent individuals seeking to work out a course of action to achieve what is appropriate both for the individual firm and for the world economy in the face of conflicting interests ... is ... at the most optimistic naïve, and probably a scoundrel, no matter which point of view is taken. (pp. 70–71)

There are valid *economic arguments* against multinational enterprises – monopoly exploitation, threat to local infant industries, barrier to foreign industrialization and unequal sharing of benefits – but *emotional arguments* will warp the judgments and decisions of policymakers in many cases:

> Scratch any of us deeply enough and you will find instincts of nationalism or xenophobia, overlain though they may be with layers of civilizing repression, and[,] equally, instincts of peasant attachment to the soil [particularly aroused when natural resources are involved]; also populist fear of outside capital, mercantilist pleasure in expanding exports ... The reactions are understandable, but they are not on that account to be approved. (p. 6)

Kindleberger observed that people and governments thrive on "prestige [which] is a curious commodity: its possession is not nourishing, but its absence is debilitating" (p. 86). In the case of the oil industry, governments do not want to destroy its monopoly aspects and replace it with competition from more entrants but to take over the monopoly – replacing war between two participants (the states and the oil companies) with collusion against third-party consumers (pp. 154–155). There are a few other nuggets, as in his analysis of attitudes toward joint ventures: "The foreign company ... wants 100 percent control to avoid conflicts of interest. The host government wants minority participation in order to create them" (p. 142).

What of international business–government relations under such imperfect and uncertain conditions? Well, there are no recipes for them:

> There is a temptation on the part of many well-meaning persons to suggest that the direct investing company should bargain gently and generously ... Perhaps. But the bargaining process is unpredictable. A cooperative attitude exhibited by the company may elicit cooperation or

it may lead the host country to increase its demands. If it works, it was cooperation. If it fails, it turns out to have been appeasement. (pp. 157–158)

Kindleberger was introducing here some of the elements of the bargaining strategy which was more fully developed by Gladwin and Walter (see below) and would later benefit from game theory. He was quite prescient about the future of the nation-state which "is just about through as an economic entity" (p. 207) because "the world is too small and too easy to get about" (p. 208); all sorts of technological developments "will not permit sovereign independence of the nation-state in economic affairs" (p. 208) – all often quoted conclusions (by Stephen Kobrin among others). However, the nation-state, along with the state (province, canton), the city, and the town, will survive and flourish as political entities with both decentralized and centralized features, as will also be the case with multinational enterprises (p. 208) which are moving faster than national governments in girding themselves for the world to come (p. 210).

Kindleberger dreamed of a supra-national system to harmonize national policies toward multinationals, that would reduce disputes between MNEs and governments as well as among governments. Whether this proposal represented a lapse in his usually keen evaluations of the course of events or a valid prophesy for the long run remains to be seen. Meanwhile, Kindleberger's 1969 book remains eminently perceptive and enjoyable about what fools we are when we think we know very much about MNEs' operations and contributions as well as what governments should do about them.[6]

At last, a conceptual framework

All of our authors declined to develop a full theory of international business–government relations, but John Fayerweather was the only one to come up with a conceptual framework that put IBGR into a context of economic, social, political, and organizational factors, in his 1969 book *International Business Management: A Conceptual Framework.*

---

[6] Kindleberger did quote Jack Behrman about capital formation (p. 3) but was totally silent about Ray Vernon's contributions – particularly his international product lifecycle theory published in 1966.

If he did not have the verve of Vernon, Fayerweather shared his lucidity as he developed a very tight argument built like a spiral as each of the above factors is first analyzed separately and then woven into the analyses of the other ones. Two of his favorite words were "sound" and "rational" (behavior, policy, etc.), with none of Robinson's and Behrman's "fire and brimstone." His calm tone and complex argumentation, together with his book's lack of cases, probably explain why it never became a textbook for the nascent international-management area.[7]

Fayerweather felt that the time had come to define and blend "the limited number of basic themes" regarding the operational problems of the international firm, that had been presented in books, articles, and cases in a fragmented way. People in management and academia were looking, he said, for "a conceptual base which will comprehend the international components of all the functional fields [production, marketing, finance, personnel, etc.], a synthesis of what international business management is as an entity unto itself, not just an extension in different forms of each functional field" (p. 2). What was that "synthesis?"

Fayerweather's conceptual framework

From economics, he drew the notion of unique resources that could be fruitfully transmitted by international firms to host nations. Putting these resources to local use required adaptations to foreign cultures and systems of social relations, which are analyzed in the social sciences. These two processes of "resource transmission" and "relations with host societies" are "interconnected" and constitute "the distinctive aspects of an international business as distinguished from a domestic one." They result, on the one hand, in "mutually beneficial, constructive activities for both the multinational firm and the interests of the affected nations" and, on the other hand, in "elements of conflict related to the confrontation of the interests of the firm with different national interests and nationalistic attitudes" – the political dimension of his conceptual framework. These transmissions, relations, and conflicts in individual foreign countries lead toward "a fragmented,

---

[7] Fayerweather had published the first international-management textbook in 1960, but there were few international-management courses and teachers that could use it at a time when most IB programs still centered on export and import management.

diversified pattern of policies and activities [that] weakens the effectiveness of the multinational corporation whose unique potentials vis-à-
vis local national firms lie largely in its unified, global capabilities. The
achievement of balance between fragmentation and unification therefore composes the final [organizational] element in the conceptual
framework" (1969, p. 12).

Et voilà! All the essential parts of the study of international business
management as a topic in itself were both neatly differentiated and
connected, drawing from all the basic disciplines. *Such a synthesis had
not been presented before and it remains valid to this day.* You have here
the seeds of subsequent works by Yves Doz and C. K. Prahalad as well
as Christopher Bartlett and Sumantra Ghoshal on "global integration
versus national responsiveness," by international political-behavior
researchers on various aspects of "conflict resolution" (Thomas Brewer,
Thomas Gladwin and Ingo Walter, Stephen Kobrin, myself, and
others), by those who focused on "resources" and "advantages" (John
Dunning, Alan Rugman, and others), and by scholars studying the
structure and functioning of multinational enterprises (Yair Aharoni,
Yves Doz, Richard Robinson, Stefan Robock and Kenneth Simmons,
John Stopford, and others). I do not mean to say that they all explicitly
borrowed from John Fayerweather, if at all, but rather that their
research can be comprehended in the context of his conceptual
framework – at least, this is what he has done for me.

Conflict resolution

Drawing from a number of sources, including political science and
studies of nationalism, Fayerweather provided some key pieces for
the development of international business–government relations, that
culminated in the masterful 1980 study by Thomas Gladwin and Ingo
Walter and its key variables of stakes, power, interest interdependence,
and relationship quality, which I will apply retroactively to
Fayerweather's analysis.

Regarding *stakes and interest interdependence*, Fayerweather argued
that "[t]he basic source of the conflicts encountered in cross-border
business processes lies in the fact that the multinational firm is caught
between and is an active participant in the conflicts between the
nationalism and national interests of the countries with which it has
business relations" (p. 88). As far as *relationship quality* is concerned,
this firm attempts to exercise from some central point a degree of

control over activities which extend into several countries, so that "it is by definition an 'outsider,' something to be distrusted and repelled ... an aggressive outsider seeking to enter and control a portion of life within the national group" (p. 91). This conflictual situation is exacerbated by nationalistic feelings, misconceptions, ignorance, and prejudice (p. 131).

The use of *power* in resolving conflicts by international firms is inevitable and quite proper. Fayerweather took some pains to point out that many "conflicts in human affairs are settled by power, sometimes by raw force, but more typically by the exercise of economic, legal, and political strength [as in labor relations] ... [although some people are disturbed by the] idea that a foreign company's status in a host country is the result of the exercise of power" (p. 114). Fayerweather would have none of that reservation, and he parted company with Richard Robinson by stating that:

There are those who propose that companies operating abroad must go all the way to satisfy the valid interests of host governments, asserting in effect that the exercise of power by the multinational firm in this context is improper ... But looking at the matter objectively, one can see no logical reason why power should not be just as normal and proper a basis for settling conflicts in the relationships of the multinational firm as in any other type of conflict. (p. 114)

Fayerweather offered a detailed analysis of the respective power bases of MNEs and governments (pp. 115–129). Multinationals have valuable resources and markets to offer, they can withhold them if the investment climate is poor, they can usually rely on the support of their home governments and of other international firms, and they have hostages in the form of foreign investments in the parent country. Politically, the power of host countries lies in their sovereignty, in the loyal support of most of the local companies, workers, and managers, and in nationalistic attitudes against foreigners, so that the political status of the multinational enterprise is normally weak. Economically, host governments benefit from the value of the market opportunities which they can give, withhold, and withdraw (shades of "the obsolescing bargain").

Franklin Root (1968) had already outlined three main responses to political risk – avoidance, adaptation, and transfer (of risks to others through insurance schemes) – based on whether multinationals considered the "market opportunities" well worth the "political risks." Fayerweather advocated a mixture of two approaches:

First, there is the effort to achieve maximum accommodation among the interests of the parties. This involves efforts to reduce the extent of the misconceptions of interest on the part of the management of the multinational firm, parent-country government officials, and host-country nationals ... Second, the resolution of the hard core of valid conflict must inevitably come through negotiation based on relative economic and political power relationships. (1969, pp. 131–132)

Altogether, there is substantial power available to each side, and the concept of dynamic balance-of-power positions is fundamental to the formulation of corporate policies (p. 124). Gladwin and Walter (1980) would later give a much more detailed list of thrusts and responses ranging from appeasement to confrontation and from avoidance to collaboration. They also concluded that conflict management is best achieved by means of a contingency approach because there is no one best way to manage all conflicts, and not all approaches (e.g., cooperation and assertiveness) are equally effective (p. 6).

Altogether, early writers were still groping for a systematic way of mapping out the political gaming between multinationals and governments – something Robert Grosse and Jack Behrman attempted in their 1992 article. Fayerweather contributed to its development not only by offering useful elements of a model of conflict resolution but also by always linking political problems to economic, social, and organizational ones through his four-part conceptual framework.

Additional contributors

I will highlight a few more contributors associated with business-school research. Louis T. Wells, Jr. (with D. N. Smith) analyzed the negotiation of third-world mineral agreements (1975) and he collaborated with John Stopford in 1972 on "Ironing the New Relationships." Robert Stobaugh (1969) analyzed foreign investment climates and the "go/no-go" criteria used to select countries in which to invest; Yair Aharoni (1966) stressed that economic and political stability was the first factor considered in foreign decisions; Richard Farmer and Barry Richman (1966) introduced the political–legal environment and its variations around the world in the study of international management; Lee Nehrt researched the political environment for foreign investors in North Africa (1970); Ashok Kapoor published a book on international business negotiations in India (1970); Peter Bennett and Robert T. Green dealt with the impact of political instability on foreign direct investment (1972); and Michael Brooke and Lee Remmers' *The Strategy of Multinational Enterprise* (1971) dealt perceptively with the influence of governments on decision making.

Jack Behrman, Ashok Kapoor, and I analyzed the roles of US embassies and various intermediaries (lawyers, consultants, American Chambers of Commerce, local trade associations, etc.) in the relations between MNEs and governments (1975); together with Ashok Kapoor, I wrote a monograph on international business–government relations (1973); I studied the organization of "corporate external affairs" in MNEs (1973), and I wrote with E. F. Cracco on "The Political Game in World Business" (1972).

In 1973, John Fayerweather's edited book on *International Business–Government Affairs* – "confrontation" was on its way out – gathered writings from many of the contributors to this field toward the end of the period covered here. It included several notable researchers previously unmentioned: David H. Blake, Alan Litvak and Alex Murray. Very influential was Theodore H. Moran's 1973 article, "Transnational Strategies of Protection and Defense by Multinational Corporations," which showed how MNEs could counter the obsolescing bargain. Less well known was F. T. Haner's *Multinational Management* (1973) which contained an excellent chapter on "Business Negotiations in Foreign Countries" (he was the founder of the Business Environment Index (BERI) service for measuring political risks abroad).

Conclusion

The 1960 to 1975 literature on international business–government relations remains relevant first and foremost because it discovered and dissected the multinational enterprise that remains the key IBGR player in the early twenty-first century as well as the child and progenitor of imperfect markets for goods and factors of production that concern governments.

Besides, these authors' analyses of nationalism and of what Kindleberger called "emotional arguments" are as profound and useful as they get. Their prediction that the MNE would continue to constitute an elusive phenomenon and institution hard to police effectively, even with the best of intentions, was on the button. They provided some of

the rudiments of a theory of international business–government negotiations, and they added "national interests," "investment climate,"
"the obsolescing bargain," "political exposure and risk," "legitimacy,"
and "sovereignty at bay" to our lexicon and analytical tools.

At the American Graduate School of International Management conference of January 2004, Jack Behrman stressed that the IBGR issues and
tensions identified and analyzed by early writers have not fundamentally
changed but that the quantity and quality of business–government relationships have, on account of: (1) the multiplication of political actors
(new nations, international organizations, NGOs, business associations,
etc.), and (2) the demand for value-based behaviors on the part of MNEs
that must act transparently, responsibly, and accountably – shades of
Richard Robinson! John Dunning and Dennis Rondinelli added that
there was a corresponding need for governments to improve the "institutional infrastructure" that allows these relationships to develop beyond
the mere calculation of costs and benefits when reconciling national and
corporate interests.[8] Therefore, the legacy of our early scholars remains
vital in new contexts that require both innovation and responsibility. To
conclude with Jack Behrman:

> The [multinational enterprise] has been described as an entity with its arms in
> several countries and its brains in one country; but acceptability depends on
> where its heart (loyalty) lies. (1974, p. 32)

Acknowledgments

The comments and suggestions of Jack Behrman, John Fayerweather,
Richard Robinson, and Franklin Root, who are highlighted in this
chapter, were particularly welcome. John Dunning drew my attention
to many scholars of the period, whose works often provided the raw
materials for the early writers' analyses.

---

[8] John Dunning's recently edited 2003 book deals with values and includes a
chapter by Jack Behrman.

2 | Institutional reform, foreign direct investment, and European transition economies

JOHN DUNNING

Introduction

This chapter addresses the role of institutions and institutional reform as a country-specific competitive advantage affecting the location of inbound foreign direct investment (FDI). Our focus of interest will be on European transition economies. Our thesis (backed up by a limited amount of econometric and field research) is that the extent and quality of a nation's institutions and its institutional infrastructure (II) are becoming a more important component of both (a) its overall productivity, and (b) its drawing power to attract inbound FDI. This, in turn, reflects the belief by private corporations (both foreign and home based) that the role played by location bound institutions and organizations in twenty-first-century society is becoming an increasingly critical determinant of the successful deployment of their own ownership specific, but often mobile, assets.

The chapter proceeds in the following way. First, we shall offer a simple analytical framework which might help us to explore the thesis set out above. Second, we shall identify the more significant firm-specific strategies and those affecting host transition economies, brought about by changes in the world economic and political scenario over the past decade or so; and how these are affecting the locational pull and push of multinational enterprise (MNE) activity. In particular, we shall examine the evidence of the links between the upgrading of the II of the Central and Eastern European region and its propensity to attract inbound FDI (vis-à-vis other areas in the world). Can we, in fact, identify the kinds of institutional upgrading which are likely to exert a greater pull for new FDI? Third, we shall examine the experiences of some ten Central and Eastern European transition economies. In particular, we will explore the proposition that any attempt to assess the willingness and capability of particular countries to upgrade their II must take account of their unique economic, cultural, and social characteristics, and their competitive position vis-à-vis that of other nations, as they affect the kind of inbound MNE activity they are aiming to attract.

The framework for analyses

Why is II an important locational asset?

We start by defining the more important terms we use. We shall take Douglass North's (1990) concept of institutions as the formal conventions (typically called rules), as well as the informal conventions (typically called standards) of society;[1] and that of individuals and organizations as the entities which devise and implement these institutions. These entities comprise each of the stakeholders (firms, civil society, consumer groups, labor unions, and governments) that make up a society. In North's view, the purpose of rules and conventions (institutions) is to define the rules by which the game (in this case upgrading competitiveness and attracting FDI) is played, monitored, and enforced. But the objective of the players (the organizations) is to use the institutions in a way which will win the game.

By the II we mean the overarching environment in which the institutions and organizations operate. Taking a recent definition by Mudambi and Navarra (2002, p. 638), the II of a country embraces its "political institutions such as regime type, the national structure of decision taking and the judicial system, economic institutions, such as the structure of national factor market and the terms of access to international factors of production, and socio-cultural factors such as informal norms, customs, mores and religions."

The key feature of institutions and the II of which they are part is that they are location-bound extra-market instruments designed to facilitate economic activity (including inbound FDI) by reducing the transaction costs of such activity. Such transaction costs are well known to international business scholars. They represent the "hassle" costs of doing business, and the uncertainties arising from possible opportunism, moral hazards, and incompleteness in commercial dealings. They include search, negotiation, and enforcement costs. The purpose of an effective and market facilitating II is to reduce these costs, which inter

---

[1] Examples of such rules and conventions include formal contracts and guarantees, bankruptcy laws, the legal system, property rights, trademarks.

alia include inadequate property rights, the absence of a properly regulated banking system, widespread corruption, imperfect or undeveloped financial markets, and weak incentive structures; and by so doing, both enhance the trust, reciprocity, and commitment among social and economic agents, and upgrade the competitiveness of firms.[2]

There has been a good deal of research on how an underdeveloped or inefficient II might inhibit FDI into host economies; and be just as much a deterrent as inadequate economic opportunities, high production costs, or inappropriate macroeconomic or micro-management policies of governments.[3] Building an efficient and socially acceptable II is likely to be particularly challenging in the case of transition economies – unused as they are to market-based institutions; and the speed with which and extent to which this can be efficiently achieved with minimum social disruption is likely to be a critical factor in influencing the capability of a country to adjust to the demands of global capitalism and to attract inbound FDI.

The analytical framework

We start by making reference to three figures. The first (figure 2.1) identifies three generic groups of variables which empirical research has shown to influence inbound FDI into all economies. It also indicates that the principal economic determinants (and, to some extent, the other two) are influenced by the motives for inbound MNE activity or growth of such activity, and also its mode of entry, e.g., by greenfield venture or by merger or acquisition (M&A).

As classified, the institutionally related determinants are spread over each of the three groups. Indeed, in a real sense, they are the 'umbrella' which affects the efficiency of each of the other determinants. Those

---

[2] For an excellent survey of different types of institution and how their upgrading might enhance economic development and the transition process see the chapter by Dennis Rondinelli in this volume. For an examination of the reasons for private enterprise development posed by the transition from state planned to market economies in Central and Eastern Europe see Behrman and Rondinelli (1999). For an application of the investment development path to the restructuring of Central and Eastern European economies, see the chapter by Meyer and Jensen in this volume.

[3] Bevan, Estrin, and Meyer (2000), Bevan and Estrin (2000) and see especially Meyer (2001a).

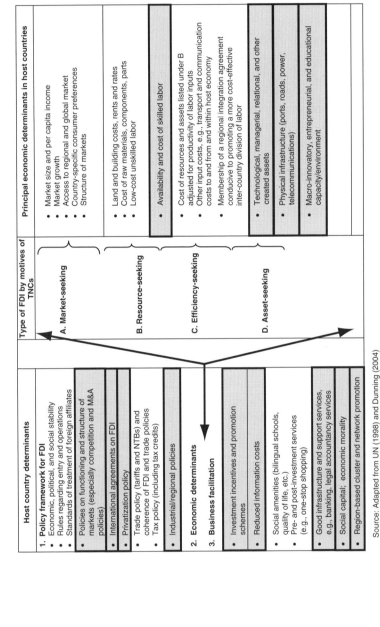

Figure 2.1 Host country determinants of FDI

Host country determinants	Type of FDI by motives of TNCs	Principal economic determinants in host countries
1. Policy framework for FDI • Economic, political, and social stability • Rules regarding entry and operations • Standards of treatment of foreign affiliates • Policies on functioning and structure of markets (especially competition and M&A policies) • International agreements on FDI • Privatization policy • Trade policy (tariffs and NTBs) and coherence of FDI and trade policies • Tax policy (including tax credits) • Industrial/regional policies **2. Economic determinants** **3. Business facilitation** • Investment incentives and promotion schemes • Reduced information costs • Social amenities (bilingual schools, quality of life, etc.) • Pre- and post-investment services (e.g., one-stop shopping) • Good infrastructure and support services, e.g., banking, legal accountancy services • Social capital; economic morality • Region-based cluster and network promotion	**A. Market-seeking** **B. Resource-seeking** **C. Efficiency-seeking** **D. Asset-seeking**	• Market size and per capita income • Market growth • Access to regional and global market • Country-specific consumer preferences • Structure of markets • Land and building costs, rents and rates • Cost of raw materials, components, parts • Low-cost unskilled labor • Availability and cost of skilled labor • Cost of resources and assets listed under B adjusted for productivity of labor inputs • Other input costs, e.g., transport and communication costs to and from and within host economy • Membership of a regional integration agreement conducive to promoting a more cost-effective inter-country division of labor • Technological, managerial, relational, and other created assets • Physical infrastructure (ports, roads, power, telecommunications) • Macro-innovatory, entrepreneurial, and educational capacity/environment

Source: Adapted from UN (1998) and Dunning (2004)

which are directly under the control of governments also come within the ambit of the policy framework, which, itself, reflects one of the modalities which both help create and monitor the II. However, the extent and pattern of business-facilitating variables, notably minimal bureaucracy and good infrastructural support services, are even more critically dependent on the quality of a society's institutions; while most of the market-oriented economic determinants themselves depend on the underlying incentive structures and enforcement procedures.

In figure 2.1, we have highlighted by shading those determinants which research has suggested have become relatively more important in the last decade, due inter alia to technological development, globalization, and the advent of alliance capitalism (Dunning, 1998); and how these, in turn, have widened the options open to MNEs in their choice of locations, not only between countries but within countries.

Although figure 2.1 does not relate the suggested determinants of FDI to particular stages of the value chain, e.g., pre-production and post-production of the investing companies, it may be used in this way. Nor does it distinguish between particular kinds of host or home economies. We make this point because it is important to acknowledge that the significance of the determinants of FDI including the composition and influence of a country's II is likely to be highly context-specific.

Figure 2.2 is adapted from an interesting article published in the *International Business Review* (Sethi et al., 2002). Exhibit 2 may be broken down into two parts. The top identifies the push-and-pull factors influencing the siting of MNE-related activity.[4] Although there is nothing particularly novel in its contents, they do serve to emphasize that the capability and willingness of countries – including transition economies – to attract inbound FDI rests not only on an adequate knowledge of the resources, capabilities, institutions, and markets which comprise their unique location-bound competitive advantages, but on an appreciation of the particular siting needs of (different kinds of) MNEs, and the forces affecting their global production and marketing strategies. Countries which are successful in matching their own location-bound assets to the ownership (but often mobile) advantages of firms (both foreign and domestic) are likely to achieve the best results in upgrading or restructuring their indigenous resources, capabilities, and social capital to

---

[4] We use the expression "MNE-related activity" to embrace *both* FDI and non-equity cooperative forms of cross-border value-adding activity.

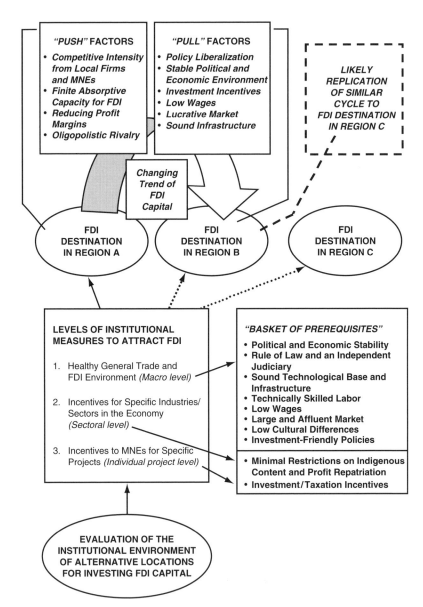

Figure 2.2 Push and pull factors and institutional measures attracting FDI

meet their developmental objectives. The second and lower part of Figure 2.2 sets out these institutionally related variables under the control of host governments which research has suggested are a necessary (but not a sufficient) condition for attracting inward FDI. The specific measures identified are not very different from those set out in Figure 2.1, and many are policy oriented.[5] However, the figure does additionally classify these measures by the context of the level of action – whether, for example, it is macro, sectorally, firm, or project based – each of which, to be effective, requires a different combination of institutional and organizational experience, and technical expertise.

The third scheme is an adaptation of one earlier prepared by a British consultancy group which aims to assess the special features of FDI and its likely impact on the competitiveness of the UK economy. We have adapted this flow chart in figure 2.3 to take into account some of the specific characteristics of transition economies. We present it here, as it suggests a useful template by which host governments – including those of transition economies – can judge not only the worthwhileness of inbound FDI, but also the appropriateness of their economic policies, and the adequacy and quality of the business environment under their jurisdiction. Again, we have shaded the components of the schema which (seem to us) to be most clearly dependent on, or reflective of, the indigenous II and related support mechanisms.

So much for our analytical framework. The next section of the chapter looks at the interaction between the push and pull factors by considering some of the more important changes in (a) the strategies of foreign investors or potential foreign investors, and (b) the competitive position and policies of economies, and does so in the light of changes in the global economic and political scenario over the last decade or so.

---

[5] We accept that the distinction between a policy and an institutionally related variable is not always easy to draw. However, the content and boundaries of each are distinct. Policy usually refers only to government action, and it is partly dependent on the character and quality of the institutions in which it is embedded. One may imagine a case of inappropriate policies within a sound II; but also of sound policies made ineffective by inadequate institutions. At the same time, while many organizations affecting institutional capability and FDI are nongovernmental, e.g. civil society, business organizations, etc., by their policies, governments may affect the adequacy and impact of their actions on their own competitive enhancing agenda.

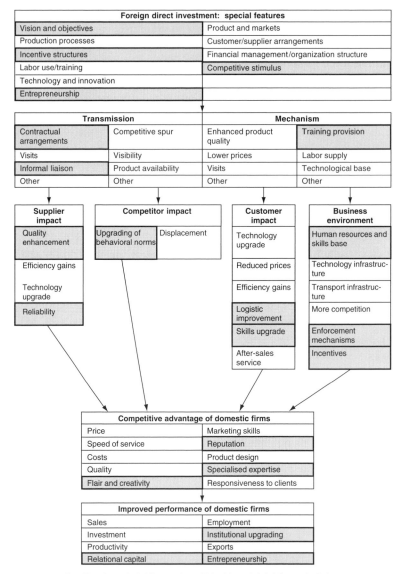

Foreign direct investment: special features	
Vision and objectives	Product and markets
Production processes	Customer/supplier arrangements
Incentive structures	Financial management/organization structure
Labor use/training	Competitive stimulus
Technology and innovation	
Entrepreneurship	

Transmission		Mechanism	
Contractual arrangements	Competitive spur	Enhanced product quality	Training provision
Visits	Visibility	Lower prices	Labor supply
Informal liaison	Product availability	Visits	Technological base
Other	Other	Other	Other

Supplier impact	Competitor impact		Customer impact	Business environment
Quality enhancement	Upgrading of behavioral norms	Displacement	Technology upgrade	Human resources and skills base
Efficiency gains			Reduced prices	Technology infrastructure
Technology upgrade			Efficiency gains	Transport infrastructure
Reliability			Logistic improvement	More competition
			Skills upgrade	Enforcement mechanisms
			After-sales service	Incentives

Competitive advantage of domestic firms	
Price	Marketing skills
Speed of service	Reputation
Costs	Product design
Quality	Specialised expertise
Flair and creativity	Responsiveness to clients

Improved performance of domestic firms	
Sales	Employment
Investment	Institutional upgrading
Productivity	Exports
Relational capital	Entrepreneurship

Note: Those items shaded illustrate those which might particularly influence the II of a country.
Source: Adapted from PA Cambridge Economic Consultants (October 1995).

Figure 2.3 Assessing the features and impact of FDI: a flow chart

The strategies of (foreign) MNEs

All national or regional governments, in seeking to devise appropriate institutions, organizations, and policies to upgrade their domestic competitiveness, need to be cognizant of the evolving strategies of existing and potential foreign investors, as they seek to advance their own objectives. For it is in the pursuance of these strategies that the locational attractions of possible host countries are evaluated.

Here, we would highlight some strategic changes of the last decade or so, each of which is tending to affect the push toward more FDI in transition economies which is now occurring. Some of these are reactive to exogenous changes in the global technological, economic, and political scenario; others are reflective of industry- or firm-specific changes. Some specifically affect the institutional capacity of particular organizations; others the broader political and economic framework within which MNEs operate. A useful examination of the specific institutional imperatives of globalization is set out in Rondinelli and Behrman (2000). In particular, the authors identify the role of ethical norms, property rights, private enterprise development, support of competition, equality of opportunity and safety nets, and democratic governance. The moral challenges of global capitalism are also the theme of Dunning (2003). We present these briefly and without detailed comment.[6]

1. Due both to the opening up of the global marketplace (including regional integration) and technological advances (particularly in cross-border communications) there is a movement by most MNEs to integrate and rationalize their foreign value-added activities on regional or global lines. Inter alia this means an increased inter-country specialization of products, processes, and functions, which, in turn, is leading to more cross-border transactions of goods, services, and assets. In particular, as far as the European transition economies are concerned, this suggests they must view their own location-bound competitive and comparative advantages, not only in terms of how far these might advance the global or European strategies of MNEs – especially their innovation

---

[6] For an extensive discussion of the changing global or regional strategies of MNEs see the annual *World Investment Reports* published by UNCTAD (1991–2004).

and sourcing options, and the extent to which they are prepared to devolve decision taking to their affiliates – but of how competitive their II is in relation to that of other similar economies seeking to attract the same kind of FDI.

2. In the last decade or so, due again to the added competitive pressures resulting from globalization and technological advances, MNEs have increasingly engaged in outward FDI to protect or augment their global competitive advantages.[7] Up to the present time, most of this asset-seeking FDI (see figure 2.1) has occurred between the advanced industrialized nations, and has taken the form of M&As.[8] However, there are signs that, at least as far as the more advanced European transition economies are concerned, the importance of this kind of MNE activity is increasing. Undoubtedly, some FDI in privatization schemes is of an asset-augmenting nature; and such investment may well become more important in the future. The point which needs stressing, however, is that both the consequences of and the policy and institutional-related variables which may affect such FDI are likely to be very different from that of asset-exploiting investment (Wesson, 2003).

3. Hand in hand with a more centralized control strategy demanded of MNEs engaging in integrated international production has come a decentralization or subsidiarity of some kinds of decision taking, and the rise in the entrepreneurial capabilities of MNEs' subsidiaries as creators as well as exploiters of assets. Birkinshaw and Hood (1998), Pearce (1999), and Rugman and Verbeke (2001) are among those economists who have written extensively on this issue. But for our purposes, it poses the question "What institutions, organizations, and policies of transition economies are most likely to encourage MNEs to sustain, build up and upgrade the value added of their subsidiaries' capabilities – including the higher grade administrative and innovatory functions – in a way which is consistent with the resources, capabilities, and goals of those economies?" Lessons from Singapore and Hong Kong about the II necessary to attract and sustain regional offices and the Bangalore region in India

---

[7] By the same token an increasing proportion of inbound FDI has been of this kind.

[8] Some 75 percent of M&A purchases between 1990 and 2000 took place between the US, Europe, and Japan. See, e.g., UNCTAD (2001).

for computer software development are apposite here.[9] This issue of subsidiary development is also related to the geographical clustering of interdependent activities which, itself, may be thought of as a form of II infrastructure.

4. Finally, such "shocks" as September 11, 2001 and related events are having, and are likely to continue to have, an effect on the global and regional value-adding and marketing strategies of MNEs. For example, the impact of terrorist activities directed to countries which are perceived to be the most likely to be targeted, and/or are least sympathetic to the policies of the home governments, is likely to be a very negative one. The concept of psychic distance has always been well embedded in IB studies. A new dimension of this concept – viz. institutional distance – is likely to affect the investment portfolios of MNEs as to where they might wish to site their higher value and more sensitive activities, e.g., research and development and some forms of subcontracting. As of the last decade or so, however, it would seem that the institutional distance between the European transition economies and the major source investing countries is not increasing on this account.

The opportunities and challenges offered by transition economies

Technological advances and sweeping changes in the global economic scenario have no less influenced the country-specific opportunities and challenges affecting the pull of FDI; and none more so than those within the transition economies of Central and Eastern Europe. At the same time, there are responses to these events which to a greater or lesser degree are affecting all countries. Chief among these are the increased competitive pressures among firms brought about by the new openness in the regional and/or global trading and investment regimes. This has underlined the need of previously protected economies both to upgrade the efficiency of, and to restructure, their production and marketing capabilities in line with their (perceived) long-term comparative advantages. To promote these objectives, and to do so quickly, the technology, management and organizational skills, and markets offered by foreign MNEs have been particularly welcomed. But to attract such

---

[9] As, for example, described in several chapters in Dunning (2000).

assets, host countries, and particularly the transition economies, have had to reconfigure both their macroeconomic and micro-management policies and their IIs in such a way as meets the needs of investing corporations. Bearing in mind the relatively footloose nature of some kinds of FDI – particularly those of a market or efficiency seeking kind within a regionally integrated area – what then are the unique location-bound advantages – and the II underpinning them – which a particular country or region can offer both existing and potential foreign investors seeking to advance their own strategic goals?

The second critical new development of the past decade, which is influencing the ability of countries to attract inbound FDI – and in particular the role of institution building and related government policies – is the advent of new means of communication, especially E-commerce and the internet, which, by lowering many spatial transaction costs, is having a major effect on the locational preferences of MNEs.[10] This is seen to be particularly the case with respect to their sourcing of standardized, but relatively labor intensive, goods and services. And it is these areas (e.g., motor vehicle components, garment manufacturing, call centres) in which the transition economies, along with other countries at the intermediate stages of their investment development paths (Dunning and Narula, 1996), have a comparative advantage. At the same time, viewed from a developmental perspective, it is important that the transition economies learn from the experience of such Asian economies as Singapore, South Korea, and Taiwan[11] of the need to continually restructure and upgrade their location-specific endowments (especially their institutional human resource and innovatory capacity); and in so doing not only attract a better quality of FDI, but help their own indigenous firms to become outward foreign investors.[12]

A third element of the changing characteristics of country-specific advantages concerns the increasing attention now being paid to

---

[10] For a detailed examination of the effect of E-commerce on IB activity see Dunning and Wymbs (2001).

[11] For a study of the relationship between the investment development path and the structural upgrading of Korean and Taiwanese industries between the mid-1960s and early 1990s see Dunning, Kim, and Lin (2001).

[12] For one of the first careful examinations of the outward FDI by Central European transition economies, see Svetličič and Rojec (2003).

sub-national clusters of economic activities, particularly in large and medium-size economies. Here the work of Porter (1998) and Enright (2002) is particularly germane. It is quite clear from the research into the intra-national location strategies of both domestic and foreign firms that the extent and content of the II of particular regions or districts – and especially the incentive structures, the quality of educational institutions, the communications infrastructure, the entrepreneurial culture, social capital, and the provision of industrial and science parks – is one of the most powerful pull factors they can offer. This is particularly likely to be so when such inducements are "tailor made" to the kind of FDI they are seeking to attract.

Clearly, there are very specific opportunities and challenges now being faced by the ex-communist countries. None is more relevant than those arising from the change in the ownership of productive assets demanded by the market economy; and the consequential need to drastically lower the transaction and coordination costs of doing business. This, perhaps more than anything else, requires a wholesale reconfiguration of the organizational and economic management of the transition economies. We have already referred to some of these, and there is a substantial literature on the subject (see especially Meyer, 2001a, b; Bever, Estrin, and Meyer, 2004). For now, however, we are interested in seeing how important the various competitive-enhancing measures just described have been in affecting recent FDI inflows into the transition economies.

The empirical evidence

Let us then turn to review the empirical evidence of the significance of institutional- and policy-related variables on the pull factors influencing the location of FDI – both in European transition economies taken as a group, and within particular transition economies.

The research studies so far conducted fall into two main groups. First there are the statistical and econometric exercises which seek to quantify the relationship between FDI flows (or changes in the stock of FDI) and selection of explanatory, including institutionally related, variables. These normally use published data, largely from official sources such as the European Bank for Reconstruction and Development (EBRD), the OECD and the United Nations (UN). Second, there are the field surveys which are primarily designed to extract the opinion of existing and/or potential foreign investors about the location-specific opportunities and challenges offered by the transition economies, and to rank in importance (what they perceive to be) the critical determinants of recent past, and likely future, FDI commitments.

In the paragraphs which follow, we shall focus on two recent empirical exercises, both of which are comprehensive in scope and detail, in as much as they draw heavily on data and opinions used in previous studies.

The statistical and econometric exercises use mainly multivariate regressions to assess the significance of either a proxy for institutions as a whole, or particular institutional-related variables as determinants of FDI flows. Both time series and cross-sectional studies, or a combination of the two using panel data, are commonly deployed. For the purposes of this chapter, we detail just one of the most recent studies (Bevan, Estrin, and Meyer, 2004). This draws upon a panel of information for the years 1994–1998 compiled by the major source investing countries (the EU countries, the US, Japan, Korea, Switzerland) in respect of FDI in ten transition economies seeking accession to the EU,[13] plus Russia and the Ukraine.

As to the general impact, it was found that, after eliminating the effects of a number of control variables such as market size, cultural, linguistic, and geographic distance and labor costs, there was a positive but (at 6 percent) not a highly significant relationship between the level of inbound FDI and a composite index of II.[14]

Of the specific II variables, both change of ownership (in the form of privatization) and private sector development were seen to be positively, though not significantly, correlated to FDI flows, again once control variables were taken into account. In particular, the creation of new markets, including those relating to FDI and cross-border alliance formation, were shown to reduce transaction costs associated with uncertainty and bureaucratic opportunism. Rather more significantly, the quality and transparency of the financial sector and banking reform were seen to be significantly correlated with FDI flows; but non-bank institutional upgrading, e.g., with respect to capital markets, appeared

---

[13] These are, Bulgaria, the Czech Republic, Estonia, Hungary, Latvia, Lithuania, Poland, Romania, Slovakia, and Slovenia.

[14] The European Bank for Reconstruction and Development (EBRD) regularly compiles such an index for each of the transition economies. See, e.g., EBRD (2000).

to be less so. However, the liberalization of domestic markets, the strengthening of competition policies, and a movement toward a more open trading regime were seen to have had a strong positive effect, as too was the upgrading of the legal system. One further conclusion of this study was that foreign investors appeared to be more concerned with the quality of formal institutions than that of informal ones.

These results all point to the importance of institution building as a necessary prerequisite for FDI. They confirm and extend those of earlier studies such as those by Lansbury, Pain, and Smidkova (1996), Bevan, Estrin, and Meyer (2000), Holland, Sass, Benacek, and Gronicki (2000) and the Economist Intelligence Unit (EIU) (2001).[15] The EIU statistical exercise, based on FDI flows into twenty-seven Central and East European countries between 1996 and 2000, found that, among the significant explanatory variables, the quality of the business environment and the privatization variable were both highly significant, along with market size, wage costs, and a natural resource variable (EIU, 2003).[16] This study also suggested that preparation for their (proposed) accession to the EU, and all this implies, is compelling countries to upgrade their II, and, in so doing, to reduce both domestic and intra-European transaction and coordinating costs. However, the example of Greece, which did not sufficiently engage in institutional and policy reform at the time of its entry into the EC, shows that accession does not automatically result in increased FDI flows (Kekic, 2002).

One other recently completed study of FDI in some thirteen Central and Eastern European economies between 1990 and 1999 is also worthy of note. Using panel data and various statistical models Grosse and

---

[15] A recently published study on FDI in Latin America also concluded that "privatization was the most highly significant independent variable to help explain inward FDI in Latin America" (Trevino et al., 2002). (Also significantly positively related to FDI inflows was the liberalization of capital markets.) The methodology of this study is of particular interest as the authors' measure of privatization subtracted out FDI in the privatized sector. The results then implied that a change of ownership as an institutional reform does much more than simply attracting FDI to a previously closed sector.

[16] According to the model "market-size, the quality of the overall business environment, wage costs, natural resource endowments and privatisation methods statistically explain almost the entire inter-country variation in FDI receipts in the region in 1996–2000" (EIU, 2002, p. 87).

Trevino (2003) found that while institution building tended to follow similar patterns in the economies studied to that in other emerging markets, it tended to play a rather more significant role. In particular, the authors noted the right kind of bilateral investment treaties, the degree of enterprise reform, repatriation rules, and the reduction of the level of government corruption were particular pulls in attracting FDI.

Complementing the statistical studies are the surveys of the opinions of business executives. These, in the main, confine themselves to identifying (a) the strength or weakness of different locational determinants (usually on a Likert Scale) and changes in these, and (b) how any particular determinant differs in its perceived significance across countries.

Let us illustrate from just one major annual survey undertaken by the EIU which attempts to calculate a Business Environment Index (BEI) for some sixty countries. This index is essentially a composite of data and opinions culled from other published sources,[17] and a series of business surveys conducted by the EIU itself. The index is derived from the rankings obtained for ten broad determinants of competitiveness which then are further sub-divided into seventy particular components.[18] The most recently compiled information was collected for two time periods. The first was for the years 1998–2002 and the second 2003–2007 (EIU, 2003).

We consider two sets of data. The first are those which relate to the rankings assigned to some specific II in all countries – and how they compared with those given to Western Europe and Latin

---

[17] As described by EIU(2002), p. 134. Regrettably this report does not identify the number of firms completing the fourteen-page Business Rankings Questionnaire the answers to which formed an important part of the BEI.

[18] These could quite readily be reclassified using the seven kinds of institutions identified by Dennis Rondinelli (see chapter 17 of this volume). These are institutions of economic adjustment and stabilization, e.g. macroeconomic adjustment policies; institutions strengthening economic motivation, e.g., FDI policies, labor markets; institutions of private property protection; institutions promoting freedom of enterprise, e.g., political liberalization, quality of financial regulatory system; institutions of rule setting and societal guidance, e.g., effectiveness and fairness of legal system, policies for controlling corruption, quality of bureaucracy; institutions promoting competition, e.g., trade and investment liberalization, competition policy; and institutions promoting social equity and access to employment opportunities.

America[19] – and policy-related determinants for the European transition economies as a whole. The second classifies the ten economies into two groups and compares the significance of II-related assets with more traditional location-specific variables[20] covered by the survey. Table 2.1 sets out scores – on a range of 1–5, 5 being the most conducive to competitiveness and 1 the least conducive – for a selection of the seventy variables which best identify with II and policy-related variables. These data show:

1. For 1998–2002, the overall BEI score for the transition economies was 2.7, compared with 3.8 for Western Europe, 2.9 for Latin America, and 3.4 for all countries. Between 2003 and 2007, the corresponding scores are expected to rise to 3.1, 4.0, 3.6 and 3.5 respectively, with the East European countries recording the greatest absolute percentage increase.

2. The scores assigned to the II variables for East European countries were, on average, ranked lower than the non II variables; and also to the scores of the II proxies assigned to Western European and Latin American countries. Those II variables ranked the lowest included the quality of the financial regulatory system, bureaucracy, the transparency of the legal system, corruption, the consistency and fairness of the tax system, stock market capitalization, access to finance for investment, the reliability of the telecommunication network, the infrastructure for retail and wholesale distribution, the protection of intellectual property rights, and the promotion of competition. Looking forward to 2003–2007, the scores of each of these variables was expected to rise – and again proportionately more so in Central and Eastern Europe than elsewhere.

3. Turning now to the business attitudes toward more policy-related variables, other data published by the EIU (not presented here) reveal that both the macro- and micro-management policies – taken as a group – were ranked more favorably than were the II variables (EIU, 2003). More especially labor-related policies, the tax burden, and the corporate tax rate were three of the policy variables in which Central and Eastern Europe were perceived to have comparative locational advantage vis-à-vis Western Europe and Latin America. The main

---

[19] As an example of a developing region.
[20] Further details on each of the individual ten countries are presented as an Appendix to this chapter.

Table 2.1 *Indicator's scores for selected institution-related variables in the EIU Business Ranking Model (i) 1998–2002 (ii) 2003–2007*

	1998–2002				2003–2007			
	World	Central and Eastern Europe	Western Europe	Latin America	World	Central and Eastern Europe	Western Europe	Latin America
(A) OVERALL BEI SCORE	3.4	2.7	3.8	2.9	3.5	3.1	4.0	3.6
(B) POLITICAL/SOCIAL								
• Risk of social unrest	3.4	3.0	4.5	2.6	3.5	3.2	4.5	2.4
• Government policy toward business	3.6	3.2	3.9	3.5	3.6	3.3	3.9	3.5
• Quality of bureaucracy	3.0	1.9	3.5	2.9	3.1	2.2	3.9	2.8
• Effectiveness and fairness of legal system	2.9	1.9	4.1	2.5	3.1	2.6	4.2	2.6
• Corruption	2.9	2.0	3.9	2.4	3.0	2.1	4.1	2.4
• Distortions arising from lobbying from special interest groups	2.8	2.1	3.6	2.8	3.0	2.4	3.8	3.0
• Distortions arising from state ownership or control	3.2	2.8	4.1	2.9	3.5	3.4	4.2	3.4
• Risk of expropriation of foreign assets	4.3	3.8	4.9	4.1	4.3	3.8	4.9	4.1
(C) ECONOMIC								
• Policies toward foreign capital	3.6	33.4	4.1	3.9	3.9	3.7	4.4	3.8
• Quality of financial regulatory system	3.1	2.4	3.9	2.8	3.6	3.0	4.6	3.5

• Consistency/fairness of tax system	3.1	2.0	3.9	2.5	3.4	2.7	4.2	2.6
• Stock market capitalization	2.9	1.7	4.2	2.3	3.2	2.0	4.6	2.4
• Access to finance for investment	3.3	2.2	4.4	2.5	3.5	2.5	4.5	2.6
• Quality of telecoms network	3.1	1.9	4.2	2.9	3.6	2.7	4.6	3.3
• Infrastructure for distribution	3.1	1.8	4.2	2.4	3.5	2.7	4.5	2.9
• Degree to which private property rights are protected	3.9	3.1	4.8	3.1	4.0	3.5	4.9	3.1
• Intellectual property rights protection	3.2	2.2	4.4	3.1	3.5	2.9	4.6	2.8
• Promotion of competition	2.9	1.9	3.6	2.8	3.4	2.9	4.0	2.9
• Tariff and monetary protection	3.5	3.2	3.9	3.0	3.7	3.6	4.0	3.4

Source: Economist Intelligence Unit (EIU) (2003).

exceptions were competition and anti-corruption policies. However, taken as a whole, the policy scores were lower than in all other parts of the world except the Middle East.[21] Again, in the 2003–2007 period, the rankings for each of these variables in Central and Eastern Europe are expected to improve, both absolutely and relative to those in other regions.

Table 2.2 sets out some further details for the ten European transitional economies for which the EIU published data. For each country, scores of 1–10 were assigned to each of the ten categories of the BEI for 1998–2002 and 2003–2007. Based on their GDPs per head,[22] we classified these countries into two groups. The Czech Republic, Hungary, Poland, and Slovakia comprised the first group (the more advanced transition economies); Azerbaijan, Bulgaria, Kazakhstan, Romania, Russia, and the Ukraine the second (the less advanced transition economies). We also added India and China for purposes of comparison.

We might highlight three main points from this table, and also from table 2.3 which gives average scores for the II and other variables for each of the ten countries.

1. For the more advanced TEs, the scores for the institution-related categories[23] were slightly above those of the other – including policy-related – categories in the 1998–2002 period. For the less advanced TEs, the II variables were ranked quite a bit lower than the other variables. Broadly, the same picture emerged in respect of the 2003–2007 scores.

2. There is a strong suggestion that, as development proceeds, the scores likely to be assigned to the institution-related variables not only rise, but rise relative to those assigned to the other categories. Particular examples, as shown in table 2.2, include the quality of institutions promoting private enterprise, the political environment and financing (mostly, one suspects, the quality of the financial

---

[21] These scores were not broken down for each country for each of the seventy individual items.

[22] Calculated in $ at purchasing power parity.

[23] We have had to be rather arbitrary in classifying the components, as, in some cases, policy- and institution-related variables were difficult to distinguish from each other.

Table 2.2 Business environment scores for transition economies (TEs), India, and China (i) 1998–2002 (ii) 2003–2007

	1998–2002				2003–2007			
	More advanced TEs ($9,998)[1]	Less advanced TEs ($4,457)[1]	India ($2,735)[1]	China ($6,034)[1]	More advanced TEs ($13,618)[2]	Less advanced TEs ($6,390)[2]	India ($4,211)[2]	China ($96,890)[2]
(A) INSTITUTION-RELATED VARIABLES								
Political environment	6.5	4.0	5.5	4.5	7.0	4.6	5.3	4.3
Political stability	7.8	5.4	6.4	5.5	8.0	5.7	5.5	4.6
Political effectiveness	5.5	2.9	4.8	3.6	6.2	3.7	5.1	4.0
Policy toward private enterprises and competition	6.0	3.5	4.4	3.3	7.4	4.6	5.8	4.9
Policy toward foreign direct investment	8.2	5.0	5.5	6.1	8.3	5.5	6.6	7.2
Taxes	5.0	3.9	5.7	5.1	6.1	5.0	6.9	5.2
Financing	6.6	3.4	4.4	3.6	7.0	4.9	5.5	5.5
Infrastructure	5.4	4.1	2.4	2.6	6.4	4.9	3.7	3.9
(B) OTHER DETERMINANTS								
Macroeconomic environment	6.5	6.1	8.1	9.7	7.6	7.5	7.4	9.7
Market opportunities	4.9	4.7	6.4	8.4	5.3	5.0	7.3	8.3
Foreign trade and exchange controls	8.0	5.7	4.9	4.9	8.8	7.2	7.8	7.8

Table 2.2 Business environment scores for transition economies (TEs), India, and China (i) 1998–2002 (ii) 2003–2007 (continued)

	1998–2002				2003–2007			
	More advanced TEs ($9,998)[1]	Less advanced TEs ($4,457)[1]	India ($2,735)[1]	China ($6,034)[1]	More advanced TEs ($13,618)[2]	Less advanced TEs ($6,390)[2]	India ($4,211)[2]	China ($96,890)[2]
Labor market	6.7	6.0	5.4	5.3	6.8	6.4	6.2	6.1
Overall score	6.4	4.4	5.3	5.4	7.1	5.6	6.2	6.3

Notes:
[1] GDP per capita (US$ PPP) 2002.
[2] Estimated GDP per capita (US$ PPP) 2007.
Source: EIU (2003): scores range from 1 to 10, a score of 10 being perceived as the best for business.

regulatory system and distortion [or the absence of same] in financial markets). Again, as table 2.3 shows, the most impressive II upgrading is predicted to occur in the less developed TEs, especially in Azerbaijan, Russia, and the Ukraine.

3. Looking at the comparative strengths and weaknesses of the institution-related categories for the ten countries identified, we see that, in the 1998–2002 period the perceived strengths of the less developed TE countries were their political stability and their policies toward FDI. The weaknesses identified were a high level of bureaucracy, corruption, distortions arising from lobbying by special interest groups, lack of political effectiveness, and lack of organizational infrastructure. For the more advanced TEs (which currently receive the great bulk of inbound FDI), the perceived strengths were their attitudes toward FDI and exchange controls, political stability, environment, the labor market, and the financing framework; and their weaknesses the lack of consistency and lack of fairness of the tax system, physical infrastructure, and (perceived) lack of market opportunities.

Table 2.2 also shows the relative strengths and weaknesses of two Asian economies undergoing significant structural transformation. In India's case, its main strength was perceived to lie in its macroeconomic environment and political stability, and its main weaknesses were the poor quality of its transport and power infrastructure, and of its banking and financing framework. In China's case there were similar strengths and weaknesses;[24] though China's policy toward private enterprise was thought to be less conducive to inbound FDI than that of India.[25]

Finally in table 2.3, we relate the business environment ranking of the ten TEs to their GDP per capita and their inbound FDI per capita. The data show that not only is there an extremely close positive correlation between the II scores for FDI per capita and GDP per capita in both 1998–2002 and 2003–2007, but this correlation is significantly higher than in the case of the other, i.e., non II variables. The lesson

---

[24] China's main comparative advantage rested on its market opportunities and macroeconomic environment. In both cases China was ranked second of the sixty countries covered by the EIU survey.

[25] Again, it is difficult to generalize for large economies like India and China as there are large differences in the institutional environment between the major industrial conurbations and the rest of the two countries.

Table 2.3 Business environment rankings (BER), FDI per capita, and GDP per capita for ten transition economies (i) 1998–2002 and (ii) 2003–2007

	1998–2002					2003–2007				
	BER			FDI per cap $	GDP per cap $	BER			FDI per cap $	GDP per cap $
	TOTAL	INST	OTHER			TOTAL	INST	OTHER		
MORE ADVANCED TEs										
Czech Republic	6.5	6.7	6.2	548	11,294	7.3	7.6	6.9	611	14,904
Hungary	6.7	6.9	6.3	328	8,858	7.3	7.5	6.8	372	12,026
Poland	6.4	6.5	6.1	178	7,664	7.0	7.2	6.8	183	9,786
Slovakia	5.8	5.9	5.6	312	8,572	6.6	6.7	6.6	367	11,386
ALL	6.4	6.5	6.1	349	9,097	7.1	7.3	6.8	383	12,026
LESS ADVANCED TEs										
Azerbaijan	4.4	3.5	5.9	72	1,548	5.3	4.7	6.4	176	2,512
Bulgaria	5.4	5.4	5.4	89	5,240	6.3	6.3	6.2	105	7374
Kazakhstan	4.8	4.4	5.8	118	4,056	5.2	4.6	6.5	151	6,644
Romania	4.6	4.9	4.1	60	4,748	5.7	5.7	5.6	79	6,508
Russia	4.5	4.0	5.7	19	4,956	6.0	5.2	7.5	69	6,948
Ukraine	4.1	3.5	4.7	14	2,456	5.2	4.7	6.1	27	3,554
ALL	4.6	4.3	5.3	62	3,834	5.6	5.2	6.4	101	5,590
ALL TEs	5.5	5.4	5.7	177	6,323	6.4	6.3	6.6	214	8,165

Key

BER = business environment rankings.

FDI per cap ($) = inbound FDI flows per capita averaged over two five-year periods (viz 1998–2002 and 2003–2007).

Inst = II variables, periods (viz 1998–2002 and 2003–2007).

Other = other variables in BER.

GDP per cap ($) = GDP per capita at purchasing power parity averaged over two five-year periods (viz. 1998–2002 and 2003–2007).

here seems to be that at a certain GDP per capita level the relative importance of the II as a variable influencing FDI inflows decreases.

Conclusions

This chapter has sought to assess the significance of institutional infrastructure and development as a determinant of FDI flows into the European transition economies. It began by examining the critical role of the institutional environment (comprising both institutions and the strategies and policies of organizations relating to these institutions) in reducing the transaction costs of both domestic and cross-border business activity. It then set up an analytical framework identifying the determinants of FDI, how these had changed over recent years, and which were likely to be the most important in influencing new business investment in transition economies.

The next section went on to describe the reconfiguration of the main push factors affecting the current strategy and behavior of MNEs brought about by recent changes in the global economy; and also the main pull factors determining the location-specific advantages of countries and regions wishing to attract the resources and capabilities which foreign investors were perceived to possess. This section concluded with some observations as to the type of asset-based advantages transition economies should strive to develop.

The third section turned to consider the results of two major empirical exercises on the particular role of II as a determinant of FDI flows into transition economies. The econometric study showed that, after allowing for control variables, the quality of the II was positively and, for some kinds of institutions, significantly related to FDI flows. The field study indicated that (proxies for) the quality of II in the less advanced transition economies were generally thought to be less conducive to FDI than those possessed by other economies, and also of the non II determinants of FDI. However, it was generally expected that, over the period 2003–2007, the quality of II of both groups of transition economies would improve relative to that of other economies, and that, in consequence, they would gain an increasing share of inbound FDI.[26]

---

[26] The EIU's prediction is that the share of the world's inbound FDI stock directed to the ten Central and Eastern European economies will increase from 2.2 percent in 2000 to 3.2 percent in 2007 (EIU 2003, pp. 135–136).

Other data also suggest that the prospect of accession to the EU, and the benefits likely to be conferred, is becoming an important inducement to many (if not all) transition economies to upgrade their II. The final part of this chapter also made some comparisons and contrasts between the competitive advantages (and disadvantages) of European transition economies and those of India and China as a location for inbound MNE activity.

Appendix 1 Business environment rankings for ten transition economies for (i) 1998–2002 and (ii) 2003–2007

	Institutionally related (i) 1998–2002										Other business environment variables					
	PE	PS	PI	PPE	FDI	FT/E	T	F	LM	I	MACRO	MO	FT/E	T	LM	OVERALL
MORE ADVANCED TEs (MATEs)																
Czech Republic	6.9	8.75	5.5	6.1	8.9	8.3	4.5	6.3	6.4	6.0	7.6	4.5	8.3	4.5	6.4	6.5
Hungary	6.5	7.3	5.9	6.6	8.9	8.3	5.9	7.0	7.1	5.5	6.1	5.5	8.3	5.7	7.1	6.7
Poland	6.9	8.2	5.9	6.1	8.3	7.2	4.8	7.0	6.2	5.1	6.4	6.0	7.2	4.8	6.2	6.4
Slovakia	5.7	6.9	4.8	5.2	6.6	8.3	4.6	5.9	6.8	5.1	6.0	3.7	8.3	4.6	6.8	5.8
All MATEs	6.5	7.8	5.5	6.0	8.2	8.0	5.0	6.6	6.6	5.4	6.5	4.9	8.0	5.0	6.6	6.4
LESS ADVANCED TEs (LATES)																
Azerbaijan	2.8	3.3	2.5	2.7	4.4	5.5	3.7	2.1	5.9	3.3	7.6	5.4	5.5	3.7	5.9	4.4
Bulgaria	5.3	6.9	4.0	4.9	6.6	6.6	4.4	4.0	5.4	5.3	6.9	3.4	6.6	4.4	6.4	5.4
Kazakhstan	4.1	5.5	2.9	3.5	4.9	6.1	3.8	4.0	6.0	3.7	8.3	6.1	6.1	3.8	6.0	4.8
Romania	5.3	6.9	4.0	4.1	6.1	5.5	4.2	4.0	5.9	4.4	2.9	3.6	5.5	4.2	5.9	4.6
Russia	3.0	4.2	2.1	3.3	3.3	6.1	4.0	3.6	6.6	4.2	4.8	6.6	6.1	4.0	6.6	4.5
Ukraine	3.7	5.5	2.1	2.7	4.4	4.4	3.2	2.9	6.0	3.9	6.3	3.3	4.4	3.2	6.0	4.1
ALL LATEs	4.0	5.4	2.9	3.5	5.0	5.7	3.9	3.4	6.0	4.1	6.1	4.7	5.7	3.9	6.0	4.6
ALL TEs	5.0	6.4	3.9	4.5	6.3	6.6	4.3	4.7	5.0	4.6	6.3	4.8	6.6	4.3	6.2	5.3

Appendix 1 Business ranking for ten transition economies for (i) 1998–2002 and (ii) 2003–2007 (continued)

	Institutionally related (ii) 2003–07						Other business environment variables									
	PE	PS	PI	PPE	FDI	FT/E	T	F	LM	I	MACRO	MO	FT/E	T	LM	OVERALL
MORE ADVANCED TEs (MATEs)																
Czech Republic	7.5	8.7	6.6	7.8	8.9	8.9	5.4	7.4	6.9	6.9	8.1	5.4	8.9	5.4	6.9	7.3
Hungary	6.9	7.8	6.3	7.8	8.9	8.9	6.6	7.4	7.1	6.6	6.9	5.6	8.9	6.6	7.12	7.3
Poland	7.1	8.2	6.3	7.2	8.3	8.3	6.3	7.4	6.4	6.0	7.4	6.0	8.3	6.3	6.4	7.0
Slovakia	6.3	7.3	5.5	6.9	7.2	8.9	6.0	5.9	6.9	6.0	8.1	4.2	8.9	6.0	6.9	6.6
All MATEs	7.0	8.0	6.2	7.4	8.3	8.8	6.1	7.0	6.8	6.4	7.6	5.3	8.8	6.1	6.8	7.1
LESS ADVANCED TEs (LATEs)																
Azerbaijan	3.5	3.7	3.3	3.8	5.5	7.2	5.5	4.0	5.5	4.6	7.6	5.7	7.2	5.5	5.9	5.3
Bulgaria	5.9	7.3	4.8	6.3	7.2	7.8	5.6	5.5	6.7	6.2	7.8	3.9	7.8	5.6	6.7	6.3
Kazakhstan	4.1	5.5	2.9	4.1	4.4	7.2	3.2	4.8	6.0	4.2	8.3	6.1	7.2	3.2	6.0	5.2
Romania	5.5	6.9	4.4	5.5	6.6	7.8	5.2	5.1	6.3	4.8	5.3	4.6	7.8	5.2	6.3	5.7
Russia	4.3	5.1	3.6	4.9	4.4	7.2	5.5	5.1	7.2	5.1	7.4	4.9	7.2	5.5	7.2	6.0
Ukraine	4.1	5.5	2.9	3.8	4.9	6.1	4.7	4.8	6.4	4.6	8.3	4.5	6.1	4.7	6.4	5.2
ALL LATEs	4.6	5.7	3.7	4.6	5.5	7.2	5.0	4.9	6.4	4.9	7.5	5.0	7.2	5.0	6.4	5.6
ALL TEs																

Source: EIU (2003): scores range from 1 to 10, a score of 10 being perceived as the best for business.

Key: PE = Political environment; PS = Political stability; PI = Political impact; PPE = Policy toward private enterprise and competition; FDI = Policy toward foreign direct investment; FT/E = Foreign trade and exchange control; T = Taxes; F = Financing; LM = Labor Market; I = Infrastructure; MACRO = Macroeconomic environment; MO = Market opportunities.

NB. Some variables are a mixture between those which are institutionally related and those more generally affecting business environment. For these cases, we have included them in both groups of variables.

3 Corporate governance in the global economy: international convergence or continuing diversity?

LEE E. PRESTON

Introduction

The corporation in all its forms is ultimately a creature of the state. Whatever its origins and purposes, the corporation is an artificial institution, granted certain status and privileges, and usually limited in its activities in various ways. This chapter focuses on the status and direction of business corporations within the political jurisdictions ("polities") that constitute their host environments and that establish the bases and limits of their powers. The issues involved can be best understood as aspects of *corporate governance*, which includes both the pattern of enterprise ownership (including state ownership) and the ways in which ownership, regulation, and other bases of control are utilized to legitimate the corporation as an institution and direct/restrict its activities.[1]

---

[1] The literature on corporate governance, both in individual countries/regions and internationally, has exploded over the past couple of decades. Some of the most sophisticated contemporary ideas on this topic were presented at a conference at Tilburg University in 1999 and subsequently published in McCahery et al. (2002). The papers in this 700-page fine-print volume synthesize much of the previous literature and are strongly recommended to all scholars interested in corporate governance. The classic international-comparative analysis of corporate governance is Charkham (1994), which covers five major economies (Germany, Japan, France, USA and UK). *The New Palgrave Dictionary of Economics and the Law* (Newman 1998) contains many entries related to this topic, particularly Zingales' theoretical explanation of the need for "Corporate Governance" and Roe's essay on "Comparative Corporate Governance." *A Special Topic Forum on Corporate Governance* recently appeared in the *Academy of Management Review* Daily, Dalton, and Canella (2003); one paper in this collection (Aguilera and Jackson, further discussed below) analyzes international diversity in terms of variations in stakeholder roles and institutional factors. The essays collected in Cohen and Boyd (2000) also cover major international governance issues. The most recent

The question addressed here is this: "Are the systems of corporate governance prevailing in the diverse environments of the contemporary "global" economy becoming, or likely to become, more similar; or are national and regional differences in corporation–polity relationships being preserved, or even increased?

This question is of particular interest to managers of multinational corporations. If significant differences among countries continue to exist, they may be exploited for strategic purposes; on the other hand, increasing similarity among corporate governance systems may simplify government–business relationships and decrease reporting and regulatory costs.

If we focus this question exclusively on the distinction between (a) state ownership and control of economic activity vs. (b) all forms of non-state ownership and governance, then it is obvious that there has been an increase in similarity (reduction in diversity) over the past couple of decades. Global diversity in the status and role of corporations *increased* immediately after the Second World War, when the state-owned enterprise became the dominant model not only in the USSR, where it was already established, but also in Eastern Europe, China, and other countries within the Soviet sphere. Moreover, even within the more market-oriented economies of Western Europe, Latin America, and Japan, various forms of state control and sponsorship ("national champions," "developmental" enterprises, and neo-protectionism) proliferated during the immediate postwar period.

By contrast, since the early 1980s the extent of state ownership and control of business and economic activity has been declining nearly everywhere in the world. These changes are most conspicuous in areas like Russia and China where state ownership was until recently most extensive. But, in addition, many EU and Latin American states have given up owning and running businesses in older sectors of their economies, and have allowed new sectors to develop without direct government control. The successive rounds of GATT–WTO negotiations have also contributed to ad hoc harmonization of public policies and business behavior in some instances.

international policy document is OECD (1999), amplified by a formal statement by the International Corporate Governance Network (ICGN) (reprinted in Monks and Minow, 2000, pp. 253–258). Several new journals (both print and online) and websites maintain up-to-date coverage of governance issues and trends.

However, privatization and the decline of state control throughout the world have not led to convergence among corporate governance systems. Indeed, the persistence of differences in the status of corporations in various polities is clearly evidenced by the strong emphasis on "national treatment" as a goal of international investment agreements.[2] That is, if there were no substantial differences in corporation–polity relationships among countries, there would be no concern about legal and policy parity between domestic and foreign enterprises. Just the opposite, however, is the case. And the increasing integration of the global economy has contributed to greatly increased interest in governance questions, with particular emphasis on the *differences* among both formal structures and functional realities in various countries.

Before turning to an examination of the convergence–divergence debate, we need to clarify a few important preliminary points:

First: The question of whether corporate governance is becoming more similar among various jurisdictions is not the same as the question of what kind of governance is best (or even better), either for an enterprise or for a polity. As discussed below, these questions, and their answers, are certainly related, but they not identical.

Second: Systems of corporate governance could become more similar among jurisdictions in many different ways. Some pre-existing system might become dominant, with other systems changing to conform to it. Or, alternatively, a hybrid model, involving elements from several systems (and perhaps new elements as well), might evolve. Some of the contemporary convergence–divergence debate is muddled by a failure to distinguish between *similarity* among systems and *conformity* to one or another existing model.

Third: In analyzing governance systems and trends, it is important to maintain a focus on effective functional relationships, not simply on formal legal or regulatory arrangements. Several Tilburg conferees stress the point that diverse legal forms and requirements concerning governance may be "functional substitutes."

---

[2] The term "national treatment" means that all enterprises operating within any particular jurisdiction – including subsidiaries of foreign multinationals – are granted the same privileges, status, etc. This idea contrasts sharply with earlier demands for "extraterritoriality," i.e., that rules of a corporation's home country should apply to all of its operations.

An expanded view of corporate governance

Corporate governance is a broad concept, not easy to define in a few words. My own definition is as follows: Corporate governance is the set of institutional arrangements that establishes the status of the corporation within its host polity and directs/restricts it in the performance of its functions. In their widely cited volume, Monks and Minow define governance as "the relationship among various participants in determining the direction and performance of corporations"; their primary emphasis is on shareowners, management, and the board (2001, p. 1). Blair (2001) says governance "refers to the legal rules, institutional arrangements and practices that determine who controls business corporations, and who gets the benefits that flow from them" (p. 2797). Daily, Dalton, and Canella (2003) emphasize "determination of the broad uses to which organizational resources will be deployed," and "resolution of conflicts among participants" (p. 371). The importance of conflict resolution is also stressed by Zingales (1998), who emphasizes that corporations necessarily operate through incomplete contracts, and sees the governance system as the framework for ex post bargaining after all complete contracts have been fulfilled (p. 497).

Governance has recently become a major topic in the field of corporate finance. Shleifer and Vishny (1997) describe governance as the way investors control managers and "make sure that the managers do not steal the capital they [the investors] supply ... " (p. 737). However, John and Senbet (1998), although also developing a finance-based analysis, define governance more generally as "the mechanisms by which stakeholders of a corporation exercise control over corporate insiders and management such that their interests are protected" (p. 372). Jensen (2000) describes the public corporation as "the nexus for a complex set of voluntary contracts among customers, workers, managers and the suppliers of materials, capital, and risk bearing" (p. 1). He emphasizes that these contracts, taken together, control and direct the corporation, whatever the formal "governance" arrangements may be. Thus, even among leading finance scholars, it is widely (although not universally) acknowledged that a thoughtful analysis of corporate governance requires a larger perspective than the principal–agent model – with its heavy emphasis on ownership patterns, property rights, and board structures – characterizing much of the conventional literature, e.g., Business Roundtable (2002). Aguilera and Jackson

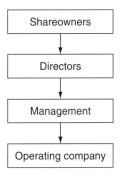

Figure 3.1 Conventional corporate governance model

(2003) point out, in particular, that "agency theory fails to account for key differences across countries" (p. 448).[3]

In the Anglo-American tradition, the private for-profit corporation is conceived as a pool of assets belonging collectively to its shareowners. According to the conventional scenario, after establishment of the organization has been authorized (i.e., chartered) by the state, shareowners elect a board of directors to represent their interests, and the directors in turn select managers who take responsibility for the actual operation of the enterprise (see figure 3.1). Much of the contemporary corporate governance literature, including many current "reform" proposals, is framed within this model and focuses on the composition and structure of corporate boards and on principal–agent problems among shareowners, directors, and managers. The ultimate concern and goal of the set of arrangements is the well-being of investors.

This conventional view of corporate governance, although formally correct, is of little value as a description of the actual status and role of the corporation, particularly of the large enterprise with widely dispersed ownership. In the first place – and as recent corporate scandals in the US, Europe, and Japan have clearly shown – the flow of influence within large firms with dispersed ownership is typically just the reverse of that shown in the model. That is, the managers usually have primary control, recruiting directors who support their goals and policies; and the shareowners are passive investors with little knowledge of the company and no basis

---

[3] For further insight into the nature of corporate governance, see the sample of definitions from European and international sources in appendix 1 and the list of critical aspects of governance in appendix 2 at the end of this chapter.

for evaluating the qualifications and activities of directors. The attention attracted by activists and policymakers (Robert A. G. Monks, and former and current Securities and Exchange Commission chairmen Arthur Levitt and William Donaldson, for example) who have tried to make the theoretical shareowner-dominant model a functioning reality suggests how difficult that is to achieve, and how rarely it is observed.

More important, common observation reveals that a host of influences, both adversarial and collaborative, impinge on the actual operations of the corporation, directing or limiting the ways in which it carries out its functions – and therefore participating in its governance (cf. Preston, 2003). These include both specific requirements of governments (e.g., tax laws) and government-mandated practices within the private sector (e.g., environmental regulations, recognition of unions), as well as commitments entered into voluntarily by the firm (e.g., commitments to employees, inter-firm alliances and contracts). Monks and Minow observe, for example, that although "the [formal] governance structure of Japan's major stock companies ... is identical to that of the US corporation, ... [in fact] the boards of Japan's major corporations currently represent the interests of the company and its employees as a collective ... , not the interests of shareholders" (2000, p. 265).

The point here is that the conventional shareowner-dominant model of corporate governance not only (a) presents a set of relationships that are not typically observed, but also (b) omits a host of relationships that are of great importance for the actual governance of corporations. A simple model of this complex situation is presented in figure 3.2. It is within *this* configuration that we need to address the issue of international convergence or divergence in governance systems.

The importance of these diverse factors is well illustrated by Charkham's list of the distinctive features of corporate governance in the five major countries included in his classic study (1994, p. 4):

- "Networking" and the role of banks in both Germany and Japan (C in figure 3.2)
- Co-determination in Germany (A in figure 3.2)
- Minor role of boards in Japan (B in figure 3.2)
- Fluid mingling of government and business in France (A)
- Prevalence of "adversarial" relationships, checks and balances, within governance structures in the US and UK (A, C)
- Typical CEO dominance and, in contrast, ease of takeovers, in US and UK (B)

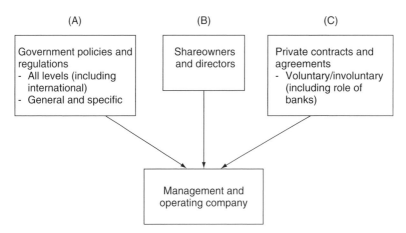

Figure 3.2 An expanded view of corporate governance

Alternative governance systems

Broadly speaking, there are three kinds of corporate governance systems in use in the world today. One of these is state ownership and control. As noted above, state ownership is less prominent than in the recent past, and the state sometimes fails to control management, even when it is the nominal owner. However, the role of the state in regulating corporate behavior in various ways is important in all jurisdictions.

The two systems of governance for corporations outside the state-owned/controlled sector may be described as "market based" and "monitoring based."[4] (This is essentially the "liberal" versus "coordinated" distinction made in the broader political science perspective presented by Hall and Soskice [2001].) Most of the Tilburg conferees tend to contrast "market-based" and "blockholder" systems,

---

[4] Some authorities also contrast "outsider" and "insider" systems. "Outsider" systems involve control by external interests, whether dispersed or concentrated, and possibly including a dominant role for banks, as in Germany; inter-linkage with other firms, referred to as *keiretsu* in Japan; or effective control by governments. "Insider" systems involve ownership and control by interests that are actively engaged in the management of the firm (e.g., managers and boards in most large US and UK firms; managers of formerly state-owned firms who acquire controlling interests during the process of privatization). This is an important distinction, but it is not the same as the market-vs.-monitoring distinction stressed in most of the literature.

emphasizing the difference between (a) widespread stock ownership within highly liquid capital markets and (b) highly concentrated, and often institutional, ownership that necessarily reduces liquidity. However, ownership patterns are not as different among countries as this dichotomy suggests (cf. Wymeersch, 2002, and many other contributors to the Tilburg volume). And, with fiduciary institutions now controlling more than 50 percent of the total value on the New York Stock Exchange – and becoming increasingly active in their monitoring activities – the notion that "market-based" corporate governance is necessarily linked to widespread stock ownership becomes increasingly questionable. Moreover, differences among governance systems may also be associated with differences in monitoring activity and authority by non-owning institutions (e.g., unions, stock exchanges), governments (both home and host), and international agencies. Hence, it is the difference between the modes of oversight and influence that distinguishes the two systems, not the difference in ownership patterns per se (cf. Hansmann and Kraakman, 2002).[5]

In theory, the "market-based" system, traditionally dominant in the US and prominent in the UK, involves widely dispersed stock ownership and relies on signals from the capital market to validate or correct the decisions and actions of managers. If shareowners (or their fiduciaries) do not like the way the company is performing – for whatever reason – they can sell their shares; and if more shares are offered for sale than people want to buy at the current price, share prices will fall and management will be pressed to take corrective action – or will be replaced. Although established corporations do not usually rely on the stock market itself as a major source of additional capital,

---

[5] Maher and Anderson (2002) describe the corporate governance alternatives as "shareholder" and "stakeholder" systems, where the former emphasizes shareholder value and the latter emphasizes corporate responsibilities to a wider constituency. Although these authors acknowledge that the stakeholder model presents some problems of implementation, they appear to endorse its goal of encouraging "socially efficient levels of investment by all major stakeholders" and "active co-operation amongst stakeholders to ensure the long-term profitability of the corporation" (p. 390). John and Senbet also stress that "the ultimate goal should be to maximize "allocational efficiency" by all stakeholders, and that "protecting the rights and claims of non-financial stakeholders" may be critical (1998, pp. 396 and 398).

movements in stock prices strongly affect the behavior of potential lenders, both banks and bondholders. Legal requirements for share-owner voting, two-way communication, and other attributes of "corporate democracy" are intended to support the functioning of these arrangements within a highly liquid capital market, with an ultimate emphasis – at least in theory – on the welfare of shareowners.

Corporate governance systems based on extensive formal "monitoring," whether by private parties, governments, or combinations thereof, are more common in Continental Europe and Japan, and are of great importance in transitional economies throughout the world. The Tilburg conferees emphasized primarily systems relying on extensive supervision by individuals and institutions holding large blocks of stock. In effect, large "blockholders" (including fiduciaries) sacrifice liquidity and assume significant burdens of supervision in order to gain the advantage of direct influence on management. However, other forms of formal monitoring can be required by the state – as in the German two-tiered board system (now also required in China, see below) and the required consultation of employee committees on certain issues in France, as well as compulsory recognition of unions, legally required employee benefits, etc., in many jurisdictions. And non-governmental regulation (as by the New York Stock Exchange and other important bourses, cf. Coffee, 2002) can also play a significant role. (Non-governmental governance codes are the focus of the European Commission, 2002.) There are strong similarities of interest between minority shareowners and many non-owning stakeholders (e.g., customers, communities), and these interests are more likely to be protected through monitoring than through the marketplace. Monitoring is ultimately focused on the well-being of the corporation as an ongoing institution, ordinarily viewing the well-being of share-owners as one, among many, objectives to be considered. As Vives (2000) states, within a broader concept of the corporation, "governance refers to the design of institutions to make managers internalize the welfare of [all] stakeholders in the firm" (p. 1).

Economies in the process of transition from socialism and state ownership to various forms of "privatization" have tended to adopt a mixture of market-based and monitoring arrangements. And the state continues to take a strong role in establishing the policy framework and serving as a back-up monitor. According to Aoki and Kim (1995), the privatization of large, formerly state-owned, enterprises typically results in a pattern of "insider control," which cannot be effectively regulated by private investors. They recommend the development of substantial investment banks, somewhat on the Japanese model, that would be capable of exercising "outsider" monitoring and control functions, even within very thin capital markets. Berglof and von Thadden (2000) go even further, arguing that in transitional economies the corporate governance model should incorporate "multilateral negotiations and influence-seeking among many different stakeholders" (p. 280).

The varied experience of the transitional economies is a strong reminder that the "convergence" of corporate governance systems may involve innovation as well as replication, and hence may result in new hybrid systems. This is nowhere clearer – or more important – than in the case of China, where corporate governance has been identified by the government as the core element of the "modern enterprise system" (Tenev and Zhang, 2002, p. vii). About 80 percent of the small/medium enterprises in China have been transformed by sale to their employees or outside investors; and the stock of about 1,200 large companies is now publicly listed and traded. A code of corporate governance applying to all "listed" companies was issued in 2001 by the China Securities Regulatory Commission and the State Economic and Trade Commission. This code specifies a two-tier board structure, and includes a recommendation for independent directors on the management board (as well as the customary independence of supervisory board members). The code also gives special attention to responsibilities for collaborative relationships between the firm and various stakeholder groups (China Securities Regulatory Commission, 2001). Further evolution toward a "hybrid" market-monitored governance model was recently predicted by a Chinese expert (Li Zhaoxi, 2002).

However, in spite of these recent developments, in China there are still strong links between businesses and governments at every level. A company's board chairman (like the general manager in a state-owned firm) is often also the head of its Communist Party committee; and information tends to be assembled and made available primarily to meet the needs of taxation authorities rather than investors. A World Bank and International Finance Corporation study team strongly recommended continued reduction in state ownership and control, expanded use of independent directors in listed companies, the development of an institutional investor base, and an increased role for banks in both financing and monitoring business operations. The

Table 3.1 Comparison of systems of corporate governance[*]

	Market	Monitoring
Primary focus	Welfare of investors	Welfare of ongoing corporate institution
Active supervision by shareowners, fiduciaries or others	Moderate	Strong
Shareowner legal rights	Strong	Limited
Diversification of investment	Favorable	Unfavorable/neutral
Liquidity of investment/ involvement	High	Low
Management perspective	Short-term	Long-term
Emphasis on growth	Usually strong	Often weak
Attention to stakeholder concerns	Moderate	Usually strong

Notes:

[*]Bratton and McCahery (2002, p. 29) present a similar comparison of "market" and "blockholder" systems, with a strong evaluative flavor (i.e., "plus–minus" ratings). However, the criteria they use in making these evaluations are not entirely clear, and my broader concept of "monitoring" differs from their emphasis on substantial share ownership ("blockholding"). Hence, this table contains descriptive comparisons rather than evaluative judgments.

importance of increasing flexibility and continuing opportunities for diversity in governance arrangements was also stressed (Tenev and Zhang, 2002; see also Yeung and Olds, 2000, and Li, 2002).

Nearly all analysts appear to agree that there is no "best" system of corporate governance, suitable for all types of enterprises and all political jurisdictions. Even Shleifer and Vishny (1997) acknowledge that, in spite of their diversity, the US, Germany, and Japan all have "the essential elements of a good governance system." Hence, "the available evidence does not tell us which one of *their* governance systems is the best." For most other countries, the question is not which of these systems to emulate, but "how to introduce significant legal protection … so that mechanisms of extensive outside financing can develop" (p. 739).

To facilitate important comparisons and contrasts, table 3.1 presents a summary of some of the features of market-based and monitoring-based systems of governance. For emphasis, we note here again that the primary function of all the attributes of the market-based system is to protect the welfare of investors; whereas the focus of monitoring-based systems is on the well-being of the corporate institution as a whole, including its critical stakeholders.

Does governance matter?

There is serious debate in the literature about whether, or how much, the system of governance actually "matters" as an explanation for corporate behavior, performance, sustainability, etc., and for macroeconomic development (cf. Emmons and Schmidt, 2000; Vives, 2000). Some authorities appear to be convinced that one particular set of arrangements is most effective for achieving "economic efficiency" goals. Others point out that there are conspicuous examples of "success" and "failure" under all systems, and that corporate experience is most strongly influenced by general business conditions, international developments, technological change, etc. And still others note the importance of multiple goals – political cohesion, compatibility with national legal frameworks, etc. – in assessing the appropriateness of governance arrangements from the viewpoints of both firms and host jurisdictions. Aguilera and Jackson (2003) stress the importance of interaction between stakeholder roles (particularly those of capital, labor, and management) and institutional arrangements, both of which vary greatly among polities.

If there were some obvious Darwinian "best" – or even "better" – system of governance, one might anticipate that the various polities of the world would evolve toward it over time. Both international economic competition (including competition for investment) and policy analysis of alternative options and experiences (referred to by the Tilburg conferees as "cross reference") would contribute to this result. However, Bratton and McCahery (2002) conclude that there is "no empirical basis for ascribing comparative advantage to either system" (p. 25). By contrast, Hansmann and Kraakman (2002) believe that the market-based model is economically superior and will ultimately prevail. However, they also state, "All thoughtful people believe that corporate enterprise should be organized and operated to serve the interests of society as a whole, and that the interests of shareholders deserve no greater weight in this social calculus than [those of other stakeholders]" (p. 58). Thus, these authors appear to endorse both the shareholder and the stakeholder perspectives; most of the other market-vs.-monitoring comparisons found in the literature are similarly equivocal.

Stanwick and Stanwick (2002) summarize a number of recent empirical studies aimed at discovering whether or not some corporate governance practices might be associated with some indicators of corporate performance – and hence might "matter," in that sense. (A similar summary is provided, along with extensive description of various governance-rating schemes and services, in Van den Berghe and Levrau, 2003.) Not surprisingly, the results of these studies are quite mixed. Some show no association. Others report perverse results: e.g., that majorities of outside board members (usually considered a "good governance" characteristic) are associated with inferior performance. Others are more consistent with "good governance → good performance" predictions. Furthermore, it appears that institutional and long-term investors favor firms with strong "good governance" attributes; hence, "good governance" might pay off in the stock market, whether or not it has any impact on short-term bottom-line results (cf. European Commission, 2002, p. 2). In their own original study, Stanwick and Stanwick find associations between some "good governance" features and return on assets among firms on the *Business Week* lists of twenty-five "best" and "worst" boards of directors for 1997 and 1999.

Emmons and Schmidt (2000) present an extensive aggregative analysis of the performance of companies based in countries with a "common law" tradition (US, UK, Canada, etc.) in contrast with those based in "civil law" countries (continental Europe and Japan). They find that the former group surpasses the latter in terms of new company creation (IPOs) and several measures of financial mobilization and performance. However, they note that some of these differences may be associated with differences in the industry composition of various economies. They may also be due to explicit social preferences for a "milder" form of capitalism involving long-term external monitoring, greater emphasis on allocative efficiency, and a desire for "socially beneficial intertemporal smoothing of risk" (cf. pp. 89–91).

In his classic 1994 study, Charkham suggests two criteria for evaluating corporate governance systems (pp. 354–355):

Dynamism   Ability of managers to take actions without excessive restraint by government.

Accountability   Managers are sufficiently accountable that "neces-
                    sary standards" can be maintained, and "appropri-
                    ate remedial action" taken when necessary.

Charkham does not directly specify to whom managers should be
accountable, although the implication suggests society as a whole, or
at least all major stakeholders. He remarks that "accountability" covers standards of behavior as well as standards of competence. He
rejects the use of a third criterion based on "social performance,"
although he emphasizes that "a company must contribute to society's
well-being, or at the very lowest must not impair it." Charkham
believes that each system studied has its own strengths and weaknesses,
but finally concludes that the German system, with some qualifications, offers the best combination of features. A similar conclusion is
reached by Prowse (1995), although he notes that "the structure that
supports a more efficient corporate governance mechanism may be too
rigid to be viable in the long run" (p. 1).

Conclusion: convergence or divergence?

Since there are substantial differences among corporate governance
systems in various jurisdictions – and little, if any, evidence that one
system is superior to another – one might conclude that the diversity
that has evolved to date might be likely to persist into the future.
However, the lists of convergence and divergence factors in table 3.2A
and 3.2B suggest that there is clearly room for argument on the point.
Of the six Tilburg papers specifically addressing the convergence/diver-
gence issue, four (Hansmann and Kraakman, Coffee, Cheffins, Maher
and Anderson) predict convergence – although the last acknowledges
that convergence will never be "complete," and Coffee stresses the role
of "functional substitutes" rather than identical rules and procedures.
Two papers (Bratton and McCahery, and Roe) predict that significantly diverse corporate governance systems will continue to prevail.[6]
In his earlier essay Roe (1998), Roe acknowledged that "the forces for

---

[6] Many other papers in that collection touch on this issue but are difficult to
classify. And, in spite of the word "convergence" in its title, the Budapest
conference papers (Balling et al., 1998) primarily describe the distinctive
features of various governance systems rather than their potential
similarities.

Table 3.2 Factors contributing to convergence/divergence

3.2A: Factors contributing to convergence *

1 Global competition will lead to convergence through a Darwinian process because the same governance arrangements (whatever they are) will contribute to competitive success in most environments.

2 Access to global financing will require uniformity (again, of whatever kind) in the legal status, protection, and treatment of investors.

3 Evolution of international accounting standards will lead to uniformity in other areas.

4 Cross-border stock listing and share ownership will lead to convergence on a firm-by-firm basis, although it might not lead to convergence in national laws and codes.

5 The increasing share of the US securities market controlled by large institutional investors creates a situation very similar to European and Japanese "blockholding," and suggests the possible evolution of a common monitoring-based regime in the largest and most important sectors of the corporate global economy.

6 Trends toward regional harmonization of securities markets, financing arrangements, etc. (within, for example, the EU) – and continuous interaction among policy actors involved in these processes – will gradually lead to a convergence of legal and policy frameworks.

3.2B: Factors contributing to continued/increased diversity

1 So long as financial institutions, ownership patterns, legal traditions, and national economic policies continue to vary considerably among jurisdictions, different governance structures will continue to be appropriate for different environments. Competitive pressures (whether in capital or product markets) will lead each firm and each polity toward the governance arrangements most likely to contribute to its own success, and these are unlikely to be the same in all cases. (Indeed, difference from other jurisdictions may become an advantageous feature in itself, as in the case of tax havens.)

2 The elements of corporate governance systems are indivisible and intimately linked with other features of a nation's legal structure, and the whole set of arrangements is heavily path dependent. Hence, the piecemeal adoption of elements of alternative governance systems is infeasible, and wholesale adoption of complete new systems extremely unlikely.

Note:
*The points on this list do not all point toward convergence in any particular direction.

convergence among the advanced nations are powerful and readily identified," but emphasized that governance systems are "embedded with institutional complementarities" – and hence difficult to modify without disrupting society-wide political and economic arrangements (pp. 343–344).

However, Van den Berghe (2002) contends that increased use of international capital markets by large firms from all parts of the world is pushing them toward common policies with respect to the treatment of investors, a trend which in turn influences policies with respect to other interests involved in governance. The European Commission (2002) study concludes that, at least within the EU, "trends toward convergence ... appear to be both more numerous and more powerful than any trends toward differentiation" (p. 3). Emmons and Schmidt (2000) find continuing diversity "unsurprising," but also observe "limited evidence of convergence" (p. 60). On the other hand, Halpern (2000) anticipates continuing diversity, and emphasizes that the market-based system is "not a viable alternative" in transitional economies.

All of the major studies reviewed here go to great pains to describe the differences among governance systems in various countries and the importance of "path dependencies" (i.e., historic evolutionary processes) in explaining the specific characteristics of the various systems and the barriers to change among them. Although Monks and Minow (2000) believe that global economic trends have "led to a remarkably effective dialogue concerning governance reform" (i.e., toward convergence), they also emphasize that "local practice remains a powerful force," and that even between the US and UK, important differences remain (pp. 295–296). Roe is the strongest exponent of the belief that governance systems are so deeply embedded in national political and social structures – indeed, are important supporting elements within such structures – that international convergence is probably an impossibility. (The more general analysis of Hall and Soskice [2001] also concludes that "national distinctive forms of capitalism" [which would, of course, include governance arrangements] are permanent features of the global economy [p. vi].) However, Aguilera and Jackson (2003) believe that contemporary governance systems are more "hybrid" than most descriptions indicate, although social and historical differences will prevent full convergence. This viewpoint is echoed in various ways by many other writers (cf. Leblanc, 1999).

At the risk of walking "where angels fear to tread," I am going to offer a prediction about the evolution of corporate governance systems throughout the world over the next few decades. I believe that the trend is toward convergence, although not toward the universal adoption of any pre-existing model, and particularly not the Anglo-American model so admired in some quarters. I find highly persuasive Charkham's conclusion that the German model – two-tier boards, with prominent large-investor involvement – combines several desirable features:

a. Financial stability – from the banks;
b. Social legitimacy – from employee and external representation on the supervisory board;
c. Adequate scope for managerial initiative – as indicated by the vigorous global activity of European, particularly German, firms.

The attractiveness of the two-tier board model, with a "supervisory board" dominated by outsiders and a "management board" consisting of directly involved parties (managers, owners, customers, etc.), is suggested by interim chairman John Reed's recent recommendations for the reorganization of the New York Stock Exchange (*Wall Street Journal*, 2003). The two-tier board model was recently adopted for all publicly listed companies in China in 2001 (China Securities Regulatory Commission, 2001).

Two faults of the current German system in its historical form are generally recognized: excessive rigidity and inadequate public disclosure. Rigidity comes mostly from the formal requirement of codetermination, which is actually quite limited within German industry and which shows no signs of being adopted elsewhere (although it may be politically difficult to remove in Germany). Apart from the codetermination feature, German two-tier boards actually differ from unified boards with a majority of outside directors only in that in the former a certain level of employee representation is required by law. Regular employee consultation within other governance structures – as in the French "committée d'entreprise" and in long-term collaborative union–management relationships in the US and elsewhere – accomplishes much the same result. German and Japanese corporate governance systems are often considered comparable because of the importance of large banks and inter-company ownership in both. However, it is notable that Japan has avoided a formal codetermination requirement in favor of what has been termed a "socially endogenous" model based on "reciprocal responsibilities, obligations and trust" between a firm and its employees (Learmount, 2002, p. 150).

With regard to disclosure, the requirements of the Sarbanes–Oxley Act (adopted in the US in 2000) will have global impact because of the number of major foreign firms registered in the US and the pressure of international investment competition. Indeed, more adequate (and more accurate!) disclosure may be the most important US contribution to the evolution of the new "hybrid" governance model. Daimler-Chrysler – a firm with headquarters in both Germany and the US, and important alliances with Asian multinationals (Mitsubishi, Hyundai) – endorses "international stock exchange regulations" equivalent to the Sarbanes–Oxley requirements in the six-page "Corporate Governance" section of its 2002 annual report.

These comments suggest that a gradual convergence of corporate governance systems toward the German model, but without its least desirable features, is at least possible, but is it likely? Two developments suggest that it may be:

First: Enlargement of the EU to include jurisdictions within which financial markets are still relatively weak and social-stakeholder involvement traditions relatively strong suggests evolution toward a "monitoring-based" system of some kind. In the New Europe, both unitary and two-tier boards will probably persist, but gradually become functionally equivalent, and a level of "social accountability" for the corporate role in society will certainly be preserved. European Commission (2002) emphasizes that inter-country differences in "best practice," as defined by non-governmental codes, are already considerably smaller than differences in formal corporate law.

Second: Recent initiatives by the OECD (1999, and related documents) combine both (a) a strong emphasis on shareowner rights and protections (particularly for minority and foreign shareowners) and (b) a comparable emphasis on the rights and roles of non-owner stakeholders (e.g., employees), and their inclusion in governance processes where appropriate. Again, disclosure – and not only of past experience but also of intention, as with the greatly increased global emphasis on "codes of conduct" – is a requirement for effective governance within all systems, as well for access to global capital markets and for social and political legitimacy. The growth of monitoring-based corporate governance systems may help to allay some fears about the "evils" of the entire globalization process.

The US, with its current fixation on short-term shareowner value, may remain an exception to a more "politically correct" corporate governance structure for many years; just as China may remain an outlier on the government ownership/control side. However, if Greater Europe, along with much of Latin America and Asia, evolves toward a hybrid market-monitored system of corporate governance over, say, the next half century, it will be hard for even these two large and powerful economies to resist the pressures toward global convergence. As Michael Useem (1998) has remarked, "[T]he days of divergent governance systems presiding over convergent organizational forms … are likely to be numbered … " (p. 57).

Appendix 1   Some definitions of corporate governance

Corporate governance is …
- the system of rules by which companies are directed and controlled (UK).
- the organization of the administration and management of companies (Belgium).
- the goals according to which a company is managed, and the major principles and frameworks which regulate the interaction between the company's managerial bodies, the owners, as well as other parties … Stakeholders include employees, creditors, suppliers, customers, and the local community (Denmark).
- the legal and factual regulatory framework for managing and supervising a company (Germany).
- the set of rules according to which firms are managed and controlled, … the results of norms, traditions, and patterns of behavior developed by each economic and legal system (Italy).
- a code of conduct for those associated with the company … consisting of a set of rules for sound management and proper supervision and for division of duties and responsibilities and powers effecting the satisfactory balance of influence of all the stakeholders (Netherlands).
- the system of rules and procedures employed in the conduct and control of listed companies (Portugal).
- a set of relationships between a company's management, its board, its shareholders and other stakeholders. [It] also provides the structure through which the objectives of the company are set, and the means of attaining those objectives and monitoring performance are determined (OECD).

Source: European Commission, 2002, pp. 28–29. (See original source for complete citations.)

Appendix 2   Some critical aspects of corporate governance systems

Status of the corporation

Incorporation procedures – registration, stock issue, and transfer conditions
Reporting and disclosure requirements
Tax treatment

Directors/boards

Structure of boards and board-related institutions (e.g., two-board structures, mandated practices such as codetermination, employee committees, union representation, etc.)
Qualifications and election of directors
Required board committees and their composition

Management

Formal reporting, disclosure, and communication requirements – with regulators, shareowners, potential investors, creditors, credit rating agencies, and others
Takeovers – conditions governing, and permissible responses (poison pills, etc.)
Definition of and limitations on insider trading
Responsibilities toward non-financial stakeholders

Shareowners

Ownership structure – concentrated or dispersed; role of banks, fiduciaries, other firms
Shareowner voting rights – protection of minority shareowner interests
Opportunity and requisite conditions for presentation of shareowner initiatives and lawsuits

Shareowner access to information (including shareowner lists)
Limitations on foreign ownership; foreign exchange convertibility

Creditors

Legal status of creditor claims; bankruptcy laws
Strength of limited liability principles

Sources of governance standards

Statute law and related court decisions – national, state, international
(e.g., EU)
Corporate and securities market regulation (e.g., SEC)
Regulation of roles of other entities vis-à-vis corporations (e.g., bank
regulation)
Non-governmental regulation (e.g., role of NYSE, NASDAQ, etc.)

4 Revisiting rival states: beyond the triangle?

JOHN STOPFORD

W HEN Susan Strange and I looked into the relationships between firms and States during the late 1980s, we were primarily concerned to signal that the rivalry among States for control over the means of wealth creation had grown to the point where it had overtaken such traditional concerns as control over territory, to become the predominant driver of diplomacy. We argued that States had moved far from the days when suspicion of the multinationals' power had interfered with bargaining relationships, to a position where incentives were being showered on the firms to influence their decisions about where to invest. These were also the days when the UN was still struggling to complete a Code of Conduct for the MNEs (it never succeeded) and when trade talks within the General Agreement on Tariffs and Trade (GATT) were beginning to link trade relationships with the consequences of foreign direct investment (FDI).

We called this "new" diplomacy "triangular" to highlight these growing interrelationships. This was occurring in an era when bargaining power and opinion had swung toward favoring the notion that the MNE was essentially a benign force for economic development. Fears of corruption in the bargaining among executives and government officials had receded. So too had fears about the MNEs' undue interference in internal, domestic policy.

Under these seemingly benign conditions, attention could (usefully, we argued) be focused on all three sides of the triangle to gain greater understanding of the dynamics of the relationships and the conditions for competitiveness. One side of the triangle represented firm–firm issues in global competition. A second side of the triangle represented the specific bargaining issues between a MNE and a host country. The third side represented the competition among governments for the scarce international investment dollar. Our contention was that if analysis was restricted to a single side of the triangle, then much of the dynamic of the reality was omitted. Analysts would therefore be in danger of drawing false conclusions. Conventional strategy analysis of competitive advantage typically restricted attention within a single industry. Much of the work on business–government relationships was focused on one government at a time, normally the host government for a proposed investment. International relations considered government–government rivalry typically in terms of older notions of diplomacy and of relationships dominated by Cold War issues of power.

A close study of many investments in developing countries – primarily Brazil, Kenya, and Malaysia – had convinced us that the dynamics were frequently determined by the interplay among all three sides of the triangle. An example suffices to make the point. During the 1970s, the US government threatened Brazil with a super-301 trade embargo unless the Brazilian government stopped its "unfair" subsidies to Embraer, then a fledgling aerospace company trying to break into the US market for regional jets. To cut a long story short, one consequence of the bilateral negotiations that ensued was Brazil's repeal in 1977 of its Infomatics Law. This law had greatly restricted the operations of all computer and information MNEs in Brazil. The easing of restrictions allowed IBM and others to transfer new technology to their Brazilian operations. With new-found access to digital control technology, Autolatina began to make and export a new generation of fuel- and emission-efficient automobile engines. What began as a US–Brazil dispute in aerospace opened up a new series of developments in the digital industries and in turn the automobile industry, affecting both trade and investment among the US, Europe, and Latin America.

The world market had become much more complex as these interrelationships linked more industries and more States in novel and seemingly unpredictable ways. Our proposition was that by considering all aspects of the "new" diplomacy, both firms and States were likely to reach better and more durable bargains than they would have achieved had they retained narrow perspectives and attitudes of mutual suspicion. Partnership in progress seemed possible on a scale previously unimaginable.

Post-Cold War globalization has changed the rules

Globalization, combined with the end of the Cold War, has acted to upset what turned out to be a short interlude of partnership. The multiple forms of globalization have dismantled more than the Berlin

Wall; they have eroded many of the means by which governments attempt to regulate affairs.

Triangular diplomacy operated in a world of "division," where power was determined by the sovereign state. We are now moving into a world of "integration," where the triangle needs significant alteration. Today, one can argue that three critical balances increasingly determine power.[1] The first balance of power is based on relations among other states and the relationship of any one state with the USA, the only superpower left. The second is the balance of power between States and markets. Susan Strange talked about the growing power of the markets to erode sovereignty. The impact of the capital market on Indonesia in 1998 is but one recent manifestation of the fact that even governments are not immune to the influence of what Thomas Friedman calls the "electronic herd."[2] The third balance is between individuals and States. For example, Jody Williams, who won the Nobel Peace Prize in 1997, was able almost single handedly to persuade 120 governments to sign up to the treaty outlawing landmines. Her one weapon was the internet. The World Wide Web is beginning to show that no one is quite in charge.

The metaphor of the Wall (a world of divisions) giving way to the Web (a world of integration) is useful to focus attention on how the unit of analysis for commercial diplomacy today has extended far beyond the simple notions of States and firms competing and collaborating for resources. The treatment of the State needs to be broadened to include both civil society and the implications of the growing importance of "clusters" of resources in cities and regions within a State. The firm needs to be treated as more than a single legal entity, to include the consequences of the growth of multiple strategic alliances and constellations of alliances. Moreover, the concept of the firm in the knowledge economy as a series of bundles of capability distributed in the metanational form raises new questions about how the firm deals with host States.[3] Furthermore, the very

---

[1] The first exponent of this concept of balance in a world of "integration" was Thomas Friedman (see Friedman, 1999).

[2] The crash of the Indonesian stock market and the sharp increase in the risk ratings for Indonesian debt were credited as having a strong influence in hastening President Suharto's departure.

[3] Doz, Santos, and Williamson, 2001.

nature of the capitalist system needs inspection. Without some stronger bonds of morality or procedural justice, the instabilities inherent in a world of growing technological scale can become destructive. An extended unit of analysis is needed to help explain the dynamics of negotiation when the range of possible outcomes from any one negotiation has grown dramatically.

Extending the notion of the nation-state

Much of the international-business literature has focused on the concept of the nation-state as defined in the Treaty signed in Westphalia in 1648. This was designed to bring peace, security, order, and stability to Europe after the devastation of the Thirty Years' War. The treaty established what have become the principles underpinning international law today: sovereign states are equal and independent. European history during the following three hundred years shows how little the treaty succeeded in bringing peace and security. Pragmatism of the kind represented by the Congress of Vienna in 1815 and the ensuing balance-of-power regime seems more salient than the universalistic ideas of the treaty. Nonetheless, over time, the idea of what constitutes a sovereign state gradually formed around three characteristics: a permanent population, a defined territory, and a functioning government. These principles were defined and enshrined in the United Nations Charter in 1945, again a period when the restoration of peace and order was the priority. They are a touchstone of principle for many sovereign states today, most strongly supported in the developing world.

Article 2.1 of the Charter recognized the sovereign equality of States as an absolute principle globally. The UN, the new organ of international governance, was explicitly prohibited in Article 2.7 from interfering in matters that were essentially within the jurisdiction of any State. The same held for all States, thus effectively ending colonialism. The implication was that everyone was living in a sovereign nation-state. The later development of regional groups, most especially the EU, has begun to challenge the absolute nature of the definition. So too have the more recent developments in US foreign policy and the war on terror.

Perhaps more important for the purposes of this analysis is the paradoxical challenge to the concept of the sovereign State posed by the

1945 Declaration of Human Rights. In this Declaration, the UN began what some people, including Secretary General Kofi Annan, have described as a competition of State sovereignty on the one hand and individual sovereignty on the other. The implication is that there are limits to what the State can do. Sovereignty is not so much about internal control as it is about the responsibility of the State both to its own citizens and to all other players in the international community.

John Dunning's recent work on the Moral State is an extension of this argument. Dunning has written extensively about the conditions needed for the survival of the global capitalist system. In Dunning (2003), he argued that global capitalism, the product of many forces, most recently triangular diplomacy, is falling short of its promise. Despite being the most efficient system for creating and sustaining wealth, it falls short on three grounds. "The first is its institutions – and particularly the market – are less well designed for the production and exchange of *public* goods and services than *private* goods and services ... the former are becoming a rising component of our daily welfare. The second is that there are a series of 'technical' failures in each of its institutions judged by their ability to meet the demands of democratic capitalism *per se*. The third is that the moral underpinning of these same institutions needs reconfiguring and upgrading" (p. 32).

Dunning's plea to executives and scholars of international business alike is that they should include some explicit consideration of the moral dimension in their thinking as they seek to create wealth and to explain how global capitalism might benefit, and become more acceptable to, a much larger number of people across the planet. The implications for governments are obvious. Those that rely on global capitalism must listen more carefully to their own citizens if they are adequately to judge their responsibilities. Many people around the world now regard the multinational as deleterious to their own interests.

Civil society and the NGOs

From the protests about the WTO trade talks in Seattle in 1999 onwards, NGOs have emerged as a new force in the bargaining about how resources are created and allocated. The international NGOs, as Lal and others have argued, may be an altruistic force in that they are not seeking benefits for themselves but for mankind, yet they may also do great harm (in Dunning, 2003, p. 55). Many of the NGOs are concentrating their attention on three areas: labor relations, human rights, and the environment. In all three areas, MNEs are seen to be the adversary.

The effect of this change – which seems now irreversible – is to make corporate policymakers and negotiators re-think their approach to their commercial diplomacy. They must now confront the paradox enshrined in the concept of the sovereign State. The NGOs are, in effect, asking firms to intervene in domestic matters when the local government is falling short of its responsibilities.

Is this pressure irresistible? By whose standards should responsibility be measured, and by whom? Should a firm intervene in a country in the interests of the local society by setting policies that are legal, yet in opposition to the government's approach? These are questions that require some exploration before an answer can be attempted.

The dilemmas implicit in these questions were apparent long before Seattle. The abortive attempt to write a UN Code of Conduct for Transnational Corporations that started in the early 1970s contained the following provision:

Transnational Corporations should/shall not interfere [illegally] in the internal [political] affairs of the countries in which they operate [by resorting to] [They should refrain from any] [subversive and other [illicit]] activities [aimed at] undermining the political and social systems in these countries. (UNCTAD, p. 154)[4]

Similar clauses were included in the OECD 1976 Guidelines for Multinational Enterprises and in the International Labour Organization (ILO) Declarations. Yet, the difficulty of setting any absolute standard of non-interference was demonstrated by the position of South Africa under apartheid. Any corporate effort to oppose apartheid could be construed as involvement in internal politics. Moreover, the UN wanted to ban corporations from any dealings with racist regimes (and colonial administrations). To complicate matters, there was a long-running argument in the UN among governments as to whether South Africa was a legitimate regime.

---

[4] Note that the use of the square brackets is a diplomatic device used in drafting committees to produce a text that carries some meaning but has yet to gain the concurrence of all members of the committee. In this case the square brackets were never removed.

The seriousness of the position in South Africa meant that something more tangible than debate had to be initiated. Where governments hesitated, the civil society movement stepped in. The movement pressurized MNEs to act against apartheid, but was itself divided. One faction wanted disinvestment to damage the regime and hasten its fall. Any MNE decision to quit would necessarily have a political consequence, regardless of whether the reasoning was to bring political change or merely to leave a deteriorating market. The other faction wanted MNEs to stay, provided they adopted the Sullivan Principles of avoiding racial discrimination and investing in black workers' communities.[5] To adopt Sullivan was, of course, to break the laws of apartheid. Both factions of civil society showed how far they had moved from governmental guidelines. For example, when the US State Department later adopted the Sullivan Principles as a standard of conduct for firms to qualify for trade assistance programs, the principle of being committed to political activities for equal rights had been neatly omitted.[6]

The South African experience shaped subsequent developments of the agenda of MNEs' social responsibilities. Social groups learned that they could not expect much direct support from governments and shifted their attention to pressing large, powerful MNEs to exert their

---

[5] For details, see the writings of John M. Kline, especially Kline (2003), pp. 1–26.

[6] On a personal note, I was involved in another dimension of this dilemma of responsibility. At the time I was a director of Shell (UK), a subsidiary that had responsibilities over South African operations. We were faced with the threat of UK sanctions against Rhodesia (now Zimbabwe). The UK Foreign Office had instructed us that we were, as a UK company, to comply with the UK embargo of all energy supplies to Rhodesia. At that time, the South African government had decreed that any corporate decisions to withhold supplies from Rhodesia were criminal actions. Because the Shell refinery in Durban was a principal supplier of oil products to Rhodesia, our tanker movements were under close surveillance. If we were to comply with the UK government instruction, our managers in Durban would go to jail. There was no question in our minds that our prime loyalties lay with our employees. We ignored the UK government. Were we right in our decision? Were we honorable? These were questions that occupied considerable time at our board meetings and gave me an early baptism into the realities of managing beyond the comfortable confines of traditionally defined products and markets.

influence on events around the world. From direct action, the NGOs were exploring the alternative of indirect action, or influence.

From the perspective of an MNE, the call for exerting influence opened a Pandora's box of problems. John Dunning's call for the explicit management of values and "higher" morality might help establish a sustainable way forward. The problem, however, is an absence of any sense of agreement about whose morality. Should firms accede to the strictures of the Interfaith Center on Corporate Responsibility? Or should they favor the requirements of the World Development Movement? Or Amnesty International's "Human Rights Checklist?" All claim the moral high ground. All advocate forms of political intervention in the name of human rights that contravene the local laws and policies of numerous sovereign States. Who could resolve the dilemma? The International Chamber of Commerce (ICC) has formulated a set of policy guidelines for international investment, but these have no more than a bland recommendation that investors should respect "national laws, policies and economic and social objectives of the host country in the same way as would a good citizen of that country."[7] How could the ICC help an investor in Myanmar or similar pariah states when home governments are becoming increasingly hostile, but lacking any policy initiatives?

Investors' dilemmas

The NGOs' call for more responsible action to offset the actions of governments that fail to live up to international standards of respect for human rights (however defined) poses a severe problem for investors. On the one hand, they are mindful of Milton Friedman's strictures that "there is only one social responsibility of business ... to increase profits, so long as it stays within the rules of the game" (Friedman, 1962). On the other hand, they are mindful that they are citizens too. As Lord Browne, the CEO of BP, put it in a recent speech, "We don't make our profits and then go and live somewhere else. This is our society too. We cannot isolate ourselves. We have to be engaged in public policy issues. We have to be constructive." In other words, Milton Friedman

---

[7] I am indebted to John Kline for reminding me of these dilemmas, in Kline (2003).

cannot be right, unless society is prepared to grant some notion of a permit to operate.

The dilemma worsens when one compares the CEO's perspective with that of operating managers who do not have the luxury of such global perspective. As one manager in BP stated recently in a debate about human rights, "We do not engage in advocacy, nor are we campaigners. This is not our role" (Rice, 2002). The same manager goes on to say, "We have options ... we have political influence ... everything is handled on a case-by-case basis." Yet BP has publicly positioned its global policy as being a "force for good" (LBS, 2001). Rodney Chase, an executive director, has claimed that BP has a default structure in, for example, its environmental policy such that where there is doubt, the manager has no option but to ensure no damage to the environment ensues from his or her actions. Similarly clear lines of demarcation are lacking in the more troubled waters of human rights, though BP is pioneering the use of a comprehensive societal audit for many of the communities in which it operates.

Some MNEs – Shell, for example – have signed up to the UN's Global Compact. This compact asks firms to "support and respect the protection of internationally proclaimed human rights within their spheres of interest" and to "make sure that they are not complicit in human rights abuses." The compact also asks for voluntary adherence to principles affecting labor standards and the environment. In Shell's case, the effect has been to change the company's General Business Principles to include endorsement of the UN Declaration on Human Rights "within the legitimate role of business." Shell now routinely conducts seminars to help operating managers figure out how to behave within these new parameters. In other words, there are small developments in the process of how MNEs conduct their decision making.

The key development here is that there is a growing awareness of the need for social engagement between firms at local levels within their host societies and governments. The dialogue could, advocates hope, yield positive gains on both sides, even though the fundamental dilemma of limiting the political role of firms remains unresolved.

Clusters of resource

Should such engagement be conducted at national level or at the level of the economic "clusters" that are so important in generating wealth and competitiveness?[8] Perhaps both, thus adding some of the complexity mentioned earlier. The thesis of the emergence of the metanational firm suggests the same trend toward a more dispersed organizational context for negotiation. As Doz, Santos, and Williamson (2001) put it, "The metanational pioneers ... are already showing the way forward. They have begun to leave behind the corporate world dominated by the omnipotent headquarters and powerful national subsidiaries. To these companies, national boundaries are no longer a useful proxy for market segments or technology but little more than an administrative nuisance" (p. 242). Add to this internal trend the external trend of an increasing reliance on alliances as a way to build new competitive strength and get access to resources that are not for sale and one glimpses a different landscape.[9]

The determining relationship for the future may not be exclusively based on bargaining between the global headquarters of a firm and a national authority. Instead, these clusters of resource may have to develop a myriad of relationships at grass roots levels as well.

Mastering multiple, complex relationships

The durable MNE of the future may well be the firm that can manage to build strength and exercise influence through consistent action at multiple levels of context, from grass roots to the White House. It will, of course, be able to exercise power in many of the conventional ways. Scale of assets and employment will continue to attract attention, as will technological strengths. Intel, for example, will likely continue to be a more attractive "catch" for governments than is McDonald's, for it creates more valuable jobs. The power of the threat of moving to a new location will continue to be important, as the airfreight companies routinely demonstrate. So too will be the power of the home government when there is a case for intervention. The power of the US will continue to tilt the bargaining field in favor of

---

[8] The importance of clusters rather than nation-states was first signaled by Kenichi Ohmae in Ohmae (1995). Many scholars such as Michael Porter have reinforced the concept and its importance in shaping development as well as competitiveness.

[9] See, for example, the works of Hamel and Doz, Gomes-Casseres, and many others.

US companies. The bargaining power of government will continue to be affected by the size and growth of the home market, by resources (natural and human), and by the competence of its administration.

Triangular bargaining will continue to explain a good deal of the interactions of all these considerations. However, there are obvious additions needed to bring the model up to date. First, the role of the NGOs must be added, even though they are far from a homogeneous set. Alongside these organizations must come international institutions like the World Bank, the International Finance Corporation (IFC), and the WTO. Their role in influencing outcomes, both directly and indirectly, has been magnified by the social protests at a time when they are becoming ever more salient in dispute settlement, not just in developing countries. This class of institution, both official and non-official, has emerged as a force in the global commons, perhaps as a consequence of changing perceptions of the power and legitimacy of the nation-state.

Second, the power of individuals to mobilize protests and boycotts of particular brands or specific investments (such as unpopular infrastructure projects, dams and the like) must be added to any explanatory model. Corporate websites are only just beginning to react to a burgeoning traffic of criticism and complaint; few firms have gone beyond thinking of the website as a portal of information and passive receipt of criticism to developing the site as a tool for social engagement and dialogue.

As the hard edges of a world of divisions shifts slowly toward a world of integration, the sources of power and influence are becoming more diffused. Advanced industrial countries will continue to exert great power in influencing location decisions, and the major MNEs will continue to lobby them about their own interests. "The technical sovereignty of the state is not at issue. However, the explicit and implicit bargaining power of corporations sets limits to the policies that governments can actually impose. Sovereignty is not precisely at bay, but it is being somewhat bruised around the edges" (Turner, 2003). Similarly, the MNEs are discovering new limits to their own power and influence. A failure to engage adequately in social dialogue can be punished by attacks on the brand, as many firms like Nike have learned to their cost. Reputational risk is now a factor in shaping behavior, both during negotiations and in the subsequent implementation.

If reputational risk is primarily downside risk, there is a complementary upside risk. Firms that fail to perceive the need to broaden their perspective on products and markets to include social engagement risk losing opportunities to grow in new ways. Shell now calls this the risk of missing the license to grow. An example of how this can work to the benefit of all is the community engagement program of the property development company British Land. They spend a great deal of money on what might be considered merely charitable donations to the communities where they operate. The rationale, however, is that these programs build strong relationships with the local municipal authorities who issue the permits to build. Moreover, the programs are very popular with employees, allowing British Land to have one of the best reputations as an employer, with consequent effects on their ability to attract and retain talented employees.

There are thus signs of green shoots of new forms of durable partnerships, rooted in an enlarged view of the scope of negotiation and action. Real durability, however, is likely to require much further progress in developing a mass acceptance of the moral foundations of a capitalist system that can deliver greater perceived justice.

PART II

The shifting international business–government partnership

5 Foreign direct investment and government policy in Central and Eastern Europe

KLAUS E. MEYER AND CAMILLA JENSEN

Introduction

Relationships between multinational enterprises (MNEs) and governments in Central and Eastern Europe (CEE) have been shaped by the region's struggle to shed legacies of central planning, and create prosperous market economies. This context has created special challenges for both MNEs and local governments to establish relations with each other, understand each other's needs, and to engage in mutually beneficial negotiations.

Due to path dependency of institutions, extraordinary politics during this period and the inheritance from the previous regime shape the future institutional frameworks (North, 1990; Stark, 1992). Policy decisions during the period of radical change around 1990, such as methods of privatization, had long-lasting effects on institutions, and moreover on the distribution of wealth and power. In many countries, the institutional vacuum and weak legal framework in the early 1990s permitted a large extent of opportunistic behavior, rent shifting, bribery, and corruption. In some countries, vested interests have inhibited the pace of reform (EBRD, 1999; Stiglitz, 1999). Consequently, the process of building institutions in transition economies has taken more time than most reform scenarios envisaged in 1990.

The duration of extraordinary politics and the pace of reform depend on each country's economic and institutional legacies. Some countries were considered among the developed economies prior to the Second World War while others went directly from a feudal or early capitalist system to a socialist system. These distinct cultural and systemic inheritances influence informal institutions such as norms and values in these countries.

In this environment, government policy and changes in the institutional framework are of pivotal concern to foreign investors. The transition has created specific policy-induced entry barriers, but also windows of opportunity for investors that established good relations or negotiated successfully with host governments. During radical institutional change, businesses cannot base their investment decisions on present institutions, as they are often transient and in some cases even inconsistent. Thus strategic flexibility and the ability to adapt to volatile rules and regulations can become crucial competitive advantages.

Recent research in both economics and business strategy has, in part through the analysis of transition economies, recognized the importance of institutions for business development and thus economic growth (Djankov et al., 2002; Murrell, 2003; Meyer and Peng, 2005). The international-business literature has long analyzed the impact of government policy on the volume of foreign direct investment (FDI) inflow and the strategies pursued by foreign investors. Institutional variables such as intellectual property rights protection (e.g., Oxley, 1999) or political risk (e.g., Henisz, 2000) have been incorporated in the study of foreign investment strategies, notably entry-mode choice. However, the interaction between national economic institutions and enterprise level organizational strategies is still under-researched (Mudambi and Navarra, 2002). This is particularly relevant for transition economies because the underlying economic mechanisms are typically underdeveloped.

Foreign investors are firstly concerned with how governments drive the general process of creating institutions for the market economy and lowering barriers to entry. However, MNEs entering a country by acquisition of a local firm interact with local authorities in different ways from greenfield investors. Investors by acquisition are concerned with privatization policies and with the regulation of markets for corporate equity (Meyer, 2002). They often face bilateral negotiations, or multiple potential investors bidding for the same asset. Greenfield investors, in contrast, can often choose between many alternative sites for investment. They would thus have stronger bargaining positions vis-à-vis central or local authorities eager to attract FDI (Jensen and Mallya, 2003; Meyer and Nguyen, 2003).

This chapter is structured as follows. In the next two sections, we place the policy environment in CEE in a comparative context, before reviewing the impact of institutional development and government policy on foreign investment. The two sections after that focus on policy issues of concern to different types of investors depending on FDI entry mode: acquisition vs. greenfield. We conclude with an outlook on EU enlargement, and point to the need for further research on the effect of policies on alternative types of FDI. We support our arguments with data on the policies adopted in the region, and with case studies to illustrate the relevance of the issues at firm level.

A comparative perspective

Despite their distinct heritage, the countries of CEE appear to be converging toward development paths of other emerging economies at similar levels of income and development. According to the investment development path (IDP), government policies are in part predetermined by the country's level of development (Dunning, 1993; Dunning and Narula, 1996). The IDP stipulates a macroeconomic relationship between FDI, governments, and development. Countries advance through the stages of development following five typical stages, yet their path is moderated by their policies toward international businesses.

The IDP proposes an endogenous relationship between the net-outward investment position (NOI) per capita of a country and its level of development proxied by GDP per capita. Transition economies are at different stages of this process. Bulgaria, Romania, and the CIS (Commonwealth of Independent States) countries for which we have data (Belarus, Ukraine, Moldova, and Russia) are at stage 1 or stage 2 of their development process (table 5.1). Their location advantages, inclusive government policies and the sophistication of market-oriented institutions do not suffice to attract major inflows of FDI, while they have little if any outward FDI. An outlier is Russia, which received considerable FDI in its oil and gas sector, while Russian MNEs in this sector started investing abroad (Andreff, 2003). Yet relative to the size of the country, both inward and outward FDI in Russia remain small.

The Central European countries have reached a mature phase of stage 2, as they continue to receive large amounts of inward FDI. Outward FDI started, but primarily in the form of 'indirect' FDI by affiliates of MNEs, for instance Hungarian affiliates of Western MNEs undertaking investment in Romania or Ukraine (Andreff, 2003). The Baltic countries fall between the two major groups of countries, with Estonia belonging to a later phase of stage 2, while Latvia and Lithuania are still at early phases of stage 2. Slovenia falls into a category of its own, reaching stage 3 on the IDP with outward FDI taking off (see also Svetliçiç and Bellak, 2002).

Table 5.1 FDI and institutional development, 2001

Country	FDI stock per capita, US$	NOI per capita, US$	EU membership	External liberalization*	Privatization (large)*	Competition policy*	Legal effectiveness*
Stage 1–2 countries							
Albania	240	-215	No	4+	3	1	2
Belarus	140	-135	No	2	1	2	3
Bulgaria	490	-475	Cand.	4+	4-	2+	4-
Latvia	920	-820	In 2004	4+	3	2+	4
Lithuania	725	-710	In 2004	4+	3+	3	4-
Moldova	140	-140	No	4+	3	2	4-
Romania	340	-335	Cand.	4	3+	2+	4
Russia	150	-50	No	3-	3+	2+	4-
Ukraine	95	-90	No	3	3	2+	3
Stage 2–3 countries							
Czech Republic	2610	-2525	In 2004	4+	4	3	3
Estonia	2290	-1980	In 2004	4+	4	3-	4
Hungary	2375	-1935	In 2004	4+	4	3	4-
Poland	1100	-1075	In 2004	4+	3+	3	3
Slovak Republic	1130	-1060	In 2004	4+	4	3	3+
Stage 3 country							
Slovenia	1415	-1012	In 2004	4+	3	3-	4

Notes: Cand. = candidate country, membership forecasted for 2007. No = not member and membership not expected in the near future. * EBRD transition indicators, based on annual assessment by the Chief Economist's office of the EBRD, scale 1 = socialist system feature, 4 = standard and performance norms of advanced industrial economies.

Source: EBRD (2002)

The IDP literature suggests that countries start to liberalize their trade and FDI regimes as they advance in their stage of development (Dunning, 1993; Dunning and Narula, 1996). In other words, policy choices are to some extent endogenous to the IDP and hence the development process. Policies are typically import-substituting and inward-looking at stage 1 and stage 2, when FDI inflows are moderate. Policies start to become more open and oriented toward attracting and incorporating FDI into the development process as countries approach stage 3. Investment incentives geared toward foreign investors may be adopted at this stage. At stages 4 and 5, policies toward outward investments may take on importance.

The EBRD's external liberalization index provides an indicator of the extent of liberal and non-interventionist investment regimes in terms of national rules and legislations. Table 5.1 shows the level of external liberalization (foreign trade and exchange) in CEE countries on a scale from 1 (socialist system features, e.g., foreign trade is controlled by the state and the current account is not liberalized) to 4+ (standard for the most advanced industrial economies). These figures, albeit only a weak proxy for foreign investment legislation, indicate that liberal and outward-oriented trade regimes are the rule rather than an exception among the former socialist countries, earning them the highest score in the EBRD assessment: 4+. Only Belarus, Russia, and Ukraine remain relatively unreformed or inward-looking.

A more detailed picture is provided by particular rules and legislations related to FDI (table 5.2): free establishment, equal treatment, foreigners' ability to purchase land, non-selectivity, access to privatization, and repatriation of profits. The rules and laws of the investment regimes in CEE largely confirm the evidence of the EBRD indices. Most countries offer highly liberalized regimes and often are ahead with legislative reforms relative to their level of development. Again the CIS countries stand out as the most inward-looking and unreformed regimes with respect to foreign investment laws. However, this picture may still be too optimistic with respect to CIS in view of the actual investment barriers experienced by investors (see below).

Free establishment and profit repatriation are the norm across the region. Purchase of land by foreign investors is feasible in most countries except Bulgaria, Belarus, and Ukraine; while non-selectivity of the regulatory regime is still a concern in Russia and Ukraine. Other countries, like Slovenia, chose privatization methods that transferred ownership to

Table 5.2 *Investment rules and legislation in individual CEE countries*

		Free establishment	Equal treatment	Purchase of land	Non-selectivity	Access to privatization	Profit repatriation
Stages 1–2	Albania	√	√	(√)	(√)	√	√
	Belarus	√	(√)	(−)	(−)	(−)	√
	Bulgaria	√	(√)	(−)	(√)	(√)	√
	Latvia	√	√	√	√	(√)	√
	Lithuania	√	√	(√)	√	(√)	√
	Moldova	√	√	√	(√)	(√)	√
	Romania	√	√	√	(√)	√	√
	Russia	√	(√)	(√)	−	(−)	√
	Ukraine	√	(√)	(−)	−	(√)	√
Stages 2–3	Czech Rep.	√	√	√	(√)		
	Estonia	√	√	√	√	√	√
	Hungary	√	√	√	√	√	√
	Poland	√	√	√	(√)	(√)	√
	Slovak Rep.	√	√	√	(√)	(√)	√
Stage 3	Slovenia	√	√	(√)	√	(−)	√

Notes: √ = Fully applicable, (√) = Applicable with some exceptions, (−) = Not applicable with some exceptions, − = Not applicable.
Source: UNCTAD (2003).

domestic new owners and did not offer direct opportunities for foreign investors. However, in the late 1990s, opportunities for greenfield FDI and acquisitions from private owners increased, such that the privatization methods become less important for the volume of FDI attracted by any country (Bevan, Estrin, and Meyer, 2004). New opportunities may emerge for acquisitions as insider-privatized firms in CIS may at some point in time need to raise capital, and thus seek foreign investors.

Survey-based research, such as that carried out by the Confederation of Danish Industries (2003), demonstrates various barriers to investment: non-tariff barriers, red tape, the quality and applicability of laws, and corruption. Based on in-depth interviews conducted with forty-five Danish investors in Eastern Europe in the period 2002–2003, the study shows an increasing gap between barriers to entry in Central Europe and Eastern Europe respectively. Barriers are even higher in the CIS countries. For example, in Russia nineteen licenses are necessary to operate a business, one of the highest barriers in the world, whereas in Poland the number is eleven and in Denmark only three. A similar example is corruption, with Denmark being the second least corrupt country in the world, Poland coming on rank forty-five and Russia at the bottom of the list in seventy-first place.

Transition began from relatively similar starting points; however, the paths of institutional development vary considerably. Differences arise from both inherited features of the institutional framework and the institutional reform of the 1990s. Government policy has played an important role in shaping the evolution of new institutions regulating FDI.

Institutional development and international business in CEE

The process of institutional development and divergence has arguably been the most important aspect of government policy affecting FDI in CEE. Economic institutions establish the rules and regulations for domestic economic actors as well as foreign investors. Institutions cover both formal institutions such as laws and regulations and informal institutions such as business practices and customs (North, 1990).

For businesses operating in CEE, institutions are much more than background conditions. Eastern Europe has gone through a process of fundamental institutional change under pressure of both internal and external political, economic, and social changes. Yet the remaining inconsistencies of institutions increase transaction costs, especially for new business relationships, and thus inhibit many potential business relations, in particular those of a complex or long-term nature. The resulting coordination failure has been a major cause of the deep recession of the early 1990s (Swaan, 1997). Yet it also affects international businesses with the transition economies. Western MNEs lack information on their partners; and they have to confront unclear regulatory frameworks, inexperienced bureaucracy, and the weak enforcement of property rights (Meyer, 2001a; Bevan, Estrin, and Meyer, 2004).

The weaknesses of market institutions, and constraints on internalizing transactions, led to the widespread use of alternative, intermediate mechanisms of exchange through informal networks in CEE (Stark, 1996), and even more in Russia (Puffer et al., 1996). Moreover, privatization created new forms of private ownership, including insider-owners and dispersed shareholders without effective stock-market governance. Some of the largest firms in the region are subject to weak governance while benefiting from close contacts to government and, in some CIS countries, considerable barriers to entry. Yet other firms have progressed far in shedding these legacies of the twentieth century. This diversity of governance mechanisms and of ownership patterns in the region may persist for many years.

Foreign entrants have to accommodate local institutions when designing an entry strategy. At an aggregate level, the stage of development of institutions is crucial to attract FDI, by reducing the transactions costs of setting up a local operation. Empirical research about the impact of host country institutions on the volume of FDI indicates the general impact of the institutional, social, and legal framework. For example, Brenton, Mauro, and Lücke, (1999) show an economic freedom index to be positively related to FDI flows in CEE.

Moreover, institutional variables influence specific strategic decisions such as the control, timing, and location of foreign operations. Formal rules establish the permissible range of entry modes, for instance, with respect to equity ownership, and set the stage for possible bargaining between investors and authorities. Both formal institutions, such as the legal framework, and informal institutions, such as managerial networking, shape transaction costs in CEE, and consequently foreign investors' preferred mode of entry (Meyer, 2001a).

Institutions and policy are particularly important when it comes to foreign investment by acquisition. In CEE, the institutions surrounding privatization set the context for foreign acquisition, as privatization policies and the policies affecting privatized firms have a direct bearing on the post-acquisition strategies (Meyer, 2002) and performance (Uhlenbruck and De Castro, 1998, 2000). We elaborate on these implications in the next section.

Bevan, Estrin, and Meyer (2004) investigate the impact of institutional development on FDI in transition economies and identify key factors by disaggregating subsets of institutional development. The results suggest that several institutional changes have particularly enhanced FDI receipts to transition economies:

- Development of private-owned businesses in place of state-owned firms;
- Development of the banking sector, but not necessarily the non-banking financial sector;
- Liberalization of foreign exchange and trade, but not necessarily of domestic markets and prices;
- Development of legal institutions, but not necessarily competition policy.

Contrary to their expectations, Bevan, Estrin, and Meyer (2004) find that domestic price liberalization and the development of competition policy do not appear to be significant in motivating FDI. This may be because the possibility of earning monopoly rents attracts foreign investors, yet often without benefiting local customers in the host economy. Thus, policymakers also have to be aware that what is good for domestic economic development does not necessarily attract more foreign investors, though it may attract different ones. For example, competition policy eases entry, but it makes it less attractive to acquire an incumbent monopolist. Governments privatizing telecommunications often face a trade-off, as liberalization would reduce prices for consumers, but also reduces receipts from selling the incumbent state-owned service provider.

Competition is regarded as at least as important as privatization for enterprises to improve their efficiency – a result fully consistent with empirical research on privatization in the West (e.g., Vickers and Yarrow, 1991). Yet while many major Western privatizations are in industries with natural monopolies that require complex regulation to create competition, most firms privatized in CEE in the 1990s enjoyed monopoly powers courtesy of past or present government policy. After privatizations it is essential that market forces are set free by removing administrative constraints. Firms in transition frequently face soft budget constraints and obtain protected market positions of various sorts. In Russia, a particular problem appears to be the lack of domestic entry, and thus contestable markets, in part due to protective intervention by regional authorities (Broadman, 1999).

The development of informal institutions may co-evolve with the establishment of formal institutions. This makes it difficult to show the *additional* impact of informal institutions. Bevan, Estrin, and Meyer (2004) find one result that can be explained by discrepancies between the development of formal and informal institutions. A Russia dummy variable, while negative and significant under most model specifications, loses value when combined with legal effectiveness. The lack of effective law enforcement may therefore help to explain the poor FDI performance of Russia. Thus, investors may be more concerned about formal institutions than about informal ones, unless informal institutions show highly unusual features.

In conclusion, government policy has been pivotal in creating new legal frameworks in transition economies, and indirectly influenced the social change that led to more gradual changes in informal institutions. Foreign investors have been affected by this institutional evolution while at the same time influencing institutional development. However, the research on which institutions are most conducive to economic development, or likely to attract FDI, does not yet allow conclusive answers. Below, we suggest that it may be more appropriate to disaggregate FDI by project characteristics to better understand the link between government policy and FDI inflows.

Box 1: Overcoming barriers in Russia – the Dandy way

Despite reports of severe entry barriers in Russia, there are also many examples of investors that have successfully overcome them and turned initial barriers into first-mover advantages. The Dandy case (a Danish chewing gum manufacturer acquired by Cadbury-Schweppes in 2002) demonstrates this well. The company itself ascribes a great part of its success to the devotion of endless working hours toward establishing strong networks in Russia. This was done at all levels of the company–country hierarchy from the national to the regional and local levels in the early 1990s. The CEO of Dandy initially spent months on establishing relations with Russian politicians at the highest level through private meetings, attending trade fairs, and foreign investor promotions. Subsequently Dandy's expatriate local management team turned its attention to the regional level whilst negotiating a special incentive package and analyzing the success of other companies having located in the Novgorod region. Having opened the factory, focus turned to local administrators and not least to the extended community of the factory's workers through sponsorships, the media, arranging parties, and participation in charities.

Sources: Hansted (2003); and interview with former CEO of Dandy Russia, Carsten Bennike.

Acquisition entry, and the privatization processes

At the onset of transition in 1989, state enterprises dominated CEE economies, and the legal framework lacked provisions for the operation of firms in private ownership, let alone foreign ownership. This changed gradually, yet the institutional legacies induced many investors to form partnerships with state enterprises. Joint ventures and acquisitions in the early to mid-1990s were generally related to the privatization process as foreign investors cooperated with, or took over, state-owned firms. Especially large FDI projects were implemented by acquiring equity stakes in state-owned enterprises. Privatization thus offered unique opportunities for acquiring potentially lucrative assets at low prices.

Yet early acquisitions also carried special risks: the valuation of former state enterprises in a rapidly changing environment was subject to high uncertainties, and the turnaround of the acquired business required major post-acquisition investments (Meyer and Estrin, 2001). The failure rate of acquisitions is high, even within and between mature market economies. Yet managing an acquisition is even more daunting in transition economies, where acquirers operate in unstable institutional contexts and may be subject to governmental interference at all times.

The acquisition and the subsequent restructuring of former state-owned enterprises necessitate intensive interaction between the investor and government authorities, primarily the privatization agency. Moreover, the process typically involves many stakeholders in addition

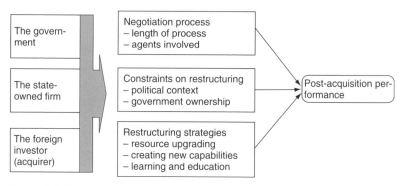

Figure 5.1 A process perspective on privatization acquisitions
Source: Meyer (2002).

to the government. Groups such as employees of the firm, the management, local authorities, national unions, and the media often take an active interest in privatization (Antal-Mokos, 1998; Meyer, 2002). Moreover, governments rarely act as homogeneous units, but different agencies and politicians – like a local town major – pursue their own objectives. Managing the complex network of relationships is crucial for the success of the acquisition process (figure 5.1). Local stakeholders have diverse objectives, which may not always be compatible with those of profit-oriented investors. In addition, local governments, management and workers' councils with *de jure* or *de facto* influence on the negotiations complicate negotiation processes (Antal-Mokos, 1998):

Governments not only maximize their financial revenues, but also pursue broader social objectives. Consequently, privatization negotiations generally involve wider issues such as investment plans and employment guarantees. Formally, potential buyers negotiate with the privatization agency. Yet a large number of agents inside and outside the firm try to influence the agency through formal or informal channels. This could degenerate into internal 'politicking,' where agents pursue individual goals to the detriment of the organization and potential foreign partners. Frequently, managers and/or employees have attained considerable influence, especially in Poland and in many CIS countries.

The involvement of multiple stakeholder groups often prolongs the negotiation process. As time passes, the competitive situation changes due to events both within the target firm and in its environment, as management may be unable to pursue strategic leadership while future ownership remains uncertain. Thus, the market position may erode, and tangible and intangible assets may deteriorate as insiders extract assets, key people leave, or the organization fails to invest. Such deterioration would diminish the firm's prospects after privatization.

Yet the governmental influence does not end with the formal privatization. Influences may be retained both direct, based on equity stakes of a state entity, and indirect. Political agents set regulatory policy, and they may exert moral suasion and political pressure in addition to interference based on specifically agreed terms in the privatization contract. State-owned enterprises often require deep organizational and strategic restructuring to be integrated in the investor's global organization. This creates major managerial challenges for acquiring firms as the process and its political context are more complex than for conventional acquisitions (Meyer, 2002). MNEs would normally prefer to design and implement such strategies without outside interference, to be able to focus on economic objectives.

Governmental agencies other than the privatization agency can assert influence via formal institutions. Industrial regulation and competition policy have a particularly profound influence on market structure and, therefore, on post-privatization performance (Uhlenbruck and De Castro, 1998). Privatization-related acquisitions from the late 1990s onward have been primarily in sectors that require substantive governmental regulation, such as telecommunications, banking, and utilities. In these industries, the regulatory frame is key to privatization negotiations as the privatized firm may hold a monopoly position. Vigorous industry liberalization and competition policy would not be in the interest of a foreign investor that took over an incumbent firm.

Governmental influence is most explicit where the state retains a minority equity stake. Many acquisitions in the privatization process occurred in a staggered pattern, and were thus registered as joint ventures although from the beginning the investor attained management control and envisaged the acquisition of full ownership. Such an arrangement permits acquisitions in a particular institutional context, and has little in common with conventional joint ventures. A temporary minority stake of a government may offer advantages to both partners. The government obtains some control over the firm's restructuring, and thus externalities created for the local economy, while capitalizing on the probable appreciation of the share value as the transition economy becomes less uncertain. Governments may also be reluctant to transfer control over firms deemed strategic, or those trading with governmental institutions (Wright, Thompson, and Robbie, 1993).

Investors normally aim for full control of acquired businesses not only to reduce transaction costs but also to enforce faster turnaround. In this respect, foreign investors may dislike the possible government interference in strategic decisions, but would appreciate the risk sharing, the lower amount of capital to be raised at the outset, and the access to local institutions and networks. If the acquirer attains management control, the influence of the co-owner on operational management may be limited.

Furthermore, the interests of the regional or local authorities may become more aligned with those of the acquiring firm if they share the profits. This should reduce undue bureaucracy and regulatory interference, while providing access to important public and private networks. Such informal networks are vital for businesses in transition economies, especially in Russia (Puffer et al., 1996; Holden, Cooper, and Carr, 1998) and China (Peng and Heath, 1996).

Hence, minority government ownership can have contradictory effects. In mature market economies, firms in mixed ownership may generate lower profits because governments aim at social rather than financial returns. Yet this does not translate to transition economies, where for example Tian (2003) finds an inverse-U-shaped relationship between state-ownership stakes and corporate performance. Residual state ownership thus has both positive and negative effects.

Even without equity stakes, the authorities may retain rights in the privatization process. The privatization contract can create a principal–agent type relationship between the government and the acquirer beyond the privatization (Stark, 1992). Deal terms can, for instance, stipulate employment guarantees, investment commitment, partial local ownership, or that the management team be staffed with nationals. The enforcement of such contracts, which were widely used for instance by the East German Treuhandanstalt, is, however, problematic and may lead to ongoing negotiations.

Informal institutions may moderate the new owners' control over the acquired business. Public opinion and, in consequence, political agents frequently take an interest in formerly state-owned firms. This may trigger governmental intervention if the new owner's actions are thought not to be in the country's best interest. In addition to social objectives, politicians and bureaucrats may pursue personal objectives and engage in various form of rent-seeking behavior. This may foster corruption, as seen in Russia. Foreign investors have to distinguish legitimate social concern from individual rent-seeking behavior.

Acquirers thus have to be aware of potential conflicts with political agents, and of the social consequences of their corporate activity. Where legal and regulatory frameworks are not yet fully developed, politicians may feel called upon to interfere in former state-owned firms in case of social conflicts.

In conclusion, foreign investors entering CEE by privatization-acquisitions typically have to negotiate with multiple stakeholders in the firm, the government, and society. The relationship between government and the foreign investor extends beyond the time of formal takeover of the firm as acquirers pursue the often necessary deep restructuring of the acquired firm, while governments or political groupings are concerned with the social consequences of such restructuring processes.

MNEs aiming to enter a foreign country by acquiring a local firm thus are most concerned with the institutions governing markets for corporate control, which in CEE implies privatization policies, and policies vis-à-vis privatized enterprises. They are also concerned with a range of other policies, such as regulatory policies vis-à-vis market incumbents, and informal means of exerting political influence on business.

Greenfield entry, and the bargaining for subsidies

In contrast, greenfield investors do not normally have to deal with privatization agencies or the regulation of natural monopolies. Their investment rarely conflicts with existing power structures in bureaucracies or incumbent firms.

Greenfield investors' relationships with authorities are more likely aimed at realizing mutual benefits. Local governments welcome investors that promise employment opportunities, technology spillovers, and taxable revenues. Their eagerness to attract FDI may translate into competition between different authorities offering investment incentives, and provides considerable bargaining power to some potential investors, notably those considering large projects and aiming to serve more than a local market.

Incentive schemes abound in CEE at the beginning of the twenty-first century. A variety of incentives are offered to potential investors, the most common being tax holidays. These schemes are likely to converge to the EU rules[1] as the CEE countries enter the EU, a process that began with eight new member countries in 2004. As EU members, CEE countries will be allowed to offer incentives within the EU for some time either within the rules of the EU, or because of the transitory arrangements that are part of the accession process (Commission for the EU, 2003). Hence, such schemes will continue to be important and may affect decisions of greenfield investors offering large manufacturing projects in particular locations. Moreover, the CEE countries within the EU have access to new resources through the structural funds, which may be used also for investment incentives. However, this may induce the new members to use more systematic and transparent rules and to abstain from anti-competitive or illicit practices.

Investors seeking to establish production facilities for global markets often face a wide choice of locations. To produce goods that are subject to low transportation costs and distributed easily to worldwide markets, investors can search worldwide for an optimal site. They can use their leverage to negotiate with local authorities to obtain favorable conditions, especially if they do not require specific local inputs, but offer substantial potential spillovers to the local environment. Local or national authorities may not only offer financial and fiscal incentives (i.e., tax exemptions), but also promise investment in infrastructure development.

For investors, these incentives offer direct financial advantages and may even add to the strategic assets of the company. For instance, policy may create the basis for dynamic economies of scale in locations through provision of temporary incentives or protection from import competition as in the Central European car industry (Werner, 2003).

---

[1] Under EU rules, incentives may be used primarily for regional policy (including labor market and R&D policies) under the EU structural funds. For example, only the relatively poor regions (with GDP below 75 percent of EU average at present) are allowed within the EU to use incentives as a way to attract new businesses to their location. But many regions in Eastern Europe will fall into this category during the first decade of membership. For general exemptions for granting State Aid in the EU, see www.europa.eu.int/comm/competition/citizen/citizen_stateaid.html.

On the other hand, recipients of subsidies put their reputation on the line if, for example, they fail to balance government objectives connected to the incentive schemes and their own business objectives. Firms that participate in an incentive scheme, but subsequently do not live up to its conditionality, can expect negative press reaction. This also holds true for firms that enter into a non-transparent deal with a government, which may make the public wonder what is kept secret. Incentive schemes are often linked to performance requirements, made attractive by a gift package of dollar bills. Failure to live up to the performance criteria may damage a firm's reputation and lead to complex legal issues and possibly a need to repay received subsidies.

Most CEE countries use special economic zones (SEZs) as part of their FDI policies. They come in two formats:

- **Free economic zones,** where investors are exempted from paying customs duties or other taxes, possibly conditional on certain performance requirements related to employment or exports, and
- **Industrial parks** or "technology parks," where the aim is to build clusters of industry that will generate spillovers to the local economy.

Table 5.3 gives an overview of incentive schemes in Eastern Europe, based on a study by Dresdner Bank (2003), complemented with qualitative information obtained from the homepages of national investment agencies.[2] Almost all countries in CEE offer some type of incentive scheme. The only exceptions are Estonia and Lithuania, which, however, offer some of the lowest corporate tax rates in the world. This shows how CEE countries seek to market their regions in the investor community in terms of cost advantages.

Box 2: The emergence of a car industry cluster

The car industry is the most prominent example of how brownfield investment into existing state firms and greenfield investments into new industrial zones, supported by incentives, work together to create a geographic cluster of producers. Research shows how the

---

[2] For example, in the case of Russia, the information provided by Dresdner Bank is very scant. Visiting the official investment site of Russia (www. invest.ru) reveals that Russia has adopted a case-by-case approach as the rules under which incentives may be provided are expressed rather vaguely.

car industry in Poland, the Czech Republic, and Hungary is located within a radius of only 200 km. These clusters have created considerable agglomeration economies. They have been built on existing industrial assets that have been enhanced by government policies, and competition among neighboring locations in different countries.

The symbiosis between government and international business in the car industry has created a critical mass in the industry. This policy opened opportunities for both acquisition and greenfield FDI during a window of opportunity. It allowed investors to overcome the high barriers in the beginning of the transition process and facilitated larger and more risky projects. The early entrants in turn created new windows of opportunity for later investors such as sub-suppliers in the car industry. Investment barriers came down faster than in other industries because of a fit between government and investor objectives. The Czech authorities recognized early that they would only be able to overcome their technological gap with the world car industry by attracting foreign investors, and inducing them, in particular VW, to locate substantive value-adding activity there. Ten years later, this has become the basis for one of CEE's strongest industry clusters.

Sources: Werner (2003), Meyer (2000).

On a less regular basis, several countries also use incentives in relation to SEZs. These policies primarily focus on the provision of infrastructure or pools of labor with a specific skill structure. Most countries combine both types of incentives. However, in table 5.3 the usage of regular incentive schemes has been put in parentheses in those cases where a case-by-case approach has been the overwhelming one, as in Latvia and Lithuania.

Incentives are tied to SEZs, especially in the countries furthest to the east, e.g., in Romania, Bulgaria, and Poland, and in CIS countries. The main performance requirements relate to job creation, and in some countries such as Hungary and the Czech Republic also to the amount of capital invested. In practice, the requirements may not differ much, as all countries aim to attract large investors with manufacturing projects to the least developed regions, either directly by setting job creation objectives or indirectly by creating SEZs in the least developed regions with high unemployment. Hence performance requirements

Table 5.3 Overview of regular incentive schemes offered in Eastern Europe

	Tax holidays or subsidies (regular basis)	Tax rate %	Strategic incentives	Special economic zones[1]	Performance requirements/ special objectives
Bulgaria	(Yes)	28 (20)	No	6 zones	Tied to zones Job creation Case-by-case
Romania	Yes	25	Yes	30 parks	Size Tied to zones
Russia	(Yes)	24	No	5+ free zones	Size Tied to zones Case-by-case
Ukraine	(Yes)	30	No	15+ zones	Tied to zones Case-by-case Partly decentralized Size
Estonia	No	26	No	Ports only	No
Latvia	(Yes)	19	No	Ports only	Case-by-case Hi-tech
Lithuania	(No)	13–15	Yes	3 free zones + 2 parks	Very large size Case-by-case
Czech Republic	Yes	31	Yes	13+ zones and parks	Size

Table 5.3 *Overview of regular incentive schemes offered in Eastern Europe* (continued)

	Tax holidays or subsidies (regular basis)	Tax rate %	Strategic incentives	Special economic zones[1]	Performance requirements/ special objectives
Hungary	Yes	18	Yes	75+ zones and parks	Job creation Corp. services and R&D Partly decentralized Size Structurally weak areas Environment
Poland	Yes	27	Yes	14+ zones and parks	Tied to zones Fully decentralized
Slovak Republic	Yes	25	Yes	9+ parks	Job creation
Slovenia	Yes	25	No	8+ free zones	Job creation Partly decentralized Case-by-case

Notes: [1]In "free zones" (in short: zones) investors mainly benefit from lower taxes and trade duties. "Industry parks" (in short: parks) have objectives beyond cost-cutting, such as trying to attract particular types of industry that match with already existing industries in the area or the skill-structure of the region.

Source: Dresdner Bank (2003) and the homepages of the national investment agencies in the Czech Republic (www.czechinvest.cz), Poland (www.paiz.gov.pl), and Russia (www.invest.ru).

are overall not a major constraint for business, except perhaps in some of the countries applying a case-by-case approach where part of the package negotiated may include strict local content requirements. If the company subsequently divests prior to the termination of the incentive contract, it must be prepared to pay back the value of incentives which may amount to as much as 50 percent of the original investment (Jensen and Mallya, 2004). Whether such contracts are enforceable is another matter.

The scant empirical evidence on success with adoption of SEZs in Eastern Europe suggest only a marginal impact on the location strategy of investors (Jensen and Mallya, 2003). As greenfield investments increase where privatization is completed, zones may become more important for investors' location strategy. But with rising income and wage levels in the EU accession countries, zones have to offer both incentives and attractive resource endowment, especially human capital, to attract investors.

Some countries offer incentives at several levels of government. In the Polish system, probably the most decentralized, incentives can only be negotiated with the local governors of the SEZs. Such decentralization offers opportunities for entrepreneurial local authorities to create a more investor-friendly environment where central reforms are sluggish or inconsistent, as observed in Vietnam (Meyer and Nguyen, 2003).

In other cases (Czech Republic and Ukraine), the additional layers of government may pose both a blessing and a curse to the managers at the negotiation table. Investors may be able to negotiate higher subsidies if multiple sources of funds are available. At the same time, the danger of multiple requests for special favors increases, such that the net gain from obtaining incentives can be difficult to foresee, and costs of negotiating may exceed received benefits. Hence in countries where the incentive–negotiation environment is very complex (case-by-case approach, large size of informal economy, and several layers of nego-tiation), such as Ukraine, competent legal counselors may be a pre-requisite to negotiating for incentives.

The provision of incentives related to trade, e.g., import protection in combination with incentives, can be an important strategic aspect to investors not only in the CIS, but in all CEE countries (Werner, 2003). Hence table 3 gives only indicative information about the prevailing nature of incentive schemes, while a case-by-case approach has been adopted all over the region vis-à-vis very large investors.

Incentive schemes can broadly be divided into two groups: the transparent and the publicly visible schemes and the less transparent schemes negotiated between top government and (typically very large) multinational investors on an individual case-by-case basis (UNCTAD, 2003). Transparent incentive schemes available to all investors meet certain criteria and attract mainly medium and large investors with cost-oriented motives. The non-transparent incentives are often associated with major multinational firms building government relations, which then can be viewed as a strategic asset. However, to our knowledge, there exists very little research on how multinationals can build and exploit government relations in CEE, in part probably because of the non-transparent aspects of these deals.

In the countries that are not (yet) acceding to the EU, the case-by-case approach to investors might lead to more corrupt behavior by government representatives (UNCTAD, 2003). Since these countries are beyond the immediate reach of institutional spillovers from the EU, and have a high estimated share of informal economy (Johnson and Kaufmann, 2001), they may be more prone to adopt non-transparent incentive schemes.

In conclusion, investment incentive schemes are widespread in CEE, and often relate to the creation of SEZs. They aim to attract capital and employment to particular regions, and focus on greenfield manufacturing projects. Next, we turn to the question whether these schemes have had any visible impact in terms of crowding-in FDI.

Most studies, even at the national or local level, suggest that incentive programs generally fail to crowd-in FDI (Morriset and Pirnia, 2000; Oman, 2000). In a panel analysis of the transition countries, Beyer (2002) finds that the announcement of incentive programs has among other factors little impact on their attraction of FDI. An earlier review of tax incentives in transition countries by Holland and Owens (1996) also concludes that incentives appear to play a marginal role in attracting investors. In a study of the Czech Incentive Scheme, Mallya Kukulka and Jensen (2004) find, based on survey data for 135 investors in manufacturing, that at most the scheme succeeded in crowding-in total investments with 3–5 percent per year. However, within the target group of greenfield investors in manufacturing, the marginal impact is somewhat greater at 10 percent per year.

The strongest impact of incentives schemes has been reported in the car industry, in combination with a host of other location advantages

(Werner, 2003 – see also Box 2 above). This pattern may be replicated in other industries, if incentives help develop industrial clusters that might become regional hubs for production in the enlarged EU. However, the type of deal that the Czech government struck with Volkswagen in the early 1990s, which included, for instance, temporary infant industry tariff protection, would not be permissible under WTO rules, let alone EU membership.

The main effect of incentives offered on the rim of the EU appears to be to attract investments to one country under the nose of its neighbor, rather than raising overall investment in the region. This competition for FDI intensified before accession to the EU (UNCTAD, 2003). A similar battle for FDI is still raging among countries of the "old" EU. With high unemployment, slow economic growth, and the relative insecurity about what Enlargement would bring in terms of geographical reorganization of industries, governments resort to incentive schemes as leverage when negotiating with potential investors.

This empirical evidence suggests that investment incentives schemes have become more systematic (transparent) and marginally more important to the location decision of greenfield investors in large manufacturing projects in CEE. However, these incentives have mainly influenced the marginal cost of locating in one CEE country rather than another.

Incentives will continue to influence the location strategies of greenfield investors after EU accession, since most of the CEE region will be eligible to use such incentive schemes in the foreseeable future. Moreover additional funds may be available when the EU programs are extended to accession countries. Countries with the administrative capabilities to manage incentive schemes, such as the Czech Republic, Poland, and Hungary, may offer a major benefit to investors negotiating for incentives.

Conclusion

The transition economies have gone through a rapid process of institutional development. This period combines with extraordinary politics that have created unique business opportunities for investors who were able to manage government relations in a rapidly changing context.

With the EU Enlargement in 2004, the period of extraordinary politics is coming to a close. Yet this does not imply an end to proactive

FDI policies; rather, future policies will be adapted to the overall legal EU framework. The policy agenda is shifting. While some windows of opportunity are closing, others are opening up. Rather than privatization, the main policy questions of the near future are likely to center on regional policy within the EU frameworks, and EU competition policy in an enlarged Union. New opportunities in the CIS countries depend on their progress with internal reforms and enterprise restructuring.

The relevant policy issues of concern to investors vary over time, and with the type of FDI. This feature should also apply in other regions, and we thus propose that policy researchers differentiate more clearly the impact of policy and institutions on different types of FDI, for instance by mode of entry between FDI, by acquisition, and by greenfield respectively. This chapter has shown that acquisitions in Eastern Europe are a highly complex issue both for investors and governments in view of the relationship between policy, FDI, and institutional development, and the difficult balancing act of getting them all right to secure and maximize mutual benefits; whereas for greenfield investments the mutual benefits among the various stakeholders involved are more obvious and apparently conflictless with other objectives in transition and economic policy.

For FDI by acquisition, key concerns relate to the bargaining with privatization and regulation authorities and the restructuring of formerly state-owned enterprises. However, foreign investors increasingly acquire private firms. This reduces the intensity of their interaction with the authorities, yet when buying a recently privatized firm, they may still face deep restructuring to shed the legacy of a firm once run as a socialist enterprise.

Foreign investors pursuing greenfield entry have more degrees of freedom with respect to their intra-country location choices. This gives them high bargaining power vis-à-vis local municipalities, and the opportunity to take advantage of special incentives in SEZs and industrial parks. For local policymakers, this raises the challenging policy issue of whether they want to attract FDI by offering special incentives, which might benefit the specific location but come at the cost of overall social welfare. Empirical evidence suggests that incentives are only effective for certain types of FDI, i.e., large-scale manufacturing greenfield projects that do not depend on specific locational advantages.

Underlying such differences are different relative bargaining positions of authorities and MNEs. Governments aiming to attract foreign investors by selling a strong local firm, such as an incumbent telecom operator, have a valuable asset and thus often a strong bargaining position. It is less strong if they seek a partner for a loss-making firm in a declining industry, such as steel. To attract greenfield investors, countries offering distinct locational advantages such as an industrial cluster or human capital have stronger negotiation positions then those offering only financial incentives.

6 Global warming and climate change: new issues for business strategy, government policy, and research on business–government relations

THOMAS L. BREWER

Introduction

Estimates of the social and economic impacts of global warming indicate that it will become an increasingly salient issue for firms and governments – and for scholars who study international business–government relations – for at least the next several decades. For instance, an estimate based on a study by a team of scholars at the London School of Hygiene and Tropical Medicine is that global warming is now causing approximately 160,000 deaths per year from disease, malnutrition, and malaria, mostly in developing countries (Doyle, 2003). As for economic costs, the 2003 annual report of Swiss Reinsurance (available at http://www.swissre.com/) on developments in 2002 notes that the European storms and floods in Austria, Germany, the Czech Republic, and other countries of that year caused damages in excess of €18 billion. Further, a forecast by Munich Reinsurance (2003) suggests that the worldwide cost of climate changes associated with global warming will be approximately $150 billion per year by 2009.

Despite the inherent uncertainties in such estimates, there is a consensus among specialists in the science and economics of global warming that the trends for these and other costs will increase for decades into the future (more in the next section about these trends). Estimates such as these, as well as continuing advances in the scientific understanding of global warming and its impacts, have put global warming on the agendas of firms and governments. As an official of a major international business organization observed, global warming is "a problem that will not go away."[1]

---

[1] The organization and official must remain anonymous, as the comment was made in the course of a confidential conversation.

Issues on firms' agendas

A survey of the FT Global 500 firms found that "More than 50 percent of FT 500 companies have already recognized climate change as a serious issue and are developing strategies to reduce greenhouse gas emissions" (Carbon Disclosure Project, 2003, p. 10). The same survey concluded more specifically as follows (p. 2; italics added):

Climate-driven risks [for firms] will continue to grow: Looking ahead, a series of secular 'mega-trends' will continue to amplify the financial impacts of climate change.
• Strengthening evidence about the reality, gravity, and causes of climate change;
• Increase in extreme weather events;
• *Further regulatory action by government at local, national, regional, and global levels*;
• Continuing growth of renewable energy and clean technology markets;
• Improved understanding of the variability of company-specific impacts;
• Improved quantification of the potential financial impacts of inaction;
• *Increasing exposure of investors to overseas regulatory regimes*;
• Growing institutional shareholder activism on corporate carbon risks;
• *Global momentum for improved disclosure on corporate risks.*

There are additional tangible indications that global warming is already an issue that many firms are addressing, including most large multinational firms; and they are responding in diverse ways. Evidence that the problem is on firms' agendas is observable in many respects – in their participation in carbon markets, the submission of shareholder resolutions at annual meetings, the development of partnerships between firms and environmental NGOs, the involvement of firms in government programs, and the public positions that firms and industry associations take on government policy issues. Examples and data for each of these types of responses follow.

Carbon markets. Because carbon dioxide emissions from burning fossil fuels are a principal cause of global warming, the trading of carbon dioxide credits (and other greenhouse gas emission credits) and the participation in carbon-offset projects are becoming more common business activities. Reflecting these developments, there are now two major industry associations focused on emissions trading – the International Emissions Trading Association (IETA) and the Emissions Market Association (EMA). In the US there is a privately organized Chicago Climate Exchange (CCX) with voluntary corporate members, plus the city of Chicago and Mexico City. In Denmark, there has been a mandatory emissions-trading scheme in the electric power sector since 2000. In the UK, there is a voluntary emissions-trading system involving corporations from many sectors. In the EU, beginning in 2005 a new mandatory emissions-trading system that covers thousands of facilities in the electric power, energy, chemical, cement, and other industries became operational. The World Bank has several programs, including the Prototype Carbon Fund, to facilitate the development of carbon markets and early transactions involving trading credit allocations and offset projects.

Shareholder resolutions. There is also evidence of increasing shareholder interest in how firms are responding to the issues posed by global warming. In particular, the Carbon Disclosure Project sponsored by thirty-two institutional investors with $4.5 trillion in assets is collecting and disseminating information on firms' exposure to carbon-related issues associated with carbon emissions that contribute to global warming. Resolutions concerning firms' responses are now regularly presented at the annual meetings of many corporations on behalf of institutional investors in the Interfaith Center for Corporate Responsibility, with several hundred billion dollars in assets, which represents the pension funds of several religious organizations. Yet another group of institutional investors, the Investor Network on Climate Risk, was formed in late 2003; its founders include the treasurers of the states of California and Connecticut, and the comptroller of the state of New York.

Partnerships with NGOs. Many firms have become partners with environmental NGOs in their programs to advance particular types of global-warming-mitigation measures. These programs are international in scope and include multinational firms from all economic sectors and all regions of the world. The NGOs include ED (formerly Environmental Defense), the Pew Center on Global Climate Change, the World Resources Institute, and the World Wildlife Fund.

Government policy positions. Firms have also been taking positions on government policies concerning global warming – whether because of emissions trading schemes such as those above; voluntary programs of diverse types such as emissions reporting; potential policy changes such as participation in the Kyoto Protocol; new domestic subsidy programs, or taxes, or other regulatory changes; or international technology transfer, investment and trade policies concerning energy, transportation, and other sectors. In the US for instance, firms are encountering government policy issues at many levels and in many forms.

The wide-ranging (but not comprehensive) list of issues below conveys the diversity of issues that firms are facing. The emphasis is on issues related to government policy and firms' interactions with governments in order to reflect the focus of this volume on business–government relations. These issues include the following:

- whether the US government should participate in the multilateral Kyoto Protocol;
- whether there should be a new NAFTA-based international regional emissions-trading system;
- whether the bilateral US agreements with China, Japan, Italy, and other governments will facilitate or inhibit international cooperation in the long term;
- what the implications would be for firms based in the US if other governments, under pressure from rival firms in their countries, imposed "border measures" in international trade to offset the short-term competitive advantages of US-based firms operating in a low-cost fossil-fuel economy because the US government has not taken effective measures to reduce carbon dioxide emissions;
- how multinational firms should adapt their operations to a fragmented international regulatory environment in which some countries have mandatory greenhouse gas emission limits, while others do not;
- what positions local subsidiaries of foreign-based multinational firms should adopt on international issues such as the development and implementation of international agreements on climate change, when the local host government and the parent firm in the home country have taken opposite positions;
- what the competitive consequences are for a parent firm that is headquartered in a country whose regulatory systems are lagging behind those of its rivals' home countries;
- whether to support or oppose transnational state–provincial arrangements such as the one among northeastern US states, Ontario Province, and the Atlantic provinces of Canada;
- how to respond to the proliferation of state-level regulatory regimes, some of them involving mandatory measures for firms, and others involving voluntary measures;
- what to expect from the US national judicial system, as law suits from city and state governments are filed against the national government

and firms for neglect of the health and other consequences of carbon dioxide and other greenhouse gas emissions, and as firms and industry associations and labor unions file suits to try to prevent governmental action at the local, state, regional, and national levels;

• what the emphases and funding levels will be of the large number of national governmental R&D subsidy programs such as tax credits and direct grants for demonstration projects, and whether to participate in them;

• what the prospects are for increases in gasoline taxes or carbon taxes, such as those in place in some European countries and under consideration in Japan.

Underlying issues of science, economics, and politics

The specific issues that firms and governments face and that are the focus of their interactions can only be fully understood in the context of the pervasive and underlying issues of science, economics, and politics that are earmarks of the phenomenon of global warming and its implications. The analytic issues of research and theory on business–government relations are shaped by these three sets of underlying issues. These key features of the science, the economics, and the politics of global warming are combining to create new issues of business strategy, government policy, and business–government relations.

Science. There is a strong core consensus among climatologists and other scientists concerning certain patterns and trends about global warming, and about its causes and its consequences, as reported below in the section on global warming trends, pp. 145–146. At the same time, there are inevitably some uncertainties – both about interpretation of data on the past, and about projections into the future. Some of the uncertainties, for instance, are about the relative contributions to global warming trends of human activities versus naturally occurring phenomena; others are about the relative magnitudes of change since the onset of the industrial revolution as compared with previous centuries and millennia. Further, many of the uncertainties are about the precise magnitudes of changes in the future, but not about the direction of change during the next several decades. These and other scientific uncertainties are important in the politics of global warming, and in firms' strategic decision making, as we shall see below.

Economics. The underlying economic issues concern the magnitudes of costs and benefits associated with global warming and responses to it, and the distribution of costs and benefits over time and among groups of people. Because the concentrations of greenhouse gases that cause global warming are globally distributed in the atmosphere, all areas of the world are exposed to the warming trend and its consequences.

The impacts of the warming trend, however, are unevenly distributed across regions, across countries, and across industries. For instance, desertification has been spreading in southern Europe. Low-lying Atlantic coast areas in the southeastern US and the Gulf of Mexico coast are vulnerable to more frequent and more severe hurricanes. Areas in North America and Western Europe that depend on the attraction of glaciers and/or snow for skiers and other tourists have already begun to experience problems associated with late autumns and early springs.

Poor countries are more vulnerable than wealthy countries because the costs of adaptation are more onerous in the former than the latter. Small island countries in the Caribbean and South Pacific, and low-lying countries such as Bangladesh are vulnerable to inundation from sea-level rise, as are fishing villages in many parts of the world. Agricultural regions in the tropics are particularly vulnerable to droughts. There are some beneficiaries of global warming, mostly agricultural parts of temperate areas that experience longer growing seasons, though with attendant costs stemming from changes in farming methods and increased pests.

The costs of global warming and its socioeconomic impacts will increase over time, so there are inter-generational asymmetries as well. The economic costs of global warming are particularly problematic in this respect because the costs can extend over many decades, even centuries, into the future. This is because a molecule of carbon dioxide entering the blanket of greenhouse gas (GHG) emissions in the atmosphere typically stays about a century. (Some other GHGs last longer, others less long. The impact on global warming of a molecule of a GHG is typically measured in terms of its global warming potential relative to a molecule of carbon dioxide at 100 years.) The costs of global warming are thus distributed over the lifetimes of current generations and many future generations as well.

Similarly, the benefits of reducing global warming trends – through measures to be discussed below – tend to be relatively long-term (potentially extending to decades and generations beyond the end of the twenty-first century). In simple economic terms, the discounted present value of future economic benefits thus depends on the discount rate that is used. Further, the benefits are relatively widely dispersed, though analogously as noted above in regard to the costs of global warming, with some areas and groups of people benefiting disproportionately from measures taken today to reduce the rate of increase.

The costs of addressing global warming, on the other hand, tend to be more short term and more concentrated among groups whose economic interests are tied directly to fossil fuels in particular. Internationally, this includes countries with large deposits of coal such as Australia, Canada, China, India, and the US or large reserves of oil and natural gas such as Saudi Arabia and Russia. Within those and other countries, certain regional economies are particularly dependent on the extraction of fossil fuels; in the US for instance, these include Illinois, Indiana, Ohio, Kentucky, Pennsylvania, and West Virginia in the case of coal, and Texas, Louisiana, and Oklahoma in the case of oil and natural gas.

Politics. Such asymmetries in the distribution of costs and benefits drive the politics of global warming issues – both internationally among countries and domestically within them. The two Kyoto Protocol Annex I countries that have not ratified it are Australia and the US – both of them with large fossil-fuel reserves. Similarly, Saudi Arabia has been among the non Annex I countries that have been particularly hostile to the Protocol. On the other hand, the correlation is not complete; Canada, for instance, has been a leader in international efforts to combat global warming, though its Kyoto Protocol ratification process revealed strong inter-regional conflicts based on differences in economic dependencies on fossil-fuel reserves, with some western provinces with oil and coal reserves opposed to ratification. More generally, each of the principal categories of government policy responses – and all of the specific measures in each of the categories – inevitably involve economic costs and benefits, and they are not distributed equally among groups.

The principal policy responses of firms and governments to global warming are commonly summarized as: (1) business-as-usual, (2) mitigation, and (3) adaptation. Business-as-usual, of course, refers to a continuation of business activities and government policies along current paths. However, there is room for disagreement about whether to classify as business-as-usual, for instance, a trend in some countries of declining greenhouse gas "emissions intensity" (i.e., units of emissions such as metric tonnes of carbon dioxide equivalents, divided by units of economic activity such as GDP), which nevertheless results in increasing amounts of emissions and concentrations of GHGs. Mitigation refers to efforts by firms, governments, other organizations, or individuals to reduce the net rate of emissions of GHGs, including through increases in the rate of carbon sequestration or other measures to capture GHGs. There is a diverse array of such possibilities – among them increasing energy efficiency, switching energy sources away from fossil fuels in transportation and electricity production, reducing deforestation/increasing reforestation, changing production processes and products, and many others. Adaptation refers to such measures as improving storm early warning systems, building dikes, inoculation against malaria, shifting farming methods, and other activities to reduce the impact of the second-order socio-economic effects.

Externalities. As with other environmental issues, there are negative economic externalities associated with the production and consumption activities that result in increases in the concentration of GHGs in the atmosphere. Examples of such externalities are the costs to society which are not internalized in the private costs of producers or consumers of:
- electricity or motor vehicles and their fuels – to the extent they use fossil fuels and thus emit carbon dioxide;
- cement – the production of which emits methane (another GHG);
- running shoes with air bubbles containing CFCs (another GHG);
- and other products of mining, manufacturing, and agricultural activities.

Such externalities reflect market failures that lead to inefficient allocations of scarce resources.

Market prices do not include the full costs to society of these types of production and consumption; groups other than the producers and consumers are thus paying part of the costs of producing and consuming these goods and services. There is therefore a rationale, on the grounds of economic efficiency, for government intervention to internalize the costs. There are three types of government measures that in principle can internalize the costs: (1) taxes on GHG-emitting production and consumption activities, (2) subsidies on mitigation/sequestration activities, and (3) the development of mandatory or voluntary emission/sequestration targets. Specific measures and issues concerning these forms of government intervention are discussed below in the section on government regulatory systems. Here we can simply note that the interests, actions, influence, interactions in the political system vary across these three "issue areas" (Brewer, 1992).

The literature – a brief review of the most relevant studies and resources

Although there are sizable and rapidly increasing bodies of literature on the scientific, macroeconomic, and public policy issues posed by global warming, there are not many studies about firms' responses to the issues. Two introductions to issues for firms, with a strong emphasis on the Kyoto Protocol, are available in O'Neill and Reinhart (2000). A special issue of *Greener Management International* (2002) includes a series of industry-specific studies. Levy and Kolk (2001) have focused on the major oil and auto firms. Reinhart (2000) presents a case study of BP's development of an internal emissions trading scheme. An extensive analysis of issues and responses among Japanese firms is provided by the Development Bank of Japan (2003). Two recent surveys of firms' practices are reported in Carbon Disclosure Project (2003) and CERES (2003). In addition, there is a vast literature on emissions trading (see especially Kopp and Toman, 2000; and IETA, 2003). There are numerous brief anecdotal and case study materials from periodicals and collections of articles. These include yearbooks and collections of cases by Cutter Information (Arris, 1997, 1998, 2000; DiPaola and South, 2000; Arris, 2001; also see RTCC, 2003). Several studies by the Pew Center on Global Climate Change are relevant.

For monitoring current developments, two periodicals are particularly useful: *Environmental Finance* and *Global Environmental Change Report*. Several electronic newsletters and periodicals are also useful – especially *climate-l of the International Institute for Sustainable Development in Canada* (www.iisd.org); *World Environment News, Planet Ark* published by Reuters (www.planetark.org); *Point Carbon and Carbon Market Europe* published by Point Carbon in Norway (www.pointcarbon.com); *Greenwire* published by Energy and Environment News in the US (www.eenews.net). Also see the websites of the World Business Council for Sustainable Development (www.wbcsd.org) and a new web-based service for firms, www.climatebiz.net. Information about regulatory systems is available at the websites of the International Emissions Trading Association (www.ieta.org).

Previous and forthcoming publications by the present author have focused on: identifying and classifying types of firms' responses (Brewer, 2003a); theoretical issues concerning firms' responses, including their positions and actions in the US political system (Brewer, in progress); development of data sets of responses by industry leaders and laggards; regulatory systems, including interactions with the international trade-investment regime centered in the WTO (Brewer, 2003b, 2004a). A study of "Regulatory Uncertainties and Transaction Risks in Greenhouse Gas Markets" is also under way. These and other studies are available for downloading at www.msb.georgetown.edu/brewer, and www.ceps.be.

In the present study, the next section provides data on the trends and projections of temperatures and carbon dioxide emissions, the industry sources of such emissions, and economic and insured losses from extreme weather events. The following section identifies key features of the regulatory systems at all levels of political institutions (from multilateral to sub-national), including subsidy and tax systems as well as mandatory and voluntary programs, with an emphasis on the complexities and uncertainties of the systems. The next section describes the carbon markets, with a focus on transaction risks for participants in them. The penultimate and final sections of the chapter discuss the implications for theory and research.

Global warming trends and their economic impacts

There is a strong consensus among environmental scientists that global warming has been occurring since the industrial revolution; that it has been occurring at an increasing rate during the past three decades; that it is substantially caused by carbon dioxide and other GHGs that are emitted as a result of human/business activity; and that its consequences include more frequent and severe extreme weather events, droughts, sea-level rise, shifting agricultural and disease patterns, and associated socio-economic costs.[2]

---

[2] Attributing economic value to premature deaths – in some studies, with variable values depending on the income levels of countries – has become a particularly nettlesome issue, not only in climate change studies but also in other studies of the health consequences of social choices. I do not intend to enter that discussion in this chapter, except to note that there are economic consequences of premature deaths and that they can be taken into consideration in estimates of the costs of global warming. However, there are also ethical, social, and political considerations that are centrally

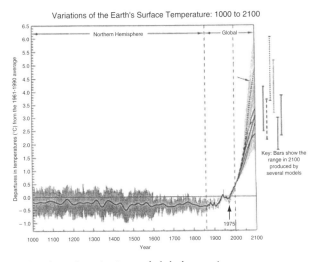

Figure 6.1 Trends and projections of global warming
Notes:

- 1000 to 1861, N. Hemisphere, proxy data;
- 1861 to 2000, Global, Instrumental;
- 2000 to 2100, projections

Source: IPCC (2001).

Figure 6.1 provides data on the trends and projections of global temperatures.

The data of table 6.1 concerning the sources of carbon dioxide make clear the relative importance of fossil fuels (coal, oil, and gas) in the production of electric power and in transportation, as contributions to global warming.

The basic patterns in the cause–effect relationships between global warming and conditions such as sea-level rise and events such as severe storms, droughts, and floods are well known; therefore, the direction of change in many indicators of the economic consequences of global warming is also widely known. However, it is not scientifically sound to attribute *any one particular extreme event* to global warming, and this makes measurement of the economic impact of global warming problematic.

Yet, it is scientifically sound to note that particular extreme events are the types of events that tend to become more frequent and more severe as

important – and indeed for many observers, of transcendent importance, compared with the economic costs.

Table 6.1 Sources of carbon dioxide emissions

	Million metric tonnes	Percentage carbon equivalent
Electricity production	614	29
Transportation	496	23
Industry and agriculture[a]	481	23
Residential and commercial[b]	534	25

Notes:
[a] Of the industry subtotal, 81 percent was from petroleum refining, chemicals and related, primary metals, paper, food, and stone–clay–glass.
[b] Heating, hot water and other direct services from gas, oil, coal – not including electricity.
Source: US Department of Energy, Energy Information Administration, www.eia.doe.gov/oiaf/1605/ggrpt/index.html#carbon, accessed August 14, 2001. Data are for 2000.

global warming occurs. Thus, it is appropriate to observe that a variety of recent extreme events are the types of events that can be expected to be more common as global warming continues. These include in Europe, for instance, the floods in the UK in 2001 that were the worst in more than 400 years, the floods in Germany, Austria, and the Czech Republic in 2002 that were the worst in more than 100 years, the heat waves in France, Spain, Portugal, and other European countries in 2003 that were the worst in decades and killed approximately 35,000 people. In the US increasing severity of hurricanes and of forest fires can be attributed in part, respectively, to changing temperatures of the Atlantic Ocean and prolonged drought in western regions of the country.

Of course, the economic consequences of such events depend on a combination of factors. In the case of losses from hurricanes, these include increases in coastal real estate development and real estate market prices, as well as the frequency and severity of the hurricanes. Similarly, the economic consequences of forest fires also depend on suburban real estate developments and prices, as well as the frequency and severity of droughts. Yet, the fact of increased losses from the combination of these factors is of much interest to casualty insurance firms – and government emergency relief agencies. Data such as those of table 6.2 are therefore increasingly noted in discussions of the economic consequences of global warming.

Table 6.2 Economic and insured losses from natural catastrophes[a]

Time period	Number of events	Economic loss – constant 2002 US$, billions	Insurance loss – constant 2002 US$, billions
1950–1959	20	42.1	N/A
1960–1969	27	75.5	6.1
1970–1979	47	138.4	12.9
1980–1989	63	213.9	27.0
1990–1999	91	659.9	124.0

Note:
[a] "Great natural catastrophes" causing thousands of casualties and significant damage to national economy.
Source: Munich Re (2003, p. 15).

In short, the economic stakes in global warming are substantial, and they are increasing. The next section of the chapter focuses on government regulatory issues, particularly complexities and uncertainties in the emerging regulatory systems at several levels of government.

Regulatory systems

There are numerous regulatory systems at various stages of development and operation at the international, national, and sub-national levels, including the multilateral Kyoto Protocol which entered into force in early 2005. In short, regulatory regimes at several levels have begun to emerge, and firms in diverse industries and countries have undertaken strategic and operational decisions in response. Further, key features of the emerging regulatory regimes for the mitigation of climate change are apparent, and they pose specific, tangible strategic and operational issues for firms.

Regulatory complexities

Three principal dimensions of the emerging climate regulatory systems that contribute to their complexity are that they are:
1. variable across levels, i.e., include governmental policies at the multilateral, regional, bilateral, national, and sub-national levels;

2. variable across countries, i.e., reflect cross-national differences, for instance, in the scopes of coverage and regulatory ideologies as well as other features;
3. variable across industries, i.e., apply to a varying extent across industries, such as energy and transportation.

The variability is particularly pronounced in the US. Because the state and local governments in a federal political system have been active filling a perceived void in national-level policymaking, a complex array of regimes at several levels has begun to develop. In particular, many states have developed regulatory systems. One is an arrangement involving five northeastern states in the US and four Atlantic provinces in Canada. Their goal is to reduce GHG emissions to 1990 levels by 2010, followed by an additional 10 percent reduction by 2020. The plan is not legally binding, but its bi-partisan and transnational features have made it otherwise politically significant. Other US state initiatives include California legislation to establish state regulation of GHG emissions by motor vehicles. This is intended to be the first state-level effort to restrict vehicle GHG emissions – and a potentially economically significant one since Californians buy about 10 percent of the new autos sold in the US each year. Governor Pataki of New York has suggested that his state also adopt carbon dioxide emissions standards for motor vehicles. It is politically significant that the two largest states, on opposite coasts, and with Republican governors, have both begun to move toward such limits. Thirteen states have established renewable portfolio standards (RPSs), according to which the electric utilities in their states must produce or purchase minimum percentages of electricity from renewable sources. California has established a 20 percent minimum by 2017; New York has established a 25 percent minimum by 2013; and Texas has a 2.2 percent minimum by 2009.

In addition, numerous US cities and other local jurisdictions have been adopting climate-change policies. At the local level, sixty-seven cities have joined the Cities for Climate Protection Campaign, and have thus committed to undertake various mitigation efforts such as increasing building energy-efficiency standards. Two cities – Oakland, California, and Boulder, Colorado – have joined with environmental NGOs in a lawsuit against two federal government agencies for supporting fossil-fuel projects without adequately assessing their contributions to global warming. The agencies would be required to undertake such assessments in the future according to the requirements of the national environmental policy acts. The agencies being sued are the Export–Import Bank and the Overseas Private Investment Corporation. The local damages being cited to justify the suit are potential salt water contamination of aquifers and flooding of the airport and sewer system as a result of sea-level rise, in the case of Oakland; and water supply and forest fire problems as a result of reduced snow, in the case of Boulder.

While the Bush administration opposed participation in the Kyoto Protocol and more generally eschewed cooperation in multilateral arenas, it pursued other forms of international cooperation, in particular, a series of bilateral international agreements that are focused on technology development and transfer. The national administration also developed a series of "domestic" programs, which are voluntary in nature. Two of these extend previous programs of the Department of Energy and the Environmental Protection Agency. Finally, the administration created a "Climate VISION" program involving voluntary participation by industry associations and their individual firm members.[3] This is a program in which industry associations have agreed to encourage their members to undertake actions that would facilitate the achievement of the administration's target of an 18 percent reduction of GHG emissions "intensity" by 2012, compared with 2002 levels. Those that have signed up to participate include seventeen associations from numerous sectors, including energy and transportation, plus the Business Roundtable, whose membership includes 150 large firms from many sectors. There is much variability across industries in the nature and extent of their commitments; most involve only relative reductions as indicated by emissions "intensity," while a few involve absolute reductions.

Institutional uncertainties

There are several different types of uncertainty associated with the climate regulatory systems. This section highlights three in particular.

The Kyoto Protocol. A basic institutional uncertainty is whether and when the US might ultimately participate in the Kyoto Protocol, or at least

---

[3] Although participation is "voluntary," there were reports of concerted and coercive actions by the administration to induce firms to participate (*New York Times*, 2003).

negotiations about the terms for its "second commitment period," which would begin after the end of the "first commitment period" in 2012. (This issue is addressed in Brewer, 2003e; also see Grubb et al., 2003.)

The EU regulatory system. A new EU emissions trading system (ETS) was approved by all the necessary institutions (Commission, Council, and Parliament) during 2002–2003, and the initial allocations to installations and firms were formulated during 2004. By January 2005, more than four thousand facilities in the oil refining, smelting, steel, cement, ceramics, glass, paper and pulp industries had allowances to emit carbon dioxide. Many uncertainties about the allocation of permits and the subsequent operation of the ETS remained; for instance, it was possible to "opt out" of the EU system if the same or larger emissions reductions were being achieved through other means. Thus, at least some sectors of German or UK industry might decide to follow that path.

The importance to firms of the reduction of regulatory uncertainties by the EU Parliament's approval of establishment of the ETS was evident in business reactions during 2003. A statement by Philippe de Buck, secretary general of the EU employers confederation UNICE, is illustrative; he commented, "This [EU Parliamentary approval] provides European business with the certainty it needs to begin planning for emissions trading which starts in January 2005."[4] See Brewer (2005).

Interactions between the climate and trade systems. Another set of concerns about the multilateral climate regime revolves around interactions between the provisions of the Protocol, its implementation by an international secretariat, and the national policies and measures that individual governments adopt, on the one hand, and the rules and procedures of the World Trade Organization (Brewer, 2003a, 2003b, 2004a). The

---

[4] Similarly, the announcement by a group of eight US electric utilities that they favored mandatory limits on their carbon dioxide emissions marked an important shift for a key sector of US industry (CERES, 2003). It also reflects a decision about how to approach the strategic issues associated with regulatory uncertainty, namely to encourage the implementation of new regulations sooner rather than later, once they are regarded as inevitable at some point in the future. The firms were Calpine, Con Edison, Keyspan, Northeast Utilities, PG&E Corporation, PPL Corporation, Public Service Enterprise Group, and Wisconsin Energy Corporation. Yet, at the same time, other firms have remained opposed to the same mandatory limits, and thus there is variability among firms in their approaches to the regulatory issues posed by climate change mitigation.

WTO agreements that are potentially relevant to climate-change issues include many of the individual Uruguay Round agreements and subsequent agreements as well. The stated objectives of the two multilateral regimes converge, and the two are officially expected to be mutually supportive. These themes are evident in key documents for both regimes. In the context of these generalized expressions of mutual support, specific activities of the two regimes offer a range of potential tangible outcomes for climate-change mitigation and trade liberalization. While some interactions of the two regimes offer the prospect of win–win outcomes, others pose the possibility of less benign outcomes.

The principal elements of the Kyoto Protocol that are particularly relevant are its provisions concerning emissions trading, the Clean Development Mechanism, Joint Implementation, enforcement, and parties' policies and measures. In combination, therefore, there are numerous potential points of intersection between the elements of the Kyoto Protocol and the WTO agreements. Questions concerning the types of international transactions in goods, services, and other business activities involved in implementing the Kyoto Protocol that are covered by WTO agreements can be answered only if the emission credits and other elements of the Kyoto mechanisms can be defined in the context of WTO agreements. Thus a key question is: What kinds of "things" does the Kyoto Protocol entail that might raise issues in the WTO? Are the Allocated Allowance Units, Emission Reduction Units, and Credit Emission Reductions envisioned in the Protocol "goods" or "services" or both or neither in the context of the WTO?

An issue of special concern is whether offsetting "border measures" might be imposed on imports from the US because its firms will have a low-cost energy advantage over their rivals in countries with mandatory GHG emissions targets (Biermann and Brohm, 2004; Brewer, 2003a, 2004a; Swedish National Board of Trade, 2004). These and other issues about climate-regime–trade-regime interactions pose a wide range of legal, political, and economic uncertainties about the regulatory environment for firms with international interests.

Markets for trading greenhouse gas emissions allowances and offset projects

The emerging markets in GHG emission allowances and in offset projects have been evolving for only a few years, and they are still in

their infancy. Except for Denmark and the UK, they initially developed
without governmental regulatory frameworks. Yet, the volumes of
transactions in 2003 had approximately doubled over 2002 – which
had doubled over 2001. Moreover, there were prices typically
expressed in terms of a standard unit, namely metric tonnes of carbon
dioxide equivalents, and denominated variously in terms of US dollars,
or euros, or pound sterling, or Danish kroner. As noted in the previous
section, the entry-into-force of the EU's ETS on January 1, 2005 led to
significant increases in trading volume. Some observers predicted
trades in the right to emit carbon dioxide among the 4,000 plants in
the EU that would be affected could be worth as much as €8 billion
a year by 2007. Such a magnitude, however, is relatively small compared
with estimates of the worldwide market on the order of $100 billion or
more per year if the US were participating in the Kyoto Protocol.

The novel, and somewhat evanescent, nature of GHG emission
reduction allowances and financial transactions regarding them is
suggested by the following observations in an annual report of the
Prototype Carbon Fund of the World Bank:

Carbon finance is inherently risky. It involves contracting to purchase an
asset created by documenting the absence of invisible gases, generated by
projects located in emerging markets, over a period of many years, where the
host country must consent to transfer the asset to the buyer. Even if all goes
well and the ERs [emission reductions] are delivered, their value is highly
speculative and their liquidity is not assured.

In addition to the institutional and other regulatory uncertainties
noted in the previous section, there are transaction risks that affect the
prices of the various "commodities" (i.e., units or sometimes "currencies")
that are the basis of the trades or offsets in the GHG markets. Thus, it is
useful analytically to identify two related and somewhat overlapping
categories: "regulatory uncertainties" and "transaction risks." Whereas
the former focuses on the largely subjectively estimated probabilities
associated with unique or nearly unique events in the evolution of
regulatory systems, the latter focuses on the more empirically based
probabilities associated with a variety of types of events that can
affect the value of individual transactions. An example of a regulatory
uncertainty as of late 2003 was whether Russia would ratify the Kyoto
Protocol during 2004 so that it would enter into force by early 2005
(which it did). An example of a transaction risk is how much the

monetary value of a particular allowance in the UK system purchased in December 2003 would change by December 2005. There are many sources of transaction risks, as noted in Eurelectric (2002, 2003).[5]

Implications for theory and research

Global warming has emerged as one of the most challenging and contentious problems facing multinational firms and governments. This chapter identifies the associated issues for business strategy, government policy, and research on business–government relations, with an emphasis on the international aspects of the issues. The specific issues facing business executives and government officials, as well as scholars, can only be understood in the context of underlying issues of science, economics, and politics, which are briefly reviewed.

Markets and regulatory regimes. Among the business and government activities of special interest are (1) government regulations that create markets; (2) government interventions in markets in order to counter inefficiencies in the allocation of scarce resources because of market failures in the form of economic externalities; (3) firms' transactions involving international emission allocation trades in carbon markets and international GHG offset projects; (4) transnational coalitions of multinational firms, national governments, sub-national governments, and NGOs to design, create, and implement new regulatory systems; (5) international bilateral, regional, and multilateral technology development-and-diffusion agreements that interact with international trade and investment agreements.

Firms' and governments' responses to the issues are creating new markets for greenhouse emission credits and carbon sequestration projects to reduce the rate of increase in the concentration of GHGs

---

[5] An announcement for a course on Risk Management for Emissions Traders indicated that it "is the course for traders, compliance planners, asset managers and back office staff that will help you manage a portfolio of emission assets more effectively. This workshop will put risk management in context and discuss issues including regulatory, political, counter party, operational and price risk. Students will explore available tools and methods to quantify and manage risk including the use of options, swaps, forwards, cross commodity and indexed transactions" (www.emissions. org/et201.html, accessed July 3, 2003).

in the atmosphere. They are also creating new government regulatory systems that include taxes and subsidies as well as emission/sequestration targets and rules.

New issues. Global warming and its implications are therefore relatively new issues on the research agenda for scholars of business–government relations and international business. But how are the issues different from those on the traditional research agenda? And how do the differences matter to theory development and to empirical and normative research? One way to answer these questions is to recall three features of these issues that were identified briefly in the introduction to this chapter and in more detail in subsequent sections.

Science. First, the issues for firms and governments are driven by scientific issues and the results of scientific research. The science of global warming is marked by a combination of (a) an increasingly strong consensus based on massive amounts of accumulating data and a longstanding understanding of the basic scientific phenomena in the past and plausible projections into the future, on the one hand, and (b) still unresolved uncertainties about some key relationships and the ranges of reasonable estimates of some variables in the future. The science is therefore concerned about the long-term effects of current economic activities, including their potentially catastrophic consequences. Research on international business–government relations can thus be predicated on the recognition that global warming is likely to persist – and even become more salient – as an issue of international business for both firms and governments. At the same time, as the science continues to evolve and some of the implications for firms and governments accordingly become clarified, the uncertainties of long-range forecasts will nevertheless inevitably remain.

Economics. Second, the economics of global warming is also different from the traditional concerns of international business–government research. There are substantial economic externalities from many of the major business activities in the manufacturing, agricultural, and mining sectors of economies; and the externalities are inherently global in scope. Market failure is central to the problems associated with global warming. As compared with many of the traditional issues of research and theory in international business–government relations, therefore, the issues concerning markets are about their failures and what to do about them in order to achieve a more efficient allocation of resources. At the same time, there are new markets emerging, particularly markets for trading GHG emissions credits. These markets are being created as a result of a combination of voluntary actions by firms, often in partnership with environmental NGOs, and government actions that mandate that firms take action.

Politics. Third, the politics of global warming is marked by issues about the introduction of new government policy instruments that intervene in markets to achieve greater efficiencies. Hence, new regulatory systems at all levels of government from sub-national to multilateral are of concern to multinational firms. The new regulatory systems include new taxes and new subsidies as well as new command-and-control regulations and new regulatory frameworks for carbon markets and other markets in tradable GHG emissions credits and offset projects. To a lesser extent, there are also issues about whether and how to phase out existing government interventions, such as barriers to international trade and investment in goods and services for climate change mitigation, or government subsidies of fossil fuels that distort international trade.

Paradox: market failure and market efficiency. There is, therefore, a seeming paradox in the trends in business–government relations: (1) governments are intervening in many business sectors in order to counter the inefficiencies resulting from market failures, and (2) at the same time, governments are helping to create new markets by imposing emission targets on firms in order to achieve emissions reductions relatively efficiently.

Analytic frameworks

These scientific, economic, and political features of global warming issues suggest the need for the application of different analytic frameworks from those that have been evident in the international business–government relations literature (Brewer, in-progress). In particular, the following macro-level models of political economy offer promising directions for further research: the public choice model, the pluralistic politics model, and the regulatory capture model. There are also micro-level models of firm behavior – shareholder, stakeholder, and organizational behavior – that are potentially useful. Among these models, the regulatory capture model (e.g., Stigler, 1971) is the most clearly applicable; but at the same time, its narrow analytic scope and inability to distinguish between quite different corporate approaches to the same regulatory issues suggest that the extent of its analytic insights may be rather limited.

Despite the differences from the usual concerns of previous studies of international business–government relations, there are several bodies of the existing literature that are relevant. These include studies of political risks in international business, which are particularly relevant to the regulatory uncertainties and transaction risks that firms encounter in the GHG markets for tradable emission allowances and carbon offset projects. The former are similar in some respects to commodities that are traded internationally, and the latter are similar in some respects to FDI projects.

An expansion of these familiar concerns to new analytic domains in order to address issues about the implications of global warming could enrich the theoretical literature of business strategy, government policy, and business–government relations. It could also contribute to the solution of one of the most daunting problems facing firms and governments at the dawn of the twenty-first century.

7 Business–government relations in the cultural industry: the evolution of the government's role in Korea

DONG-SUNG CHO AND WIJIN PARK

Introduction

The Korean economy has experienced dramatic change in just four decades, and recent developments have focused increasing attention on the future path for this dynamic economy (Kraar, 1992). Firms in any society can be analyzed in general by their interactions with other organizations such as the government, stockholders, workers or labor unions, consumers, environmentalists, and others. Hence, the general framework of the firm in a society can be schematically shown as figure 7.1. However, this general framework should be modified for countries where the government plays dominant roles through an industrial policy and other means.

In Korea, the government not only affects activities of firms directly, but it also intervenes in the relations between firms and other organizations within the society. For example, in the past in Korea's film industry, a film producer was required to attain the government's approval before producing a movie. The government was endowed with the powerful right provided by law to unilaterally prohibit a film production in consideration of market conditions. Furthermore, the government also wielded unfettered power in film imports. Government recommendation was a mandatory requirement when a foreign film was imported, and the government could choose to recommend only those film producers that had good track records in producing Korean films. In other words, the direct distribution of foreign films was prohibited until 1986, so multinationals in the film industry such as Warner Brothers, 20th Century Fox, Columbia, etc. had no choice but to export their films through Korean film producers in order to penetrate the Korean film market. With the revision of the Film Act in 1986, however, the Korean film market was opened to foreign firms, which enabled major multinationals to establish sales subsidiaries in Korea from 1988 and proactively begin sales in the Korean market. Thereafter, foreign movies – mostly Hollywood

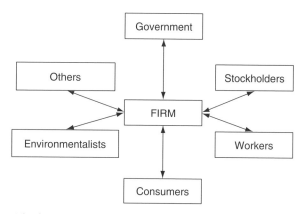

Figure 7.1 The firm in society – general framework

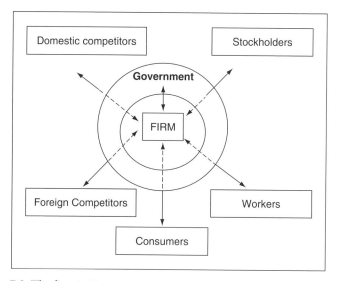

Figure 7.2 The firm in Korean society

movies – eventually increased their market share in the Korean movie market. Alarmed by a sense of crisis, the Korean film producers came to demand a strong enforcement of institutional mechanisms such as the screen quota and government support, which the government provided. Therefore, understanding the impact of the government on the firms, or – to put it differently – the relations between firms and the government, is of paramount importance in managing business in Korea. Figure 7.2 shows the framework of the firm in the Korean film industry within the context described above.

Cho (1992) showed the business–government relations in Korea by analyzing the top ten business-related news stories of each year from 1945 to 1991 of the two major newspapers. This study focused on the business–government relations throughout all Korean industries. In this paper, however, we analyze time-series data on regulations and subsidization of the cultural industry, an industry that is increasingly being recognized as the new growth engine of the twenty-first century. The following examines the concept of the cultural industry and the Korean government's perception of it, reviews previous studies and theoretical ideas about the government's approach toward business, and then sets up a hypothesis on the government's role on the basis of business–government relations models, and lastly, tests the hypothesis through an analysis of time-series data on regulations and subsidization in the Korean cultural industry.

The cultural industry and the Korean government

The concept of a cultural industry first emerged from the study of Adorno and Horkheimer (1944), who argued that cultural products such as movies, radio broadcasting, and magazines were spreading rapidly, and this mass production and consumption of cultural products was ultimately creating a uniform mass culture, becoming a major social problem. However, in the 1960s and thereafter, the commercialization of culture was seen from an economic perspective, and mass production and consumption of culture through its commercialization began to be taken for granted. Now the creation and appreciation of culture, which was once seen as an "elite culture" enjoyed only by the select few, has evolved into a "mass culture" in which everyone participates (Korean Ministry of Culture and Tourism, 2000). The cultural industry is called the creative industry in the UK, the cultural industry in Canada as in Korea, the entertainment industry in the US, the largest cultural product supplier in the world, and frequently referred to as the audio-visual industry by the UN. Regardless of its nomenclature, the cultural industry encompasses film, music, performance, video, games, and the characters and toys that derive from these sectors. Global multinational companies dominate films, music, and game markets, which indicates that films, music, games, video, and performance are at the center of the cultural industry. According to the Korean Basic Act for the Promotion of the Cultural Industry (1999), the "cultural industry" is related to the services such as development, manufacture, production, distribution, and consumption of cultural products, and incorporates industries related to films, music, video, games, publications, periodicals, broadcasting contents, cultural assets, animations, designs, advertisements, performances, art works, and craftworks. "Cultural products" in the Korean Basic Act for the Promotion of the Cultural Industry refers to tangible and intangible goods (including digital cultural content) and services as well as their combinations that embody cultural elements and thus create economic value. Of these, "digital cultural content" refers to digital content that embodies cultural elements and thus creates economic value. Today, most cultural products can be digitized, and even films, music, animation, and characters that were produced in the analogue mode can easily be transformed into digital content. So there is no significance in distinguishing analogue and digital cultural products; rather, the term cultural content industry is used more often to stress the IT-based content technology that is emerging with the advance of information technology. In 2001, the Korean government proposed six T industries as the subject of pan-governmental support in preparation for the twenty-first century and announced that these six industries would be the focus of future industrial policies. The six Ts are culture technology, information technology, biology technology, environment technology, nanotechnology, and space technology. In the past, culture was simply an object of appreciation as a part of leisure, but now the designation of six Ts by the government implies that the cultural industry has been selected as the new growth engine of the twenty-first century. Although the government is opening its eyes to the importance of the cultural industry and is providing active support, this has not always been the case. As can be seen in the following sections, there was a period of laissez-faire with no regulations or subsidization followed by a period with only regulations and no subsidization. Then from the mid-1990s, the government realized the industrial importance of culture and began to make policy changes to reflect its new-found significance. This study analyzes the evolution of government regulation and subsidization policies for films, music, performance, video, games, and copyright from 1959 to 2002.

Government roles toward business

The history of a capitalist system can be expressed as the history of changing relations between the government and businesses. In the macroeconomic dimension, business–government relations are an important factor in characterizing the economic system of a nation and its international competitiveness (Porter, 1990).

We can identify three categories of government roles in businesses. The first category is the role of a subsidizer. The government may choose certain industries as systematically important for the national economy. Then the government may provide firms wishing to enter these industries with various subsidies. For example, it may provide capital needed for investment and operations, tax exemption, and reduced administrative requirements. If necessary, the government could support firms with business information to help penetrate overseas markets. For large-scale projects, which an individual firm would have difficulty in organizing, the government may play the role of an organizer. With the government at the center, various firms would get together and work for nationally important large-scale projects. For example the Korean government played the role of an organizer in the HDTV (High Definition Television) projects by catalyzing R&D consortia among firms.

The second role the government plays in business is that of a regulator. In this capacity, the government legislates various regulatory acts and measures, which are instrumental in controlling private businesses. In addition, the government uses administrative directives to regulate business activities. As a regulator, the government sometimes organizes "counter-firm" activities. A case in point is the organizing of consumer or environmental groups by the government on behalf of private citizens.

The third role of the government in business is that of a rule-setter, in which capacity the government arbitrates between firms and the counter-firm groups. It also legislates the "rules of the game" in the market, and enforces the competitive market conditions which private businesses have to obey.

Besides these three basic types of roles, there are various others. One is that of a producer which independently produces various products and services in competition with private firms or as a monopoly. As such, the government purchases commodities or services on a large scale as a buyer. Sometimes it forms a consortium or joint venture with private firms as a partner or co-decision maker.

Among the various roles of government in business, the roles of a subsidizer and a regulator make the characteristics of a government distinctively different from others in business–government relations, because these roles may have a more direct impact on the management of businesses. Competitiveness among firms may be changed according to the way the government functions as a subsidizer or a regulator in a certain business. However, when the government acts as anything else, its impact on overall business management is neutral. In this respect, this chapter is more concerned with the role of government as a subsidizer or a regulator.

Many scholars have emphasized the regulatory element in the government's role toward businesses. Elkins and Callaghan (1975) stressed the impact on the managerial decision-making processes of government policies and regulations used to guard fair competition, regulate price and market entry, and promote social welfare. Weidenbaum (1980) pointed out the role of government, especially in the United States, in regulating the relations between consumers and producers, employees and employers, and the society and private firms over various matters such as pollution.

By contrast, few have emphasized the government's ability to directly support businesses. This phenomenon has obviously resulted from the conventional thought that business is inside the boundaries of market mechanisms, and the government is on the outside forming the context for commerce. Nevertheless, governments have actively communicated their beneficial roles to businesses. In the US, for example, the Johnson administration in the mid-1960s stressed the importance of partnership between government and business in order to cope with the difficulties facing the American economy. Specifically, it showed the government's role in creating and maintaining a stable economic environment to facilitate business activities. That role was again highlighted following the civil unrest in Los Angeles and other cities in early May, 1992.

These two views have been synthesized by Steiner, who acknowledges the government's dual role. On the one hand, the government supports business activities of firms in the role of a maker and guide of economic plans, as well as a source of financing. On the other hand, it functions as the guardian of social welfare and the controller and redistributor of resources (Steiner, 1975). In Schelling's black-box model, the government executes its policies in order to direct business firms to fulfill their social responsibilities satisfactorily. Schelling argues that a balance should be maintained between the voluntarism of firms and the coercion of the government (Schelling, 1979). Friedman sees the government as fundamentally a rule maker and an umpire, and considers the roles of enforcer and paternalistic guardian as supplementary (Friedman, 1962). While Friedman's model is based on a developed country, Jones and Sakong (1981) describe the government's role in a developing economy as a rule maker which intervenes actively in business affairs through direct commands and the manipulation of various discretionary and nondiscretionary measures.

Porter's model, which describes a government's industrial policy, takes a liberal approach, where the government plays an extremely limited role, such as eliminating obstacles to competition, and generally follows the practice of not intervening in the market. A nation's firms themselves must ultimately create and sustain competitive advantage compared to rivals from other nations. Governments have been notably unsuccessful in managing firms and in responding to the fluid market changes that characterize international competition. Even when staffed with the most elite civil servants, governments make erratic decisions about the industries to develop, the technologies to invest in, and the competitive advantages that will be the most appropriate and achievable (Porter, 1990). However, Okimoto (1989) emphasized the role of the MITI (Ministry of International Trade and Industry) in the Japanese development process. He argues that governments everywhere have had to respond to political cries for help in maintaining acceptable levels of employment, generating jobs in depressed regions, administering labor retraining programs, and slowing down the speed of structural change. Not only the government of Japan but also that of Korea have in the past selected a few growing industries to make a large contribution to the national economy and provided active support to a select few.

Models of business–government relations and research hypothesis

Using the roles of a regulator and a subsidizer as two forms of government action, we can develop a model of business–government relations.

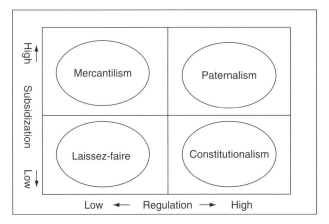

Figure 7.3 A framework for analyzing business–government relations

Using the degree of regulation by the government on the horizontal axis, and the degree of subsidization on the vertical axis, we can construct a four-celled diagram as shown in figure 7.3. This four-celled model was originally proposed by Cho in the article, "Incentives and restraints: government regulation of direct investments between Korea and the United States" (Cho, 1984).

The government which neither provides too many subsidies nor imposes too many regulations would be regarded as a laissez-faire government, as depicted by the lower left box in the four-celled diagram. The government which plays a supportive role with various subsidies, but does not enact regulatory measures, is a mercantilist one, as represented by the upper left cell. The government which regulates rather than subsidizes is considered a constitutional government, as noted in the lower right cell. Finally, the government which provides many subsidies and institutes many regulations at the same time is considered a paternalistic government.

The four models in figure 7.3 – laissez-faire, mercantilism, constitutionalism, and paternalism – are basically conceptual, but historical examples of each model are easily found. In the Western world, we observe a progression from mercantilism, through laissez-faire policies and constitutionalism, to paternalism.

Figure 7.4 shows a historic review of business–government relations. Governments were directly involved in the business activities of sixteenth-century Europe, when the economy was regarded as a

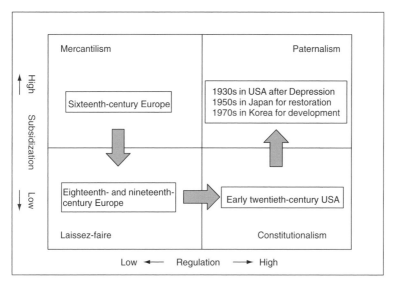

Figure 7.4 A historic review of business–government relations: a global picture

foundation of political sovereignty and a source of the military strength of a nation. In that environment the task of the government was to adopt a mercantilist approach in supporting, strengthening, and encouraging the business sector. With the coming of the Industrial Revolution, the previously mercantilist governments began to abjure their involvement with business in favor of a capitalistic market system, resulting in laissez-faire governments. Another result was the gradual formation of very large corporations, which established barriers and discouraged the entry of competitors. The constitutional pattern of business–government relations emerged in the late nineteenth century in the US as a reaction against the monopolistic exploitations of big business firms. Anti-trust laws were passed, regulatory agencies established, and criminal sanctions applied to business transgressions. The final transition of business–government relations was to the paternalistic model, and took place as the government supplemented its regulatory activities with supportive policies. The US government's adoption of several incentive programs to stimulate business during the Depression of the 1930s illustrates this transition. Presently, in the midst of declining international competitiveness and a chronic trade deficit, the US government is continuing its paternalistic approach by

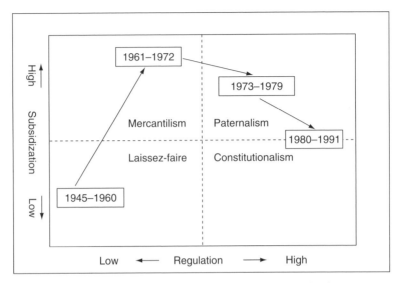

Figure 7.5 Empirical test of the evolution of overall industrial policies in Korea

taking the initiative in its relations with businesses through various administrative mechanisms.

The previous study on the changes of the Korean government's role through an analysis of the top ten business-related news stories in major dailies based on a four-celled model indicated that the Korean government's role evolved from laissez-faire to mercantilism to paternalism, and then finally to constitutionalism in the early 1990s (Cho, 1992). Figure 7.5 shows the evolution of overall industrial policies in Korea.

As we have seen thus far, a government's major means of industrial policy are regulations and subsidization. Should a government's role in industry be limited to that of a rule maker and there is no need to intervene directly in the market, the amount and intensity of regulations and subsidization would not be different from those of the past. Applied to the cultural industry, this would imply that since major cultural industries such as films, music, and performing arts have a long history and thus industry rules are already firmly established in the market, the regulations and subsidization provided by the Korean government over the past forty years would not show any significant differences among the few stages identified.

Null hypothesis: The government's regulations and subsidization in the cultural industry do not differ from one time period to another.

Research method

Data

The above null hypothesis assumes that regulations and subsidization will not differ in any statistically significant way between time periods. To find the data for the hypothesis test, this study analyzed laws regulating major cultural industries and the government budget allotted to culture and the arts. The law is the only permitted means through which the government can regulate and limit the people's freedom and rights in a democracy. Therefore, regulations pertaining to the cultural industry and the evolution of the government's role can be deduced from the number of regulations relating to the industry. This study analyzed yearly changes in the number of regulations from the year that various regulations were enacted in films, music, performance, game, video, and copyright sectors up to the year 2002. In 1959, even before the Film Act, the Performance Act, and the Music Recording Act were enacted, the Copyright Act was first enacted to protect copyrights of films, music recordings, performance, and publications, and to regulate the industry as a whole. This implies that market order and regulations in the cultural industry before this time were not based on legal foundations. However, the Performance Act was soon enacted in 1961, the Film Act in 1962, and the Music Recording Act in 1967; all legal regulations were in place by the middle of the 1960s and most of these acts had been revised more than ten times by 2002. The number of regulations examined in this study includes all regulations that were enacted, revised, and abolished up to 2002. The number of such regulations was analyzed for each year and was organized in a time series. In addition, although there are many forms of government support, no form of support is feasible without an adequate budget, so changes in the government budget allocated to the cultural industry over the past forty years could be the focus of study in terms of subsidization. A government budget is specified in numbers, and, since the meaning of a budget size would differ depending on the market size, a standardized index based on annual movie-theater ticket sales for the last forty years has been established. This standardized index was then multiplied by the budget related to culture and arts, which provides groundwork for relevant data gathering and analysis under the assumption that the market size is identical.

Variables and analysis

Films, music, and performing arts were introduced to the Korean people in the early twentieth century, although the Korean government was only founded in 1945. The Copyright Act was enacted in 1959, the Performance Act in 1961, the Film Act in 1962, and the Music Recording Act in 1967. This is to say that there was virtually no systematic legal framework before the enactment of the Music Recording Act in 1967, and the government made no special budgetary considerations for the industry. In 1967, the legal framework for major cultural industries was established and the intensity and number of regulations has been continually rising. In 1994, a government organization exclusively responsible for the cultural industry was established and dubbed the Cultural Industry Bureau. This marked a sharp turn from laws that centered mainly on regulations and censorship. In particular, before the cultural market was opened to foreigners in 1986, culture was perceived as a political tool or propaganda apparatus that could have a direct impact on people's thoughts and emotions via its content and delivery method, and could thus form public opinion. This meant that governmental regulations took the form of strict entry restrictions through approval, registration and censorship, examination and imposition of cultural content. Government subsidies were also limited to the operational expenses of a few culture-related institutions or support for a selected number of artists. But since the establishment of the Cultural Industry Bureau in 1994, not only has the cultural market expanded substantially but government subsidies have increased even more.

A close look at this development process allows us to identify three distinct period classification variables: the period before 1967 when both legal regulations and subsidization were meager, the period from 1967 to 1993 when legal regulations far outnumbered subsidization, and lastly the period from 1994 to the present when both regulations and subsidization increased. In this study, these three period classification variables were selected as independent variables and the number of government regulations and the amount of standardized government subsidization over the past forty years were established as dependent variables. By verifying whether any statistically significant difference could be found among the three periods, this study examines the changes in the government role toward the cultural industry. In as much as the two dependent variables (number of regulations and amount of subsidization) are correlated (e.g., $r = .717$, $p<0.001$) and the period classification variable is categorical, multivariate analysis of variance (MANOVA) was relied on for analysis.

Results

The results of the MANOVA (table 7.1) for the operational hypothesis suggest robust differences between dependent variables. Univariate F tests (table 7.2) also indicate significant differences.

As can be seen in the test results, there is a distinct difference in the number of regulations and amount of subsidization between the periods. As indicated in table 7.3, multiple comparisons between adjacent groups show statistically significant differences. Therefore, we can

Table 7.1 Multivariate test results

	Value	F	Hypothesis df	Error df	Sig.
Pillai's trace	1.401	47.966	4.000	82.000	.000
Wilks' lambda	.059	62.301[a]	4.000	80.000	.000
Hotelling's trace	8.140	79.369	4.000	78.000	.000
Roy's largest root	7.032	144.160[b]	2.000	41.000	.000

Notes:
[a] Exact statistic.
[b] The statistic is an upper bound on F that yields a lower bound on the significance.

Table 7.2 Univariate test results

Dependent variable	Sum of squares	df	Mean square	F	Sig.
Regulation	1.228	2	.614	67.975	.000
Subsidization	2.829	2	1.415	129.626	.000

Table 7.3 Multiple comparisons

Dependent variable		PERIOD	PERIOD	Mean difference	Sig.	95% confidence interval	
						Lower bound	Upper bound
Regulation	Tukey HSD	1.00	2.00	-.3163 *	.000	-.4094	-.2233
			3.00	-.5360 *	.000	-.6483	-.4237
		2.00	1.00	.3163 *	.000	.2233	.4094
			3.00	-.2196 *	.000	-.3086	-.1307
		3.00	1.00	.5360 *	.000	.4237	.6483
			2.00	.2196 *	.000	.1307	.3086
Subsidization	Tukey HSD	1.00	2.00	-.1129 *	.028	-.2151	-1.0612E-02
			3.00	-.7069 *	.000	-.8304	-.5835
		2.00	1.00	.1129 *	.028	1.061E-02	.2151
			3.00	-.5941 *	.000	-.6919	-.4963
		3.00	1.00	.7069 *	.000	.5835	.8304
			2.00	.5941 *	.000	.4963	.6919

Note:
* The mean difference is significant at the .05 level.

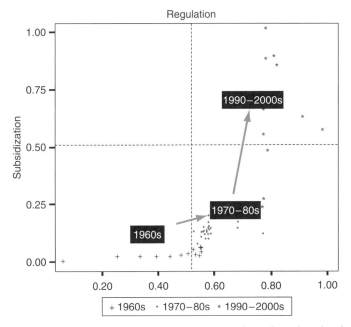

Figure 7.6 Evolution of the Korean government's role in the cultural industry

conclude that government regulations and subsidization have changed drastically in the diffent policy settings. Based on this conclusion, we can draw a diagram shown as in figure 7.6. This indicates that the period until 1966 was the time of laissez-faire, from 1967 to 1993 was a period of constitutionalism when regulation was the main policy employed, and 1994 and thereafter is a period of paternalism when active subsidization was added to regulations.

Discussion and conclusion

The previous study on the changes of the Korean government's role through an analysis of the top ten business-related news stories in major dailies based on a four-celled model indicated that the Korean government's role evolved from laissez-faire to mercantilism to paternalism, and then finally to constitutionalism in the early 1990s (Cho, 1992). It was an analysis based on media reports and was not tailored to a specific industry but covered all industries. In contrast, this research focuses on a specific industry and makes a detailed analysis in that the actual number of regulations and the amount of standardized government subsidization were used to examine the scale of government subsidization. It can be said that this research uses a more direct proxy for regulations and subsidization compared with the previous study.

This paper reached a somewhat different conclusion from that of Cho (1992). On the basis of the conclusions of these two papers, we can examine why the government's stance toward the industry as a whole and the cultural industry specifically evolved in different directions. The Korean government's industrial policies in the 1960s and the 1970s were mainly focused on domestic industries, manufacturing in particular, and the export of domestic products was seen as the best means for accumulating national wealth. Consequently, export companies were provided with large subsidies so that they could enjoy economy of scale, while at the same time regulations were cut to the minimum so that those companies would be free to grow in size. However, with the arrival of the 1990s, the abuses of manufacturing conglomerates became a social issue, and calls for environmental and fair trade regulations grew louder with economic democratization. In addition, government subsidies were cut dramatically, which allows us to view the 1990s as a period of constitutionalism by and large.

Until the 1990s, however, the cultural industry was perceived as a political propaganda tool or as a form of leisure life for the select few, which explained excessive government regulations and meager subsidies. In fact, since regulations in the 1970s and 1980s consisted of various entry barriers to the market, there were detailed rules for granting approval or qualifications in accordance with strict government criteria. The government also wielded great power with the right to censorship, investigation, and correction orders in the name of maintaining national security and good customs. The Ministry of Culture branched out as a separate ministry from the politically biased Ministry of Culture and Public Information in 1990. Since then, the cultural industry has been free from political implications and understood in the industrial sense. The establishment of the Cultural Industry Bureau in 1994 spelled the beginning of substantial policy subsidization for the cultural industry.

On the whole, many industries including the cultural industry have suffered under a constitutionalist government with strong regulations since the early 1990s, as is indicated in the 1992 study by Cho. But around 1994 and 1995, the cultural industry was recognized as a high value added industry and consequently earned large subsidies from the government. In that process, business–government relations regressed toward paternalism from the general pattern of constitutionalism.

Through industrial policies, the government tries to play a central role in developing an industry as well as improving the competitiveness of domestic firms. Ever since the enactment of the Film Act, the government has enforced various policies such as restricting the penetration of foreign movies and promoting the production of Korean movies in an effort to increase the market share of Korean films. However, the government geared up for a more open economic policy in preparation for the 1988 Seoul Olympics, which eventually forced it to open the gates to foreign films in 1986.

Figure 7.7 shows the evolution of the market share of Korean movies. From 1986 when foreign movies were allowed to be directly distributed in the domestic market, foreign films increased their market share in leaps and bounds. Before the open-door policy was adopted, the government recommended the import of foreign movies only to producers with an excellent production track record and foreigners were not permitted to enter the Korean market directly, which explains

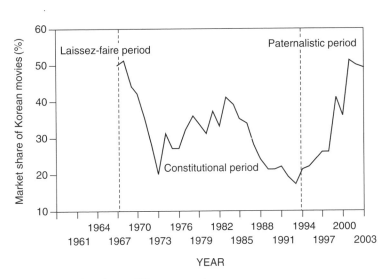

Figure 7.7 Market share of Korean movies
Source: Annual Reports on Film Industry since 1965

the high number of Korean movies and their high market share. However, the Korean film market share started to rise again from 1994 when the government started to support the cultural industry in earnest.

As such, the government, like a strategist of a firm following the principle of selection and concentration with limited resources, selects its strategic industry based on a comprehensive consideration of national human and material resources, growth potential, competitiveness and entry barriers of the industry on the grounds of environmental and core competence analyses. The cultural industry in the mid-1990s was the industry that was strategically selected by the government. This study suggests that firms that conduct business in the cultural industry, both domestic and foreign, have a much higher possibility of success when they establish business strategies after having examined business–government relations of the past, present, and future. This can be extended to infer a need for an understanding of business–government relational developments before business strategy settings not only in the Korean cultural industry but also in all industries of all countries.

This study is not without flaws. First of all, the number of legal regulations may not necessarily indicate the degree or amount of regulations per se. Some regulatory acts may include incentives and even protective measures for those inside the government-protected barricade. Managers, however, may side with us arguing that all regulatory acts are by definition regulatory in nature. Second, we may need to prove that the business–government relations are not affected by the fundamental changes in the nature and content of the industrial policy ranging from industry-specific policies to technology-specific policies. Since this issue deserves a separate analysis, we simply assume here that the change in the nature of industrial policy does not have an impact upon business firms.

8 Multinational enterprise, public authority, and public responsibility: the case of Talisman Energy and human rights in Sudan

STEPHEN J. KOBRIN

Recognizing that even though states have the primary responsibility to promote, secure the fulfillment of, respect, ensure respect of, and protect human rights, transnational corporations and other business enterprises, as organs of society, are also responsible for promoting and securing the human rights set forth in the Universal Declaration of Human Rights.

(United Nations Social and Economic Council, 2003, p. 1)

Corporations ... are increasingly being asked to step into roles that were once the domain of governments or international bodies such as the United Nations. Defining what is properly expected of a company needs to be more clearly articulated and rigorously debated.

(Jim Buckee, CEO Talisman Energy. Corporate Social Responsibility Group, 2001, p. 5)

In November 2001 a $1 billion class-action lawsuit was brought against Talisman Energy, a large Canadian independent oil and gas producer, on behalf of the Presbyterian Church of Sudan and a number of individual plaintiffs. The plaintiffs allege that Talisman violated the human rights of Christian and other non-Muslim minorities in Sudan as part of its oil exploration, development, and production operations in that country. Specifically, the suit accuses Talisman of conducting a campaign of ethnic cleansing to clear the land for oil operations (Wichita Global Coalition, 2001; D'Avino, 2002).[1]

---

[1] The suit was later amended to include the Government of Sudan as a defendant; a motion to dismiss on the part of Talisman was rejected by a

Talisman is charged with violating the human rights of Sudanese in Sudan; the alleged actions did not involve American nationals nor did they take place on American territory. The case was brought under the Alien Tort Claims Act (ATCA) which permits aliens to sue in a US court for torts committed abroad in violation of the "law of nations" or a treaty of the United States. The ATCA dates from 1789, and while it may have been enacted to combat piracy, Congress' original intentions have been lost in the mists of time (Amon, 2000; Bridgeford, 2003).

The Act lay dormant for almost 200 years until 1980 when a Circuit Court allowed two Paraguayans to sue a Paraguayan police inspector for the torture and death of a family member under the ATCA (Developments in the Law, 2001). In the last decade there has been "a growing tide of litigation" under the Act attempting to hold multi-national corporations responsible for human rights violations occurring in the course of their subsidiaries' operations. Suits have been brought against Texaco in Ecuador, Chevron in Nigeria, Exxon-Mobil in Indonesia, and perhaps most notably, UNOCAL in Burma. American courts have held that gross violations of human rights such as summary execution, torture, slavery or forced labor, genocide and cruel, inhuman or degrading treatment violate the "law of nations" and are thus actionable under ATCA (Developments in the Law, 2001; Blumberg, 2002; Olsen, 2002; Perlez, 2002).

The Alien Torts Claims Act cases raise a number of interesting questions, two of which are directly relevant here. First, what does it mean to say that a multinational corporation (MNC) is "complicit" in human rights violations? Is actual participation in recruiting or using forced labor, for example, necessary or is the fact that the company knew, or should have known, that abuses were taking place sufficient? (I will deal with this issue in much more detail below.) Second, why are these cases, some of which involve neither American nationals nor acts committed on US territory, being brought in the US, and why do American courts claim "universal jurisdiction" (Developments in the Law, 2001)?

There are practical and conceptual answers to this second question, both of which involve a "governance gap" resulting from incomplete

District Court Judge in March 2003 when the judge ruled that the case was properly brought in a Manhattan court (Neumeister, 2003).

globalization: an integrated world economy is governed by political authorities which are still primarily local and national. The nongovernmental organizations (NGOs) concerned with the impact of Talisman's operations in Sudan on human rights had a limited range of options.[2] The host country (Sudan) was obviously unwilling to pursue the matter, and the home country (Canada) either unwilling or unable to deal with what amounted to extraterritorial activities on the part of one of its companies. Furthermore, as a private firm, Talisman's activities in Sudan were beyond the reach of international organizations such as the United Nations. Thus, a case brought under the ATCA in a US court provided one of the few venues available to NGOs to pursue a MNC for alleged human rights violations in an international system characterized by fragmented, geographically based political and regulatory authority.

The modern international political system reflects its Westphalian origins: it is defined by mutually exclusive territorial jurisdiction, geographic sovereignty, and state-centrism – states as the only political actors and the only subjects of international law. Given these parameters, private actors such as business firms are objects rather than subjects; their role, authority, and responsibilities in international politics (and international law) are strictly limited.

The process of globalization brings significant changes to the organization of international politics and economics. The once clear line between domestic and international affairs has blurred and morphed into what Rosenau calls the "domestic–foreign frontier" (1997); in many respects borders are no longer either discrete or meaningful. Furthermore, states are no longer the only significant international political actors; while they may still occupy a "seat at the head of the table," advocacy groups and other NGOs, international institutions, and multinational firms have considerable power in international politics. As Cutler observes, "Westphalian-inspired notions of state-centricity, positivist international law, and 'public' definitions of authority are incapable of capturing the significance of non-state actors, like transnational corporations and individuals ... and private economic power in the global economy" (2001, p. 133).

---

[2] As will be discussed below, the advocacy groups concerned with Talisman's operations in Sudan mounted a very successful campaign aimed at institutional investors and shareholders which, in large part, was responsible for Talisman withdrawing from Sudan in 2003.

If multinational firms have become significant actors in international politics, they definitionally command some degree of "authority." It is a short step from acknowledging multinationals as commanding some degree of "public authority" to holding them responsible for public functions such as the protection of human rights. The ATCA cases in American courts can be seen as a tentative, if very controversial, step in that direction.

I next turn to a more complete discussion of the question of public authority and responsibility in the international system, both in general and as regards MNCs. I will then review the experience of Talisman Energy in Sudan, especially in regard to the charges brought against it by a variety of groups that it was complicit in the very severe violations of human rights that have occurred in that country during its brutal civil war. I will then attempt to use the Talisman case to try to generalize about multinational firms' responsibilities for human rights. I conclude by exploring questions of the limits of public responsibilities of multinational firms.

Private actors in international politics

While the international business literature deals with questions of fragmentation of strategy and the limits of headquarters' control over subsidiaries, the multinational enterprise is typically seen as a single transnational enterprise operating in a relatively large number of countries. We talk about Shell Oil, Sony, and Lever as coherent global entities.

The legal reality is quite different: the multinational – as such – does not exist. It is not possible to incorporate under international law: the global firm is an apparition (Cutler, 2001), a coalition of companies incorporated under the laws of many different states. Thus, under accepted principles of international law, "each of the constituent corporations of a corporate group is a national of the nation-state in which it has been incorporated and subject to the laws of that state" (Blumberg, 2002, p. 494).

For private firms operating transnationally, "legal personality is conferred under national and municipal laws, and corporate rights, duties, and remedies remain a function of national law." As a result, the legal (and political) rights and obligations of multinational firms are derivative; they flow from their status as national firms responsive to national governments (Cutler, 2001, p. 141). Thus, the fact that private multinational firms lack "legal personality" renders them unaccountable under international law. "TNCs benefit from their international nonstatus. Nonstatus immunizes them from direct accountability to international legal norms and permits them to use sympathetic national governments to parry outside efforts to mold their behavior" (Charney, 1983, cited in Cutler 2001, p. 143).

States are the only "subjects" of *traditional* international law, the only entities with legal rights and duties. International law does not either articulate the obligations of corporations with regard to human rights or provide a mechanism for regulating, or even monitoring, corporate behavior in that area (Developments in the Law, 2001). Multinational firms are private actors who owe an obligation to their shareholders to produce profits and whose obligation to the state is defined by law and regulation. "[P]rivate non-state actors, such as MNEs, do not have any positive duty to observe human rights. Their only duty is to obey the law. Thus it is for the state to regulate on matters of social importance and for MNEs to observe the law" (Muchlinski, 2001, p. 35).

This sharp distinction between the public and private spheres is not inherent in the human experience, but rather a property of the Westphalian international system and the development of the sovereign territorial state. During the feudal period, political authority was diffuse, ambiguous, interwoven, and non-territorial (Kobrin, 1998; Cutler, 1999). There was no clear line between the public and private spheres, between political and economic authority. The public/private distinction developed with the rise of the territorially sovereign state and the development of private property and property rights (Cutler, 1999).

Modern ideas about the distinction between public political authority and private economic markets and actors developed in the nineteenth century with the rise of the self-regulating market. As Cutler notes, the market "perfected the association of 'political' and legal authority with the public sphere of governments and the association of 'apolitical' economic relations with the private sphere of individuals and markets" (Cutler, 2001, p. 138).

In the traditional liberal view, only "public" entities – states and other governmental units – have political authority. Markets and firms are private, commanding economic but not political authority or responsibilities. During the twentieth century, what Muchlinski (2001, p. 36) has called "a remarkably resilient model of a liberal market society" developed, characterized by a clear distinction between the public and private spheres. Liberalism "renders *private authority* an impossibility by creating the distinction between public and private activities and locating the 'right to rule' or authority squarely in the public sphere" (Cutler, 1999, p. 73, emphasis in the original).

That once clear distinction has blurred considerably with the political and economic changes that have accompanied globalization. In a rapidly evolving post-Westphalian world it has become reasonable to talk about private political authority and private political obligations. The standard Westphalian assumptions about power and authority are no longer capable of explaining contemporary reality (Cutler, 2001).

Globalization – defined in terms of deep, networked integration of economies, societies, and polities – involves significant systemic changes in the structure or organization of international economics and politics (Kobrin, 1997). Political authority has become fragmented and inter-woven once again with the emergence of non-state entities such as civil society groups (NGOs) and multinational corporations as significant actors in international politics, the increased salience of international institutions such as the World Trade Organization, and the rise of supra-national powers such as the European Union. While states may still be the dominant players in the system, the state-centric model has broken down and states have lost power to other actors and to markets (Strange, 1996). States function, at least in part, as economic actors, and multinational firms influence political outcomes (Cutler, 2001).

The result is a complex evolving international political system in which sovereign states are still dominant, but non-state entities are significant, authoritative actors (Burke, 1999). Much of the literature on private authority argues that the international integration of mar-kets has affected the ability and willingness of states to intervene in economic affairs and is concerned with the role of multinational firms and other private actors in standard setting, the impact of privately arbitrated dispute resolution, and, more generally, the role of firms in the governance of international economic affairs (Cutler, Haufler, and Porter, 1999; Haufler, 2001, p. 5). In addition, as Muchlinski (2001, p. 40) observes, the fact that MNCs participate directly in the activities of international institutions such as the WTO and EU creates "the clear perception of MNEs as entities capable of exerting power over public policy."

My concern here is not the exercise of public authority by multi-nationals but rather the corresponding public *responsibilities* of MNCs in a number of important issue areas. One example is the global battle against AIDS where private multinational firms are being pressured to take on increasingly important public roles (Beattie, 2003). Another is human rights where responsibility, and perhaps liability, follows from MNCs' role in the "global order" (Bridgeford, 2003). "The traditional notion that only states and state agents can be held accountable for violations of human rights is being challenged as the economic and social power of MNEs appears to rise in the wake of the increasing integration of the global economy that they have helped to bring about" (Muchlinski, 2001, p. 31).

Human rights has become a significant international issue and, notions of sovereignty aside, human rights violations within countries are now deemed to be the responsibility of the "international community." United Nations Secretary General Kofi Annan argues that traditional notions of sovereignty can no longer do justice to people's aspirations for human freedom; that nothing in the UN charter "precludes a recognition that there are rights beyond borders" (Littlejohns and Buchan, 1999, p. 5).

The problem at this point is that the "international community" is still an ambiguous construct. While less so than in the past, in all but the most egregious circumstances states are reluctant to cross borders to intervene to protect human rights. International organizations have neither the resources nor the capabilities to enforce human rights or even to monitor violations. As a result, the primary responsibility for monitoring human rights violations, publicizing problem areas, and advocating remedial action often falls on private civil society groups or NGOs such as Amnesty International and Human Rights Watch, among many others.

As Haufler (2001, p. 29) observes, "When governments do not govern, the private sector does – often in response to the demands of public interest groups who find themselves unable to move national govern-ments." As noted above, MNCs are increasingly perceived as significant, authoritative actors in international politics, actors with meaningful political power. However, political authority is a two-sided coin. On the one hand, MNCs are perceived as having the political power to positively affect human rights regimes in host countries. On the other hand, they are increasingly being held responsible – as quasi-public actors – for human rights violations occurring in conjunction with their subsidiaries' operations.

Advocacy groups increasingly target MNCs directly (Broad and Cavanagh, 1998). NGOs monitor human rights violations occurring in conjunction with corporate activity, publicize them widely and often very effectively, and bring pressure to bear on home-country governments, but more importantly, managers, shareholders, and investors, to effect change. MNCs are being held "liable" – at least in the forum of public opinion and perhaps in the courts – for "complicity" in human rights violations. More interestingly, as the quote at the start of this chapter illustrates, MNCs are increasingly seen as having a positive responsibility or duty for promoting and securing human rights, for using their power and influence to change a given regime's human rights policies and practices.

That raises some critical questions. First, if MNCs are to be held responsible for complicity in human rights violations, what does complicity entail? Is simply entering a country where human rights violations are the norm complicity or, at the other end of the scale, does a firm have to actually participate in activities that violate the rights of individuals? Second, who is to establish the parameters of corporate responsibilities for human rights, and how are violations to be monitored and judged and penalties for transgressions enforced? The experience of Talisman Energy in Sudan is directly relevant and provides a rich case study in which to ground further discussion of these issues.

War in Sudan[3]

Sudan has been engaged in civil war for thirty-six of the forty-seven years since it gained independence from Great Britain in 1956. The "second civil war," which began in 1983, has been characterized by a vicious brutality that has resulted in two million deaths – the majority of them civilians – and over four million displaced persons (International Crisis Group, 2002; Martin, 2002). Sudan sits squarely on the divide between primarily Arab and Muslim North Africa and the primarily Black, Christian and "Animist" area south of the Sahara; the southern provinces are ethnically diverse containing a large number of tribes and linguistic

---

[3] See Kobrin (2003) for a more complete discussion of the origins of the civil war in Sudan.

groups (Idahosa, 2002). A focal point of the war has been the Upper West Nile region in which Talisman's operations were located.

The rebellion in the southern provinces at independence intensified in 1958 when a campaign by the government in the north to forcibly extend Islam to the south resulted in a full-fledged civil war (International Crisis Group, 2002). The "end" of the first civil war came in 1972 with the Addis Ababa agreement which provided security guarantees and some degree of political and economic autonomy to the south. However, by the end of that decade, the government in Khartoum came under pressure from hardliners to re-exert control over the south and the regime embraced strict Islamism (Sudan Update, 1999; Gagnon and Ryle, 2001; Idahosa, 2002).

The situation in Sudan was complicated by the discovery of oil (in the southern provinces) during the 1970s which (eventually) altered the balance of power in that country and provided an additional motivation for the conflict. In 1980 the regime in Khartoum redrew the boundaries of the Upper Nile province to include the areas where oil had been discovered within the north, and in 1983 it issued an order abrogating the Addis Ababa agreement, returning powers to the central government, eliminating the south's autonomy and dividing it into three administrative provinces. Shortly thereafter, Sudan was declared an Islamic state and *sharia* the law throughout the country. Southerners then mobilized around the Sudan People's Liberation Army (SPLA), rebelled and the second, and even more destructive, civil war began (Harker, 2000; Gagnon and Ryle, 2001).

While there was a brief window where peace appeared possible in the late 1980s, after General Umar al-Bashir took power through a coup in 1989, the war was pursued with a vengeance with the regime in Khartoum attempting to impose "God's law" throughout the country (Sudan Update, 1999; International Crisis Group, 2002; Martin, 2002). While there have been various attempts at settlements, and recent (late 2003) hopes for peace, at this writing the situation in Sudan remains unsettled and dangerous.

The Sudanese civil war is complex and can no longer be characterized as a conflict between the Islamic north and Christian, Animist and tribal south. While the government's attempt to impose Islam and Islamic law on the entire country continues to fuel the conflict, the longstanding marginalization of the southern provinces, an attempt by the government to extend its control over the disputed areas, and a struggle among several groups for control over Sudan's territory and resources are all important reasons for the continued fighting.

During the 1990s, the war evolved from its roots as a largely north–south conflict "into a contest for power that involves groups from across the nation." In addition to the forces of the government in Khartoum and the SPLA (now the SPLM), it involves a relatively large number of militias and inter-tribal factions, some of whom change sides as it is advantageous (United Nations Office for the Coordination of Humanitarian Efforts, 2000; Gagnon, Macklin, and Simons, 2003, p. 15).

The war involves massive attacks on and displacement of civilians and human slavery as a result of raids by Khartoum-supported mur-ahaleen militias on southern tribes. "The vast majority of Sudan's casualties are not combatants killed in battle but southern civilians who fall victim to famine and disease" (Martin, 2002; Gagnon, Macklin, and Simons, 2003). While both sides are guilty of atrocities and attacks on civilian non-combatants, there is general agreement that the primary responsibility for the destitution, death, and destruction in the south lies with the government of Sudan.

Oil and Talisman's entry

While oil exploration and development began in Sudan in the early 1960s, serious efforts started with the entry of Chevron which was granted a concession in 1974 (Shell later took a 25 percent interest). Although Chevron made a number of significant discoveries and Sudanese oil appeared to have considerable potential, the company suspended operations and withdrew in 1984 after a rebel group kidnapped and killed three expatriate employees. Chevron relinquished its concessions in 1990 having spent $1 billion in Sudan (Sudan Update, 1999; Harker, 2000; Energy Information Administration, 2003; Gagnon, Macklin, and Simons, 2003).

As a result of an acquisition, Arakis Energy (a Canadian independent) gained control of a large part of Chevron's concession in 1994; at that point the project involved both oil exploration, development, and production, and the construction of a pipeline to the Red Sea. Arakis, however, could not finance the project on its own and in late 1996 it entered into a consortium, the Greater Nile Petroleum Operating Company (GNPOC), in which it held a 25 percent share, the Chinese

National Petroleum Company 40 percent, Petronas of Malaysia 30 percent, and the Sudanese national firm 5 percent (Arakis Energy Corporation, 1998; Chase, 1998; Sudan Update, 1999).

Arakis still found itself in a very difficult situation. The US imposed sanctions on Sudan in 1997, as a result of concerns over both that country's support for terrorism and human rights violations, that prevented American participation in Sudanese oil and limited Arakis' ability to raise funds in US markets. Furthermore, there was an eight quarter decline in crude oil prices from $23 a barrel to a low of $13 in the summer of 1998. In any event, when it became clear that Arakis would not be able to raise the $200 million necessary to fund its share of the project, it encouraged offers from other companies (Cattaneo, 1998; Jones, 1998b; Sudan Update, 1999; Gagnon, Macklin, and Simons, 2003).

On August 17, 1997 Talisman Energy acquired the outstanding shares of Arakis, and thus acquired that company's 25 percent share of GNPOC in Sudan. Talisman, which originated as a spin-off of British Petroleum's Canadian subsidiary, was the second largest Canadian independent oil company by 1997 (Cattaneo, 1998; "The Human Factor," 1999; Sudan Update, 1999).[4] Despite the American missile attack on the al-Shifa plant in Khartoum a few days later, the takeover took place as scheduled on October 8 (Jones, 1998).

A number of analysts saw the project as a high-risk–high-return investment that made sense for the company. Despite the ongoing civil war and the location of the concessions in the midst of the disputed area, Talisman obtained a 25 percent share of five fields with an estimated production of 150,000 bbls/day, and a pipeline and marine terminal expected to be completed by late 1999 (Alden, 1998; Cattaneo, 1998; Talisman Energy, 1998).

Talisman's short, unhappy, Sudan experience

Despite oil production and profits that far exceeded expectations, Talisman withdrew from Sudan in March 2003, selling its 25 percent share of GNPOC to a subsidiary of India's national oil company

---

[4] An independent has only "upstream" operations, it does not refine petroleum or own retail outlets.

("Talisman Closes Sale of Sudan Oil Stake," 2003). While Talisman was able to handle the political situation in Sudan and produce petroleum in spite of the civil war – production in Sudan was estimated to reach 300,000 bbls/day in 2003 and the pipeline reached capacity in 2003 ("Exploration Hums as Sudan's Output Reaches Pipeline Capacity," 2002; "Sudan," 2002) – its stock price fell at the announcement of the deal and sold at a 10 to 20 percent discount during the time Talisman was in Sudan as compared with a 20 percent premium (to net asset value) before the investment (Carlisle, 2000; Dabrowski, 2002; Olive, 2002).

While Talisman encountered considerable opposition from both the United States and Canadian governments, its difficulties were due, in large part, to a very successful campaign waged by a coalition of advocacy groups and NGOs who persuaded a number of institutional investors to sell their Talisman stock and maintained a continual barrage of pressure on Talisman's shareholders and managers. Sudanese production, which never amounted to more than 12 percent of Talisman's operations, was not worth the considerable political costs it incurred. As CEO Jim Buckee noted after the sale, "Shareholders have told me that they were tired of continually having to monitor and analyze events relating to Sudan" ("Talisman to Sell Sudan Assets for C$1.2 Billion," 2002).

The divestment campaign, led by the American Anti-Slavery Group, was directed at the major institutional investors holding Talisman's stock. Advocacy groups linked the company directly to the brutal violations of human rights in Sudan including forced displacement of civilians and the slave trade. They accused the funds owning Talisman's stock of supporting genocide. During 1999 and 2000 at least six American pension funds sold millions of share of the company's stock including TIAA-CREFF, CALPERS, The Texas Teachers' Retirement Fund, and the New York City Pension Fund (Gillis, 1999). While it is difficult to gauge the success of similar efforts mounted against mutual funds such as Fidelity and Vanguard, it is reasonable to assume that the activists' efforts had a significant effect on purchases and sales of Talisman's stock (Scherer, 2001).

Oil production has always been a risky business and, given the very active civil war and the location of Talisman's operations, it is clear that the level of political risks associated with the project were very high. What drove Talisman from Sudan, however, was not in-country risk: they managed a difficult situation well and, as noted above, production exceeded expectations. Rather, Talisman sold its Sudanese operations because of "political risks" arising in North America from activists' successful efforts to associate it with complicity in human rights violations in Sudan. As will be discussed below, the company argued that it fully complied with local law and engaged in significant efforts to improve the lives and livelihoods of Sudanese in the affected areas.

That raises the more general question of exactly what "complicity" means, what the obligations of multinational firms are with respect to human rights violations in the countries in which they operate. I will argue that MNCs are now regarded as international political actors with "political" authority and responsibility, and that directly affects both the perception and reality of their human rights obligations. As a first step in developing that argument, I turn to a more detailed examination of Talisman's role, and the role of oil more generally, in Sudan.

Talisman, oil, and human rights in Sudan

While an oversimplification, it is reasonable to characterize the differences between Talisman and its critics in terms of differences in the interpretation of events within Sudan and the extent of the company's responsibilities for human rights within that country. In general, the company tended to minimize the extent of the conflict, argue that it was overblown in the media, and see its responsibilities in terms of contributing to overall economic growth and to the well-being of Sudanese in the area through construction of schools, clinics, and the like. It is also fair to say that the company's view changed somewhat over time. There were a number of concerns expressed by a wide variety of observers about the impact of the company's operations on human rights in Sudan.

Oil production exacerbated and changed the nature of the conflict.

A wide range of observers argue that oil production and the opening of the pipeline by the GNPOC intensified the war and has changed its dynamics by providing significant new resources to the government in Khartoum. The investigation undertaken at the request of the

Canadian Ministry of Foreign Affairs concluded that "oil is exacerbating the conflict in Sudan" (Harker, 2000, p. 14).

Oil production transformed the conflict from a fight over control of territory to a fight over control of a valuable resource and the benefits it produces. In 2002, a UN Special Rapporteur (Gerhart Baum) noted that "oil exploration is closely linked to the conflict ... which is primarily a war for the control of resources, and, thus, power" (cited in Human Rights Watch, 2003, p. 58). More important, it transformed Sudan from one of the poorest countries in Africa to an exporter of petroleum. Oil revenues, which were negligible in 1998, increased dramatically from $61 million in 1999 – the first year of significant production – to almost $600 million in 2001 (Energy Information Administration, 2003; Human Rights Watch, 2003); by 2001 oil revenues accounted for around 40 percent of Sudan's total income (Gagnon, Macklin, and Simons, 2003). There is little question that Talisman provided the technology and experience necessary for GNPOC to exploit Sudan's oil reserves; as noted above, oil production increased significantly within a year after the company's entry (Gagnon and Ryle, 2001).

The oil revenues were spent on arms and military equipment, including the purchase of modern weapons and helicopter gun ships. Sudan can now manufacture its own light arms and munitions and is planning to build tanks and artillery (International Crisis Group, 2002; Martin, 2002). The Khartoum regime's military expenditures and military capabilities increased dramatically as a direct result of successful oil exploration, development, and production; by 2001 the war cost the government over $1 million a day (International Crisis Group, 2002). That level of expenditure would have been unthinkable before 1999.

Measures taken to provide security to oil operations have resulted in serious human rights violations.

Talisman's operations (as part of the GNPOC) are located in the midst of the war zone, an area disputed by rebel forces and the government in Khartoum. They are an obvious target and have been for some time. As discussed above, an attack on Chevron's operations in 1984 resulted in the deaths of three expatriate employees and led to that company's eventual withdrawal from Sudan. When Talisman first entered in 1998, the SPLA publicly declared the company's operations to be a legitimate military target (Gagnon and Ryle, 2001).

The importance of oil to the government's war effort has led to increased attacks on oil operations by rebel forces and increased the intensity of the war, on both sides, in the area of Talisman's operations. The government's response has been brutal, including attacks on civilians, forced displacement of very large numbers of people, and the burning, looting, and destruction of villages in the area (Gagnon and Ryle, 2001).

The government is engaged in an attempt to depopulate the area around the oilfields.

A UN Special Rapporteur (Leonardo Franco) concluded that a "swath of scorched earth/cleared territory is being created around the oil fields"; the Harker investigation agreed with Franco's findings (Harker, 2000, p. 11). In fact, Human Rights Watch concludes that "forced displacement of the civilian population, and the death and destruction that have accompanied it, are the central human rights issues relating to oil development in Sudan" (2003, p. 36).

Similarly, an article in *The Economist* (2001, p. 41) notes that the government of Sudan has "adopted a brutal new policy of clearing the oil areas." Before the marked increase in oil production in 1999, the government armed Arab militia groups and encouraged them to raid southern villages for cattle and to take slaves. While this certainly resulted in widespread suffering, it did not entail the massive displacement of the civilian population seen since oil production became an issue. As noted above, oil operations are in disputed border areas and the government wants "the southeners out" (*The Economist*, 2001). The Human Rights Watch (2003) report on oil and human rights in Sudan contains an extensive discussion of the displacement of civilians from the oil-producing areas both before and after Talisman's entry.

Talisman's facilities were used to stage military action against both rebel and civilian targets.

Talisman itself agreed that there were at least four instances of the use of its airstrip at the Heglig field for "non-defensive" military purposes (Talisman Energy, 2000; Gagnon, Macklin, and Simons, 2003). The Harker Report (Harker, 2000, p 15) noted that " ... flights clearly linked to the oil war have been a regular feature of life at the Heglig airstrip ... It is operated by the consortium, and Canadian chartered helicopters and fixed wing aircraft which use the strip have shared the facilities with helicopter gunships and Antonov bombers of the GOS [Government of Sudan]. These have armed and re-fuelled at Heglig and from there attacked civilians." Furthermore, a number of observers have concluded that the government used the infrastructure built by the oil companies – the roads and bridges – to launch attacks on civilians in the area (Human Rights Watch, 2003).

Complicity

I suspect that most observers, including Talisman Energy, would agree that the military use of corporate facilities – especially for non-defensive operations – is inappropriate and renders the company complicit in the ensuing human rights violations. Once one moves beyond this sort of direct involvement in the violations of human rights, however, the situation gets much more ambiguous. Talisman is a private company whose obligation to its shareholders to generate revenue and profits requires it to explore, develop, and produce petroleum. It is certainly not unusual for oil reserves to be found in difficult environments, both physically and politically. Does Talisman, or any other company in a similar situation, have obligations which go beyond avoiding direct complicity in human rights violations and obeying the law of both host and home countries? The regime in Khartoum is recognized as sovereign internationally and one could argue it was appropriate for Talisman to rely on the government of Sudan to defend its operations against rebel attacks.

I will argue that as multinationals emerge as significant actors in international politics, their new-found "private" political authority will bring with it "public" political responsibilities. The line between public authorities and private economic actors has blurred to the point where MNCs may begin to be held liable for a much broader definition of complicity in human rights violations, which may even include a positive responsibility to effect a change in the host country's human rights policies. There have been a number of recent attempts to define "complicity" or to suggest the extent of MNCs' responsibilities for human rights.

Gagnon, Macklin, and Simons (2003, p. 8) use Canadian and international law to define complicity in the commission of acts of a perpetrator (of human rights violations) as:

- Acts or omissions that provide material assistance in circumstances where the TNC [Transnational Corporation] knew or should have known that its acts or omissions would provide such assistance.
- Acts or omissions that abet the perpetrator in circumstances where the TNC knew or ought to have known that its acts or omissions would encourage the perpetrator.
- Where a TNC enters into a commercial relationship with one or more parties in a conflict zone, and any of those parties commits acts in violation of the Code in furtherance of that commercial undertaking, the TNC is complicit if it knew or ought to have known that the commission of the acts would be a probable consequence of carrying out the commercial relationship with that party.

In their extensive review of oil and human rights in Sudan, Human Rights Watch (2003, p. 61) puts it more directly: " ... [Talisman] had a responsibility to ensure that its business operations did not depend upon, or benefit from, gross human rights abuses such as those that have been committed by the government and its proxy forces in Sudan."

The UN Global Compact, which is a voluntary initiative to promote "responsible corporate citizenship," devotes two of its nine principles to human rights (Global Compact, 2003b). Principle One states that businesses should "support and respect the protection of internationally proclaimed human rights within their sphere of influence." In its elaboration of Principle One, the compact argues that, at a minimum, business should "ensure its operations are consistent with legal principles in the country of operation." It also notes that businesses may have an opportunity to promote human rights and raise standards in host countries. Businesses can prevent the "forcible displacement of individuals, groups and communities," and have a right and responsibility to express their view on human rights to governments (Global Compact, 2003b).

Principle Two states that businesses should make sure that they are not complicit in human rights abuses. Complicity is defined in the following terms (Global Compact, 2003b):

- Direct Complicity occurs when a company knowingly assists a state in violating human rights. Assisting in forced location is given as an example.
- Beneficial Complicity suggests that a company benefits from the abuse of human rights. Violations by security forces guarding installations are given as an example.
- Silent Complicity involves the failure by a company to raise the question of systematic violations of human rights with authorities.

Last, the "UN Norms on the Responsibilities of Transnational Corporations ... " is, perhaps, most explicit about the extended human rights responsibilities of MNCs. While noting that states have the primary responsibility for human rights protection, including ensuring the compliance of MNCs, it goes on to state that transnational corporations have " ... the obligation to promote, secure the fulfillment of, respect, ensure respect of and protect human rights recognized in *international as well as national law* ... " (United Nations Social and Economic Council, 2003, p. 3, emphasis added). Furthermore, transnational corporations are held to recognize applicable norms of international law, national law and regulation, the rule of law, the public interest, development objectives, etc. (United Nations Social and Economic Council, 2003, p. 4).

Two points are obvious from this brief summary. First, most if not all of these statements go well beyond the traditional view of the MNC as a private actor, an object rather than a subject of international law and politics. MNCs are held to a positive duty to promote and secure human rights that transcends obeying national law and regulation. Furthermore, these statements – especially the UN "Norms" – appear to point toward MNC liability for human rights violations under international law. Second, it is far from clear what any of these strictures mean in practice. Do any operations in a conflict-ridden country "benefit" from human rights violations as a matter of course?

Complicity or constructive engagement?

As the criticism of its operations in Sudan mounted, Talisman Energy established a dedicated Corporate Social Responsibility Group in March 2000; as a result, two Corporate Social Responsibility Reports were published in 2000 and 2001. In the second, CEO Jim Buckee notes, "Some express the opinion that we should leave Sudan, however, many people we speak to believe that the appropriate moral response is to stay and use our corporate resources in a broad and responsible manner to encourage peace, provide economic opportunities and support the communities in the areas in which we operate" (Talisman Energy, 2001, p. 5). The Company consistently took the position that its presence in Sudan was beneficial, even as it sold its operations in 2003.

It should be noted that one of the major points of contention between Talisman and its critics is the extent of forced dislocations of the civilian population in the area of the oil concessions. As noted above, the human rights organizations active in Sudan, the UN Special Rapporteurs, and the Canadian government's Harker Report all found that there was massive forced displacement of civilians in the Upper West Nile Region. The company tended to dismiss local conflict as tribal in origin, and after commissioning a satellite photo study concluded that "there was no evidence of appreciable human migration – in other words displacement – within the concession areas studied" (Talisman Energy, 2001, p. 16). They did go on to note that "many people hold a differing opinion on this issue."

It does appear clear that the company either knew or should have known the full extent of the situation it was getting into. The "second civil war" in Sudan had been raging for fifteen years when it entered in 1998; most of the rural areas in the oil concessions had been outside of government control since that time (Gagnon and Ryle, 2001). The government's strategy of "division and displacement" of the southern population had been in place since the 1980s (Human Rights Watch, 2003). Furthermore, Chevron had been forced out by rebel activity and the SPLA had made it clear that they considered the oil concessions a target.

Canadian NGOs approached Talisman immediately upon its announcement of its takeover of Arakis to protest its involvement in Sudan, citing the considerable human rights abuses in that country. By late 1999, the Canadian Minister of Foreign Affairs (Lloyd Axworthy) had expressed strong reservations about Talisman's involvement in Sudan (Bowley, 1999; Foster, 1999). Talisman's response, at least at first, was to deny the mass displacement of civilians; there is no evidence that they made an effort to mount an investigation of the allegations of human rights abuses before entering the country (Human Rights Watch, 2003).

There is no doubt that Sudan during the time of Talisman's investment represents an unusually stark and difficult environment in which to operate responsibly with regard to human rights. I suspect that there would be general agreement about what constitutes direct complicity in human rights violations: consenting to the government's use of the airstrip to mount "non-defensive" operations, for example, or assisting in the forced dislocation of civilians to clear a concession area.

At the other extreme, Gagnon and Ryle (2001, p. 39) argue that "a company operating in the war zone of Sudan cannot be neutral. Every aspect of its operation benefits one side – the government side – in a conflict where human rights violations are the norm. In these conditions, all aspects of oil development contribute to the worsening situation for the inhabitants of the Upper Nile." It is not unreasonable to ask whether the act of entering the country, in this case producing and transporting oil in Sudan, renders the company "complicit" in human rights violations. Given the need to secure facilities and the very high probability of a rebel attack on oil operations and some knowledge of the government's strategy and tactics to date, should it have been clear that the company would be dependent on the government to protect its concessions and that human rights violations would be probable in the course of government operations? Could any oil company enter Sudan in 1998 without becoming "beneficially complicit?"

While Talisman has tended to minimize the forced dislocations taking place as a result of oil exploration (as noted above), one of the UN Special Rapporteurs has been quoted as saying that "if the oil companies don't know what's going on, they're not looking over the fences of their compounds" (Harker, 2000, p. 14). Assuming that the Harker Report and other human rights monitoring in Sudan are correct, it is reasonable to argue that any oil firm entering Sudan should have known that the concessions were in the midst of a war zone, that the government had engaged in human rights abuses in attempting to clear that area previously, and that the company would be dependent on government forces accused of human rights abuses to defend their concessions from attack. It is hard to avoid a conclusion that any oil firm entering Sudan had to accept that it was likely to both benefit from human rights abuses on the part of the government and depend on them for survival.

Direct complicity and determining that merely entering the country constitutes complicity are two ends of a continuum; there is a great deal of ground in between. One possibility is certainly constructive engagement, where a company undertakes a positive obligation to influence the policy of the regime and mitigate human rights abuses. As the Harker Report concluded (Harker, 2000, p. 17), " . . . if the company is either unwilling or unable to constructively influence the GOS [Government of Sudan], perhaps it should not be in Sudan at this time."

My point here is that defining "complicity" specifically or the obligations of MNCs with regard to human rights more generally is complex and may well be beyond the capabilities of a given firm at any point in time. As multinational firms take on "public" authority and "public" responsibilities, including potential liability for human rights violations, determining the extent of those responsibilities and liabilities becomes critically important. I will return to this topic below.

Talisman's response

As discussed above, Talisman Energy responded to the mounting wave of criticism of its operations in Sudan by establishing a Corporate Social Responsibility Group in early 2000. One result was the publication of two Corporate Social Responsibility Reports (2000 and 2001) which focused on the Company's operations in Sudan. In his introduction to the first, CEO Buckee noted that "as a business we should focus on delivering shareholder value and to do this effectively, we must achieve high standards of social and environmental performance. In all countries where we operate, we believe that we have a duty to advocate respect for human rights where there are abuses" (Talisman Energy, 2000, p. 7). While the reports are controversial and the company's response has been disputed by advocacy organizations, what is of interest here is that they indicate an acceptance of responsibilities that go far beyond focusing "on delivering shareholder value" and obeying the law.

By the time of publication of the 2000 Report, Talisman had "accepted" the need to comply with the International Code of Ethics for Canadian Business and to support the principle of the UN Declaration of Human Rights. It also accepted as "objectives" the need to use its corporate influence to ensure that GNPOC infrastructure was not used for offensive military operations, to promote "to the Government of Sudan the formalization of the provision of security that complies with the pertinent UN Codes of Conduct," and to advocate support for the Universal Declaration of Human Rights with the government. It did note that security of its operations and personnel was a primary concern and that the government of Sudan had "primary responsibility for the protection of oilfield staff and property" (Talisman Energy, 2000, pp. 9 and 14). The report also describes the more traditional community development efforts such as funding for schools, water development, and clinics as well as human rights monitoring efforts.

During 2001 Talisman reported an attempt to develop an agreement between GNPOC and the government of Sudan that contained provisions dealing with respect for human rights, the appropriate use of oilfield infrastructure, and the prohibition of the use of irregular

Sudanese military forces for oilfield protection. It also asked that the Government ensure that all security forces comply with appropriate United Nations codes. The government of Sudan "ultimately rejected the draft security agreement ... on the basis that the provision of security is the prime responsibility and prerogative of governments and that these issues were not appropriate to be addressed by a company residing in and operating under the laws of Sudan" (Talisman Energy, 2001, p. 17).

The Canadian government backs off

In late 1999 Madeleine Albright, the US Secretary of State, sent a strongly worded letter to Lloyd Axworthy, the Canadian Foreign Affairs Minister, urging him to ask Talisman to withdraw from Sudan (Frank, 1999). While Axworthy was initially somewhat miffed over US involvement in Canadian affairs, he quickly called CEO Jim Buckee in for consultations and launched a high-profile investigation of Talisman's involvement in Sudan, culminating in the Harker mission and report. He threatened sanctions if the investigation found that oil money was either perpetuating the conflict or contributing to human rights abuses (Bowley, 1999; Drohan, 1999; Foster, 1999; Nikifouruk, 1999).

While the Harker Report stopped short of explicitly recommending sanctions, it found that oil had become a key factor in the war, that oil exacerbated the conflict, and that "it is difficult to imagine a cease-fire while oil extraction continues, and almost impossible to do so if revenues keep flowing to GNOPC parents and the GOS ... " (Harker, 2000, p. 16). The Canadian government, however, did not impose any sanctions or restrictions on Talisman.

Mr. Axworthy had discussed the possibilities of sanctions a number of times. In March 1999 he told a conference on religious persecution he had met with oil executives about the situation in Sudan, noting "We've been engaged recently in the role we play in Sudan, partly because I think that there is a responsibility of Canada because of the activities of some of our private-sector companies" (Human Rights Watch, 2003, p. 393). Somewhat later he warned that "if it becomes evident that oil extraction is exacerbating the conflict in Sudan, or resulting in violations of human rights or humanitarian law, the government of Canada may consider, if required, economic and trade restrictions ... " (cited in Human Rights Watch, 2003, p. 401). On

February 14, 2000 Mr. Axworthy announced that Canada would not impose sanctions on Talisman.

The turn-about resulted from a massive public relations campaign mounted by Talisman, including at least implicit suggestions that it was important to keep the head office of a major Canadian firm in Canada, and pressure from the Canadian oil industry in general. Axworthy later noted that he had gotten ahead of himself: "when I set up the Harker Commission I said, 'look, we'll do something about it.' And then I got the rug pulled out from under me because I didn't have the legislative authority I thought I did … And I'm not sure I could have done it politically, because I got a lot of pressure around town" (Drohan, 2003, p. 271).

A governance gap

There are a number of critical points to be drawn from the case of Talisman Energy in Sudan. First, in a very real sense, the company activities in that country were beyond the reach of any "public" political authority. The government of Sudan had no interest whatsoever in restraining human rights abuses in that country and rebuffed even Talisman's rather tepid effort at an agreement in that area. The Canadian government was either unable or unwilling to extend its reach to the extraterritorial activities of one of its companies to protect non-Canadian citizens outside of its territory. Last, the firm as a private actor was beyond the reach of existing international organizations or international law. As Gagnon, Macklin, and Simons conclude, "At present, corporations are not directly accountable at international law for their activities and operations that violate human rights standards. While an increasingly sophisticated regime of corporate rights is developing under various free trade agreements … none of these agreements link corporate rights or the rights of the states parties to obligations to ensure respect for human rights in the conduct of business" (2003, p. 51).

Second, defining the human rights obligations of multinational firms in situations such as that in Sudan is complex and extremely difficult. Once one accepts that the obligation of the firm goes beyond obeying local law, such as it is, it is not easy to draw boundaries around the firm's responsibility or set standards for behavior. In this case one could argue that simply entering into oil production in Sudan entailed some degree of complicity in human rights violations. The point is that once one moves beyond a narrow definition of responsibility to the shareholders, defining that responsibility cannot be left to the individual firm. It becomes a task of society at large.

Third, the mechanisms used in the case to attempt to force Talisman to accept responsibility for its actions in Sudan, and eventually to withdraw from that country, were less than satisfactory from a governance perspective. The Alien Tort Claims Act cases in United States courts are an ad hoc and cobbled-together attempt at global governance by extending the jurisdictional reach of a single country. While the NGOs' advocacy efforts with institutional investors eventually drove Talisman to sell its operations in Sudan, that surely is not the best way to establish the rule of law internationally. At a minimum, it relies on primarily Northern NGOs and multinational firms to make policy in third world countries.

As noted above, Kofi Annan argues that definitions of sovereignty have changed and that human rights violations within countries are now the responsibility of the international community. Furthermore, as should be clear from the arguments and case detailed in this chapter, the rights and responsibilities of multinational firms can no longer be considered purely derivative: as they gain political authority in the international arena, MNCs will increasingly be held to responsibilities, and potential liabilities, beyond that of the traditional private economic actor.

The problem at this point is that systems of global governance are ill-formed and incomplete. Attempting to hold multinational firms accountable through campaigns by advocacy groups or action in US courts is not fair, democratic, or effective. There is every indication that multinational firms are increasingly being held to broader, public standards in the area of human rights and other issue areas. If that is the case, then coordinated international action is needed to establish standards, monitor compliance, and enforce sanctions. Given the evolution of the political system, that will require cooperation between a number of actors including the firms themselves, states, civil society groups, and international organizations. Holding firms accountable under some agreed-upon form of international law or regulation will be both more effective in dealing with human rights abuses and fairer to the firms involved.

9 Direct private foreign investment in developing countries – the judo trick

PAUL STREETEN

Introduction

Direct private foreign investment, the total of which reached $1.3 trillion in 2000, has been fairly concentrated on the middle-income developing countries. Under thirty middle-income countries account for over 90 percent of total direct private foreign investment to the developing countries, and within this group Brazil and Mexico, joined more recently by Singapore, Malaysia, and especially China, dominate the figures. In 2002 China has become the leading recipient of direct foreign investment, exceeding that of the USA, previously the largest recipient.[1] But 2001 and 2002 have seen a reduction for most other recipients, though not as large a reduction as that to developed countries. But the small flow of investment (of the order of 5 percent of total OECD flows) to the poorest countries does not necessarily reflect its importance. First, even these small flows may be quantitatively important in relation to the economy of a particular poor country. Second, even quite a small amount can be more important than the quantity indicates if it contributes a missing component, breaks a bottleneck, or has spread effects on the rest of the economy in technology generation, employment creation, or foreign exchange earnings. Since it cannot be expected that the total quantity of investment to the lowest-income countries will increase by much very quickly, or that host governments can do much to influence it, it is all the more important to concentrate on measures that get the maximum multiplier effects from whatever small investment there is. One proposal of this kind is discussed below under the label of "the judo trick." Other forms of new institutions also are discussed. An invitation to explore such approaches is the main theme of this chapter.

---

[1] Department of Economic and Social Affairs and United Nations Conference on Trade and Development (2003), pp. 26–27.

Much has been written about the role of private foreign investment and the multinational corporation in development, both in its creative aspect as a package combining capital, management, marketing, and technology, and as a harbinger of exploitation. Without wishing to defend or attack either the proposition that the Ford Motor Company is the nearest thing to the Ford Foundation, or, on the other hand, that the transnational company is, if not the devil incarnate, the devil incorporated, some useful guidelines for private foreign investment in the least developed countries can be laid down.

Before doing this, it may be useful to remember that there are two different approaches to direct private foreign investment: the analysis in terms of financial flows, and that in terms of industrial organization. The former is the older approach, but became important again during the debt crisis and the search for finance. But it should be remembered that (a) the financial contribution is bound to remain small and (b) although it has the virtue of sharing in losses as well as profits, one would expect the net returns in the long run to be higher, and the foreign exchange burdens to be heavier, than those on fixed-interest borrowing. The second approach is the more modern one, and it is based on the integration of the theory of international investment with that of industrial organization. The emphasis in this paper will be on this approach and on institutional innovations, partly for the reason that the interest in finance arising from the debt crisis is relatively unimportant for the poorest countries, and partly because the quantitative importance of this form of financial flow is bound to remain small. The principal guidelines to these are the following.

First, it is clear that private foreign investment, to be successful, calls for complementary and supplementary action in the public sector. Roads, railways, ports, airports; education and research; nutrition and health services for farmers and factory workers are preconditions for productive and remunerative private investment. Few private investment projects can flourish if there are no schools or no clinics. And the government normally provides the physical and social infrastructure. There is "crowding in," in the sense that the profitability of a private investment project depends on, or is enhanced by, public investment. This applies also to the schemes proposed in this chapter.

Second, the foreign firm should not replace or drive out but should encourage the growth of domestic enterprises. In particular, small-scale family enterprises, micro-businesses, cottage industries, and the informal sector should be encouraged to produce inputs, components, spare parts, repairs, and ancillary services for the normally large, foreign firm. More of this will be said below in the section on how to make the foreign firm complementary to the informal sector enterprise.

Third, institutional innovation and hybrids can often combine the virtues of different types of traditional institutions. An important area of policy is the imaginative exploration of new legal and business institutions that combine the considerable merits of the transnational corporation with the maximum beneficial impact on development objectives. This area comprises joint ventures, i.e., joint both between private and public capital and between domestic and foreign capital, which go further than window dressing by giving the developing host country access to information and decision making, and various provisions for divestment and gradual, agreed transfer from foreign ownership and management to the host country. Thus, countries that wished to curb the power of large foreign groups in their manufacturing sector have found investment reduced. This may make it advisable to institute a "joint sector" in which public capital is combined with private national management with or without an equity stake, or public capital is combined with private international capital. Another possibility would be a management contract with a transnational firm.

Thought and action in this area have suffered from a poverty of the institutional imagination. It has lagged behind the advance of the scientific and technological imagination, and the global vision of transnational firms. Discussions have turned on the ideological dispute between private and public enterprise. Yet the real issues have little to do with the locus of ownership. The large, privately owned companies are run on lines not very dissimilar from those of public institutions. The challenge is to design mixed or hybrid companies that simultaneously harness private energy and initiative yet are accountable to the public and carry out a social mandate. The British Commonwealth Corporation, at least until recent changes have brought it more in line with a purely private company, can serve as a model. In Britain it is claimed as a wonderful example of private enterprise by the Conservatives, because it is run by a board consisting of businessmen and bankers, without interference by any government department, and is acclaimed by the Labour Party as a model of socialism, because it is in the public sector and draws some of its funds from the British Exchequer.

Equally arid has been the dispute over the virtues and vices of private foreign investment. Some developing countries dislike private profits, some dislike foreigners, and foreigners earning private profits can be an explosive mixture. But here again, the task should be to identify the positive contributions of foreign firms, and the social costs they impose on the country, and to explore how the former can be increased and the latter reduced. A proposal of one type of arrangement in which there is a gradual transfer to national (or regional) ownership and management is discussed below. There is a need for a legal and institutional framework in which social objectives that are not normally part of the private firm's objectives can be achieved, while giving the firm an opportunity to earn profits by contributing efficient management, marketing, and technology.

The quantitative contribution of private foreign investment and transnational firms in the poorest developing countries, outside mining and plantations where these have not been nationalized, is probably bound to remain small. But its qualitative role as a center round which to cluster small domestic enterprises, as a potential mobilizer of domestic enterprises, and as a contributor of particularly valuable missing components in technology, marketing, and market access, remains to be explored and exploited. Some suggestions will be made below.

There has been by now a good deal of experience in the growth of lending to very small and poor businesses. The Grameen Bank in Bangladesh has been one of the first, but the experience has been replicated in many other countries. One important lesson is that even without collateral, poor people tend to repay loans, particularly if peer-group pressure exists. Another is that, combined with some training in accounting, bookkeeping, and management, these loans have multiplier effects that create jobs for other poor people. They break the grip of the usurious moneylender and enable people to start businesses who could not have done so without these loans. There is a potential role here for foreign banks.

The judo trick or "crowding in": the role of micro-enterprises

The relatively recent emphasis on the role of private enterprise and free markets has been useful. It has been partly a healthy reaction against excessive early faith in the power of governments to direct the economy, to manage businesses, and to correct market failures. But unregulated markets can be both inefficient and cruel. Joan Robinson once said that the Invisible Hand can work by strangulation. We know that both markets and governments may fail, and that the failure of one does not automatically constitute a case for the other. It is now widely accepted that market failure is not necessarily a case for government intervention. It is less generally realized that government failure does not necessarily constitute a case for private enterprise. There is no a priori presumption as to which is preferable.

The possibility of government and bureaucratic failures suggests that it is important to concentrate the activities of the government on areas in which private efforts fail even more. Government activity often is complementary to private enterprise and efficient markets. The aim should be to avoid crowding out, and to achieve "crowding in." Government intervention should provide the conditions in which markets and enterprise can flourish. Market orientation and state minimalism, far from going together, are incompatible. A well-designed policy calls for interventions to maintain competition and avoid restrictive practices, monopolies, and cartels, to provide physical and social infrastructure, and some research efforts. It may also require new types of institutions, about which more later. Governments should also take care of the victims of the competitive struggle, both for humanitarian and for efficiency reasons. The informal sector can play an important part in providing a safety net. But the policy of looking after the victims of the competitive struggle by encouraging the informal sector to provide a safety net (it should not become a safety hammock) can be carried out beyond this point and can make a substantial contribution to production and productivity growth.

The informal sector has been much discussed. It comprises four quite distinct groups. First, there are the self-employed, sometimes working with unpaid members of their families. They are a heterogeneous group, ranging from shoeshine boys, street vendors, garbage collectors, petty thieves, prostitutes, drug traffickers, smugglers, and self-appointed tourist guides and bag carriers to jobbing gardeners, and small-scale producers such as blacksmiths, carpenters, sandal makers, lamp makers, bricklayers, bus and taxi drivers, seamstresses, repairmen, cobblers, bakers, shopkeepers, auto mechanics, and builders who sometimes earn more than workers in the formal sector. Some formal sector workers use their savings to set up such enterprises for themselves in the informal sector.

Second, there are the casual workers, hired on a day-to-day basis in the docks, in construction, transport, and services. If the criterion for being in the informal sector is the method of hiring, then some workers hired casually by quite large firms should be counted as being in the informal sector.

Third, there are workers employed on a regular basis by small-scale, labor-intensive, not bureaucratically controlled firms outside the formal sector.

Fourth, there are the "outworkers," working in their homes under the modern equivalent of the putting-out system.

Another distinction is that between three quite different kinds of informal sector firm. First, there are the productive, entrepreneurial, often rapidly growing firms. They often graduate to middle-sized, and occasionally to large, firms. Secondly, there are the viable family firms, neither dynamic nor lame ducks, who stand midway between the first and the third category. Third, there are the absorbers of the lame ducks thrown out of the formal sector, or incapable of entering it. These are small family firms of infirm, old, or otherwise unemployable people. An elderly, infirm couple who live above their small grocery store, but are not bound by the laws about closing hours, might be entirely unemployable elsewhere. If their receipts exceed their costs, they earn a small producer's rent. They constitute the safety nets for the victims of personal incapacities and the disasters that befall people, and the shifts in demand or technology that occur in the formal sector. The second type of firm has been swollen in recent years by declining aggregate growth rates and austerity programs that have thrown people out of employment in the formal sector. The activities of these firms are anti-cyclical, swelling with a decline in aggregate demand, and declining with its growth. At the same time, the crisis also provided opportunities for some firms who belong in the first category, although if they are linked, say through sub-contracting, to the formal sector, their behavior will be pro-cyclical. Nevertheless, they benefit from fluctuations, for they will receive excess orders in booms, when the large firms run into capacity limits, and in slumps, when these firms wish to convert fixed into variable costs by hiving off employees and transforming them into sub-contractors.

Informal sector firms,[2] in the right setting, thrive on certain advantages over large-scale, formal sector firms. These advantages may be:

1. locational, when raw materials are dispersed and the enterprise processes them, or when markets are local and transport costs high;
2. relating to the process of production or the product, when the work requires simple assembly or other activities that are best carried out by hand or with simple tools;
3. relating to the market, when operating on a small scale for a local market has lower costs than larger-scale, more distant operation, or when the service has to be rendered where the customer is;
4. relating to adaptability and responsiveness to changing demand or technology, because of the absence of high fixed costs.

In the informal sector employment is largely supply driven, absorbing fairly easily additional entrants (although there are also barriers to entry into some informal sector enterprises, particularly the need for some capital, and employment is offered by small businessmen *demanding* labor), whereas in the formal sector employment is largely demand driven (although in the public sector there is a *supply*-driven component). There is also the work of women, until recently invisible in some cultures, who perform hard work without being counted as members of the labor force because their product is often not sold for cash.

According to the ILO Kenya Report,[3] informal sector activities are a way of doing things, characterized by:

a. ease of entry;
b. reliance on indigenous resources;

---

[2] The term "informal sector" is used here interchangeably with small-scale or micro-enterprise sector.

[3] International Labour Office (1972), p. 6. Among other definitions of the informal sector are the following: self-employment; unpaid family workers, domestic servants, and those self-employed who are not professionals and technicians; workers in small-scale units of production, sometimes including domestic servants and casual workers; sometimes also low-wage employees of "modern" firms; unprotected, unregulated economic activities; illegal, clandestine, and unregistered activities; "traditional" sector; "subsistence" sector; "marginalized mass"; very small economic units or micro-businesses; an abnormally swollen, overdistended tertiary sector of minimal productivity; a sector in which wage rates equal marginal productivity. For sources of these and other definitions, see Hopkins (1989), pp. 69–73.

c. family ownership of enterprises;
d. small-scale operations;
e. labor-intensive and adapted technology;
f. skills acquired outside the formal educational system;
g. unregulated and competitive markets.

It is easy to dismiss the informal sector as a useless concept.[4] It is equally easy to romanticize it and to think of it as a potential of high productivity, of competitive capitalism, harassed and discriminated against by mercantilistic, predatory, and interfering bureaucrats.

The informal sector certainly is a very heterogeneous collection of people and activities. There are some whose marginal productivity is zero or negative, because their activities only take away from the sales of others, or because they only create nuisances and then extract payment for their removal. Beggars, petty thieves, small vendors, providers of unwanted services are manifestations of disguised unemployment. Even genuinely productive firms often break the law and evade taxes. Many informal sector employers exploit their workers at least as much as formal sector employers. There is no point in glamorizing them, or in overstating their contribution to production.

Another way in which the informal sector has been misleadingly romanticized is by holding it up as a splendid example of entrepreneurial competition and free enterprise capitalism. The informal sector has its peculiar modes of behavior and formalities. As the studies of Hernando de Soto (one of the leading proponents of this form of activity) and of Judith Tendler have shown, relations between firms in the informal sector are sometimes characterized by a striking degree of cooperation.[5] They share inputs when these are in scarce supply; when one firm has a large contract and its neighbor does not, it shares the contract with the other firm by sub-contracting or hiring its owner as a temporary worker; there is work-sharing not only between firms,

---

[4] For a well-reasoned criticism of the concept see Peattie (1987), pp. 851–860. Although the critique by L. Peattie is well argued, I do not think it necessarily leads to the abandonment of the concept. The exploration of the specific linkages, some positive, others negative, between firms and policies that she asks for can surely be done within the conceptual framework suggested by the "informal sector."

[5] See de Soto (1989a) and Tendler (1987). De Soto has recently become famous for preaching the virtues of private property and for giving the poor full property rights.

but also when the demand for labor is reduced. Not much attention has been paid to this fact, partly because it contradicts the idealized individualistic picture of firms in active competition (Tendler, 1987).

While, on the one hand, the informal sector should not be glamorized, there are, on the other hand, actually or potentially highly productive small enterprises, some of whose owners earn more than some workers in the formal sector. They tend to use more labor per unit of capital and per unit of output, and often use it intensively, remuneratively, and highly efficiently.[6]

In Peru some informal sector firms absorb those who wish to, but cannot, enter the formal sector. In Argentina, on the other hand, people with secure but ill-paid jobs in the formal sector opt to earn extra income and gain additional mobility in the informal sector.

Some people who work in the informal sector also work in the formal sector. Sometimes members of the same family are engaged in both. Some characteristics of the informal sector can be found in the formal sector, such as casual hiring of labor. Some firms are informal with respect to some of their activities (not paying certain taxes, working without some licenses, casually hiring some of their workers), and formal with respect to others. We have seen that some informal sector incomes are higher than some formal sector earnings. It is impossible to count and record the informal sector, because, by its nature, no official records exist.[7] But in spite of these obstacles to a clear and neat definition, the concept meets a real need and I shall not abandon it.

There are those who believe that the informal sector is entirely the creature of mistaken government policies. "Get the prices right,

---

[6] Some caution is necessary. Obviously, not all small-scale, informal sector enterprises are efficient, or economize even in the use of capital. The working capital requirements of small enterprises are often higher than those of larger ones. And even the lower capital/labor ratio can be bought at the cost of a higher capital/output ratio. But the scheme proposed below should ensure that such waste is minimized. For evidence of the efficiency of small-scale industries (overlapping with the informal sector, though not identical), see Liedholm and Mead (1987).

[7] Since less interventionist governments will tend to include in their national accounts activities that more interventionist governments do not count, because they are illegal, it is easy to overstate the growth performance of countries that have followed the World Bank's advice to rely more on markets. World Bank reports have not always paid attention to this distortion of growth figures in comparing good and poor performers.

deregulate, decentralize, liberalize, and privatize, and the informal sector will disappear." The evidence does not show, however, that modern technology, even with the most "realistic" equilibrium prices for labor, capital, and foreign exchange, can absorb the numbers of workers who are and will be seeking jobs at wages that can support them.

There are four reasons for paying attention to the informal sector. They arise from the triple needs to increase production, employment (recognition and self-respect), and incomes, and the need to avoid political unrest and rebellion.

First, the informal sector represents a potentially large reserve of productivity and earning power. Although not all informal sector activities contribute actually or potentially to productivity and earnings, some do.

Secondly, the labor force in the low income countries is likely to grow rapidly in the next fifteen years and neither agriculture nor the industrial formal sector is capable of absorbing even a fraction of these additions, to say nothing of the large number of already unemployed or underemployed. The number of workers seeking remunerative employment is likely to grow at a rate of 2–3 percent per year in Africa. The labor surplus economies of Java and Bangladesh represent the future for Africa, where at this time there are still relatively few landless workers seeking jobs in the towns. The situation is further aggravated by the low world growth rates. The combination of population growth, urbanization, and recession has swelled the informal sector, which presents the only hope for jobs.[8]

---

[8] This approach has been criticized as excessively Eurocentric. The critics say the notion of a "labor force" comprising all able-bodied men and women between, say, fifteen and sixty is not applicable to many developing countries. The problem is not to find jobs, but to redefine "work." The "idleness" of the women in purdah, the gossips in the cafés, the begging priests and monks, the small-scale rentiers, the useless peddlers, the idle bureaucrats, should, according to Clifford Geertz, not be suppressed and these people should not be encouraged to "work," but the notions of "idleness" and "work" should be redefined, so that these "underemployed" are kept "outside the work force but inside society" (Geertz, 1969, pp. 34–54). The evidence does not seem to have confirmed that this is the preference of the workless, whenever opportunities to earn arise. It would, however, be worth exploring whether activities in the informal sector that do not show high economic returns may not be valuable by some other standards.

A third reason is that, although the informal sector should not be equated with the poor (we have seen that some members of the informal sector earn more than some in the formal sector and many poor are outside the informal sector), it is in the informal sector where many poor people are to be found. By harnessing its potential for generating incomes (and self-respect), not only is efficient growth promoted but also poverty is reduced. If its productivity and remunerativeness can be raised without depriving the high-productivity sector of resources, and hence not only of more production but also of the opportunity of future employment, there is no conflict between efficiency and equity.

A fourth reason is that prolonged unemployment leads to alienation and a sense of worthlessness, and can be a source of rebellious instead of productive activity. Particularly governments in power have an interest in not upsetting the existing order and peace, and in using the informal sector as a vote bank.

Normally one would wish the informal sector neither to be subsidized at the expense of the high-productivity formal sector firms, nor to be squeezed out by privileged formal sector firms.

The task then is to make these informal sector enterprises complementary to the larger-scale, formal sector firms, including foreign multinational corporations. Now they are often competitive, and, aided by the government, the large firms often drive out the small ones. The success of the Japanese in combining a modern and a small-scale industrial sector illustrates the possibility of successfully combining the two sectors. The East Asian success stories illustrate how the marketing of manufactured exports can be undertaken by foreign firms. In Singapore, it was transnational corporations that marketed the output of wholly or majority-owned local subsidiaries. In other countries it was the importers in the advanced countries, retail and department stores, wholesalers or trading companies that performed these functions. The Koreans used foreign buyers in the early stages of development not only to sell their goods but also to acquire knowledge about styles, designs, and technologies. The current trend toward modular manufacturing, according to which some quite small firms produce components for assembly in large firms, also encourages the growth of informal sector firms. All these are illustrations of ways of using the power of the large firms, the Goliaths, in their self-interest, for the benefit of the poor, the little Davids, rather as a judo fighter uses the power of his opponent for his own purposes. Let us call this the judo trick, partly because it uses the leverage of an initially antagonistic force with multiplied effect, and partly because it uses the force of what is usually regarded as a powerful, strong opponent for the benefit of the weak.

One model for such a symbiosis in agriculture has been pioneered by the Commonwealth Development Corporation first in the Kulai oil palm project in Malaysia and then in the Kenya Tea Development Authority. A modern nucleus estate does the management, the processing, the exporting, the marketing, and provides the extension services and the credit for a group of smallholders clustered round the estate. The activities best carried out on a large scale, with modern techniques, are done by the nucleus estate, while the growing of the crop is done by newly settled smallholders. This type of project has proved highly successful, although it is rather management-intensive and the calls on skilled professional management and extension services would have to be reduced if it were to be replicated on a large scale in labor surplus economies, such as those of South Asia. Another model is the National Dairy Development Board in India. The production of milk, largely by women, remains traditional and informal, while processing, credit, and marketing follow modern, formal sector lines.

A similar model has been followed by private foreign agro-businesses. It has been called the "core–satellite" model, or contract farming or smallholder outgrower scheme.[9] Companies like Heinz, Del Monte, United Brands, Nestlé, and Shell provide marketing, equipment, technical assistance, credit, fertilizer, and other inputs, as well as ancillary services, and smallholders grow fruit and vegetables. In order to balance bargaining power in drawing up contracts, the smallholders have to be organized. Then they can use their power both directly on the companies and indirectly on the government to give them political support. The high fixed costs of processing plant make it important for the company to secure an even and certain flow of inputs, which is ensured by the contract. It is preferable to either open-market purchases or a plantation with hired labor, though contract farming is sometimes supplemented by these other forms. The smallholders, in turn, acquire an assured market,

---

[9] Glover (1984), pp. 1143–1157, (1987), pp. 441–448. Also Goldsmith, (1985), pp. 1125–1138 and the Special Issue on Contract Farming and Smallholder Outgrower Schemes in Eastern and Southern Africa of the *East Africa Economic Review*, Economics Department, University of Nairobi, August 1989.

credit, and inputs at low costs. I do not advocate the replication of these schemes, for too little research has been done on the precise division of gains and conditions for the optimum smallholder benefit, but I suggest that these are worth exploring.

This type of institutional arrangement can combine some of the advantages of plantation farming, such as quality control, coordination of interdependent stages of production and marketing, with those of smallholder production, such as autonomy, keener incentives, and income generation for poor people. But the possibility of abuse of its monopsonistic power by the private company against the smallholders makes it necessary to have either smallholder organizations with countervailing power or public regulation.

No similar type of arrangement exists as yet in manufacturing. One can easily imagine a large, modern manufacturing plant round which are clustered informal, small, enterprises doing repairs, manufacturing components and spare parts, and providing ancillary services such as transport, handling, cleaning, packaging, catering, etc. The nearest thing to such an arrangement is the system of modular manufacturing. It has, for example, replaced or perhaps complemented the assembly line as a method of manufacturing cars. It involves designing and assembling an entire motor car as a series of sub-assemblies, or modules. Suppliers of these components (e.g., dashboards, sunroofs, or doors), with their lower labor costs, could concentrate on the nuts and bolts, leaving to the large firms styling, packaging, marketing, and distribution. Another approximation is the Japanese *kanban* system.

Such a project, to make use of informal sector enterprises, would require changes in government policies. The first step would be to stop repressive regulation, harassment, and discrimination against the informal sector; to stop, for example, demolishing informal sector houses, subject, of course, to some urban planning for open spaces. In Peru a Union of Formals and Informals has been formed to reduce government regulations and bureaucratic meddling.[10] It is an interesting example of a reformist alliance, in which formal sector enterprises

---

[10] See Riding (1988), p. 3. This article cites Hernando de Soto, head of the Institute for Liberty and Democracy in Lima, who says that 60 percent of Peru's workforce operates outside the formal economy and accounts for 38 percent of its gross domestic product; 95 percent of public transport in Lima is in the hands of informal operators; 98 percent of new homes, most

make common cause with informal ones, sharing with them their experience and uniting in exercising political pressure. The next step would be to adopt policies and to create institutions with respect to the provision of credit, training, information, and imported inputs (e.g., tariff remission for the informal sector). As to credit, innovative steps are needed for small loans and new types of collateral, such as inventories, or an unlicensed bus, or plots of land in shantytowns. Another option is the mobilization of peer pressure to repay loans, as in the Grameen Bank in Bangladesh. A third step would be to remove legislation that gives the formal sector special advantages in buying from or selling to the informal sector.

The implications of this proposal for policy are quite radical. For example, the common prescription is to lower real wages in order to raise employment. But in this model, a rise in real wages may increase employment and incomes in the informal sector. The production of spare parts, repairs, and ancillary activities, such as cleaning, transport, packaging, are carried out inside the firms in the organized sector while wages are low. When they are raised, these activities become worth contracting out to small informal sector firms not subject to minimum wage legislation. These firms carry out these activities in a more labor-intensive way, and benefit from the new contracts. Even if the workers previously engaged on these activities inside the formal sector firms were to be dismissed (rather than redeployed), and were to add pressure on incomes in the informal sector, the savings in capital and profits may be enough to produce higher incomes as well as more jobs for the sub-contractors.

of them in shantytowns, are built without permits; and 80 cent of clothing and 60 percent of furniture are produced by the informal sector. According to the same source it takes 289 days to register a new company, so most people do not bother. After this article was published, de Soto (1989a) appeared. It contains an impassioned introduction by Mario Vargas Llosa. There de Soto estimates that in Peru the informal sector makes up 48 percent of the total labor force. Its members work 61 percent of all man-hours and create 38 percent of the GDP. They have set up 274 markets in Lima; they run 93 percent of the buses; and they have built 42 percent of the houses. See also de Soto (1989b). There are, however critics of de Soto's enthusiasm. My friend Jaime Mezzera, with the International Labour Organization (PREALC) in Santiago, estimates the informal sector's contribution in any Latin American country at no more than 15 percent.

This would be the case, for example, if the self-employed small entrepreneur works harder than the same man as paid foreman or manager. A similar effect is produced by legislating for a shorter working week, to which the informal sector firms are not bound. Higher taxes, avoided or evaded by these enterprises, work in the same direction.[11]

It is true that, for such efficient and income-raising sub-contracting to occur, the initial in-house production by the formal firms may have been sub-optimal. For, it may be argued, if it pays to sub-contract at the higher wage, it would have done so also at the lower wage. In this case stubbornness, inertia, or ignorance stood in the way, and the rise in the wage wakes up the businessman. But there may have been non-pecuniary offsetting advantages in in-house production, which are more than offset when costs rise. These may be the result of transport, communication or transaction costs, or high training costs with greater probability that the trained sub-contractor may leave than the in-house worker.

Other linkages between formal and informal sector firms affecting competing and complementary inputs and products should be carefully traced.[12] If high and modern growth rates in the formal sector are not to be impeded, it is important not to deprive it of scarce factors, such as capital, management, or wage goods, in order to benefit low productivity activities. This implies that the capital and organizational capacity should be recruited from within the informal sector. At the same time, it is also important that the expansion of the formal sector should not raise the prices of goods necessary for production in the informal sector. This appears to have happened in Colombia, where a housing project for the rich was intended to generate incomes for workers. But the resulting price increase in concrete and steel led

---

[11] Ronald Dore has suggested that the same effect can be achieved by the Japanese practice of high average wages with lifetime employment and a retirement age at 50. The worker then sets himself up in a small sub-contracting business and makes use of his connection with the large firm, which regards him as loyal and reliable (private communication).

[12] Sanjaya Lall distinguishes between the following linkages: establishment, locational, informational, technical, financial, raw material procurement, managerial, pricing, other distributional, and diversification (Lall, 1985, pp. 269–270).

to price rises in sheet metal and cardboard, jeopardizing the building efforts of the poor.[13]

A second illustration is to be found in a modern version of the eighteenth-century putting-out system. Sub-contracting by large firms to small, sometimes informal sector firms or cottage industries is quite common in the developing world. But there is still much scope for importing houses in advanced countries, or retail chains independent of developed country producer interests, to apply the putting-out system to informal sector firms in developing countries. The large firm provides the materials, the designs, the credit, and the marketing, while the informal sector firm produces the clothes, the sport equipment, the electronic components, the cloth and woodwork for handicrafts, or the crops. The British retail chain Marks and Spencer have employed this modern putting-out system not only in England but also in some developing countries.

There opens up another use for the judo trick. The political power of these retail chains, such as Atlantic and Pacific Stores or Safeway, can be used to counteract the pressures for protection of the producer lobbies in the developed countries. Their interest in low-cost, labor-intensive imports coincides with those of the poor producers in the developing countries. If institutional safeguards are adopted to prevent exploitation and sweated labor, firms such as Marks and Spencer can do more for the poor of the world than Marx and Engels.

In addition to new institutions, policies will have to be revised. Thus, many economists have opposed minimum wage legislation on the ground that it prevents higher employment. But, as we have seen, if a higher wage level or a shorter working week, applied only to organized sector firms, forces them to contract out to the informal sector activities previously carried out inside these firms, this can be a gain in employment and earnings. For these activities are likely to be carried out in a more labor-intensive way in the informal sector than they were inside the large firms. One characteristic of the distinction is the flexibility of

---

[13] See Peattie (1987), p. 858. The terms of trade between the informal and formal sectors are an important determinant of the division of gains. The "reserve army of unemployed" will tend to keep incomes and prices of informal firms low, while productivity growth in formal firms will tend to be passed on in higher wages, rather than lower prices. In addition, there may be unequal bargaining power. An "unequal exchange" may result.

incomes in the informal sector compared with downward rigidity in the formal sector. Therefore the informal sector's capacity for absorbing labor is higher, and policies that make it worthwhile to give more business to the small firms are to be welcomed.

The measures needed to implement such a policy can be summarized under the following headings.

1. First, a more favorable economic environment for the informal sector should be created. At present, macroeconomic policies tend to discriminate against it. For example, investment incentives confine tax concessions to formal sector firms. Overvaluation of the exchange rate combined with import restrictions and undervaluation of the interest rate handicap the access to inputs and credit of informal firms.

2. Second, it is necessary to design new institutions of the kind indicated above. The access of the poor to assets should be improved. In agriculture this policy has worked. It is more difficult to apply it in urban industry. Steps are being taken to provide these small entrepreneurs with credit. The Grameen Bank in Bangladesh has found many imitators in other countries. The Inter-American Development Bank wants to establish itself as the bank for Latin America's informal sector. The International Fund for Agricultural Development has successfully lent to businesses without collateral. Pressures for repayment can be exercised by peer groups, and by making small loans for short periods. Loans should be primarily for working capital. Judgment of the borrower's reliability can replace conventional collateral requirements.

3. Third, returns to these enterprises must be raised. It is not enough, as is often said, to raise their productivity, for productivity gains can be passed on in the form of lower prices to often better off buyers in the formal sector. It is the earning power, the remunerativeness of the enterprise that matters.

4. Fourth, employment opportunities must be improved. Even though the informal sector is often defined as supply driven, there are obstacles to entry and to employment, which can be reduced.

5. Fifth, demand for the informal sector's production should be raised. Since poor people tend to buy the goods produced by the poor people in the informal sector, policies that generate incomes for poor people will also raise the demand for their products.[14]

[14] See Liedholm and Mead (1987) and Sinha et al. (1979).

6. Sixth, access to education, training, and health services must be improved, both as an end in itself and in order to raise the productivity of the poor. Technical training and instruction in simple managerial techniques, such as accounting and bookkeeping, marketing, and technical know-how are important. The identification and provision of missing components, such as market information, infrastructure, or technical know-how can yield great benefits at little cost.

7. Seventh, transfer payments out of public funds are also required to provide a safety net, not only for the unemployables, the disabled, the sick, the old, but also to tide people over periods of no earnings, of failure of their enterprises, or temporary inability to work.

It is customary to distinguish between primary incomes, earned through production and sales for the market; secondary incomes as a result of access to the sources of improved earning power, such as education, training, and health services; and tertiary incomes which are pure welfare payments. The unemployables would receive tertiary incomes. Even this policy may not indeed raise productivity but lower reproductivity. The need to be looked after in old age or in case of accident is one of the incentives for having many children, particularly sons. If the community looks after the disabled, infirm, sick, and old, there is less reason for having large families.

Another way of categorizing the public sector measures necessary to make the symbiosis between multinational corporations and the informal sector successful can be summarized with a mnemotechnic device. It is the seven "Ins" or Instruments.

1. Incentives: prices of both inputs and outputs must be right.
2. Inputs: both imported and domestic inputs, including credit, must be available.
3. Institutions: access to marketing institutions and credit institutions and a non-corrupt, efficient administrative apparatus must exist.
4. Innovation: the right small-scale technology, appropriate for small enterprises, often does not exist and research and search should be provided to create and find, and adapt, it.
5. Information: a knowledge bank for technology should provide means of spreading the results of research and search among the firms. Also instruction in management, bookkeeping, and recording should be provided.

6. Infrastructure: roads, communications, harbors, and utilities must be available if the output of the informal sector is to be sold in national and international markets.
7. Independence: permit and encourage self-reliance and freedom from excessive regulation and harassment.

In the manner described above, the informal sector can be made complementary to the formal with respect to access to markets, inputs, information, and technology; the small-scale firms to large-scale firms; domestic to foreign firms; public to private firms; and non-governmental organizations to governments. The putting-out system of foreign retailers or importing houses is an example of the symbiosis between foreign large and domestic small enterprises. Similarly, private voluntary organizations engaged in helping informal sector projects should find ways of cooperating with government departments and multinational corporations, which are often in a better position to finance and replicate successful projects.

Our knowledge of the informal sector in most developing countries is still rudimentary. What we need is both time series and cross-country studies of informal sector activities to show at what income levels, with what policies, which activities, actually or potentially, contribute to employment, production, productivity, earning power, and growth.

It has been emphasized that the encouragement of complementarities should not be done at the expense of the growth of the high-productivity, modern sector. On the contrary, the small units should contribute to raising the productivity of the large ones. According to Kashyap (1988, pp. 677–681), handicaps for large firms and biases in policy against them are largely responsible for the growth of small-scale enterprises in India. Nor should there be any form of exploitation, such as child labor, inhuman working conditions, sweated labor, or monopsonistic depression of the prices at which outputs are bought. Fears have been expressed that the informal sector enterprises have been reduced to a state of "peonage" by their formal sector principals (Lall, 1985).[15] Nor should there be monopolistic overpricing of the intermediate products supplied by the formal sector as inputs to the informal enterprises. Such overpricing could be the result of import

---

[15] Lall, however, concludes from his case study that "on the whole, their benefits from being linked outweigh their costs" (p. 288).

restrictions or other barriers to entry. In Sierra Leone the large-scale flour mill, which supplies flour to small-scale bakers, is protected by an exclusive import license, and therefore can sell its flour at prices over twice those of potential imports (Chuta and Liedholm, 1985, p. 144). The policies must be designed to mobilize the energies of the small-scale firms, and to make use of their lower costs, more labor-intensive techniques, greater employment creation, and wider dispersion of technology, without, on the one hand, sacrificing efficiency and innovation, and, on the other, depriving the informal sector, by underpricing outputs or overpricing inputs, of adequate rewards and humane working conditions.

Encouragement that the informal sector, or at any rate the sector containing small-scale firms, can be the dynamic sector of the future comes from an unexpected source: the literature on Flexible Specialization, mainly applied to trends in the advanced, industrial countries.[16] The move from standardized, large-scale mass production to small-scale, flexible firms is the result of changes in demand and in supply. On the demand side, the mass consumer has been replaced by a more sophisticated type with higher purchasing power and more differentiated tastes. On the side of supply, the technology for energy and information has encouraged decentralization of production and smaller size of firms. 'Mass production is the manufacture of standard products with specialized resources ...; flexible specialization is the production of specialized products with general resources ... '(Sabel, 1986, p. 40).[17] In Mexico the large number of small, decentralized workshops (*maquilas*) and household units are sub-contractors for the large firms. The uncertainties of the 1980s have encouraged the rise of these units which produce specialized products with a broadly skilled and weakly specialized labor force. The division of labor resembles the already mentioned Japanese *kanban* where many small suppliers and sub-contractors are clustered round a large firm. Similar patterns are to be found in northern Italy (the so-called "Third Italy") and other parts of Europe, with

---

[16] See Tendler (1987) and Sabel (1986, 1987).

[17] The *marxisant* terms are "Fordism" and "post-Fordism," not, of course named after the Ford Foundation but after Henry Ford and his famous remark that the American public could have their model T any color they liked as long as it was black.

their regional clusters of small, cooperating, flexible firms.[18] As demand and technology changes, skills and products can be easily switched and adapted to the new situation. The shoe industries around Novo Hamburgo in Brazil and León in Mexico are organized on this basis and have encouraged the growth of rural industries. As Judith Tendler has pointed out, there has been a role reversal, and in this literature the formal sector firms, interpreted as the traditional, large-scale, fixed-cost, mass-production firms, are seen as "sick," whereas the flexible, small firms are capable of responding dynamically to changing demand and technology. Not only have they taken over the function of leadership, but they are also more humane and responsible in their work relations. There is also a new form of cooperation between the small firms, and the old confrontation between labor and capital is replaced by one between the managers, owners, and workers in the small, sub-contracting firms, on the one hand, and the large buyers of their output on the other. In addition, supportive local institutions evolve that provide information, technical know-how, and training. All this holds out great productive and social promise for the informal sector, especially if supported by the right social policies.

Foreign investment and macroeconomic policies

It is fashionable to extol "outward-looking" trade and industrialization policies as good for growth, employment, poverty reduction, and income distribution and to condemn "inward-looking" ones. In the same vein, it is generally held that transnational corporations and private foreign investment that are attracted by a "realistic" exchange rate, a docile and cheap labor force, and good export prospects contribute more to the host country than those attracted by highly protected domestic markets, and overvalued exchange rates combined with import restrictions, high wages, and underpriced capital.

It is, however, not clear how helpful this kind of distinction is. First, if we look at the process historically, most successful outward-looking policies were preceded by a phase of inward-looking

---

[18] Recent evidence shows, however, that some of these firms in the Third Italy have gone bankrupt, others have been taken over by large firms. It seems that they have a tendency to merge into the first and second Italy.

protection. Industries that have grown up under protection, producing for the home market, then became exporters. Volkswagen Brazil
is only one of many examples of a foreign investment that originally
catered for the domestic market and later became one of the most
successful exporters. Zimbabwe, whatever the mess of its present
position, presents an illustration of a country that laid the foundations for initially successful exports during an enforced inward-looking phase. The simple division into outward- and inward-orientation
is ahistorical.

Second, much industrialization takes the form of replacing imported
inputs into the production of exports by domestic inputs. This applies
also to foreign investments. Is this to be classified as inward-looking,
because it substitutes domestic inputs for imports, or as outward-
looking because it increases the value added in exports? Of course,
those who define "outward-looking" as neutrality between import
substitution and exports, and as using free market prices as signals
and incentives, have a ready answer. But this is a somewhat biased
definition and some authors have defined "outward-looking" in a more
symmetrical way, as biased toward exports.

There are other problems with this simple distinction of trade and
industrialization policies. One is that the dichotomy may not exhaust
all directions in which the policy may look. A discriminating policy
may look to the expanding markets of the newly industrialized countries rather than at the outside world at large, just as the newly
industrializing countries in the nineteenth century that followed
England did not look primarily to England, but at one another, at
Germany, the USA, and Latin America. There is also the well-known
problem of aggregation: can all developing countries emulate the
model of the East Asian exporters? And there is the question of the
changed world environment, with slower OECD growth rates and
higher barriers of protection than in the period when exports boomed.

It is often claimed that "outward-looking" policies make labor-
intensive exports profitable, and that this is good for employment
and income distribution. But there is no reason why some forms of
import substitution should not be carried out in a labor-intensive way.
If a country undervalues its exchange rate, it makes imports more
expensive and encourages exports. Undervaluation of the exchange
rate looks outward with respect to exports, just as overvaluation
looks outward with respect to imports. Private foreign investors may

take these signals as given and adapt to them, or they may wish to influence and shape them, by exercising pressures on governments, either for protection or for tax concessions or for subsidies.

Although the recommendations based on the distinction between outward- and inward-looking are too simple as a guide to policy, it is true that foreign investments that are attracted by the low costs of available inputs, such as cheap and docile labor, a stable political climate, a well-managed economy, and perhaps some subsidies to infrastructure, such as trading estates, or a subsidy to power, or export zones, or remissions of tariffs on imported inputs, are preferable to investments that are attracted by highly protected domestic markets. This is particularly true of small countries, which have no large market to offer. In Singapore, which provides an attractive export base, foreign private direct investment is over 10 percent of gross domestic product. The horror stories of negative value added (or value subtracted), documented for highly protected import substitution (such as the Philippine car industry), can, of course, in principle also be found in export industries. Just as it is possible to combine high private profits to foreign firms with large social losses by excessive protection of the domestic market, so it is possible to oversubsidize and undertax export production, and combine private profitability with negative value added. But in practice it may be politically more difficult to practice very large support in the transparent form of subsidies to inputs than in the more hidden form of import restrictions that protect the markets for outputs. It is therefore for practical reasons that the export orientation of foreign investment found in East and parts of South East Asia such as Malaysia is to be preferred to the import substitution of Latin America and the Philippines.

An empirical study by Blomstrom, Kravis, and Lipsey (1988) shows that transnational corporations can make an important and increasing contribution to manufactured exports of developing countries. According to this study, the share of US, Japanese, and Swedish transnational firms in manufactured exports of developing countries has increased from the sixties or seventies to the present. But the lesson for the low-income countries has to be qualified in that these firms were mainly in technologically oriented industries, and in the newly industrializing countries (NICs). Even in the NICs, in less technologically oriented industries, such as food, textiles, and clothing, exports of locally owned firms were growing faster than those of transnational companies.

Regional integration and foreign investment

Regional cooperation among developing countries is much talked about but little has been achieved. The reason for this is disputes over the location of industry and therefore the division of the benefits. The most advanced country in the region, with its superior infrastructure, skills, and institutions, will tend to attract the new investments, and the poorer countries will be deprived. If, on the other hand, provision is made for compensation payments to the poorer members, the richer countries object to having to make these payments. One solution to this problem is the founding of a new form of joint venture between a foreign company and the member governments of a union. The company would locate itself and produce according to commercial criteria, where costs are lowest. Its shares would be held partly by member countries of the union. If desired, it would be possible to allocate more shares to the lowest-income members. In this way the company would combine low-cost, efficient location and operation, not subject to political horse-trading, with a sharing of the profits between member countries that would compensate the poorest members for their disadvantages.

Export processing zones

In view of the low incomes and small size of the domestic market in most low-income countries (the exceptions are India and China), the best hope of attracting foreign investment in manufacturing is in export processing zones. One of the assets poor countries have to offer is a cheap labor force. If the labor force is disciplined, ready to learn, and well motivated, it can attract foreign investors interested in producing components or engaging in processes that are labor intensive. Export zones have been set up in many countries for this purpose. And, at first sight, their existence seems to vindicate the doctrine of comparative advantage, according to which countries with a plentiful supply of labor should concentrate on the production and export of labor-intensive goods. Mauritius has had outstanding success in attracting foreign investment. Its manufactured exports are now worth more than twice those of sugar, its dominant export in the past. Its economy has been growing at 5–7 percent a year for many years. There are, however, dangers to host countries in this type of investment.

It is foreign capital, know-how, enterprise, management, and marketing that are highly mobile internationally and that are combined with the plentiful, but internationally much less mobile, domestic, unskilled, or semi-skilled labor. One set of factors (enterprise, management, knowledge, and capital) are in relatively *inelastic* supply *in total*, but easily moved around the world in response to small differentials. They are therefore in *highly elastic* supply *to any particular country*. The other factor, labor, is in labor surplus countries in *highly elastic* supply domestically, but *immobile* across frontiers. The situation is equivalent to one in which plentiful unskilled and semi-skilled labor itself, rather than the product of labor, is exported. The surplus of the product of labor over the wage, resulting from the cooperation of other factors, in less elastic supply, accrues to foreigners. The differential international and internal elasticities of supply in response to differential rewards and the difference in monopoly rents entering the rewards of these factors have important implications for the international distribution of gains from investment.

Since the firms operate normally in oligopolistic and oligopsonistic markets, cost advantages are not necessarily passed on to consumers in lower prices or to workers in higher wages, and the profits then accrue to the parent firms. The operation of this type of international specialization depends upon the continuation of substantial wage differentials (hence trade unions must be weak in the host country so that low wage costs are maintained), continuing access to the markets of the parent companies (hence stronger political pressure from importing interests than from domestic producers displaced by the low-cost components and processes, including trade unions in the rich importing countries), and continuing permission by host countries to operate with minimum taxes, tariffs, and bureaucratic regulations.

The packaged or complete nature of the contribution of the transnational enterprise, usually claimed as its characteristic blessing, is then the cause of the unequal international division of gains. If the package broke, or leaked, some of the rents and monopoly rewards would spill over into the host country. But if it is secured tightly, only the least scarce and weakest factor in the host country derives an income from the operations of the transnational firm, unless bargaining power is used to extract a share of these other incomes.

It appears to be the secret of the Korean success story that the Koreans drew knowledge from inputs and equipment suppliers and from foreign buyers, and developed their own technical capacity through reverse engineering. Export processing zones contributed only 4 percent to total manufactured exports of Korea. The Koreans unbundled the package, tolerated majority foreign ownership only in export and high-technology firms, and did not waste money on the rents in the foreign investment bundle. Technology transfer took the form of transferring knowledge from foreign brains to domestic ones.

It is sometimes said that the workers in the firms in export zones acquire skills which will later benefit the host country. But often these workers are young women who do not stay in the labor force when they get married. Moreover, the skills are often quite simple ones, such as using nimbly your fingers for sewing or assembling wires for carburetors.

The situation is aggravated if there is technical progress of the kind that knocks out the advantage in labor-intensive production of the host country. The electronics revolution makes it possible to robotize whole textile factories and to relocate to the parent country. Other processes and products than the automated ones will still be left to which the labor force could be switched. But such switching has its costs. Skills acquired are wasted, workers have to be retrained, and the bargaining power of the host country and its labor force is further reduced.

The bargaining power of the host country and of its plentiful factor – semi-skilled labor – in such a situation is likely to be weak and the question is whether such a division of gains between parent firm and host country, between the foreign investment "package" and domestic labor, remains acceptable. The gains to the host country are confined to the wages of those employed if the alternative is unemployment. The fact that these earnings are in foreign exchange may put them at a premium, if the country suffers from a foreign exchange shortage. There may, in addition, be linkages, but these may be positive or negative.

A possibly more hopeful note can be struck if we remember that the electronics revolution economizes not only in labor, but also in supervisory and managerial talent. Since this is scarcer in developing than in advanced countries, the developing countries' comparative advantage in some of these lines may be reestablished. It would no longer be employment-creating, but would still earn foreign exchange which could be used for job creation through public works or productive, labor-intensive investment. A number of research projects are devoted to finding out what the locational implications of recent technical progress are, but the empirical evidence is not yet in. While the type of foreign investment discussed has attractions for some countries faced with labor surpluses or foreign exchange shortages and poorly endowed with natural resources, the potential gains have to be weighed against the social costs and social risks, including a form of dependence and dualistic development of a new kind, different from that of the colonial mines and plantations, but similar in its distributional impact.[19]

What are the lessons for policy? The most obvious conclusion is that developing host countries should share in the monopoly rents by appropriate tax policies. But this requires *joint* action of countries with similar attractions for the foreign firm in order to reduce the elasticity of supply with which any one country would be faced if it acted in isolation. Such joint action is difficult to achieve. The more successful the agreement on not giving tax concessions promises to be, the more attractive it is for any one country to break away, or to make the concessions outside the agreement. And the fear of someone breaking away is a deterrent for others to reach, or, once reached, to adhere to the agreement.

Thought should be given to how to introduce sanctions and penalties that would prevent such defections. The European Union and the Association of South East Asian Nations have provisions against concessions above an agreed level. The situation may, however, be asymmetrical, if increasing tax concessions were not to attract additional investment, because it would be followed by other countries. The situation would then be like the kinked oligopoly demand curve. Both raising concessions and reducing them would reduce the foreign investment.

Apart from sharing in the gains through tax collection, the host country can impose various conditions on the company. One would

---

[19] There is a secondary problem. Assume the host country were able to provide some of the technicians or managers normally provided by the transnational corporation. It would then have to reward them with incomes not too much out of line with those received by the rich foreigners, or they would emigrate. Local replacement would make an egalitarian incomes policy more difficult or impossible. This threat to social objectives may be worse than the actual brain drain of professional manpower.

be to undertake the retraining should it decide to relocate elsewhere, or more generally to provide training outside its own workforce for a flexible labor force. Another would be various ways of making the foreign factors complementary rather than competitive to indigenous factors. Some of these possibilities were discussed above: joint ventures, local participation in board membership, training requirements, etc. Others are discussed below. The aim would be to use the foreign investment as an instrument for the mobilization and improvement of local resources. The question is whether without protection of markets, without tax concessions, and without heavy subsidies to inputs, such conditions remain within the bargaining range that satisfies the objectives of both the foreign firm and the host country. Outside this range, more or less foreign investment has to be weighed against the still largely unexplored costs and benefits of this investment.

Government intervention and performance requirements[20]

The generally prevailing view is that specific incentives to attract private foreign investments and transnational corporations, or to direct them into specific sectors or projects or locations, such as tax concessions, are not very effective. The reason for this may be that they tend to be small and that the investor does not regard them as permanent. Instability is regarded as a deterrent. On the other hand, the expectation that incentives may be provided in the future (e.g., restrictions on competing imports and new foreign investment) could work as an incentive to invest now. Another reason for the apparent unimportance of specific incentives is that many similarly situated countries offer them. If only one country were to withdraw them while the others maintained theirs, it might well lose a good deal of investment (Guisinger, 1986).

Probably more important than specific incentives, which are small and unstable, is the general investment climate, which is influenced by government policies, although not those directed specifically at the investment. Government attitudes to transnational corporations, macroeconomic policies with respect to a realistic exchange rate, a fairly uniform and not too high tariff structure, and low wages play

---

[20] For a full list of host country incentives and disincentives to foreign investment, see table 1 in Guisinger (1986).

an important part. Reliable infrastructure, good administration, political stability, and absence of arbitrary and rapid changes in regulations are usually cited as more important than the regulations themselves.

At the same time it should be remembered that there are justifications for departures from such a uniform and open system. There is the well-known terms of trade argument for tariff protection when a country has monopoly power; this is stronger for poor countries, for which the redistributional effect of such monopolistic action can be justified in the absence of adequate direct income transfers. There are learning effects and infant industry encouragement, both to import substitutes and to exports. And there are justifications for import restrictions combined with restrictions on domestic production of certain types of consumer goods, the demand for which is heavily influenced by advertising, or by other people's consumption, or by habit, or by ignorance or false beliefs.

In contrast to incentives, developing countries impose performance requirements on foreign firms. These may relate to raising exports or lowering imports, offsetting import content of inputs by export earnings,[21] use of local materials, employment, participation in management and ownership, local research and development, transfer of technology, training, etc.[22] They may, if effective, offset the incentive effects of the concessions. Alternatively, if they are well designed and reduce monopoly rents, they may only amount to a shift of benefits to the host country, without affecting the amount of foreign investment.

Some countries use general principles that apply to all foreign applicants; others use discretion for particular cases. The World Bank found an inverse relationship between market size and universal (as opposed to discretionary) performance criteria.

Learning by doing is often cited as an argument for protecting or, better, subsidizing the learning activity in an infant industry. The subsidy is justified only if the benefits from the learning process do not accrue to the firm but are passed on to others in lower prices. The argument applies, in principle, as much to import-substituting as to export-promoting investments. Indeed, it also applies to subsidizing foreign firms, if their learning process yields lower-priced imports into the subsidizing country in the future.

---

[21] See the discussion of inward- and outward-looking foreign investment.
[22] For a list of such requirements, see Streeten (1981), p. 283.

PART III

Bargaining theory and the obsolescing bargain

10 From the obsolescing bargain to the political bargaining model

LORRAINE EDEN, STEFANIE LENWAY,
AND DOUGLAS A. SCHULER

Introduction

The best-known model of relations between multinational enterprises and host country governments is the obsolescing bargain model (OBM), first developed by Raymond Vernon in *Sovereignty at Bay* (1971). obsolescing barguin model (OBM) explains the changing nature of bargaining relations between a MNE and host country (HC) government as a function of goals, resources, and constraints on both parties (Vernon, 1971, 1977; Kobrin, 1987; Brewer, 1992; Grosse and Behrman, 1992; Grosse, 1996). In OBM, the initial bargain favors the MNE, but relative bargaining power shifts to the host country government over time as MNE assets are transformed into hostages. Once bargaining power shifts from the MNE to the host country, the government imposes more conditions on the MNE, ranging from higher taxes to complete expropriation of MNE assets. Thus, the original bargain obsolesces, giving OBM its name. Originally applied as an explanation for widespread expropriation and nationalization in the 1970s of MNE natural-resource subsidiaries located in developing countries (Vernon, 1977), OBM was later tested in other situations such as manufacturing MNEs and developed HCs, with much weaker results (Kobrin, 1987).

The now widely held view among IB scholars is that OBM has outlived its usefulness. The many case studies testing the model suggest that MNEs were able to retain relative bargaining power and prevent opportunistic behavior by HC governments so the bargains, in practice, seldom obsolesced. In addition, today, few governments restrict inward FDI, either in the form of screening or performance require-ments, so that little formal bargaining over entry occurs between MNEs and host governments. To the extent entry bargaining does occur, it is mostly at the local level as cities compete in so-called "locational tournaments" to attract new investments. Thus, host gov-ernments have shifted from "red tape" to "red carpet" treatment of foreign MNEs. MNE–government relations are now seen as cooperative, not conflictual (Dunning, 1993a; Stopford, 1994; Luo, 2001). As a result, there appear to be few areas where OBM applies.

The purpose of this chapter is to refute this view. We argue that the essential elements of the obsolescing bargain model can and should be retained. OBM does have long-term usefulness as a theoretical model of MNE–state relations once the twin emphases on "entry" and "obsolescing" are removed. Instead, we propose that IB scholars should revitalize OBM by reconceptualizing it as a *political bargaining model*. In our PBM, MNE–state relations are modeled as iterative political bargains negotiated between MNEs and governments over a wide variety of government policies at the industry level.

Our new PBM updates the OBM by incorporating recent insights from the liability of foreignness, transaction cost economics, and the resource-based view literatures. We argue that "obsolescing bargain" can be reconceptualized as "political bargaining" if, first, we broaden the issue area from a focus on ownership shares and recognize that firms and governments engage in iterative bargaining over a wide variety of government policies at the industry level. MNE entrants want not only to maintain the original bargain but also to search for new bargains that will enhance their competitive position. Obtaining favorable outcomes in these public policy debates is critically important to firm competitiveness and performance. Second, even if MNE–state relations are cooperative and not conflictual in nature, democratic governments must also take into account the interests of other stakeholders (e.g., consumers, labor groups, NGOs) and commitments (e.g., membership in international organizations, bilateral and regional accords) so that, in practice, MNEs must bargain for favorable public policies. Many of these favorable policies may also contribute to host country economic growth and have the effect of creating more resources for both the company and the country. Lastly, the essential insight of OBM – that bargaining processes and outcomes depend on the parties' goals, resources, and constraints – can and should be retained in PBM, even if MNE–state bargains do not obsolesce. PBM is therefore a powerful tool for analyzing MNE–state relations, which includes OBM as a special case.

The obsolescing bargain model

OBM explains bargaining relations between an MNE and a host country as a function of goals, resources, and constraints on each party

(Vernon, 1971; Moran, 1985; Kobrin, 1987; Brewer, 1992; Grosse and Behrman, 1992; Vachani, 1995; Grosse, 1996).

In the original model, the goals of the MNE and HC are assumed to be conflicting. Even though their goals are assumed to conflict, OBM assumes that bargaining is a positive sum game such that both parties will voluntarily bargain and achieve absolute gains. Relative gains, however, will be positively related to relative bargaining power: the greater one party's relative bargaining power, the greater that party's relative share of the gains. Absolute gains refer to the dollar magnitude of gains realized by one party; relative gains to each party's share of the total gains. Alternatively, absolute gains can be interpreted as how close each party comes to achieving its first best goals; relative gains by comparing the two parties' success rates. The OBM literature suggests that the outcome should favor the party with the stronger resources, higher issue salience, weaker constraints, and greater coercive power.

In OBM, relative bargaining power is assumed to initially favor the MNE. Because the MNE can invest in several locations (has other alternatives) and is therefore highly mobile or has capabilities and resources to extract raw materials that the host country does not have, the HC has to offer locational incentives to attract inward FDI. The initial bargain then obsolesces over time. Once the MNE has made sector-specific investments in the host country, these resources can be held hostage by an opportunistic HC. The longer the MNE is in the host country, the more likely it is that the government's perception of the benefit–cost ratio offered by the MNE falls, particularly if the investment turns out to be much more profitable than either the MNE or the HC anticipated and there are large profit remittances to the affiliate's parent firm. At the same time, technological spillovers and economic development encourage the emergence of local competitors, so that the HC becomes less resource-dependent on the MNE over time as there are more likely to be local firms that could replace the MNE, assuming that all the resources and capabilities to create a product exist in the HC. If the host government's perception of the benefit–cost ratio turns negative, the obsolescing bargain model hypothesized that the HC would demand more commitments from the MNE, causing the original bargain to obsolesce.

The wave of nationalizations in the early 1970s are used as real-world evidence of MNE–HC obsolescing bargains, but even in vertically integrated, resource-intensive industries, there is some evidence that

MNEs have been able to protect their bargains. For example, Theodore Moran's 1973 study of the Chilean copper industry found that the US multinational Kennecott developed domestic and transnational alliances which, when the firm was nationalized by the Chilean government in 1971, were successful in getting Kennecott nearly full compensation for its investments (Moran, 1973). Anaconda, another US MNE that had not developed any domestic alliances, was nationalized without any compensation. Moran concluded that resource-intensive industries could reduce the probability of an obsolescing bargain by reducing their own risk exposure and raising the costs to the HC of opportunistic behavior. As a second example, Jenkins' 1986 study of the National Energy Policy in Canada found that the oil MNEs were able to defeat the National Energy Program by enlisting the US government on their behalf, shifting their oil rigs outside of Canada, and canceling new investments (Jenkins, 1986). Moran (1985) also provides several rich case studies.

In manufacturing industries, MNE–HC bargains are expected to be less prone to obsolescence because MNE investments tend to be smaller and more mobile, and the MNE's knowledge-based firm-specific advantages (FSAs) more difficult to copy (Kobrin, 1987). If the MNE can supply the HC with a stream of new investments (thus, keeping the country dependent on the MNE for new technology, products and/or access to export markets, and improving the government's perception of the value added from FDI), the bargain need not obsolesce. The MNE can ward off obsolescence by forming strategic alliances with local firms that have desired resources and/or capabilities, diversifying activities outside the host country by dispersing manufacturing sites across several countries to reduce the probability of being held hostage, and offering more benefits to the host government, such as involving the government in the business venture (Grosse and Behrman, 1992).

Vachani's study of nationalizations by the Indian government of foreign MNE investments in US, British, and European subsidiaries over the 1973–1985 period suggested that bargaining outcomes should be broken into two components (Vachani, 1995). He argued for differentiating between static bargaining success (the outcome of any one particular negotiation) and dynamic bargaining success (the long-run trend in outcomes over several negotiations), on the grounds that factors important for one might not be important for the other. Over the longer term, the MNE's FSAs in the form of technology intensity and size of investment were positively related to the MNE's ability to prevent the bargain from obsolescing; that is, with dynamic bargaining success.

Using percent of ownership as a measure of bargaining success, Kobrin (1987) found evidence that suggested the MNE–HC bargain did not obsolesce for manufacturing MNEs, particularly in high technology sectors, supporting Vachani's argument. Bennett and Sharpe (1979), in their study of bargaining between the Mexican government and foreign automotive MNEs, found that the Mexican government's bargaining power was strongest at time of entry because the MNEs desired access to the Mexican market. Once the MNEs had become integrated into the Mexican economy and developed strong relationships with local upstream and downstream firms, MNE bargaining power increased rather than obsolesced. The promise of additional technology transfers also kept the HC dependent on the MNEs and sustained the host country's interest in the potential benefits that the MNE could bring.

The political bargaining model

We now turn to developing our proposed PBM. We retain the core components of OBM but update them with recent insights from IB and strategic management literatures. We break our analysis into the three core components of OBM: similarity of goals and relative states, resources and constraints, and, finally, the bargaining outcome.

Similarity of goals and relative stakes

OBM assumes that both parties have goals they want to accomplish and that one party achieves goals that they believe salient at the expense of the other party. The (dis)similarity of interests between the two parties and the extent to which they frame their interests as zero sum affects the anticipated difficulty of the negotiations (Grosse and Behrman, 1992). The more similar the goals, the less difficult the bargaining process and the less need for the host government to regulate and/or coerce the MNE into activities seen as beneficial by the host country. MNEs and host governments tend to have dissimilar goals when they perceive that one will benefit at the expense of the other. OBM also assumes the MNE's and HC's goals are inherently conflictual in nature. The conflict arises because MNEs are integrated

businesses consisting of many affiliates located in a variety of countries, where all units are under common control and share common
strategic goals and resources. Nation-states, on the other hand, are
the ultimate location-bound asset, limited in their sphere of action by
geographic borders. Thus, MNEs and host countries are assumed to
have divergent goals.

How would a political bargaining model reconceptualize the first
component of OBM: the similarity of goals and relative stakes of the
two parties?

MNE goals

In OBM, the MNE has one of four specific motives for entry – market
seeking, resource seeking, efficiency seeking, or strategic asset seeking –
as outlined by Dunning (1993b). For example, petroleum MNEs typically
enter a host country looking for sources of oil (resource seeking)
whereas white-goods (e.g., washing machines) MNEs typically are
seeking new markets for their products. We identify two new issues
in the IB literature related to MNE goals, and argue that these must be
part of our new political bargaining model.

Recently, IB researchers have focused on MNEs from nontraditional
home countries, such as emerging market firms (EMFs). The motives
for internationalization of EMFs include not only market-seeking (now
referred to as knowledge exploitation FDI) but also knowledge-seeking
FDI. When MNEs go abroad to learn, rather than to exploit existing
firm-specific advantages, they enter a host country from a position of
competitive disadvantage. Chung (2001), for example, showed that the
technology spillover benefits to the United States were reduced when
FDI entrants came from countries with average technology levels
below US levels. Knowledge-seeking FDI is also the case for meta-
nationals (Doz, Santos, and Williamson, 2002; Murtha, Lenway, and
Hart, 2001) where their global competencies are derived from their
abilities to learn from their affiliates located throughout the world.

Second, underlying the MNE's specific motives for going abroad is a
more diffuse set of objectives – improving economic efficiency, increasing
its market power, and obtaining legitimacy in the host country – that
are needed if the MNE is to maximize its long-run after-tax global
profits in the host country after entry (Boddewyn and Brewer, 1994).

Efficiency and market power are well understood terms but legitimacy
may require some explanation. At the time of first entry, the MNE

suffers from the liability of foreignness (Kostova and Zaheer, 1999). Since the HC will lack familiarity or is likely to have stereotypical views about the MNE, the government will treat the MNE as an outsider, that is, as a firm without legitimate status in the host country. Legitimacy can be achieved if the MNE becomes isomorphic with the institutional environment in the host country; however, it takes time and commitment by the MNE to build a reputation and become recognized as an insider by the host country.

Legitimacy is also more likely to be enhanced when the MNE develops partnerships with local firms and institutions (Boddewyn and Brewer, 1994) that make the firm "become domestic," reducing liability of foreignness. These actions also can be related to stakeholder contract costs theory, where stakeholders exercise some social control over a firm (Wood, 1991). To manage these relationships, firms expend resources on social performance activities. Relational costs are lowered because stakeholders expect firms to deal fairly with respect to their rights and the overall distribution of outcomes. A firm that respects this implicit contract fosters social harmony and minimizes the costs of maintaining relationships with stakeholders. Firms with good social performance should realize lower costs of managing stakeholder relationships and thus earn higher financial returns than those firms with bad social practices. To the extent that the MNE can build organizational legitimacy in the host country through local partnerships and social performance activities, its potential bargaining power should atrophy less over time.

Third, the MNE's goals vis-à-vis the host country are affected by the activities that are shifted to that location and the position occupied by the foreign subsidiary(ies) within the MNE network. Traditionally, market-seeking and resource-seeking subsidiaries were established in developing countries, designed to either sell products locally or source local inputs to process or assemble elsewhere in the MNE network. As MNEs shift higher value-adding and more service-intensive activities offshore (e.g., the shifting of business processing functions to India or the Philippines), the changed nature of offshore activities should affect the MNE's goals and relative stakes.

HC goals

In OBM, the host government's goals are different from the MNE's. The host government typically hopes to accomplish broader economic, social, and political objectives through its negotiations with the foreign firm(s). Reflecting both nationalistic tendencies and rational economic attempts to secure greater benefits from FDI, the goals of developing country governments in the 1960s and 1970s were seen as wanting significant investment and technology transfers, employment creation, positive balance-of-payments effects, local sourcing of inputs, etc.

Whereas the typical "host country" in OBM was a developing country such as Mexico or Brazil, in our PBM, "host countries" should probably be decomposed into four groups, each group with governments which have different capabilities: developed market (e.g., United States), emerging (e.g., Brazil, South Korea, India), transition (e.g., former USSR members), and developing countries (e.g., Africa, Caribbean). Each group has its own institutions, cultures, and goals. One would not expect the HC goals of the United States to be identical with those of emerging market economies, in terms of inward FDI. Our PBM therefore needs to be nuanced to take into account the differing institutional characteristics, capabilities, and goals of host countries.

A second insight for PBM that comes from recent IB research is that government corruption can influence MNE–state relations. Petty bureaucratic corruption at the time of MNE entry can influence the negotiation over investment concessions and tax incentives. The larger the number of bribe collectors, the greater the political hazards of negotiating with government officials. Public corruption deters inward FDI and influences companies' choice of entry mode (Rodriguez, Uhlenbruck, and Eden, forthcoming).

(Dis)similarity of MNE–HC goals

In OBM, MNE and HC goals were seen as conflictual. In our political bargaining model, we argue MNE–HC goals do not have to be in conflict. The key point for PBM is that the goals of the two actors are different because MNEs and governments are very different entities with different objectives and a different geographic scope. Their goals may be in agreement, they may just be different, or they may actually conflict with one another. The important point is that there is some range of complementarity or overlap so that there is scope for each party to achieve its own goals through cooperation. (We are indebted to Steve Kobrin for clarifying this point.)

More recently, with widespread market liberalization and the pressures of globalization, HC goals have shifted toward the achievement of international competitiveness through the development of strong home bases. The work done over the past decade by Krugman, Porter, and others on geographic clusters and agglomeration economies as drivers of innovation stresses that governments can help create more favorable business environments for domestic and foreign firms. "The unique and critical role of modern democratic governments is to create and sustain an efficient economic system," which means that "governments and firms are best considered as partners in the wealth-creating process" (Dunning, 1997, pp. 118, 128). Because MNEs are now seen by governments as key actors in the process of transferring and facilitating international competitiveness, some IB scholars (e.g., Dunning, 1993a) argue that MNE–HC relations should now be viewed as cooperative rather than competitive, reflecting the shared goals of efficiency gains and international competitiveness. Where similarity of interests prevails, MNE–HC negotiations should be more harmonious, with both parties seeing benefits from combining the MNE's core advantages with the host country's location-bound assets.

Size of the stakes

The size of the stakes (how important the negotiations are to each party) can also affect MNE–HC bargaining and the outcome. While each party has general goals it hopes to accomplish, the importance each party attaches to the negotiations may differ. The stakes depend on the availability of alternatives to each party (i.e., the next best available alternative should deadlock occur), the importance of this particular negotiation to each party in the context of the overall MNE–HC relationship, and the importance of this negotiation in the context of each party's overall interests.

In our PBM, we recognize that numbers matter. As the number of MNEs continues to multiply, host countries should have more alternative sources of investment. The larger the host country, the smaller the importance attached to any single investment. Also, the number of suitable host countries has increased as countries have made institutional changes (or at least said they would) in response to new WTO rules liberalizing investments. For example, after 1996, the TRIPS (Trade Related Intellectual Property) accord requires governments to establish a domestic intellectual property rights regime, even if host governments find it difficult to enforce. Lastly, if we subdivide host countries into four groups (developed, emerging, transition, and developing) the alternatives in terms of domestic and other sources of inward

FDI are likely to vary considerably across the groups and across time. This suggests that the size of stakes to the HC will vary by the type of host country.

Relative resources

The second core component of OBM is the relative resources possessed by each party. In OBM, both parties are assumed to possess assets or resources that are valuable to the other. The MNE's resources are its firm-specific assets (FSAs) that are difficult to imitate, such as patented technology, brand names, and trade secrets (Teece, Pisano, and Shuen, 1997). The HC's resources are the size of its local market and its country-specific advantages (CSAs), typically subdivided into economic, sociocultural, and political–legal (dis)advantages. We use recent insights from strategic management to update the concept of relative resources in our political bargaining model, as follows.

MNE resources

Based on insights from the resource-based view (RBV) of the firm, we argue that competitive advantage is derived from the firm's FSAs or resources if they are rare, hard to imitate, have no direct substitutes, and enable companies to pursue opportunities or avoid threats (Barney, 1991). The firm's ability to earn sustainable above-normal rents (either Ricardian or monopoly rents) is dependent on its possession of hetero-geneous resources, skills, and capabilities, limits to industry competition, and imperfect factor mobility. We assume the MNE possesses three types of resources, based on the method by which they are protected from imitation: resources protected by property rights (including patents), tacit resources, and relational resources.

Property-based resources are "enforceable long-run contracts that monopolize scarce factors of production, embody exclusive rights to a valuable technology, or tie up channels of distribution . . . they buffer an organization from competition by creating and protecting assets that are not available to rivals – at least not under equally favorable terms" (Miller and Shamsie, 1996, p. 522). Exclusive ownership of a valuable resource that cannot be legally imitated by rivals means that its owner can earn superior rents on the resource. Any rival firm that wants the resource must pay the discounted future value of the expected economic returns from the resource.

Where FSAs are not protected by contracts, there are at least two other categories that may satisfy Barney's resource definition. First, tacit resources, by definition, are subtle and hard to understand, based on routines and learning by doing. Because they are hard to transfer, their value is protected not by property rights but by knowledge barriers. Second, external relationships that facilitate knowledge sharing, privileged access to resources or customers, and/or erect barriers to entry may confer monopoly rents. These relation-based resources can arise through strategic alliances between firms or business–government relationships. In this regard, Boddewyn (1988) argues that MNEs have political FSAs that can be used to generate rents for the firm; one can see these as both tacit and relation-based resources that favor firms with strong political ties to host country governments and stakeholders, reducing liability of foreignness, and generating the ability to earn above-normal rents.

In sum, the MNE's resources/FSAs are its bundle of tangible and intangible assets that give rise to long-lived rents, where the MNE either owns property rights in the asset (or complementary assets) or its value is protected from erosion due to the tacit or relational-based nature of the asset.

HC resources

The HC's resources, in OBM, are seen as its country-specific advantages (CSAs): access to the local market, abundant raw materials, cheap labor, etc. With globalization, the increasing mobility of capital and the decreasing importance of traditional resources such as unskilled labor and raw materials, the host country's resources in our PBM also need to be redefined, in the same way that FSAs have been redefined by the resource-based view of the firm. The host country's true locational advantages are its location-bound assets, in part derived from geography, that are rare, hard to imitate, have no direct substitutes, and enable firms using those resources to pursue opportunities or avoid threats. Governments can positively affect the value of their "home bases" through dynamic efficiency-enhancing investments and a regulatory environment that encourages technological upgrading, reduction of transaction costs, and openness to the global economy (Dunning, 1997).

MNE–HC valuation

In OBM, the value of each party's resources is measured, not by its owner's evaluation, but by the other party's desire for those resources.

The other party's valuation depends on the strength of desire/need for the particular resource and on what other alternatives are available should this negotiation fail. We retain this concept of valuing resources in terms of the other party's valuation in our PBM, but update the concept of valuation to take account of institutional distance as a barrier to evaluation.

The concept of institutional distance can be a useful construct for evaluating the HC's resources from the perspective of the MNE. Kostova and Zaheer (1999) argue that the institutional distance between the home and host country affects the MNE's ability to achieve external legitimacy in the host country. Institutional distance refers to difference/similarity between the regulatory, cognitive, and normative institutions of the two countries (Kostova, 1996). Institutional distance should increase transaction costs, reduce the MNE's evaluation of HC resources, and discourage FDI into institutionally distant countries (Pederson and Shaver, 2003; Eden and Miller, 2004). When cognitive institutional distance is high, governments are likely to see the MNE in stereotypical terms, increasing the MNE's liability of foreignness and making it more difficult for political bargains to be reached.

Potential bargaining power

Bargaining power comes from the ability to withhold resources that the other party wants. We argue that a PBM should incorporate insights from the resource-based view. HC bargaining power is stronger when the host country has rare and location-bound CSAs that are desired by the MNE (e.g., central location in a region for efficient logistics, large and growing national market, valuable natural resources). MNE bargaining power is stronger when the HC wants FSAs that are inimitable and in scarce supply (e.g., sophisticated technology). Thus, it is the relative resources of the MNE vis-à-vis the HC that is the underlying determinant of potential bargaining power in each negotiation.

Luo (2001) argues that resource complementarity is also an important factor influencing potential bargaining power. The greater the perceived complementarity between the MNE's and host country's resources, the higher each will value the other's resources. In the absence of other alternatives, the greater will be their bilateral interdependence, the higher the salience each party will attach to the bargaining process, and the more attention each party will devote to MNE–state relations.

In these circumstances, Luo expects more cooperative relations, higher benefits for the MNE, and stronger firm performance in the host country.

Relative constraints

The third key component of OBM is the effect of political and economic constraints placed on each party's actions. The exercise of potential bargaining power, which depends on each party's resources as valued by the other party, can be reduced by exogenous constraints. Constraints on HC bargaining power can be political (e.g., a weak, politically unstable government that lacks legitimacy or the HC's actions are restricted by international agreements) or economic (the HC suffers from balance-of-payments difficulties). Constraints on the MNE's bargaining power can also be political (previous commitments to the host or home country or legal restrictions on its activities) or economic (restrictions imposed on the subsidiary by its parent firm). Thus, constraints can be either internal (within the MNE and HC) or external (imposed by third parties or external institutions). How can we update constraints for our PBM?

MNE constraints

Transaction cost economics suggests that previous contracting arrangements can constrain current negotiations. Argyres and Liebeskind (1999) argue that previous contracts can cause governance inseparability, that is, an agent's past governance choices can restrict the range and type of governance mechanisms the agent can adopt in the future. This is because contracts are difficult to reverse; "a firm's contractual commitments tie it to specific other parties who have rights in relation to the firm" (Argyres and Liebeskind, 1999, p. 52). Governance inseparability creates two problems for the agent: the inability to engage in governance switching (changing modes) or governance differentiation (adding new modes). Thus, in repeated negotiations with the same government, or in negotiations with new governments, the MNE's options may be limited by its prior agreements with the host country or with other governments and firms.

HC constraints

Similarly, in repeated negotiations with the same MNE, or in negotiations with new MNEs, the host government may be constrained by its existing bargains. Bargains with one group of MNEs may constrain bargains with another group (Eden and Molot, 2002). The actions of nongovernmental organizations, such as environmental and labor rights groups, can also constrain MNE–state bargains.

An important constraint not recognized in OBM is the role now played by supranational institutions in constraining the policies of national governments (Ramamurti, 2001). Because most developed and developing governments are members of multilateral organizations (e.g., WTO), regulatory convergence through the multilateral rules negotiated between national governments now constrains MNE–HC bargaining. For example, the General Agreement on Trade in Services (GATS) requires member countries to schedule services for liberalization. While national treatment is not required by GATS, most favored nation (MFN) is required. To date, most developing countries have not scheduled very many services for liberalization under GATS.

Regulatory convergence is also fostered by bilateral and regional agreements. Bilateral investment treaties (BITs) guaranteeing right of establishment, national treatment, MFN status, and so on, are now widespread. Bilateral tax treaties (BTTs) constrain excessive taxation of MNE subsidiaries by revenue-seeking nation-states. Regional trade agreements such as NAFTA and the European Union regulate FDI flows within trading blocs. This web of binational and supranational agreements is creating an investment regime (Eden, 1996) that offers more protection, and bargaining leverage, to multinationals.

The bargaining outcome

Let us summarize the basic components of our PBM. MNEs and nation-states engage in political bargaining over a government policy that affects either the MNE directly or the industry of which it is a part. In the negotiations (which can include lobbying), the MNE seeks legitimacy and higher economic profits, and offers, in return for more favorable policies, improved access to the MNE's own non-location-bound resources (FSAs). The host government, as part of the policy negotiations, offers the MNE improved access to its location-bound resources (CSAs). The valuation each party places on the other's resources determines its potential bargaining power. The existence of economic, political, and institutional constraints suggests that actual bargaining power may be greater or less than potential power, depending on several factors: the resources controlled by one party and demanded by the other, the similarity of interests and relative stakes attached to the negotiation, the constraints on each party, and the ability of either party to limit the behavior of the other party directly through economic or political coercion. The final outcome of the policy negotiations should tip in favor of the party with the strongest actual bargaining power. The "winner" in the negotiations is defined by comparing the final outcome to the goals of each party; the one whose goals are most closely achieved is the winner. Both parties win if they believe the policy outcome will be ultimately beneficial for them.

Discussion

We argue that our PBM is an improvement over OBM in several dimensions.

First, PBM can handle a wider variety of issues in MNE–state relations than can OBM. In OBM, HC–MNE bargaining is over the initial firm-specific entry decision (e.g., FDI screening), subsequent monitoring of the MNE by the host government and the distribution of rents between the MNE and the HC. Our PBM is conceptualized as much broader in scope. MNEs and governments bargain over a wide variety of government policies at the industry level; in some cases, individual firms will have very different policy positions, in others they may lobby as a group. Over time, through iterative bargaining, MNEs can affect government policies toward their industry, and in turn affect the achievement of MNE goals. Bargaining outcomes in these public policy debates should depend on the relative goals, resources, and constraints of the two parties, as outlined above, with the "winner" being the party whose goals are most closely mapped by the outcome.

Second, OBM assumes that negotiations take place between one MNE and one HC government. However, the real world is much more likely to be characterized by negotiations among multiple MNEs, domestic firms, and the government over a particular policy issue (Averyt and Ramagopal, 1999; Keillor, Boller, and Ferrell, 1997). For example, Eden and Molot (2002) explored the effects of two waves of entrants (first movers and latecomers) into the Canadian auto industry. They found both groups suffered from the liability of foreignness of establishing operations in a foreign country. Each brought FSAs "to the table" at the time of entry and invested in resource-building strategies afterwards to overcome their liability of foreignness. In the case study, the first movers (the Big Three auto MNEs) achieved legitimacy as insiders in Canada and accumulated privileged access to markets and inputs. The subsequent entry of Asian auto MNEs disturbed the original MNE–HC bargain, and generated subsequent bargaining rounds where insiders and outsiders jockeyed for preferential treatment.

Third, PBM can contain OBM as a special case. Vernon's *In the Eye of the Hurricane* (Vernon, 1998) argues that MNE–state relations at the end of the 1990s were an unusual period of harmonious relations. He predicted that, in both developed and less developed countries, these relations would become more conflictual in the early years of the twenty-first century. Both home and HC governments would be more likely to ask the MNEs in their midst, "What have you done for me lately?" and to either require greater commitments from these MNEs or respond with less favorable government policies. Vernon's predictions may be coming to pass as governments new to MNEs (e.g., Russia) and governments well experienced with MNEs (e.g., Venezuela) have both, in the past year, retaliated against the MNEs in their midst. Anti-MNE individuals and NGOs now regularly mount strong protests at meetings of international organizations such as the OECD, WTO, IMF and World Bank (Eden and Lenway, 2001). Thus, the perception that all MNE–state relations are harmonious and MNE–state bargains never obsolesce is wishful thinking. There are cases where OBM can provide a useful theoretical lens. Thus, OBM can be seen as a useful but rare case within the general PBM.

Conclusions

IB literature is full of individual case studies of OBM, some supporting and some rejecting the hypothesis that MNE–HC relations are inherently conflictual and that MNE–HC entry bargains are bound to obsolesce. Even though scholars believe that OBM is dead, we have argued in this paper that core concepts from the model can and should be retained. We developed a new model – the political bargaining model (PBM) – using the concepts of goals, resources, and constraints as a theoretical lens through which to examine MNE–state relations over time, and, indeed, other IB relationships. Our model takes into account recent insights from the IB and strategic management literatures as a way to revitalize research on MNE–state relations. We argue that PBM is a powerful theoretical lens for analyzing MNE–state relations, one that includes OBM as a special case. We hope that PBM will turn out to be useful for other scholars in their research on public policy negotiations between MNEs and nation-states.

Acknowledgements

Some of the ideas in this paper were first developed in Eden and Molot (2002). We thank Steve Kobrin, Jean Boddewyn and the participants at the "International Business & Government Relations in the 21st Century" workshop for helpful comments on an earlier draft of this paper.

Table 10.1 *From an obsolescing bargain to a political bargaining model of MNE–state relations*

	The obsolescing bargain model		The political bargaining model	
	MNE	*HC*	*MNE*	*HC*
Goals	MNE–HC goals are conflictual but the bargain is potentially positive sum (both parties can gain).	Economic, social, and political goals, focusing on national welfare.	MNE wants access to HC's location-bound CSAs. Importance of organizational legitimacy, relative to efficiency and market power goals.	MNE–HC goals are different and are typically cooperative; there is positive sum bargaining. HC wants access to MNE's non-location-bound FSAs. Goals vary by type of host country. Importance of national competitiveness.
Resources	FSAs of the MNE. FDI is a bundle of capital, technology, and managerial skills.	CSAs of the host country (economic, social and political) that attract FDI.	MNE transfers non-location-bound resources that are property based and tacit/relational based.	HC offers location-bound resources (property based and relational based).
Constraints	Economic and political constraints, both domestic and international.		Economic, political, and institutional constraints. Governance inseparability constrains outcomes. International institutions and home country governments can affect outcomes.	

Bargaining	Bargain over MNE entry. Subsequent bargains with same firm(s) over access to HC resources, contribution to HC and ability to repatriate profits.	MNEs and governments bargain over public policies in industry-specific issue areas.
MNE strategies	Focus on preventing opportunistic behavior by the host government.	MNEs use economic and political strategies, lobbying for legitimacy in order to overcome liability of foreignness. MNE–HC relations can be strengthened through organizational legitimacy, political accommodation, resource complementarity and personal relations.
Outcomes	Outcomes measured by percent of ownership retained by the MNE. Outcome depends on relative goals, resources, and constraints. Initial bargains favor MNE and then obsolesce over time.	Outcomes measured by which party most closely achieves its goals. Outcome depends on the parties' relative goals, resources, and constraints. Governance inseparability, firm rivalry, and liability of foreignness are key variables affecting bargaining outcomes. Other governments and international institutions are important intervening variables.

11 The bargaining view of government–business relations

ROBERT GROSSE

T H E idea that relations between international companies and national governments can usefully be viewed as a bargaining situation is not new in the international business literature. If we limit the history of business analysis to just post-Second World War writings, then the focus on these relations probably began with someone such as Stephen Hymer (1960), who looked at multinational firms as institutions that internalize transactions costs (efficiency) and at the same time seek to dominate markets through monopoly power (equity). He did not relate the former issue to dealings with governments, but he certainly did consider the second issue, arguing that powerful international firms can pursue monopolistic goals, unless they are constrained by governments. While his perspective was ultimately critical of multinational firms, his focus included the key relationship of concern here, between national governments and international firms.

Another author writing at the same time was Jack Behrman (1960, 1962), who explored the use of foreign direct investment as a tool for economic development, and who recommended government policies to stimulate this activity. Behrman's work was far more policy oriented, with emphasis on explaining the phenomenon of foreign direct investment, and on how governments could channel (encourage) that activity to pursue development goals. Behrman clearly focused on the interests of firms and the interests of governments, and on the ways in which they could pursue mutually acceptable goals.

Richard Robinson (1964) took perhaps the broadest perspective of all, looking at the wide range of issues on which multinationals and governments interact. He argued that firms would have to take national interests into account in their activities in order to obtain legitimacy. He stated that most MNE projects did not take national interests sufficiently into consideration and were therefore "vulnerable to nationalization and expropriation in less-developed countries and to severe restrictions on their operations in developed ones" (cf. Boddewyn, this volume).

Writing on international business/government relations was given a major impetus by Vernon (1971), when he argued that multinationals faced an "obsolescing bargain" in their dealings with host-country governments. The bargaining relationship that before entry might favor the firm – due to its capabilities such as ownership of proprietary technology, access to foreign markets, and financial strength – would deteriorate once a physical investment in plant and equipment in the country was made, since such investments are "hostage" to government policies once established. This concept was explored in great detail by a wide range of authors (e.g., Moran, 1974; Bennett and Sharpe, 1979; Fagre and Wells, 1982; Jenkins, 1986; Kobrin, 1987), who generally found evidence that bargaining power did tend to shift more toward the government after market entry with physical facilities, but still showed many examples of firms that maintained bargaining strength over time through various means. This idea of a company's deteriorating bargaining power once physical facilities are committed is one of the enduring concepts that remain relevant to analyzing government–business relations.

Later studies on the bargaining relationship have attempted to explore additional facets of the issue. Vachani (1995) examined longitudinal outcomes of individual firms' relationships with the government of India, demonstrating that firm power tended to decline (obsolesce) over time. Stopford and Strange (1991) looked at the impact of multiple players on the firm–government bargain, including other governments, pressure groups, and other firms. They emphasized the importance of inter-country relations as leading to national policies toward MNEs. Ramamurti (2001) likewise looked at inter-government bargaining as an initial stage in a process, which was followed by dealings between MNEs and governments.

As demonstrated in these last references, even apart from the obsolescing bargain discussion, the analysis of government–business relations has come to recognize and explore in more detail the fact that the relationship is multifaceted, involving not only the company and the government, but each one's additional relations with other institutional players. Figure 11.1 depicts this reality.

One view in more detail – the Behrman–Grosse model

One characterization of the government–business relationship that will form the basis for extension in this chapter is the perspective developed

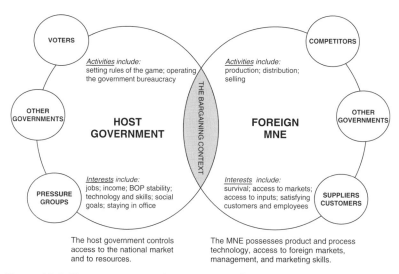

Figure 11.1 Host government–foreign MNE relations

by Behrman and Grosse (1990), in which three dimensions of the relationship are identified and utilized to design policy and strategy. These three dimensions cover the aspects of a government's sphere of concerns and activities, plus the aspects of a company's sphere of concerns and activities, that overlap and produce a bargaining context.

Each of the parties has a set of *resources* that are of interest to the other actor in the bargaining context. These resources on the side of a national government include the right and ability to give the company access to the national territory for serving the local market or obtaining inputs such as raw materials and local labor, as well as access to knowledge that is available locally. The resources on the side of a company include such things as proprietary knowledge, access to foreign markets, and financial resources, among others. Much of the early bargaining literature focused on these resources as the basis for government–business bargaining, arguing that whichever side had greater resources would obtain the better "deal," in the sense of more favorable treatment. For example, a national government could charge very high taxes, force significant knowledge transfer, and place many other restrictions on foreign oil companies in exchange for giving them the right to extract oil from the national territory. And for an example in the opposite direction, a company could demand tax exemptions, privileged borrowing opportunities, and other incentives in exchange for setting up an export-platform, computer chip-manufacturing operation to serve foreign markets.

These examples and others generally employed in the literature refer mainly to emerging markets, but the same kind of relationship applies to Triad countries as well. The Japanese auto firms faced tremendous restrictions on their car sales into the United States beginning in the early 1980s, as the US Government applied "Voluntary Export Restraints" to limit access by those firms. The Japanese companies offered high-quality, low-cost vehicles to the US, while the US offered the largest and most affluent market to the car companies. The Japanese car companies had a much weaker position than the US Government, and as a result they were forced to comply with US demands (reducing imports into the US – and setting up local production in the US as well).

And an example on the other side of the picture would be the use of incentive policies by industrial-country governments to attract manufacturers to select their jurisdictions for production facilities (often for autos), thus providing jobs, income, and often exports. This kind of policy has been used within the EU by countries such as Ireland, trying to attract EU-serving manufacture of autos, computers, pharmaceuticals, and other products. It has also been used by individual US states, trying to attract large-scale manufacturing facilities that will serve the entire country from one location.

A second dimension of the relationship is the relative *stakes* that government and company have in a given bargaining situation. This dimension refers to the possible losses that each side could incur if a successful bargain were not achieved. For example, a government would have relatively little to lose if a successful agreement with a particular fast-food restaurant were not accomplished, because many such firms exist, the product is probably not viewed as overly important to the country, and thus the government has little at stake.

Stakes for the government in a general sense would include the possible loss of access to whatever resources that company offers, plus other considerations such as worsening of relations with the company's home government, loss of participation in a regional or global trading alliance, and perhaps even the defense of public health (in the case of the fast-food restaurant, during an era when fast foods are under criticism). Stakes for a company would include the inability to gain access to the government's resources (the national market, and/or the available natural resources and factors of production), potential loss of access to a regional trading bloc, and potential loss of face for being unable to achieve successful dealing with this government.

The stakes for a government may be very high in a situation where countries are essentially competing with each other to attract company business. This is especially true among member countries of the European Union, where in most industries one location can produce output for the whole region. In another context, the stakes for the government of India may be very high if they can/cannot attract a particular foreign direct investment in production of computer software (such as from IBM) and in operation of "call centers" (such as for General Electric or Citibank) for Triad companies. India is competing with other English-speaking countries literally around the world for this business, which can be carried out anywhere via telecommunications. As another example, the stakes of the government in Costa Rica were extremely high in their efforts to attract Intel to set up a computer-chip manufacturing plant in that country, when Intel was considering a number of alternatives in Latin America. If Costa Rica's government could not convince Intel to invest, then thousands of jobs and hundreds of millions of dollars of annual exports would be lost.

Switching to the company perspective, the stakes for a company such as Citibank or Wal-Mart are enormous in China, so that in each case a successful bargain with the Chinese government to permit the company access to the world's largest market (in terms of consumers today and GDP in the future) is extremely important. Interestingly, access to China's human resources for manufacturing is also attractive to foreign investors, but there are alternatives in Asia and elsewhere with low-cost labor, so a firm such as Nike or Sony would not have as high stakes in dealing with China's government for an assembly business to serve foreign markets.

The third dimension of the government–business relationship that will fundamentally drive the bargaining between the two sides is the *similarity of interests* between them. The more similar the goals of a company and the government, the more likely a successful bargain will result from their interactions. When the goals of the company and the country diverge greatly, then a successful relationship between them is less likely. ("Success" is defined as reaching a mutually acceptable outcome to a bargain situation, with neither side withdrawing from the relationship.)

When manufacturing firms deal with the Mexican government to set up *maquila* (offshore assembly) plants that will import components, both the government and the company want to see a profitable venture that employs lots of local people, exports large amounts of goods, and transfers knowledge to local people. The company would prefer to pay less tax and have easier access to the Triad markets for selling final products, while the government would like to earn more tax revenue and have more knowledge transfer, but despite these differences both sides are interested in much the same outcome. Thus, the bargaining in this kind of situation where both sides' interests are similar is likely to produce a successful, collaborative outcome.

Contrast this situation with an extractive venture or an importing venture, in which little integration of the foreign firm into the local economy is sought, because the firm wants primarily to obtain a raw material for use elsewhere, or to sell locally products that are made elsewhere. The government in this situation wants almost the opposite of the company's interest: fewer imports, more downstream processing of a raw material, and generally more integration of the company into the local economy. The similarity of interests in an extractive venture is often quite low, and consequently the relationship is more conflictive, as seen in this example.

The three-dimensional view of government–business relations is pictured in figure 11.2 below.

This framework is useful first for understanding the pressures and perspectives that drive companies and governments in their interactions. It is valuable second for its suggestion of directions to go in pursuing a more harmonious relationship, that is, in moving toward point C on the diagram, where government and company have similar interests. In principle, any point lying on the back wall of the diagram would yield the positive feature of similar interests; point C produces outcomes of low regulation/high incentive policies, since at that point the company's bargaining position is strongest.

The bargaining relationship in a dynamic context

The analysis that can be carried out through the bargaining model described above may be faulted for lacking in dynamism and for lacking in consideration of the added complexities that are due to interactions of the government and/or the company with other stakeholders in their

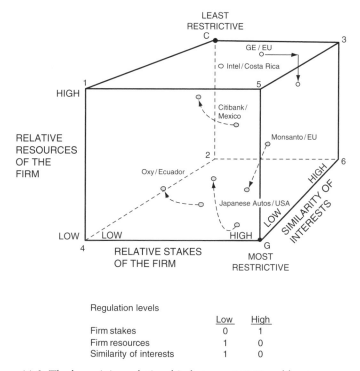

Regulation levels		
	Low	High
Firm stakes	0	1
Firm resources	1	0
Similarity of interests	1	0

Figure 11.2 The bargaining relationship between MNE and host government

environments. This is not a completely fair assessment, since the addition of further stakeholders is directly included in the question of the stakes that each party holds in a bargaining situation. And the interests of both company and government should, in principle, include interest in satisfying additional stakeholders. Even so, there is room for further development of the impact of added stakeholders on both the definition of the bargaining context and the development of strategies/policies for improving the outcomes.

On the question of dynamism, it is quite difficult to identify a model or a structure of reasoning that is analytically manageable and still reflective of the kinds of conditions that change over time and that require responses within the bargain. For example, when a country goes from a period of economic boom into a recession or depression, the government's concerns change dramatically. A bargaining context would be much more favorable to the company under the recessionary conditions than in boom times, other things equal, because the government would have a greater need for the company's business. Yet, trying to identify a model whose parameters reflect both boom and bust situations (or variations on the degree of boom or bust conditions) is difficult at best. Also, in technology cycles, when new technology (computing capability; biotech products; telecom equipment) is introduced, governments have few suppliers among which to choose. When technology becomes more mature, the number of alternative suppliers grows, and the government gains in bargaining power with any one of them. The stage of the technology cycle is another logical candidate for inclusion in modeling, but one that is quite difficult to measure appropriately.

Looking at the company side of the picture, a different but rather parallel situation is evident. During booms and recessions, a company's resources in the affected country relative to those of the government probably do not change dramatically. What is at stake for the company may shift, if a recession puts severe strain on the company's viability, or when a boom puts the company in a new position of financial capability. Additionally, when a company is diversified across many countries and several regions, the dealings with one particular government will be less critical than at another stage of the company's development when it is concentrated in only a couple of or a few countries. Certainly companies' geographic diversification can be measured; can company exposure to macroeconomic cycles in a given country be modeled usefully?

Probably more important in the company context are shifts in the competitive terrain. If a new competitor enters the market and competes strongly with the firm, more may be at stake in bargaining with a particular government. When technology changes, and puts the firm at a disadvantage or gives it a new advantage, again the importance of a bargaining situation will change. It is these changes in the competitive environment over time that are most likely to give the company a changed bargaining position, rather than changes during macroeconomic cycles.

Macroeconomic cycles and changes in the competitive environment are major challenges to the effort to create a more complete view of the government–business relationship. To arrive at an initial foundation for thinking about dynamic bargaining, let us explore a handful of examples of bargaining situations over time, and then return to thinking about the foundation.

Example 1: Banking

The banking industry provides a useful example of a sector whose technology has changed dramatically in the past ten years, whose regulation has likewise changed dramatically since the fall of the Soviet Union, and where competition has spanned both commercial and investment banking, with specialist firms in each area entering the terrain of the other. Consider the government–business relationship in Mexico, as one outstanding example of waves of conditions. In the 1980s, Mexico's economy was in a severe recession, with all domestic banks nationalized in 1982 due to their insolvency from a crushing dollar debt burden and peso devaluation. Foreign banks in the country might have had ready access to purchase domestic banks at the time, but since the major foreign banks such as Citibank, Bank of America, Morgan Guaranty, and Bank of Nova Scotia had incurred very large loan defaults, they were not interested in building a local presence in Mexico. The government became more open to foreign funding alternatives (e.g., debt–equity swaps, creation of Brady bonds, and allowing foreign banks more freedom of operation in Mexico) as the decade progressed.

In 1990–1992, Mexico's government re-privatized the banks, only to fall into the Tequila Crisis of maxi-devaluation and loan defaults at the end of 1994 (just after Mexico had joined NAFTA, paradoxically). During the second half of the decade, Mexico's government allowed all of the major local banks except Banorte to be acquired by foreign investors. And in the early 2000s Mexico operates both an extremely open financial market and an open market for ownership of financial institutions. The bargaining positions of the banks went from very weak up to the late 1980s, to stronger by the end of the debt crisis, to very strong during and after the Tequila Crisis. Perhaps the conditions will shift back somewhat to greater government intervention in the mid-2000s, as Mexico's economy grows at an acceptable pace.

Citibank, as one example, was limited to one branch in Mexico up until the late 1980s. At the end of the debt crisis, the government permitted Citibank alone among foreign banks to establish another half-dozen branches, still primarily in Mexico City. At the time of the Tequila Crisis, the government tried to entice Citibank to buy one of the mid-sized failed local banks, leading to acquisitions of

Confia in 1998. Subsequently, acceptance of foreign bank entry grew, and Citibank was allowed to buy the largest Mexican bank, Banamex, in 2001. Citibank's resources during this twenty-year period did not change dramatically relative to other foreign financial service providers, but its bargaining position evolved as the Mexican government experienced two major crises that provoked greater acceptance of foreign (especially financial) firms in the country.

If we look at the United States, a similar shift in government–business dealings was evident in the same time period, with a financial (Savings and Loan) crisis in the late 1980s leading to the government's allowing banks such as Citibank and Chase Manhattan to establish branches in multiple states, even though that activity was prohibited by the basic banking law of the country at that time (the McFadden Act of 1927 and the Bank Holding Company Act of 1956). Citibank bought failed Savings and Loan companies in Florida, Texas, and other states as a result. In the late 1990s, as new technology was permitting financial institutions to provide more and more services between states, Citibank even merged with an insurance company and stockbroker (Travelers), as an exception to the existing national law (Glass–Steagal Act of 1933). These examples show how a bank's regulation changed over time, though it is not an international example. The acquisition of Bankers Trust in New York by Deutsche Bank is an example of that kind of dramatic act, in which a foreign bank purchased one of the main US money center banks. This would not have been permitted in earlier years, but as the US deregulated the industry in the 1990s, the Deutsche Bank decision was allowed (in 1998) as part of a continuing regulatory opening (and not to favor Deutsche Bank in particular).

Both of these examples, the US and Mexico, even in extremely simple form, demonstrate how the banks' bargaining positions changed over time, due to features of the environment that led to overall government policy shifts relative to the industry, rather than relative to an individual financial institution.

Example 2: Oil

This industry has been one of the favorites for arguing the obsolescing bargain view. Once a multinational oil company was established in any country with a multi-million dollar investment in exploration and/or oil wells and/or refining and downstream activities, it was "hostage" to the local government. This situation has changed over the years, first as oil companies were established by the national governments in major oil exporting countries such as Saudi Arabia, Iraq, and other Middle Eastern countries, as well as in Venezuela, Mexico, and Ecuador in Latin America. These complemented the existing state-owned oil companies in England and the Netherlands as well. The bargaining position of foreign oil companies in the emerging markets declined precipitously during the largely anti-MNE years of the 1970s, when many were nationalized and their activities put into the hands of the local state-owned firms. This was emblematic of the global view that emerging markets should challenge foreign MNEs and pursue relatively independent development paths (Prebisch 1952).

The situation changed in the 1980s, when oil prices fell dramatically and emerging market governments scrambled to find external financial and knowledge resources such as those available from the multinationals. A few state-owned oil companies were sold into private hands (especially YPF in Argentina, Lukoil and Yukos in Russia – but also British Petroleum). Multinational oil companies were not welcomed with open arms back into the Middle East or Latin America, but they encountered increasing numbers of opportunities to participate in exploration, production, refining, and international distribution of oil and gas. During the 1990s, national policies toward the oil firms moved parallel to regulation changes in general. The United Nations (1999, p. 9) estimated that of 895 changes in regulatory policy toward foreign direct investment, 94 percent were favorable toward the firms. And this trend has continued into the early 2000s.

An example of one relationship that has developed interestingly over time is that of Occidental Petroleum (Oxy) with the government of Ecuador. In the 1970s, the Ecuadorian oil industry was nationalized, with the main foreign MNE, Texaco, selling its operations to the state-owned firm, now called PetroEcuador. Occidental Petroleum entered the country in an exploration contract, which was permitted by the Ecuadorian government in 1985 during the height of the external debt crisis that was accompanied by very low oil prices. Oxy obtained the right to explore in a major block of territory (Block 15), just like a handful of other foreign oil companies including YPF, Petrobras, and Agip. Oxy received similar treatment, with about 50 percent of revenues from any oil produced and sold going to the government of Ecuador.

Oxy found commercial quantities of oil in seven sites within the block, and has been producing oil there since the early 1990s. The relations with Ecuador's government were manageable, though probably the Oxy–Ecuador relationship would have fallen somewhere near the middle of the cube, somewhat closer to the bottom right endpoint than to any other corner. In Ecuador, oil has been the national patrimony for decades, and any foreign oil company runs some risk of criticism just for being foreign. The social view has not changed greatly over time, despite international trends for deregulation, and particularly for privatization of state-owned firms.

At the end of the 1990s, five foreign oil companies were given permission to build a second major oil pipeline from the producing fields in the Ecuadorian jungle to the coast for either refining or shipment to overseas refineries. Oxy and the other companies invested approximately US$1.4 billion during 1998–2003, and the pipeline construction was finished in November 2003.

In the early 2000s, Oxy's position has deteriorated markedly, arguably due to an obsolescing bargain. Indigenous groups began to criticize the firm for exploring for oil on tribal lands (despite prior permission having been requested and granted). Both indigenous and environmental groups protested the pipeline and its potential harm to the land. And the Ecuadorian government changed a tax-holiday agreement, leading Oxy to claim about US$50 million in overtaxation during 2001–2002. These steps have led to a situation in which Occidental has publicly stated its intent to reconsider the operation in Ecuador, and to stop producing oil if the tax problem is not resolved. The bargaining situation clearly has moved to the bottom right corner of the bargaining space.

Example 3: Computers

This final example presents a high-tech industry to contrast with the service sector and natural resource cases. Computing power and scope have developed truly dramatically since the 1970s. The launch of the personal computer at the end of the 1970s by Apple Computer is a useful mark of the beginning of this revolution.

Competition has largely been based on technological developments and on firms' abilities to market their new products and services. (This example is confined to the hardware side of computing.) Government policies have been largely supportive of computer production and sale, to allow companies to keep up with global trends.

Even so, the degree of support offered by governments to computer companies differs widely across countries, and some countries have even followed protectionist policies to try to stimulate local R&D and production of these key products in the electronic age. Brazil's protectionist computer policy (1985–1992) is an outstanding example of an attempt to keep foreign multinationals at bay and to stimulate local firms' activities in this sector. The policy required local ownership and production of PCs and minicomputers (while allowing mainframes to be imported). The intent was to foster local technology development and creation of competitive firms in this sector. For various reasons, the policy failed completely, and was dropped after seven years of frustrating and acrimonious relations between the Brazilian government and foreign MNEs, as well as between the Brazilian government and foreign governments, local users of computers, and other groups hurt by the policy (Schoonmaker, 2002).

The bargaining model of Behrman and Grosse serves well here to demonstrate that the dissimilarity of interests is what drove the government to push for localization of the computer industry, despite the large resource advantage of the foreign computer producers and their relatively low stakes in Brazil. Over half a decade the Brazilian government recognized the futility of the protectionist policy (given the local companies' initial and continuing inability to develop leading-edge, competitive computer technology). And under weak macroeconomic conditions, with pressure from the US government to eliminate the anti-competitive barriers, the government ultimately dropped the inward-looking policy and joined the rest of the emerging markets and industrial countries in promoting an open market for computer development and production.[1]

---

[1] This episode may have been one key factor in Intel's decision to choose Costa Rica, rather than its other site alternatives of Chile and Brazil, to set up a multi-billion dollar chip-manufacturing plant in 1998.

Tying the examples together

The lessons learned from these three examples may help to point out one truly fundamental point about government–business relations. It appears that the main driver of changes in regulatory/incentive policies is the macroeconomy rather than the actions of a multinational firm. That is, the conditions that change over time with respect to a country's economic health seem to be the main drivers of the changing relationship. This argues for a two-stage view of the relationship, though different from that envisioned by Ramamurti (2001). It says that an initial understanding of the government's goals and constraints must be achieved, and then the specific relationship with a multinational firm can be interpreted. This sequential process is quite visible in the examples above.

In terms of measurement, the call for modeling has been made, though no advance toward that end will be made here. It seems that a process to identify the macroeconomic and political conditions at a particular time could produce broad guidelines for the kinds of protective or incentivizing policies to be anticipated, and then a second process could be followed utilizing the three-dimensional bargaining model to see where the company–government bargain stands and to derive policy and strategy steps to improve on that position. The two-stage process would thus begin with the identification of essentially static macro conditions facing the government, for example economic boom or bust situations. The particular situation would then be used to identify the company–government relationship in the three-dimensional space. Once this process has been established, an effort can be made to project the macro conditions, which in turn lead to automatic changes in the bargaining position. Company and/or government can then undertake policies and strategies to optimize their outcomes under the current and anticipated conditions.[2]

---

[2] Boddewyn (1981) suggests a dynamic bargaining framework in which the bargaining develops over time according to the *initial conditions* (Grosse's resources, stakes, and interests), then the *motivating factors* that could lead to changes in the initial situation, and finally the *precipitating factors* that would prompt a change in policy or strategy.

Conclusions

I suppose that one conclusion here is that the idea of gaining a full appreciation of the relationship between a national government and a multinational firm would require a "general theory of social science," as proposed for centuries but never achieved (e.g., Parsons and Loubser, 1976). Failing this outcome, it does seem reasonable to conclude that a two-stage (or perhaps multiple-stage) process of evaluating the relationship can offer more understanding than a simpler, static, and narrower view.

The view suggested here, to set the relationship in a time- and situation-specific framework on the government side, hopefully moves in this direction of complicating the modeling but greatly improving the usefulness of the perspective in terms of policy and strategy. It is equally clear that the analysis should set the relationship in a time- and situation-specific context for the company, since a larger company or an older company or a company with activities in different countries will have a different outlook from the same company at a different time in its history or a different company in terms of these parameters.

These problems may lead to another interesting conclusion, based on the fact that Behrman, Robinson, Vernon, and others have shown us very useful views of this relationship, but they have pursued a non-modeling method of analysis. Their efforts to capture the multi-dimensional reality of the government–business relationship are perhaps more instructive than ever as we make additional strides to try to capture the relevant set of considerations for understanding this phenomenon.

12 Shifts of Chinese government policies on inbound foreign direct investment

YADONG LUO

Introduction

Multinational corporations (MNCs) have been increasingly active in investing and operating in emerging foreign markets such as China, Brazil, India, Russia, Mexico, and Eastern Europe. In these countries, regulatory policies concerning foreign direct investment (FDI) play an even greater role on MNCs' market expansion and financial returns than do those in more developed countries. Moreover, the regulations and policies governing MNC activities in these countries differ greatly from those governing domestic business activities. These factors are important, because the regulatory environment in which MNCs operate determines operational conditions under which they maximize risk-adjusted net returns. Specifically, regulatory policies could affect an MNC's (1) outsourcing strategies (e.g., import materials vs. local procurement), (2) production processes (e.g., requirement for local inputs and for technological commitment), (3) marketing effectiveness (e.g., restrictions on marketing approaches, channels, and destinations), (4) financial conditions (e.g., foreign exchange balance, foreign currency cash flow, local financing costs, taxation rates, and security investment), and (5) management efficiency (e.g., local employment and dismissal, union power, and costs of human resources).

Our accumulated knowledge about developing country or emerging economy FDI policies, however, has changed little from what we learned in the 1980s and early 1990s. Major previous studies include Lecraw (1984), Poynter (1985), Behrman and Grosse (1990), Brewer (1993), and Stopford (1994), among others. These studies provided enormous insights into the characteristics and contents of FDI regulations and rules established by developing country governments before the mid-1990s, when MNC–government relations were largely adversarial and were built on the basis of bargaining power (Fagre and Wells, 1982). We learned that FDI policies in this part of the world were characterized by high barriers of entry into the market or the industry, strong government control over entry mode choice and ownership level, discriminated treatments in obtaining indigenous resources, heavy burden of taxation, dominant control by central-level governments, and high volatility of policy changes (Lecraw, 1984; Grosse, 1996). MNCs with greater bargaining power arising from contributed technologies, organizational expertise, or global distribution channels have been able to maintain higher ownership stakes or gain better regulatory treatments granted by the foreign government (Lecraw, 1984; Brewer, 1992).

This profile of governmental policies has significantly changed in recent years. In most emerging markets (e.g., Brazil and Argentina in Latin America, China and Vietnam in Asia, and Poland and Hungary in Eastern Europe), the entire regulatory system has been undergoing bureaucratic transformation, reallocating more autonomy in supervising commercial activities to regional-level (provincial or city) governments. Meanwhile, structural transformation of various economic sectors has been accompanied by many unexpected changes of governmental policies, making these policies often opaque or nontransparent. In addition, decelerated economic growth in some emerging markets such as Russia, Poland, Brazil, Thailand, and Indonesia has created pressure for the nations to bring in more FDI on the one hand, and pressure for MNCs to exit from or commit less to these nations due to shrunken market demand on the other. Finally, increased pressure of global integration with the rest of the world and heightened competition for inbound FDI with other developing countries have shifted governmental attitudes in dealing with MNCs from adversarial to complementary (Stopford, 1994; Dunning, 1998). Overall, these forces have provided a mixed effect on regulatory changes on FDI: pressures for increased global integration and for more inbound FDI drive the shift from conflict to cooperation with MNCs, while continuous economic, bureaucratic, and political transformations give rise to greater unpredictability of policy changes and directions. Such unpredictability is particularly evident in newly opened yet still rigorously regulated industrial sectors.

This chapter uses China as an illustrative case. China is today the world's largest emerging economy. Its per capita income has more than quadrupled since 1978. Real growth in GDP has averaged about 8 percent since that year. For a country whose population exceeds that of Sub-Saharan Africa and Latin America combined, this has been a remarkable development. Economic reforms have advanced China's integration with the world economy, maintained a strong external payment position, liberalized markets for many goods and services, intensified industrial competition, and introduced modern macroeconomic management. According to UNCTAD's *World Investment Report* (2002), China accounts for more than 20 percent of total inbound FDI worldwide. From 1979, when China opened up, to the end of 2001, foreign investors pumped $468.46 billion into the country. Since 1993, an average of US$0.1 billion FDI has flowed into China every day, making that nation the largest FDI recipient in the world today.

FDI policy shifts

China represents well all four features that characterize emerging markets: a relatively rapid pace of economic development, high uncertainty of institutional and industrial environments, government policies favoring economic liberalization, and structural transformation toward a free-market system. Although the pace of economic liberalization and state sector privatization in China is relatively slow compared to Russia and Eastern Europe (known as the incremental approach), China has strived since 1979 to develop an economic infrastructure in which a market economy system and a competitive industry structure can grow and be sustained. Inevitably, however, institutional and industrial environments have experienced drastic changes and have created regulatory and market uncertainties for businesses. Like other emerging markets, China's legal and regulatory frameworks on inbound FDI are far from mature. As detailed below, continuous economic reform and structural transformation, together with changes of overall regulatory structure and the development of legal systems, propel a series of shifts of governmental policies on FDI. Specifically, this chapter looks at five phenomena:

1. shift from entry intervention to operational interference;
2. shift from overt control to covert intervention;
3. shift from separation from domestic policies to convergence with domestic policies;

4. shift from regulatory homogeneity to regulatory heterogeneity;
5. shift from policy rigidity to treatment elasticity.

Shift from entry intervention to operational interference

Throughout the 1980s and up to the mid-1990s, the Chinese government oversaw inbound FDI mainly through entry intervention, that is, emphasizing FDI project ratification by which the government authorities could manipulate FDI size, location, timing, and even partner selection. Due to the lack of experience dealing with MNCs and the fact that many industries remained regulated (some of them were run under the dual-track pricing system, one centrally planned and the other market determined), the government was thus mainly concerned about which industries should be opened to foreign investors and where FDI should be directed. Most laws, rules, and regulations were associated with how to control foreign company entry and how to ratify FDI applications by government agencies such as the Ministry of Foreign Trade and Economic Cooperation (MOFTEC) or their provincial departments. This emphasis was well reflected in China's early regulations, notably in the Joint Venture Law (1979 and amended in 1990), Provisions for the Encouragement of Foreign Investment (1986), Law on Foreign Investment Contracts (1985), and Provisions for Export-Oriented and Technologically Advanced Foreign Investment (1992).

Regulations in China spelled out what kinds of projects should be approved, what documents MNCs should submit, what industries MNCs could access, what entry modes MNCs were allowed to employ, and what percentage of equity ownership was permitted at the maximum. Entry intervention during this period was implemented mostly by the central government authorities including MOFTEC, the State Planning Commission, the State Economic Commission, the State Industrial and Commercial Administration Bureau, and the State Bureau of Foreign Exchange Administration. Specific measures for entry intervention included the following:

1. *Industry access control*: By classifying industries into prohibited, restricted, permitted, or encouraged and providing different accessibility to firms in different industrial categories, the government was able to control how many and what kind of MNCs would enter a specific industry. This policy was embodied in the 1995 Catalogue Guiding Foreign Investment in Industry. Each category was treated

with different accessibility. Discriminatory treatments were designed by the government to rationalize its industrial structure, alleviate resource or price distortions across industries, create foreign exchange earnings, and help develop its infant but critical industries.

2. *Entry mode control*: MNCs were allowed to enter into certain industries only through certain entry modes (e.g., joint ventures, co-production, technology transfers, or build–operate–transfer). For instance, build–operate–transfer (BOT) should be used when an MNC invested in China's utility industry. When the joint venture mode was mandated in an industry strategically vital to Chinese economy (e.g., the telecom sector), a state-owned enterprise was often introduced or designated as a local partner by the government. Some large projects involved in infrastructure development also had to include local state-owned firms assigned by the government. These firms might not have a previous cooperative history with foreign investors.

3. *Equity and size control*: Foreign investors were restricted from holding a certain percentage of equity in the joint venture. For instance, MNCs entering Chinese auto assembly industries can only maintain up to 49 percent of equity in the venture. Size control was indirectly fulfilled through project approval. Projects with different investment sizes had to be ratified by different levels of the government. The greater the size, the higher the rank of the authority that an MNC must deal with. When a project planned to increase its investment size, it usually had to get approval by the same authority that initially ratified the project.

4. *Location control*: The government required MNCs to locate projects in certain geographical regions. This requirement was expected to help boost regional economies by launching investment in certain industries, as planned by the central government. Projects in different locations were also taxed differently. Even within the same city, ventures in different locations could be subject to different treatments. For example, the Economic and Technological Development Zones (ETDZs) provided more tax breaks than non-ETDZs within the same city or county.

5. *Duration and timing control*: Each FDI project was asked to specify a term (number of years) in its joint venture contract. Although this term could be renewed, such renewal was not automatic but usually

subject to a new round of approval by relevant governmental authorities. Timing control was exerted through controlling the date of approval. The government could deliberately withhold or delay approval of certain FDI projects. This often occurred when the government had approved too many new projects, surpassing the actual need for economic development.

6. *Project orientation control*: Each project was mandated to identify in its application documents the project's orientation. (i.e., export-oriented, technologically advanced, infrastructure-oriented, agri-culture-oriented, import-substitution, or local market-focused). Each of these orientations received different treatments and support from the government, which had to approve the project's classification. In general, the first three orientations enjoyed preferential treatments, including lower income tax and tariff rates, refund of value-added taxes, lower financing costs, better infrastructure access, and cheaper land rent.

In the mid-1990s, Chinese government policies on FDI began to shift the focus from entry intervention to operational interference. The government thus enacted a large array of regulations on component localization, minimum export level, distribution restrictions, local worker unionization, environmental protection, financing criteria, and accounting standards, among others. These measures have forcefully influenced an MNC's market orientation, marketing efficiency, human resource management, outsourcing strategy, and financial management. Altogether, they affect a firm's operational process, organizational effectiveness, and financial performance (Rosenzweig and Singh, 1991). At the same time, many hurdles involving FDI entry have been eliminated. China has been gradually relaxing restrictions on foreign ownership and on establishment of wholly owned subsidiaries. MNCs have been allowed to access and to operate in more industries. Many previously restricted service sectors (e.g., retail, insurance, tourism, hospital, trading, accounting service, and banking) have been opened up to foreign companies. Restrictions in partner selection, location, and entry mode have also been significantly relaxed. Restrictions in these aspects are essentially gone for FDI projects in nonrestricted industries.

However, new measures regulating MNC operations have emerged:

1. *Content localization*: A foreign company is required to purchase and use local materials, parts, semi-products, or other supplies

made by indigenous firms for the production of its final outputs. The required level of localization varies across industries. Those involving more value-added processing or production tend to face a higher localization standard. For instance, the State Council's Automobile Industry Policy states that foreign automobile MNCs must have 40 percent local content when they start production and 60 percent within three years after commencement.

2. *Marketing or geographical restrictions*: Certain marketing approaches (e.g., direct sales) are not permitted. For example, in April 1998, China imposed a ban on all direct sales operations. MNCs in retailing and banking industries are also subject to geographical restrictions. They are allowed to provide services only in the city they are located.

3. *Foreign exchange control*: The inflow and outflow of foreign exchange are monitored by the State Administration of Foreign Exchange (SAFE). Although foreign exchange centers established in recent years make foreign exchange conversion (with local currency) and foreign exchange balance (between earnings and expenditures) easier, the cumbersome tracking and monitoring system, originally designed to eliminate fraud, corruption and illegal trade, sometimes adversely affects normal operations.

4. *Financing administration*: Bank loans in both foreign exchange and Chinese yuan are highly regulated. The People's Bank of China (PBOC) and Bank of China (BOC) are two government bodies for monitoring Chinese yuan and foreign currency, respectively. As MNCs increasingly rely on local financial resources to reduce foreign exchange exposure and risk, the government keeps a wary eye on MNC local financing. The country has enacted a number of rules and regulations on mortgage loans, loan guarantees, loan priorities and restrictions, financing criteria and procedures, and the ratio of loans vis-à-vis assets or investments. In addition, the Regulations on the Control of Financial Affairs of Foreign-Invested Enterprises (FIEs) have recently taken effect.

5. *Unionization and labor administration*: About 90 percent of FIEs in China have established unions. China's Labor Law and various rules set by the Ministry of Labor and Personnel (MOLP) and the All-China Federation of Trade Unions (ACFTU) stipulate in detail about local employee recruiting and dismissal, minimum wage; overtime compensation, working conditions, medicare, insurance

and welfare benefits, union organizing, and corporate contribution to the nation's social welfare systems.

The reasons underlying these changes are threefold. First, most veteran MNCs in China have now moved to the second stage of operations – expanding their economy of scale, market breadth, business functions (e.g., build local R&D centers), and vertical integration, all within China. In response, the Chinese government started to place more emphasis on monitoring MNC production, operation, and management activities. Second, as China has accumulated more experience in dealing with MNCs and developed relatively mature legal systems on foreign entrance, it is a natural process over time to shift regulations on entrance to those on operations. Third, China has strived to obviate FDI entry barriers to meet the requirements of WTO membership. As a result, the government eliminated many overt barriers during the entry process and enacted more covert restrictions associated with subsequent operations.

Shift from overt control to covert intervention

A shift from overt control to covert meddling occurs when governmental policies become more opaque and less open. This shift is especially evident in regulated industries (e.g., telecom, automobile, insurance, retailing, internet, banking services) and in such issues as foreign exchange conversion, regulatory standards for building investment or holding companies, outright prohibition of investment in certain industries, and developing distribution networks. In terms of foreign exchange control, for instance, China has shifted the foreign exchange balance mandate to foreign exchange flow supervision. Previously, the harsh requirement for self-balancing foreign exchange earnings with foreign exchange expenditures was indeed restrictive but was overt and clear. Every FIE was subject to the same requirement. This rule was incrementally liberalized as China opened foreign exchange centers in the major cities of Shanghai, Beijing, and Shenzhen, where FIEs and local businesses could trade or swap different currencies, including Chinese yuan for import- or export-related transactions.

After liberalizing this regulation in 1996, excessive smuggling and foreign currency leakage prompted the central government to pay closer attention to foreign exchange conversions and flows. Thus, China tightened controls on foreign exchange flows in 1998, a move aimed largely at preventing Chinese companies from sending foreign currency abroad illegally. This change, however, had unintended effects on legitimate FIE operations. Many companies saw their shipments languish at Customs for weeks as their trading companies awaited approval to convert currency. Similarly, although China did not phase out a tax exemption on imports of capital equipment used by FIEs, since 1997 it has required FIEs to meet stringent requirements, including scrupulous tracking of each piece of equipment covered by the tax exemption. These examples show that these covert measures allow the government to crack down as called for under existing rules. These covert measures also mean that these changes can come swiftly.

Covert measures are also employed in other areas. Many regulations contained in the Unfair Competition Law (1993) and the Price Law (1998) are ambiguous, greatly empowering governmental agencies such as the State Administration for Industry and Commerce (SAIC) to explain and interpret rules and policies relating to unfair competition and pricing practice. Regardless of whether the price of a good or service is market- or government-determined, these two laws permit the government to take various steps to cope with "emergencies," which are interpreted only by the SAIC. In addition to curbing unfair competition or unfair pricing practices, these two laws attempt to crack down on businesses that fail to implement government-guided prices, or temporary interference or emergency measures. Similarly, the Advertising Law (1995) provides a set of new guidelines in an attempt to weed out fraudulent advertising and requires that all advertisements correspond to the "demands of socialism," which remain in a halo of ambiguity as to the exact meaning. This ambiguity and its derivative interpretation rights give the SAIC opportunities to intervene in FIE advertising practices.

MNCs in regulated industries are facing even more covert interference. In 2000, for instance, the government published new regulations that require all companies providing internet content to apply for licenses. Under the rules, internet companies that provide news or supply information about education, health care, pharmaceutical products, and medical instruments must be approved by regulatory agencies. In addition to the Ministry of Information Industries (MII), those agencies include governmental departments that regulate news, publishing, education, public health, pharmaceuticals, industry and commerce, public security, and national defense. The rules also reiterate government bans on various forms of internet content, including anything deemed subversive, pornographic, or related to cults. The rules also require companies to maintain records of all the information that has been placed on their websites and all the users who have connected with their servers for sixty days. If asked, companies must submit those records to government authorities. Companies violating the new rules could face fines of up to one million Chinese yuan or be shut down.

Government rules make many FIEs exercise self-censorship to avoid conflicts with the government. In the telecom sector, for example, the government published regulations in October 2000 requiring a more cautious opening of basic telephone services, such as fixed and mobile telephones, data services, satellite services, and leasing network capacity. Such services must be licensed by the central government. More importantly, many detailed descriptions of these policies are opaque. Even many governmental agencies at the regional levels are unsure how, and to what extent, such rules and policies should be completely implemented.

Covert intervention also exists in environmental protection. China continues to pass or upgrade laws and regulations on environmental protection. During 1997–2000, about thirty new laws and rules were adopted, including high-impact ones such as Energy Conservation Law (1997), ISO Standards (1997), Land Administration Law (1998), Solid Waste Law (1998), Marine Environmental Protection Law (1999), Environmental Standards Management Measures (1999), and Pollution Control Standards (1999). Today, China is working on drafts of a number of pieces of key environmental protection legislation, including (1) Desertification Law; (2) Environmental Impact Assessment Law; (3) Air Pollution Prevention and Control Law; (4) Radioactive Pollution Prevention and Control Law; (5) amended Water Law; and (6) Clean Production Law. These regulations will indirectly increase operational costs and will covertly become a pitfall for some FIEs. Foreign companies cannot afford to take an approach to environmental compliance that is anything but strict, for two reasons: first, the legislation is increasingly comprehensive and based on international standards. Second, as international companies are perceived to have more resources and experience with environmental issues than domestic firms, they are often subject to more stringent enforcement.

The main reason for the shift to covert measures can be ascribed to the fact that many newly opened industries (e.g., the internet, telecommunications, insurance, and e-commerce) are growing so fast that regulators are having trouble keeping up. Many emerging practices or problems – unfair competition, direct selling, intellectual property rights infringement, and environmental protection, for example – also give rise to many new concerns for governmental regulators. On the one hand, the lack of experience in administering these emerging problems or experiment-type practices allowed by the government cause many new regulations and laws to be ambiguous and opaque. On the other hand, the opaque rules provide various authorities exclusive rights to explain and interpret these ambiguous regulations – which, in turn, provides them with opportunities to intervene in FIE businesses. It is this interpretation and explanation that makes regulatory policies particularly covert to foreign companies. It means that the written rules are sometimes just the theory, but the practices or applications are determined by the regulator's explanations, which may be quite different from what MNCs have understood and interpreted. In addition, it is worth noting that problems created by local companies plague legitimate FIE operations, and this compounds the covert nature of governmental policies. For instance, covert measures regulated in the Price Law are largely the derivatives of distorted pricing activities implemented by Chinese domestic companies. Local businesses in recent years have used price collusion, dumping, spreading rumors of price hikes, deceptive pricing strategy, manipulating prices by incorrectly categorizing commodities, illegal profiteering, and discriminating against particular business operations to gain covert advantage over MNCs.

Shift from separation to convergence in relation to domestic policies

Before the mid-1990s, most FDI laws and regulations were separated from other law documents associated with the nation's domestic economic, procedural, administrative, and civil laws. Most FDI rules were independently documented and not part of related domestic laws. Overall, these FDI rules and laws included two categories. One comprised the central laws such as the Equity Joint Venture Law (1979 and amended in 1990), the Cooperative Joint Venture Law (1988), the Wholly Foreign-Owned Enterprise Law (1986), the Contract Law Involving Foreign Investment (1988), and the Income Tax Law for Foreign-Invested Enterprises (1991). These central laws were all enacted and promulgated by China's National People's Congress, the highest legislative body in the country. The other category comprised a large number of detailed rules, provisions, interpretations, and interim regulations adopted and issued by the ministries under the State Council (mostly by the MOFTEC).

Since the mid-1990s, FDI-related rules and regulations have been in large part embodied in various pieces of domestic economic, procedural, administrative, and civil legislation. For example, the Labor Law describes what welfare benefits FIEs should provide for local employees. An article in the Company Law states that all business ethics and social responsibilities required of local companies are equally binding on FIEs. In the Partnership Business Law, an article specifies that all regulations in this law apply also to FIEs. The Advertising Law states that all businesses operating in China, including FIEs, are prohibited from using messages that "hoodwink or deceive end-users and consumers" and also are banned from using obscene or crude language or pictures, nor can they use superstition or slander in their communications. Similarly, the Price Law, the first piece of PRC legislation to broadly address unfair pricing activities, spells out that all businesses, including FIEs, are prohibited from fabrication and spreading of rumors of price hikes to force prices to rise and from attracting business through deceptive pricing. It forbids businesses, including foreign ones, from "colluding in manipulating market prices and jeopardizing the legitimate rights of competitors or consumers." Similarly, the Foreign Trade Law contains specific terms delineating import and export rules and procedures that all FIEs should observe.

The main reason leading to this shift is that China's overall regulatory framework on FDI is heading toward the national treatment – gradually eliminating discriminations against FIEs in the area of operational rights as well as removing preferential treatments offered to FIEs in the area of taxation, vis-à-vis local counterparts. The convergence of laws between domestic and foreign businesses by embodying these laws in the same legislation and treating these businesses in the same manner represents an important step in this direction and signals positive development of the regulatory framework governing FDI in China.

Shift from simplicity to complexity

It is recognized that China's FDI policies are becoming more complex than ever before. This complexity is reflected mainly in regulatory heterogeneity across regions, locations, sectors, and industries. Previously coordinated policies nationwide are increasingly becoming idiosyncratic according to these parameters. For instance, the regulatory power differs among different provincial governments, leading to substantial variations in project approval, financial treatment, and institutional support. The application of regular FDI projects may take as short as three days in some regions such as Jiangsu and Guangdong Provinces, but may take more than one year in other regions such as Jiangxi and Sichuan Provinces. While local income taxes are totally exempt in some locations (Wuxi city), others increase taxation burdens on FIEs through either levying local taxes or allocating governmental expenses. Within a province or city, governmental policies also vary. Within the same city (e.g., Shanghai), those located in an Economic and Technological Development Zone (ETDZ) or High-Tech Park enjoy longer tax breaks or more exemptions than those outside these zones. In addition, local governments in some regions may heavily tax FIEs as well as workers in these FIEs to support social security and unemployment insurance funds in their jurisdiction's territories. Others, however, may not only eliminate these taxes but also provide free services to FIEs in training and recruitment.

Significant differences in FDI policies are also present across industries. Although domestic retailing is now allowed to set up joint venture outlets in inland cities that were formerly restricted areas, international trading rights are granted only to FIEs located in Pudong (Shanghai) and the five Special Economic Zones. FIEs in restricted industries (e.g., wristwatch chips, aluminum materials, photocopiers, and cassette recorders) must export at least 70 percent of their total production. But FIEs in encouraged industries such as agricultural technologies and new material industries are not only free from this export requirement but also enjoy up to ten years of tax breaks. For FDI in cigarettes, cotton or woolen textiles, chemical fibers, film, sedan cars, TV sets, air conditioners, video recorders, and most service industries, project proposals are required to be approved by the central-level authorities under the State Council and filed with the State Planning Commission or the State Economic and Trade Commission. Other projects, in contrast, are not subject to this requirement.

The shift from simplicity to complexity is understandable as China is transforming from a centrally planned economy to an increasingly decentralized and deregulated economy. This transformation causes three consequences that lead to regulatory complexity. First, regional governments (provincial, city, and county) play an increasingly stronger role in administering FDI activities. In fact, most FDI projects today are ratified and supervised by regional authorities. This helps improve the efficiency of FDI approval and administration. On the flip side, however, decentralization creates enormous variations across regions. Each regional government often provides a different policy in its judiciary territory. Second, different industries are at different stages of development, transformation, deregulation, and competition. Accordingly, FDI policies and treatments vary among industries. More regulated industries tend to have less favorable and more complex conditions under which FIE operations can flourish. In contrast, more competitive, open industries (e.g., light industries) tend to offer a more stable and less complex regulatory environment. Third, while regional governments now maintain an increasing supervisory power over FDI in their respective regions, regional and central jurisdictions over FDI administration often overlap, causing confusion for FIEs. This problem extends to the different departments or ministries under the State Council, as well. Each department, looking at FDI administration through its own set of rules, is likely to provide different answers to the same question. Thus, different levels of governments (especially central vs. provincial) or different departments under the State Council (e.g., MOFTEC vs. SAIC) often explain or enforce the same policies in a different manner.

China – unlike the United States, where federal and state jurisdictions are clearly delineated – has a unitary system of government. A deal struck at the provincial level is not always safe from changes in policy and regulation at the central level. The machinations of Chinese power structures are not generally transparent to Westerners. As a consequence of continued power decentralization, China's government structure lacks an effective chain of command from central directive to local implementation. Local protectionism has complicated the efforts of central officials in supporting legitimate foreign businesses. For instance, in the area of intellectual property rights (IPR) protection, China is about thirty to fifty years behind the United States and the European Union in developing a modern IPR legal system. Today, China has more than thirty laws that cover trademarks, patents, copyright, computer software, technology transfer and licensing, and trade secrets. For the most part, these regulations meet international standards, including those required under WTO's Agreement on Trade-Related Aspects of Intellectual Property Rights (TRIPS). Enforcement, however, has been hindered by poor coordination among China's central and local authorities. Local protectionism makes the effectiveness of enforcement worse because IPR-violating enterprises often account for a disproportionate share of the local economy and are major employers. During periods of economic stagnation or downturn, local protectionism of counterfeiters tends to increase. In still another complication, disputes often arise about which governmental body has jurisdiction over a particular geographical region or type of IPR because enforcement authorities answer to different laws.

Shift from rigidity to elasticity

In the past, the central government dominated the law enactment and enforcement associated with FDI activities. Under this dominance, most FDI policies were rigid, and local authorities or industrial ministries did not have autonomy to change these policies during enforcement and implementation. Moreover, FDI was concentrated on coastal regions and competitive industries, where there was less variation in terms of environmental dynamics across regions and industries. Thus, FDI treatments such as foreign currency remittance, corporate income taxation rates, import tariffs, and duration and rate of land lease were virtually non-negotiable and were largely consistent nationwide.

Since the late 1990s, this situation has changed. Many FDI policies and treatments are now changeable and negotiable, depending on an MNC's bargaining power and how an MNC utilizes its bargaining power to negotiate with the central or local governments. Two main factors affect the elasticity of FDI rules: first, financial and operational treatments are negotiable with regional authorities. For those foreign investments that are fundamental to economic development in the region (e.g., infrastructure investment, high-tech development, foreign exchange creation, and a large pool of employment), MNCs are in a strong position to bargain with government authorities in that region for better regulatory stances or treatments, especially in financial areas. Those maintaining a superior cooperative relationship with regional authorities or a stronger bargaining power arising from resource commitment are now likely to have longer taxation breaks or lower rates.

Many local governments have the power to provide more preferable treatments to those FDI projects that enormously help the local economy than what is specified in the document of the central government. For instance, a handful of FDI projects in chemical and fabrics production have been offered up to fifty years' free use of land by some regional governments in inland provinces. This practice conflicts with written rules of the central government policies in land use but is now tacitly consented to by the government.

The second aspect of elasticity rests in industry access and ownership requirements. In those industries undergoing substantial structural transformation or only partially opened up to MNCs, restrictive and bureaucratic rules set by the central government are negotiable, and related ministries in charge become flexible in enforcing and overseeing these rules. For instance, in 1999, when other internet companies were restricted from launching websites in China, Yahoo built its www.yahoo. com.cn in Beijing on September 24. Despite the announced ban on foreign investment in China's online industry, Yahoo's entry and operations were unopposed by the government, a consequence that was largely attributed to its good relations with China and strong support from its local partner, Beijing Founder Electronics Co. In the insurance industry, AIG was able to control its joint venture operations in Beijing, Shanghai, and Guangzhou and share 70 percent of the joint venture profit, whereas other international insurance companies were prohibited either from entering China or from controlling joint venture operations. The first-mover advantages and cooperative relations with the government certainly helped AIG in this achievement.

The shift from rigidity arises from several reasons. First, China faces increasing competitive pressure from other emerging economies, especially four mini-dragons (Taiwan, South Korea, Singapore, and Hong Kong), South East Asian nations, and India, in attracting MNCs' investments. Today, many MNCs are strategically restructuring their Asian businesses, reallocating their centers of excellence there (e.g., R&D centers, training centers, sourcing centers), and rebuilding their globally integrated manufacturing bases in Asia. To some extent, regulatory flexibility demonstrated by the host government encourages MNCs to enter and creates more favorable conditions for MNCs' investments and operations. Second, regulatory elasticity is particularly apparent in industries that have just deregulated and opened to MNCs. In the absence of administrative experience, government policies in these industries are essentially designed on a trial-and-error basis. The regulatory framework in these sectors is still being developed, thus providing MNCs with opportunities for better bargains. Third, the differences in economic development and income levels across provinces have increased, rather than decreased, in recent years. Less developed regions require more support from the central government. Because the government already replaced the direct financial subsidy policy previously used by granting more power and more autonomy to provincial governments, these regional governments are now allowed to modify some national FDI policies, which consequently propels regulatory elasticity in such regions.

Strategic responses of MNCs

The nature of MNC–host government relations today is largely "coopetitive" – that is, cooperation and competition simultaneously function in increasingly interdependent MNC–government relations. From a governmental viewpoint, increasing pressure of global integration, heightened competition for inbound FDI, decelerated economic growth, and stronger needs for upgrading economic structure all drive up cooperation with MNCs. From an MNC viewpoint, foreign operations increasingly depend on educational, technological, industrial, and financial structures built by host governments. To MNCs, whether a host government provides a stable set of rules for business players to act within and whether the rules can be adapted to changing conditions becomes increasingly crucial for firm growth and international expansion (Kobrin, 1982; Murtha and Lenway, 1994). Governments themselves can also be important customers, suppliers, or partners of large transactions conducted by MNCs. They are sometimes an irreplaceable solver of operational and financial problems that are beyond organizational control.

On the other hand, the competition element remains in MNC–government interfaces, despite its decreasing significance in such interfaces compared to the cooperation element. Competition is mainly manifested in bargains and resource control (Grosse, 1996). Many industries that MNCs seek to enter are still significantly controlled by the government. These industries are generally the fields in which MNCs have distinctive competitive advantages over local rivals.

MNCs also need to bargain with the government for local resources, whether physical or human. Because production and operational costs are higher in emerging markets such as China, an MNC's profitability is more dependent on financial treatments by the government, reinforcing the necessity of bargain.

The five shifts that reflect the new face of China's government policies on FDI coincide with "coopetition." For example, to the extent that administrative flexibility signals governmental commitment, a shift from regulatory rigidity to elasticity represents the government's new efforts to accentuate cooperation with MNCs. This shift provides MNCs with more options in product diversification, geographical expansion, and cost reduction. In addition, a shift from separation from to convergence with domestic policies is also a positive mark toward cooperation. Generally, the more mature the legal systems and regulatory frameworks are, the greater the convergence between domestic and FDI policies. Thus, this shift indicates the Chinese government's commitment to national treatment, the regulatory domain, and the cooperative platform long awaited by MNCs. Meanwhile, the shifts also imply competition. The shift from entry intervention to operational interference escalates governmental control over production inputs required for MNC operations. This may, in turn, increase transaction costs as well as operational uncertainties. The shifts from simplicity to complexity and from overt to covert also infer the coexistence of cooperation and competition. Those MNCs equipped with greater bargaining power are likely to benefit more, rather than suffer more, from these two shifts. Contrarily, those firms without such power may confront more regulatory hazards from the changing institutional environment.

So, how should MNCs properly respond to emerging coopetition and a new regulatory environment? First of all, as global businesses are increasingly shaped by emerging markets and the cooperation element becomes increasingly important in MNC–government relations (Stopford, 1994; Dunning, 1998), MNCs should shift from a conflictual-adversary view toward a cooperative-complementary view in dealing with emerging-market governments. MNCs should endeavor to develop a better relationship with the host government. When investing abroad, they should commit resources that are complementary to the local economy's needs. This commitment increases strategic interdependence between MNCs and the government, and thus forms an economic foundation for improving an MNC's bargaining power and for nourishing cooperation with the government (Boddewyn and Brewer, 1994; Murtha and Lenway, 1994). An MNC that directs its distinctive resources toward areas that are unavailable from local companies but are required for the long-range development of the local economy will create ties of interdependence that hold for a very long time.

Second, as a result of continued bureaucratic decentralization along the horizontal dimension (i.e., stronger influence of lower level governments) and vertical dimension (i.e., stronger influence of industrial departments), MNCs should shift from a single government view toward a multi-government view within a host country. Within the host country, they must deal with multiple governments at different levels and in different regions that have jurisdiction over their commercial activities. Regional governments are gradually becoming the major regulatory force affecting foreign investments and operations. In China, these government bodies are also politically linked through centrally nominating and appointing top officials in various regions and departments, thus remaining a complex, yet coordinated, network. Therefore, MNCs should not neglect the remaining influence of the central political government while emphasizing regional administrative authorities.

Third, socially embedded personal relations between MNC managers and government officials are important. Shifts to regulatory heterogeneity, institutional flexibility, and covert involvement amplify individual officials' power in overseeing MNC activities in certain areas. Under the centrally controlled, rigid system in the past, individual officials did not have the power to maneuver government policies but could only implement them. Today, they have authority to create new policies or modify existing policies in their respective regions or departments. This makes personal connections with these officials more important to foreign companies than ever before (Luo, 2001). Personal relationships with officials can transform into organization-level relational capital, strengthening an MNC's relations with government authorities. Because most MNCs entering emerging markets such as China intend to pursue long-term strategic goals such as sustained market share and long-range investment opportunities, personal ties with officials are essential at the outset (need more social responsiveness) and, once established, are more likely to translate into social capital and trust-building (both are accumulative and time-dependent).

Fourth, as governmental policies shift from entry intervention to operational involvement, an MNC must prepare for this institutional change by establishing an umbrella company within the host country to coordinate and integrate its nationwide operations there. One major reason for this regulatory shift is that the host government has realized the evolutionary growth of MNCs, many of which have built, within a major emerging market such as China, dozens of projects in a number of locations through various investment forms. Greater operational flexibility and better organizational coordination within the host market are becoming critical in response to environmental changes. To fulfil this end, it is important for an MNC to unite various existing investments under one umbrella and establish a fully integrated network that can combine and integrate sales, procurement, reinvestment, manufacturing, training, financing, and other activities. In China, many MNCs have recently set up holding companies for this purpose. In contrast to joint ventures or wholly owned subsidiaries, which can manufacture and market only approved products, a holding company is able to unite existing investments under one umbrella to combine sourcing, production, maintenance, and marketing activities in the entire nation. It facilitates foreign exchange balances between subunits, acts as a clearinghouse for intragroup financing, centralizes training programs for all subunits, and consolidates project management. The umbrella model is especially necessary for MNCs that are multidivisional, where each division adopts different entry modes, operates in different locations, and runs independently. Uniting a multitude of operations through an umbrella company enhances individual subunits' ability to mitigate hazards and reduce uncertainties arising from governmental interference over their operations.

Finally, as world economic integration increases, many emerging country governments face an increasing anti-globalization pressure from certain groups such as labor unions and environmental protectionists. In China, its WTO entrance further reinforces this pressure because thousands of workers currently in state-owned enterprises will be laid off after more competitive foreign firms enter. When the regulatory regime shifts from rigidity to elasticity, MNCs that are more responsive and contributive to social needs will benefit more from this elasticity. Favorable policies and treatments will be given to socially accommodative MNCs that maintain a good reputation and image in the indigenous society. Typical examples of social accommodation by MNCs include local employment, job training, education of local nationals, pollution control, infrastructure development, and financial support for schools, research, sports, and other public interests. As a result of significant participation by MNCs in host industries, many governments and societies are increasingly concerned with MNCs' corporate citizenship. An MNC's bargaining position (competition element) as well as productive ties (cooperation element) with the government can be safeguarded if its business interests accommodate rather than neglect public interests. An MNC's social responsiveness also strengthens its credibility and legitimacy in the view of the public, as well as in the eye of the host government. In fact, in several emerging markets such as China, Russia, and South America, social responsiveness is a substantial public favor as perceived by officials, and it significantly heightens an MNC's face value, a financial metaphor for business–government relations.

In summary, China's regulatory policies have experienced five significant shifts in the last few years. To respond to these shifts, MNCs must themselves shift from competition with government to "coopetitive" behaviors. They should build stronger relationships with host governments, committing resources in ways that complement the local communities' needs. They should take a multi-government view of the bureaucracy, recognizing the increasing strength of regional governments. They should strengthen personal ties with government officials to navigate the new regulatory climates, establish umbrella organizations, and respond to the social needs of the host countries to ward off attacks from anti-globalization forces. These efforts will create interrelationships with host governments that will guide them through these policy shifts and put them in the most profitable position.

13 | *Has the obsolescing bargain obsolesced? Negotiating with foreign investors*

ALVIN G. WINT

Introduction

Surely there can be no questioning the fact that there has been, over the last few decades, a fundamental change in the nature of the relations between multinational corporations and the governments of host developing economies, in the direction of more welcoming attitudes toward FDI on the part of these governments? And should this change not significantly reduce the likelihood of friction in the international business–government relationship?

The fact of change is certainly unquestionable. For several years UNCTAD has followed changes in investment policies in host economies. Based on its analysis, UNCTAD contends that 95 percent of the changes in investment policies across countries between 1991 and 2002 have been in the direction of greater investment liberality (UNCTAD, 2003b).

The implications of changes in attitudes toward investors on the part of host governments on the likelihood of investment disputes and contract continuity are, however, more contentious.

Does greater investment liberality mean that disputes between investors and host governments are no longer likely? In certain sectors, in particular, might there not remain the possibility of friction between these sets of actors during the twenty-first century? (Wells and Gleason, 1995). Does the change in the environment for FDI mean that the bargaining power cycle between host governments and multinational corporations, in which the relative bargaining power shifts to the host government after investments have been made, leading at times to the premature termination of these bargains (obsolescing bargain, vernon, 1971), has itself ended its cycle of explanatory usefulness and obsolesced? Have the strictures of multilateral and bilateral investment agreements contributed to the obsolescence of the bargaining power model of international business–government relations? (Ramamurti, 2001) These research questions form the basis of the study reported upon in this chapter.

Research methodology

The study seeks to provide predictions about the likely nature of relations between multinational corporations and the governments of host developing countries in the twenty-first century. In order to do so, however, it is important to understand the factors that have affected these relationships as they have evolved in the recent past. As captured in the literature on this subject, these relationships can be conceptualized through a bargaining power lens (Gladwin and Walter, 1980; Fagre and Wells, 1982; Lecraw, 1984; Gomes-Casseres, 1990). For many countries, it is the structure and longevity of these bargains that have colored the relationships between these parties. In some cases the obsolescence of bargains between host governments and multinational corporations is reflected in formal disputes between these entities.

In an effort to assess, even if in a cursory way, the extent of changes in the extent of disputes between foreign investors and multinational corporations, I examined the structure of investment disputes registered with the World Bank's International Center for the Settlement of Investment Disputes (ICSID) from its origin, in 1966, to 2003. While the ICSID data provide an indication of trends in investment disputes, a more intensive examination of investor–host government negotiations is important to an understanding of the evolving nature of MNC–host government relations.

Accordingly, the second methodological approach adopted in this study is a close examination of negotiating activities between one host government and several multinational firms over a period of close to thirty years.

The country chosen for examination was Jamaica. This country has engaged in three sets of negotiations with foreign investors that correspond quite closely to general trends in negotiations between multinational corporations and host governments over the last three decades. At the same time, its attitude toward foreign investors, like that of many other developing countries, was one of welcome in the 1950s and 1960s, shifting to suspicion during the 1970s, followed by welcome during the 1980s, and continued welcome since then, with the qualifier that, beginning in the late 1980s, it has become far more sensitive about the need to manage carefully investment in infrastructual industries.

A longitudinal analysis of bargains between multinational corporations and the host government of one country allows for a focus on the impact of time, and the changing internal and external environment associated with the passage of time, on the nature of bargains. It further facilitates an assessment of learning on the part of the host government. The bargaining experiences of the Jamaican government, as reported in this chapter, were informed by interviews with senior Jamaican policy-makers involved in bargain re-alignments in 1974 and 1999, and in bargaining activities in 2001.

The concluding section of the chapter seeks to identify the lessons for bargaining relationships between host governments and multinational corporations, and make predictions about the nature of these relationships in the twenty-first century.

Trends in MNC–host government investment disputes

The clearly more welcoming stance toward foreign investment by host governments corresponds to the expectation that this has resulted in far fewer disputes between host governments and multinational corporations. At one level this is clearly correct. The most extreme dispute between a multinational corporation and a host government results from expropriation of an MNC's assets, without adequate compensation. Such expropriations are, indeed, an event of the past (Minor, 1994). But this does not mean that other forms of dispute do not exist between MNCs and host governments.

In an effort to understand the nature of and trends in disputes between host governments and multinational corporations, I examined disputes registered at the World Bank's International Center for the Settlement of Investment Disputes (ICSID). This institution was established as a public organization created under a treaty, the Convention on the Settlement of Investment Disputes between States and Nationals of Other States, which entered into force on October 4, 1966. The Centre's principal objective is to promote an atmosphere of mutual confidence between States and foreign investors conducive to increasing the flow of private international investment.

Table 13.1 indicates that there has been a significant increase in disputes registered with ICSID over the last three decades, with nine registered in the 1970s, seventeen in the 1980s, forty-three in the 1990s, and sixty-nine between 2000 and 2003, of which fifty-eight are still pending. Of the total of 138 registered cases in 2003, 76 had been completed and 62 were pending.

Table 13.1 Investment disputes registered with ICSID: 1966–2003

Year registered	Concluded disputes	Pending disputes	Total disputes
1972	1	–	1
1974	4	–	4*
1976	1	–	1
1977	2	–	2
1978	1	–	1
1970s	*9*	*–*	*9*
1981	2	–	2
1982	2	–	2
1983	3	–	3
1984	4	–	4
1986	1	–	1
1987	4	–	4
1989	1	–	1
1980s	*17*	*–*	*17*
1992	2	–	2
1993	1	–	1
1994	3	–	3
1995	3	–	3
1996	3	–	3
1997	9	1	10
1998	9	2	11
1999	9	1	10
1990s	*39*	*4*	*43*
2000	5	7	12
2001	3	11	14
2002	2	17	19
2003	1	23	24
2000–2003	*11*	*58*	*69*
TOTALS	76	62	138

Note: *Includes three disputes registered against the Government of Jamaica by multinationals in the bauxite and alumina industry.
Source: ICSID, www.worldbank.org/icsid

It is, of course, important to recognize what has led to such a significant increase. The increased registration of investment disputes is one important indicator of improved relations between multinational corporations and host governments. Where, in the past, the result of differences between these actors would have been acrimonious and sometimes unilateral action in the form of expropriation and other contract-terminating activities on the part of host governments, more and more countries have elected, or been pressured, (Ramamurti, 2001) to enter into bilateral or multilateral investment treaties.

The first modern bilateral investment treaty was entered into in 1959 between Germany and Pakistan. Since then 1,169 bilateral investment treaties (BITs) have been concluded, through 2002, with by far the majority, over 800, consummated since 1987 (UNCTAD, 2003b). A typical provision of such treaties is that investors are promised fair and equitable, most favored nation treatment, which typically explicitly rules out the possibility of expropriation, while providing for international arbitration of disputes under the ICSID Convention. Surely Vernon was prescient when he suggested in 1971 that "[b]it by bit, host governments have been responding to the growing presence of the foreign-owned subsidiary" (Vernon, 1971, p. 241).

Thus, an examination of trends in investment disputes registered with ICSID provides an indication of a more transparent system for settling investment disputes. Such a system favors foreign investors, because of the provision for international arbitration, rather than reliance on courts in host countries, which typified the systems of yesteryear. At the same time, these trends also indicate that there continue to be significant areas of differences between multinational corporations and host governments. Hints about the nature of these differences are captured in a sectoral analysis of the investment disputes registered with ICSID over time, as identified in table 13.2.

In terms of completed cases, the dominant sector represented is extractive industries. This is not surprising. Extractive industries have been the arena in which disputes between host economies and multinational corporations took on their most contentious form, and presented the most striking examples of obsolescing bargains. The second most significant area of dispute among completed cases, infrastructural investments, also presents little surprise.

The shift, between completed and pending cases, to a situation in which infrastructural industries become the most significant arena for

Table 13.2 Sectors represented among completed and pending ICSID cases (%)

Sector	Completed cases	Pending cases
Manufacturing	16	6
Finance	4	10
Infrastructure	20	40
Extractive industries (mining, natural gas, forestry)	30	21
Real estate and construction	17	5
Other	13	18
TOTAL	100	100

Source: ICSID, www.worldbank.org/icsid

disputes between multinational corporations and host governments also reflects patterns of activity that are well known. The 1990s and early years of the twenty-first century have seen a return to significant levels of foreign investment in infrastructure in developing countries. But the associated investment agreements, if not properly managed, create much possibility of dispute and contention between host governments and foreign investors (Wells and Gleason, 1995).

It is to an understanding of the elements of the management of negotiations between foreign investors and host governments, in these two key areas, extractive and infrastructural industries, and over time, that the study now turns. But to do so, it is critical to examine particular negotiations closely. Jamaica has undertaken important sets of negotiations with foreign investors in these industries over a period of thirty years.

Bargaining between multinational corporations and Jamaica

Since Jamaica's emergence as an independent sovereign state in 1962, three sets of bargains between Jamaica and multinational corporations have defined the country's past, and probably future, relations with the international direct investment community. These include:

- The 1957 and 1967 tax arrangements between Jamaica and several North American bauxite and alumina firms, both of which represented twenty-five-year bargains, but the latter of which obsolesced seven years after its consummation. The bargain obsolesced when the government of Jamaica replaced the existing income tax arrangements, which had resulted in little revenue to the country, by a levy on bauxite production. This change in the taxation regime was imposed subsequent to the breakdown of negotiations between the government and the firms on changes to the taxation regime designed to generate greater revenues for Jamaica from its bauxite and alumina resources.

- The 1988 contractual arrangements with Cable & Wireless, as a part of the privatization of the telecommunications system, concluded in July 1989, which granted Cable & Wireless a twenty-five-year monopoly (with an option to renew for an additional twenty-five years) on voice telephony with an agreed rate of return. This bargain obsolesced in 1999, when the 1988 agreement was renegotiated to include the introduction of competition into the telecommunications industry, fourteen years (indeed, thirty-nine years) prior to the expiration of the previously agreed monopolistic arrangements.
- The agreement in the first year of the twenty-first century surrounding the privatization of the national electricity system, which agreement continued to be intact at the time of this study.

Bargaining with extractive FDI: Jamaica and the bauxite/alumina firms

The initial bauxite and alumina bargain

Several bauxite mining and alumina processing firms from North America, including Kaiser Aluminum (bauxite mining), Aluminum Company of America (ALCOA) (bauxite mining and alumina refining), Aluminum Canada (ALCAN) (alumina refining), Reynolds Metals (bauxite mining), Revere (bauxite mining) and Anaconda (alumina refining), began bauxite and alumina operations in Jamaica, beginning with the mining of bauxite in the 1940s. In 1950, the Jamaican Government introduced the Bauxite Industries (Encouragement) Law, which provided for generous taxation arrangements, based primarily on income tax for the alumina companies and relatively small royalty payments on bauxite mined, and allowed for easy land acquisition by the companies.

In relation to the taxation arrangements, two agreements were critical elements of the bargain entered into between the companies and the

Jamaican government. In 1957, the Chief Minister of Jamaica, future National Hero, and attorney at law, Norman Manley, led a team that negotiated higher royalty rates for bauxite and income tax increases for bauxite, but not alumina firms.

But there were two side agreements to which Manley agreed: (1) the assurance given to the companies that no further taxes would be levied on bauxite; (2) the term of twenty-five years for this agreement. Manley indicated that these clauses were agreed to, despite his misgivings, because the companies refused to forgo their earlier, more generous, income tax arrangements, under any other condition. Manley also, however, went on to point out that he could make no agreement that would bind the legislative action of a future government (Davis, 1995).

The identical set of issues arose ten years later, in 1967. In a continued attempt to encourage investment in the alumina sector, in particular, an amendment to the 1950 Bauxite Industries (Encouragement) Law was enacted which stated that:

It is hereby declared that the Minister may on behalf of Government, make or confirm such agreements, and arrangements as he may think expedient for the encouragement and expansion of the alumina industry in Jamaica. (Davis, 1995)

Following this amendment the Government of Jamaica and the alumina firms entered into a bargain in a March 1967 Agreement which involved two critical clauses: Part 11, Clause 12 of the Agreement stated that:

No further taxes (including any income tax) burdens, levies, excises, customs or imposts will be imposed on bauxite operations or on alumina, or the production of alumina or any operations carried on in relation to or incidental thereto or on any raw materials, supplies, property or other assets used in connection therewith in Jamaica. (Davis, 1995, p. 239)

Part 11, Clause 13 of the Agreement followed with the stipulation that it would last for twenty-five years (Davis, 1995, p. 240).

Obsolescence of the bauxite and alumina bargain

The stipulation of Clause 13 did not bind the Jamaican government for long. Within seven years, the bauxite and alumina bargain had obsolesced. There were several precipitating factors. One was the election of Michael Manley, Norman Manley's son, as Prime Minister in 1972.

His party, the People's National Party, founded by the elder Manley, came to power advocating a philosophy of democratic socialism. Another was the 1973 OPEC-induced oil price increase, which put considerable balance of payments pressure on Jamaica, but also provided an example of developing countries seeking to generate greater returns from their natural resources. Indeed, the low level of returns from the bauxite and alumina industry may have been the most significant factor that drove the Jamaican government to seek higher returns from the bauxite and alumina firms.

The royalty and income tax returns per ton of bauxite produced averaged US$2.56 between 1960 and 1973, while the total tax returns from the industry represented, for the same period, an average of 2.1 percent of the value of the primary aluminum processed from the bauxite (Davis, 1995). Whereas the bauxite firms paid a royalty based upon assumed profits per ton mined, the alumina processing companies were liable only for income taxes. The government of Jamaica received minimal income taxes from these companies. Indeed, two of the alumina companies had paid no income taxes since their formation. The concern of the Jamaican government was the fact that companies had a strong incentive to use transfer pricing mechanisms, and significant intra-company loan arrangements, to conceal profits within vertically integrated corporate structures.

Against the background of these events, the Manley Government established, in April 1972, a National Bauxite Commission, one of whose tasks was to negotiate new taxation arrangements with the multinationals operating in this industry. After several months of preparatory work during which the Commission investigated the companies' holdings of mineral reserves, assessed the potential of Jamaicanization of the management structure of the industry, and studied the domestic and international industry, a proposal was prepared in January 1974, designed to form the basis for negotiations with the companies.

The key feature of the proposal was a shift in the taxation arrangements in the industry, away from income tax, to a production levy. Based on the production levy proposed, the companies would pay taxes to the government in direct proportion to bauxite mined and exported (at US$11 per ton) and bauxite processed into alumina (at US$15.40 per ton), representing a five- to six-fold increase in revenue relative to the 1960–1973 average returns. The proposal also included a minimum floor for taxation based upon minimum levels of production. The proposal further indicated the government's intention to increase the level of local ownership in the industry, with the government paying for acquisitions out of future earnings from the industry.

With the proposals developed, a negotiating team was formed, including Mayer Matalon, a key member of the private sector, and Alister McIntyre, a future deputy secretary general of UNCTAD, serving as lead economist. The negotiations began with a meeting between Prime Minister Manley and the senior leadership of the firms, with Manley pointing to the government's need for additional revenue in light of the international challenges, and the companies indicating that, despite their binding contracts, they were willing to discuss amendments to the revenue arrangements to help Jamaica with its financial problems in the face of the increased oil import bill.

The negotiations began in March 1974. They were contentious, with the companies indicating that they had binding agreements based upon the legislation of 1957 and 1967. On this basis, the companies issued a joint position in late March 1974, in which they indicated a willingness to pay additional taxes in the amount of US$2.50 per ton of bauxite mined and exported, or processed into alumina, while rejecting all proposals from the government of Jamaica.

The negotiations continued until May 1974, but the parties did not get much closer. Time was of the essence since Prime Minister Manley felt compelled to have a clear indication of new revenue options by the time of the budget presentation. In the absence of the budget pressure, a key technical resource person to the negotiations and current Cabinet Secretary in Jamaica, Dr. Carlton Davis, believes that a negotiated solution might have been possible (Davies, 1995, p. 182). In the event this was not to be. By early May 1974, the Jamaican government alerted diplomatic contacts in the United States and Canada that imposition of the production levy by way of legislation was a distinct possibility. Simultaneously, the Jamaican government, one of the twenty founding contracting parties to ICSID, filed a notification of its withdrawal from the Center in relation to disputes relating to mining or mineral resources.

These events were followed by the Prime Minister's budget statement in mid-May indicating that the negotiations with the bauxite and alumina companies had broken down and the government had no option but to impose the new taxation arrangements. Later in the same budget presentation, Manley was to announce that the government would be fully financing education for all students through the tertiary level.

The reaction of the bauxite and alumina companies took several forms. All expressed their outrage at the imposition. Three firms, ALCOA, Kaiser, and Reynolds, filed disputes with ICSID. Indeed, these three disputes were three of the first five disputes filed with ICSID since its formation in 1966. One company, Revere, took the government to court. This case was heard in the Jamaican Supreme Court, between 1976 and 1977, with the court finding for the Jamaican Government, on the basis that taxation is a right of state, and that one legislature cannot bind a future legislature.

Shortly after filing in the Jamaican courts, Revere made a claim for compensation to the Overseas Private Investment Corporation (OPIC), claiming that the imposition of the bauxite levy effectively constituted expropriation by the Jamaican government. The majority panelists hearing the OPIC claim found on behalf of Revere, stating that, in international law, the Jamaican Government was bound by its commitments as stipulated in the 1967 Agreement with the bauxite and alumina multinationals. The minority opinion on the other hand felt that Revere was unable to make a convincing case that the imposition of the levy constituted expropriatory action (Davis, 1995). Revere won an award of US$1.1 million from OPIC.

The other response of all the bauxite and alumina firms was to restrict their investments in Jamaica. This applied to capital investments, but companies also restricted their recurrent expenditure, leading to a downgrading of plant capabilities. Further, several companies had, by the early 1970s, begun to invest in Guinea and Australia, in particular. These investments were accelerated in the aftermath of the imposition of the levy as the relative cost of Jamaican bauxite increased. Significant investments in the Jamaican bauxite and alumina industry only began to return in the late 1980s as downward revisions were initiated in the production levy. By the late 1990s, the government of Jamaica was moving to shift the basis of taxation back to income, but in a deal with companies for capacity expansion in exchange for taxation changes.

Bargaining with foreign infrastructual firms: the 1980s and 1990s

In the 1980s and 1990s, Jamaica continued to bargain with multinationals, but the significant bargain was with investors in infrastructure, corresponding to the tremendous increase in foreign investment in infrastructural investment, beginning in the late 1980s. Jamaica's bargain with foreign infrastructural firms over this period revolved around the country's relationship with the multinational telecommunications firm, Cable & Wireless (C&W). This company had a long history in Jamaica, having invested as a joint venture partner in the long-distance telephone company that existed as a separate entity until the 1980s.

The initial telecommunications bargain

In 1987, the monopoly long-distance and local carriers were merged, as a prelude to a process of privatization in which, by 1989, the Jamaican government had reduced its shareholding in the merged company through the sale of a majority interest to C&W.

A critical precursor to the privatization of the telecommunications system was the bargain negotiated between C&W and the Jamaican Government. This bargain involved the Jamaican government issuing to C&W telecommunications licenses (All Island Telephone License and Telecommunications License) that allowed the company "exclusive rights to sell and supply domestic and international telephone services for public and private purposes in all parts of the Island of Jamaica for a period of twenty five years from Sep. 1, 1988 with provision for renewal for another period of twenty five years" (Wint, 1996). The monopoly bargain was coupled with an agreed real after-tax rate of return on shareholders equity of between 17.5 and 20 percent. The bargain allowed C&W annual adjustments in telephone rates, if necessary, in order to stay above the minimum permitted rate of return.

The chief negotiator on the government of Jamaica's side was Mayer Matalon, who had served as a negotiator for the bauxite levy negotiations, although he was later to resign from the negotiating team out of frustration with the government's unwillingness to involve him in fully in efforts to Jamaicanize the bauxite industry after the imposition of the levy (Davis, 1995). He also served as chairman of the telephone company, before and after privatization, and was described in 1995 by Alister McIntyre, Jamaica's former lead economist in the bauxite negotiations, and vice-chancellor of the University of the West Indies, "as the financial wizard handling numbers with an artistry that I had met in no one before or since" (Davis, 1995, p, xii).

The bargain struck between the government of Jamaica and C&W led to a rapid expansion in the Jamaican telephony network, at an average annual rate of 17 percent between 1990 and 2002, although the bargain had little in the way of incentives for efficiency. Further, it was a bargain that suggested insufficient background research, by Jamaican negotiators, on the global telecommunications industry, and, consequently, excessive concessions on the part of the government of Jamaica in its search for system expansion and capital inflows (Wint, 1996).

Obsolescence of the telecommunications bargain

It was against this background that the bargain quickly came under scrutiny. From the perspective of the government of Jamaica, this scrutiny began with the competition policy element of the government's operations. In the mid-1990s, Jamaica strengthened its competition policy arm with the establishment of a Fair Trading Commission (FTC) and the associated legislative competition framework.

One of the early submissions made to the FTC came from a new internet service provider seeking permission from the government to acquire the necessary equipment, and to interconnect with C&W's infrastructure, in order to allow for the electronic transmission of data to take advantage of the new market in information communication associated with the development of the internet.

The FTC approached C&W to discuss the issue of interconnection. But C&W's position was that its monopoly extended to all forms of telephony, including information transmission, which relied on the telecommunications network, and it would allow no firm to connect with its network. Indeed, C&W's initial position was that the FTC had no jurisdiction over its operations. The FTC disagreed, citing the doctrine of "essential facility," which suggests that where a public utility has a facility that cannot be readily replicated, others should have ready access to this facility.

The Executive Director of the FTC, Phillip Paulwell, an attorney at law, was to go on to become, by 1998, the Minister of Commerce, Industry and Technology. In the intervening period, in 1996, the government of Jamaica had announced a national industrial policy which sought to develop a blueprint for accelerating development in Jamaica, and which relied on information and communications technology (ICT) as a key platform for enhancing Jamaica's development prospects as the new millennium approached. Paulwell examined C&W's 1988 contract and felt that it was critical to negotiate a new agreement, allowing eventual liberalization of the telecommunications system in order for Jamaica to rapidly develop its ICT infrastructure and shift toward a more knowledge-based economy.

As the Ministry of Commerce and Technology considered the start of negotiations in order to liberalize the telecommunications industry, it was very clear on the part of Paulwell that only a negotiated outcome would be possible. He realized that, given Jamaica's experiences in the aftermath of the unilateral imposition of the bauxite levy, there would be no support in Cabinet for any unilateral abrogation of the 1988 telecommunications licenses granted to C&W.

The strategy that was developed involved moral suasion and the exertion of international pressure to support the government's position that negotiations to end C&W's monopoly status were appropriate. There was already considerable support in Jamaica as it became apparent that the 1988 license was constricting competition in areas of technology, particularly internet-related and cellular telephony, that had not been contemplated when the 1988 agreement was consummated. But to the suggestion that its license did not include cellular phones, C&W was clear that its license included all forms of telephony, and even pointed to the prescience of its name: Cable **and Wireless**.

In seeking international support, Paulwell visited London where he was promised full support from his counterpart minister in the UK. There was much support across the Caribbean as several Caribbean countries had also entered into monopolistic agreements with C&W that looked similarly anachronistic by the late 1990s. Further, the United States, which was also concerned about the monopolistic dominance of C&W in the Caribbean telecommunications industry, indicated to Jamaican negotiators support for the government of Jamaica's position.

Against this background, and in the face of its own internal pressures, C&W agreed to negotiations. C&W found itself in a rather difficult position since, as a new entrant into the UK telecommunications sector, its parent company had pressed the UK government to liberalize the UK telecommunications market to allow it to compete more effectively against the entrenched monopolist in the UK, British Telecom. C&W initially mooted the idea of hosting negotiations in the UK. The Jamaican team, however, was able to succeed in its position that negotiations should be held in Jamaica. Paulwell became chairman of the negotiations in Jamaica, with a Jamaican negotiating team, which included the Solicitor General, the Director of the Office for Utilities Regulation, one of Jamaica's foremost trade negotiators, Peter King, and one of its premier scientists, Professor Gerald Lalor, pitted against C&W's London-based negotiating party,

The negotiations began in March 1999 and covered six areas: compensation for the loss of C&W's monopoly license; the length of the phasing of liberalization; the regulatory regime that would be introduced subsequent to liberalization; the social program the government would require of the company; the system expansion goals required of C&W; and the legislation that would govern the new telecommunications system. Each of these issues was placed under the consideration of a separate negotiating team, jointly chaired by a member of the government of Jamaica's negotiating team and a member of C&W's negotiating team. By September 1999 a heads of agreement was announced that formally signified the obsolescence of the 1988 bargain between the government of Jamaica and C&W.

The agreement included: C&W's agreement to surrender its existing operating licenses, without compensation; the discontinuation of a lawsuit in which C&W had sued the Minister of Commerce, Industry and Technology for issuing VSAT (very small aperture terminals) licenses to internet service providers (ISPs); the commitment of the government of Jamaica to clamp down on unlicensed firms seeking to bypass the C&W telecommunications system; agreement to open the cellular component of the telecommunications infrastructure to immediate competition; and agreement to phased liberalization of the telecommunication system with full liberalization to be achieved by March 2003. There was also agreement that telecommunications, under new legislation to be developed in the immediate aftermath of the agreement, was to be regulated by the Office of Utilities Regulation. The OUR would incorporate performance standards and "price-cap:RPI-X" approaches to tariff regulation.

As part of the heads of agreement, C&W also agreed to social and system expansion goals, including the installation of 100,000 new telephone lines within one year and 217,000 lines within three years of the coming into effect of new telecommunications legislation, in addition to the installation of internet terminals in post offices. The government of Jamaica agreed to use its best endeavors to secure for

C&W low-cost, long-term World Bank financing to support the system expansion objectives.

Importantly for Jamaica, the agreement involved no compensation to C&W for relinquishing its monopoly licenses. C&W had shortly before entered into similar negotiations with Hong Kong, in which the government of Hong Kong had sought to extricate itself from a similar monopolistic situation. In that case, C&W had negotiated compensation in the amount of over US$1 billion for giving up its monopoly licenses.

Bargaining with foreign infrastructural firms: Jamaica in 2001

Telecommunications was not the only infrastructural industry in which privatization had been accompanied by bargains with foreign investors toward the close of the twentieth century. In the early 1990s, the Jamaican Government began to consider the privatization of the electricity industry. The privatization framework was initially developed in a study by Coopers and Lybrand, commissioned by the Government of Jamaica and financed by the World Bank. The Coopers and Lybrand study focused on separating the generation and transmission elements of the electricity infrastructure, with the distribution and transmission elements to continue to be provided by a single player, but with generation developed on a competitive bid basis, with private power generators providing electricity to the transmission company on a take-or-pay contractual basis.

The movement to privatization was halted in the mid-1990s, after the government had invited bids for the acquisition of the monopoly transmitter and distributor of electricity, the Jamaica Public Service Company (JPS), following on the government's appointment of Professor Gordon Shirley, of the University of the West Indies, to the chairmanship of JPS. Shirley, following studies on the impact of privatization conducted at the University of the West Indies, kept focusing government policymakers on the importance of establishing carefully the benefits of privatization in an industry such as electricity provision, and the need for particularly vigilant regulatory oversight, the institutional mechanisms for which, he felt, were not yet in place.

While focusing on these matters with policymakers, Shirley negotiated with the University of the West Indies to be allowed to move from chairman to executive chairman of JPS. Following his movement to full-time management of the company, he and his management team developed a business plan for the company, incorporating a performance contract, to be agreed with, and monitored by, the newly formed Office of Utilities Regulation (OUR). This contract was influenced by the management team's benchmarking of Jamaica's electricity operations against those of high-performing small economies.

By 2000, the government of Jamaica concluded that its debt profile did not allow it to borrow, or guarantee the borrowing of, the resources needed to modernize the nation's electricity infrastructure, and that its fiscal crisis would be assisted by the capital revenues associated with the sale of the Jamaica Public Service. Against this background, privatization bids were reopened and negotiations were initiated with the first-choice company, Southern Electric.

The negotiations with Southern Electric focused largely on two areas: the price to be received by the government; and the performance standards and capital expansion program to which the privatized entity would be held accountable. The benchmark performance standards were those already agreed on in the service contract between the OUR and the Shirley-led JPS. These standards incorporated customer service levels, levels of allowable technical and non-technical losses, availability of generating plant, level of allowable heat ratings and approvals for least-cost expansion.

As it turned out, in order to maximize its short-term financial returns from the privatization, the government of Jamaica and Mirant (the spin-off of Southern Electric focused on its non-US operations) negotiated lower levels of performance in certain areas, relative to those previously agreed between JPS and OUR. For example, Mirant negotiated a longer period to arrive at levels of customer service performance, indicating the need to invest in an appropriate customer service system, and additional time to arrive at specified heat rate targets. Further, existing approaches to competition in generating were shelved for a period, as Mirant negotiated the option of supplying all new generating capacity through 2004, with further tranches of generating capacity to be fully opened to competition.

The agreements created two sets of penalties for non-compliance with the standards stipulated. For breaches of the customer service standards, the privatized JPS would be required to compensate customers directly. For other standards, for example technical losses and heat rate targets, there was an inbuilt incentive to perform. JPS would not be able to obtain upward tariff adjustments to compensate for losses in these areas.

Accordingly, meeting these standards would translate directly into improved profitability for the company. And thus was concluded the Jamaican government's most significant bargain with multinational corporations since the 1970s, which continued to be fully intact in 2003.

Has the obsolescing bargain obsolesced?

It is now appropriate to revisit the question that initiated this study. Has the obsolescing bargain obsolesced? Is it no longer true that once foreign investors have initiated an investment process, there is pressure for governments to reconfigure the terms and arrangements of the investment bargain, as the costs of the investment to the country become more apparent, while the benefits generated from the investment seem less impressive (Vernon, 1971)?

The data on trends in investment disputes provide no evidence in support of such a conclusion. Disputes continue to exist between multinational corporations and host governments, and these disputes typically involve post-agreement differences between these two sets of actors. Further, these disputes are not random in their occurrence, but, instead, tend to be particularly manifest in certain types of industries. In the 1960s, '70s and '80s, the industries which dominated in disputes between investors and host governments were extractive industries. This is exactly what the obsolescing bargain perspective predicts. Indeed, Vernon introduced the concept of the obsolescing bargain explicitly in an analysis of "The Raw Material Ventures" (Vernon, 1971, p. 46).

Since the 1990s, however, extractive industries are no longer the dominant industry with respect to investment disputes. Now dominant is infrastructure, but infrastructural industries share many similar characteristics with extractive industries. Like in extractive industries, governments of developing countries turn to foreign direct investment because of the capital costs associated with investment.

But also like extractive industries, infrastructural industries present no ongoing source of technology nor significant employment, but exhibit visible foreign control of key sectors of the national economy. When one adds the monopoly status that has characterized some infrastructure projects it becomes clear why the bargains governments enter with foreign infrastructure providers seem much less appropriate once the country has received the capital investment, or capital revenues in the case of privatization.

There is little evidence from an analysis of investment disputes which suggests that bargains no longer tend to obsolesce. What is clear, however, is that there have been significant changes in the way in which obsolescence is handled. This is evident in the significant expansion in the number of investment disputes registered with ICSID. Many developing countries, as a part of their efforts to attract FDI, and in the context of pressure to liberalize FDI regimes, have signed bilateral investment agreements. Typically, these agreements specify that disputes with foreign investors need to be referred to international arbitration, in particular ICSID.

International arbitration may seem to suggest that bargains will not be allowed to obsolesce. But this is not necessarily the case because with infrastructure investment, in particular, there are diverse opinions internationally in relation to the relevance of contract sanctity. These divergent views are relevant to the issue of the obsolescence of an infrastructural bargain in Jamaica.

The Jamaican government's success in renegotiating its telecommunications bargain resulted in large part from the ability of the negotiating team to tap into mixed sentiments about the wisdom of telecommunications monopolies and the sanctity of long-lived monopolistic contracts, in the presence of significant changes in technology in this industry. C&W itself had resisted the monopoly status of British Telecom and, consequently, was concerned about the public relations effects of struggling to hold onto its monopoly status in Jamaica. The Jamaican negotiating team made diplomatic contacts in the UK and in the USA and got indications of support for its efforts to renegotiate with C&W.

The Jamaican government would not have been interested in handling bargain obsolescence in 1999 in the manner that it did in 1974, with its acute learning from the 1974 episode about the negative implications for future investment of unilateral contract abrogation. It is also not likely that the Jamaican government would have received international support for unilateral action. Nevertheless, this is not to suggest that there was no international support for handling bargain obsolescence in a less adversarial manner. The obsolescing bargain has not obsolesced, but there have been changes in the manner in which obsolescence is likely to manifest itself in the twenty-first century.

Transactional versus attitudinal relations in the twenty-first century

Bargains will continue between multinational corporations and host governments in the twenty-first century. And some of these bargains will obsolesce. But obsolescence will not manifest itself in the sweeping expropriations of the 1960s, and it will not take place because host governments have negative attitudes toward foreign investors. The relationship between host governments and multinational corporations will largely be transactional rather than attitudinal. This has already occurred. Host governments that are actively involved in seeking to court investors, and have shifted their orientation toward investors from "red tape to red carpet" (UNCTAD, 2003b) are nevertheless renegotiating existing bargains, particularly in the area of infrastructure investment (Wells and Gleason, 1995; Vernon, 1998).

These renegotiations are not occurring because of negative attitudes toward foreign investors, in general, but because of the particular problems of a specific investment transaction that has gone awry. Further, the renegotiations focus less on issues of ownership and control, and more on issues associated with national policy space: taxation, tariff rates, expansion targets for infrastructure firms, and performance levels.

In an era of general investment and economic liberalization, the issues on which governments and foreign investors are likely to experience contention are not "foreign investment issues" but transactional issues that would apply whether the other party to the transaction were foreign or domestic.

Therein also lie the circumstances under which these transactions are likely to remain intact. Careful preparation on the part of government negotiators, which anticipates changes in industry conditions and recognizes the importance of a vigilant regulatory institutional apparatus for infrastructural investment, will assist in bargain longevity.

This preparation and enhanced negotiating was evident in the contrasting cases of privatizations of telecommunications and electricity in Jamaica. In the poorly negotiated privatization of telecommunications, which granted a fifty-year monopoly, the only reference to performance standards was that "the company shall maintain standards of service which shall be no lower than those prevailing immediately before the date of the license" (Wint, 1996, p. 64).

The privatization of electricity, on the other hand, following a performance-focused period of local management of the electricity company, showed evidence of better knowledge of the industry, careful scrutiny of appropriate performance standards and incentives, and penalties provided in the bargain to ensure compliance with these standards.

To be fair, even in the 1960s and 1970s, bargains became obsolete for transactional as much as attitudinal reasons. For example, the introduction of the bauxite production levy in Jamaica in 1974 was driven partly by the ideological and attitudinal position of the Manley-led People's National Party. But there were significant transactional elements leading to the obsolescence of the agreement.

The minority panelist on the OPIC panel who disagreed with the majority on the appropriateness of Revere's claim for compensation based on expropriatory action stated that "by any reasonable standard, the levy which Revere treated as expropriatory was within the range of the proper taxing power of the Jamaican Government" (Davis, 1995, p. 278). Further, the negotiators commissioned by the Jamaican government, including leading members of the Jamaican private sector and a conservative academic, were hardly avowed socialists.

To be sure, a close reading of Vernon's initial explication of the obsolescing bargain concept (Vernon, 1971) demonstrates that, despite its development in an era of hostile attitudes toward foreign investment, Vernon was as prescient as usual, by focusing on transactional rather than attitudinal factors as the lead causes in the obsolescence of bargains.

With a focus on transactional relations, analyses of bargains between multinational corporations and host governments can be examined through the lens of transaction cost economics. Again, transaction cost economics is also useful in explaining bargains of the past. One of the reasons the Jamaican government shifted from an income tax to a production tax was the fact that it was of the view that alumina companies were being opportunistic, in a Williamsonian sense (Williamson, 1975), when they made significant losses year after year. The Jamaican government established a bauxite commission, a bauxite institute, and sought some level of national ownership of the bauxite industry, in order to reduce the level of information impactedness (Williamson, 1975) that, it felt, stymied its negotiating ability.

Thus, from this perspective, understanding bargaining relationships between multinational corporations and host governments in the twenty-first century is likely best done through an understanding of bargains that have taken place over the last several decades. The future will bring changes. To the extent that economic liberalization continues its likely advance, relations between governments and foreign investors will be less about the foreignness of the investor, and more about the particular transactional circumstances of investments. But, understanding past bargains is a useful way of preparing for the future, because, contrary to the rhetoric, past bargains may also have been more about transactional relationships than is often recognized.

PART IV

Host and home government views of international business

14 | *Global regulatory convergence: the case of intellectual property rights*

RAVI RAMAMURTI

Introduction

Multinational corporations manage relations with governments at different levels – in the home country, at the regional (supranational) level, in host countries, and, from time to time, in a coordinated fashion at the global level (see figure 14.1). The IB literature is quite extensive on MNC relations with host governments but relatively thin on how MNCs manage government relations globally (e.g., Mahini, 1988), even though MNCs have become much more proactive at working through home and host governments to change the context of control, rather than just working within a given context (e.g., see Ramamurti, 2001).[1] In this paper, I focus on one such area, intellectual property (IP) rights, and analyze how one MNC, Pfizer, worked to change the global regulatory environment. Influencing public policy at the global level is for MNCs the ultimate challenge in business–government relations. With global economic interdependence growing, there are stronger incentives for MNCs to seek harmonized global regulations in international trade and investment, and in fields such as accounting, corporate governance, health and safety, and anti-trust.

MNCs pursue global strategies and operate in global industries but the regulations governing their operations are often national or regional in scope. Regulatory heterogeneity demands matching complexity in MNCs' strategies and operations. Just as convergence in tastes worldwide creates opportunities for MNCs to produce globally standardized products, so too convergence of regulations allows MNCs to adopt globally standardized methods of operation, which can lower costs and reduce policy uncertainty.

---

[1] The notion of changing the context of control is borrowed from Pfeffer and Salancik (1978).

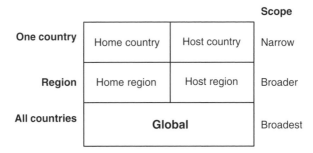

Figure 14.1 Levels of MNC–government relations

But through what process does regulatory heterogeneity give way to regulatory homogeneity? In other words, how does the convergence in regulatory policy happen? Which firms or countries are likely to lead the effort to produce global regulatory convergence? When does convergence take the form of mutual recognition and when does it take the more stringent form of harmonization, i.e., where countries adopt the same standard worldwide? And when convergence takes the form of harmonization, to which standard do countries converge, and why?

I begin with a brief look at the growing literature on global regulatory convergence, including competing views on the best way to achieve that result (Vogel, 1999; Esty and Geradin, 2001). Turning to the specific case of IP, and the landmark TRIPS agreement reached as part of the Uruguay Round trade talks, I analyze why convergence in that area was led by a US pharmaceutical firm (Pfizer) and its long-time CEO Edmund Pratt. This case illustrates at once the struggles involved in producing global regulatory convergence, the role played by MNCs in that process, industry features and company attributes that make certain firms in certain industries more likely to champion regulatory convergence, the role of international institutions in facilitating convergence, and the tactics MNC managers use to change the global business environment. I conclude with generalizations or "hypotheses" about the dynamics of global regulatory convergence.

From regulatory heterogeneity to regulatory homogeneity

The postwar global economy began in a state of regulatory heterogeneity, i.e., each country had its own laws and regulations in any given field. These were likely the product of each country's unique history, priorities, institutions, and economic circumstances. For instance, in a field like intellectual property, poor countries had weak IP laws and still weaker enforcement. Rich countries had stronger IP laws, but still varied greatly among themselves, with the US having perhaps the strongest protections for patents and countries like Canada, Spain, and Italy having relatively weaker laws (Cheek, 2001). In the United States, for instance, protection for creative works and inventions is enshrined in the constitution, whereas in Italy there was at one time no provision for pharmaceutical patents.

From the perspective of individual countries, regulatory heterogeneity has advantages. It allows them to make laws that suit their unique circumstances. For instance, countries that do not generate much intellectual property might prefer a system of lax IP laws that make it easier for local firms to "steal" IP produced in foreign nations. Poor countries used this argument in the context of drugs and pharmaceuticals, so that local firms could produce copycat generics and make health care more affordable. Regulatory heterogeneity also allows countries to use national standards and rules to protect home markets from competing imports, because local firms will readily be in compliance with local laws and regulations while foreign competitors will not be. It also reaffirms the sovereign right of governments to make laws as they see fit. US resistance to international standards/regulations is partly driven by Congressional reluctance to surrender – or at least share – policymaking rights with non-US actors and institutions. Global regulatory convergence also implies that future rulemaking will be done through international negotiation and compromise. A related advantage of regulatory heterogeneity is that national pride is not hurt by the need to discard homegrown laws or standards in favor of foreign laws or standards. Politicians may also worry that acceding to international rulemaking or sharing of national sovereignty makes them look weak to the populace.

On the other hand, regulatory homogeneity has its advantages, especially for MNCs, because it allows them to comply with global regulations at lower cost. The point is illustrated by the example of accounting, where one firm (Roche) estimates that having international accounting standards rather than multiple national or regional standards would save it $100 million a year in compliance costs (Quinn, 2003, p. 16). Similarly, drug firms estimate that international standards for drug testing could reduce substantially the cost and time of introducing new drugs. Thus, one would expect multinational firms to initiate programs to achieve global regulatory convergence. As a corollary, countries that are home to many multinationals might be expected to champion global regulatory convergence. Furthermore, countries championing such convergence might also prefer that rules converge toward their national standards.

Another advantage of regulatory convergence in some cases is that it may be necessary for interconnecting with foreign firms or suppliers. Examples include technical standards for network industries, such as telecommunications, banking, or the internet. Without global standards, countries would have to forgo network economies and reach.

Uni-national firms can be expected to resist regulatory convergence because it would rob them of one competitive advantage vis-à-vis foreign competitors and simultaneously impose the cost of making the transition to the global standard. The global standard could also be sub-optimal from the perspective of every country, because it is not tailored to their unique needs. There can also be substantial transaction costs in negotiating new standards in multilateral or plurilateral forums. Think of the seven years it took to negotiate the Uruguay Round or the delays in launching serious negotiations in the Millennium Round.

Another important question is what kind of regulatory convergence will be achieved. The weakest form is "national treatment," wherein foreign firms are required to be treated as well as local firms but laws are not aligned across countries. A stronger form of convergence occurs when countries make reforms in the right direction without going the whole distance at once, i.e. countries move toward the ideal regulatory system in stages, recognizing that in the medium term some countries will be closer to the ideal than others. In global trade, for instance, countries reduced their tariffs by equal percentages, though not to identical levels, with the expectation that eventually all countries would converge to zero tariffs. Where regulation consists of technical standards (e.g., to protect consumer health/safety or the environment), a halfway arrangement is "mutual recognition": countries maintain different rules but recognize others' tests and certifications as valid for doing business in their own countries. This arrangement risks creating a "race to the bottom," if countries compete for MNC investment by imposing lax standards. The strongest form of convergence is harmonization, that is, when countries adopt nearly identical laws and rules to govern a particular activity. When this occurs, there is the corollary question of whether the common rules are set at the highest prevailing national standard, the lowest prevailing national standard, or some point in between.

Global convergence of IP laws

One of the startling achievements of the Uruguay Round talks was the TRIPS agreement covering intellectual property (IP) rights. Prior to these talks, IP regulation was quite heterogeneous across countries. Many developing countries had very lax rules: for instance, they limited patent protection to a very short period, e.g., five years compared to seventeen in the United States; they recognized process patents but not product patents; they had rules for compulsory licensing that essentially allowed local firms to make patented drugs very soon after they were introduced in rich-country markets. Occasionally, local firms in developing countries like Argentina introduced generic copycats of patented drugs even before multinational firms had introduced their own drugs in the country. IP laws in industrialized countries were generally stronger but not uniformly so. For example, EU nations such as Greece or Italy and countries like Canada had weaker patent laws than did the US or UK. In developing countries, weak IP laws were accompanied by weaker enforcement: piracy of software, movies, books, brands, and trademarks was rampant. US firms lost an estimated $61 billion per year as a result of patent and copyright infringement worldwide (Harvey and Lucas, 1996, p. 77).

The World Intellectual Property Organization (WIPO) was the principal global agency for managing relations between countries on matters relating to IP. WIPO was created in 1967 to administer international treaties relating to copyrights (Berne Convention, negotiated originally in 1886) and industrial property or patents (Paris Convention, adopted originally in 1883). Neither agreement required global convergence of IP laws. They required national treatment but left signatory countries free to frame IP laws as they deemed fit, i.e., regulatory heterogeneity was legitimized by these treaties, making regulatory homogeneity in IP laws that much more difficult to attain.

Yet, at the end of the Uruguay Round, TRIPS provided for harmonization of IP laws in WTO member nations. Industrialized countries were expected to adopt the agreed standard within one year, developing countries were given five years to comply, and the least developed countries were given eleven years to comply. Moreover, IP laws were to converge to the highest prevailing standard, namely, those of the United States, rather than to the lowest standard or to a compromise standard. The breadth of convergence, in terms of the number of countries involved, and the type of convergence (i.e., harmonization to the highest standard), despite enormous differences among the countries involved, makes IP a particularly interesting case of global regulatory convergence.

What made this possible, and what role did MNCs play in the process?

Pfizer's role

By all accounts, one firm (Pfizer) and its CEO (Edmund Pratt, Jr.) played a leading role in bringing this about. For instance, the non-governmental organization, Oxfam, describes Pfizer's role in the TRIPS negotiation as follows:

Pfizer has lobbied vigorously and successfully in support of its commercial interests ... It has close links with government, and its personnel occupy a number of important policy-shaping roles ... It was a driving force in putting intellectual property on the trade agenda and therefore was instrumental in the eventual adoption of TRIPS. ... It has played a leading role in encouraging the US administration to use bilateral negotiations and unilateral economic sanctions against countries that it believes offer inadequate patent protection. (Oxfam, 2001)

A few things are readily apparent about Pfizer: it is a multinational firm, it belongs to the pharmaceutical industry, and it is based in the United States. All three factors were important in explaining why this firm led this fight and did so successfully. I will argue that a firm with only one or even two of these characteristics would not have led the fight; only one with all three characteristics could have done so.

Being multinational was clearly a necessary condition for a firm to champion a fight to strengthen IP laws worldwide. As discussed earlier, only firms operating across several countries are likely to notice – and have to bear – the cost of regulatory heterogeneity. A uni-national firm might fight to change IP laws within its own country, seeking to make them stronger or weaker, depending on whether it was a creator of IP or looking to pirate other firms' IP. But only a multinational firm would try to change the IP laws of other countries, so as to maximize revenues derived from its innovations or to minimize the costs of serving foreign markets. It is also a safe prediction that once a firm has become multinational, it will seek to strengthen IP laws in other countries rather than to weaken them, because IP is one of the most important competitive assets of MNCs (whether it takes the form of proprietary technology, brand names, copyrights, trademarks, or trade secrets).

But not all multinational firms have the same incentive to champion global regulatory convergence. In the case of IP, pharmaceutical firms were prime candidates to lead the charge, because their spending on research outstripped most other MNCs, including those making computers, medical equipment, or other high-technology products. In the 1980s, R&D spending, as a percentage of sales, averaged 18 percent in pharmaceuticals, compared to 4–6 percent in many "high technology" industries. Drug firms spent an average of more than ten years and $231 million on developing new drugs, testing 5,000–10,000 compounds before finding one that was a commercial success (DiMasi, 1991). Blockbuster drugs were few and far between. In contrast, the marginal cost of developing a copycat drug, using a different process than the one patented by the inventing firm, was very low, and manufacturing itself was inexpensive, compared to what the drug might retail for.

A company like IBM may have been a strong candidate to lead the fight to strengthen IP laws worldwide, but it derived most of its profits in the 1980s and earlier from hardware rather than software, and computer hardware was much harder to copy than drugs. Producers of movies or books may have been candidates too, but each faced a different situation from drugs: movies were not easily copied until they became available for home viewing in the video-cassette format and video recorders became widespread (these trends took off only in the late 1980s); books were vulnerable to copying, after photocopiers became widespread, but the publishing industry lacked the clout of IBM or the pharmaceutical firms.

But pharmaceutical firms faced another distinctive circumstance that may have caused them to lead the IP fight. Unlike copyright or trademark violations, where the problem was usually one of lax enforcement in many countries, pharmaceutical firms faced a situation where IP "theft" was actually permitted by law in many countries. Countries like Argentina and India allowed local firms to make copycat drugs within a few years of their invention in rich countries. Thus, drug firms faced an entirely different problem from other IP-based multinationals. Their outrage was that much stronger, and the IP laws of many countries were so egregious that they were good targets for attack and reform.

But did the initiative to reform IP laws worldwide have to come from an *American* pharmaceutical MNC? Why not from one of the eight European pharmaceutical MNCs that in 1991 were among the top twenty pharmaceutical firms worldwide, including three from the UK, two from Switzerland, and three from Germany (*Medical Advertising News*, 1990)? I would argue that only US pharmaceutical firms had a home government powerful enough to lead the fight to change global IP rules. None of the European nations – Switzerland, Germany, or even the United Kingdom – had sufficient leverage over trading partners to force them to reform IP laws, and getting the European Community to act in unison on any issue, including IP, would have been difficult. It might also be argued that by the 1980s the US government was much more receptive to policy advice from the private sector than was the European Commission to similar advice from firms in member countries. The importance of US leverage in trade negotiations becomes apparent when one examines the process by which the TRIPS agreement came to be negotiated.

If one accepts the arguments about why the initiative to harmonize IP laws worldwide had to come from an American pharmaceutical MNC, there is still the question of why Pfizer in particular led that fight. The answer seems to lie in an idiosyncratic factor, namely, the personal commitment and passion that Pfizer's CEO brought to this issue. For more than twenty years, as head of Pfizer, Edmund Pratt tried every method to strengthen IP laws worldwide. Pfizer was neither the largest US pharmaceutical firm nor the biggest spender on pharmaceutical R&D. However, under Pratt's leadership, the firm pursued a strategy that moved it away from being a producer of bulk pharmaceuticals and chemicals to that of a branded ethical drugs firm. Pratt also pursued international expansion vigorously, including strengthening Pfizer's network in developing countries, despite their weak IP laws. In 1990, developing countries accounted for only 10–12 percent of Pfizer's total sales, but Pratt believed these markets had high growth potential and would be increasingly important to the firm. Thus, Pfizer seems to have led the IP reform fight because of Pratt's belief that protecting IP was morally correct, and the new directions in which he was taking Pfizer made global reform of IP laws important to the firm. There is little doubt, though, that his efforts and Pfizer's efforts produced positive externalities for many US and non-US firms in IP-intensive industries. Apparently, the free-rider problem did not deter Pfizer from fighting the fight on behalf of all such firms.

Had Pratt not come along and led this fight, in all likelihood the IP reform battle would have been led by another American multinational firm, probably also in pharmaceuticals, although if the fight had started in the 1990s rather than the 1980s it might have been led by a software firm like Microsoft or by a media/entertainment firm like Disney.

Changing the global IP regime[2]

In retrospect, Pfizer's strategy for strengthening IP laws worldwide had four interesting elements.

Infiltrating policymaking bodies worldwide

Pfizer influenced policymakers at home and abroad by infiltrating policymaking bodies in several countries, including the United States, through its global organization network. Strategy for influencing government policy with respect to IP was centrally planned and coordinated, resembling what Mahini (1988, pp. 27–85) calls the "assertive mode" of managing government relations. Neither intellectual property nor government relations was seen as a specialty field to be surrendered to experts; instead, line management was heavily involved in formulating and implementing strategies in these areas. Specialized staff in the IP and government relations areas worked together rather than in isolation.

In the US, Pfizer executives occupied key positions in industry associations, corporate associations, and advisory committees to the government. Perhaps the most important of these was Pratt's membership on the Advisory Committee on Trade and Policy Negotiations (ACTPN), which, on behalf of US industry, counseled the US Trade Representative on trade issues. From 1981 to 1987, Pratt chaired this important committee. In that capacity, he helped blur the traditional distinction between trade and investment, and brought IP issues to the fore. Pfizer's chief

---

[2] This section draws heavily on facts in Santoro and Paine (1992).

counsel was active in the US Council for International Business, where he chaired the Intellectual Property Committee, and another Pfizer executive headed up its European Community committee. Pfizer's president sat on the board of the US Pharmaceutical Manufacturers Association and President Reagan's Council on Competitiveness. Pfizer executives were also involved with the National Foreign Trade Council and the US Chamber of Commerce.

Overseas, Pfizer's International president chaired the Trade Committee of the Business and Industry Advisory Committee to the OECD. Pfizer executives were involved with US Business Councils in Brazil, India, Mexico, Thailand, and Turkey. In several countries, including France, Germany, Japan, and the United Kingdom, they participated in national Pharmaceutical Manufacturers' Associations. Pfizer was also represented in European Community organizations, including the American Chamber of Commerce in Belgium. Pfizer also established links with think tanks and universities in OECD countries "to strengthen the intellectual foundation for its political efforts" (Santoro and Paine, 1992, p. 8).

Pfizer's top management explicitly worked to raise awareness of IP issues in the countries in which it operated. The government-relations function was woven into the internal management systems for planning, budgeting, and measuring performance. Santoro and Paine note:

The operating plans and budgets developed annually for each operating division also emphasized the importance of public affairs, including intellectual property protection, and identified specific objectives to be accomplished. As a result, country managers in problem countries such as Mexico, Brazil, Korea, Argentina, Indonesia, Taiwan, Thailand, and India worked to build a consensus in favor of intellectual property protection through involvement with local business, professional, academic, and government groups .... Several hundred Pfizer executives around the world spoke up for intellectual property protection through the trade associations and business organizations with which they were affiliated. (p. 8)

Building coalitions, managing fault lines, and leading governments

Pfizer and other MNCs could not have succeeded in changing IP laws without finding like-minded firms in the Triad markets with whom they could form coalitions to influence their respective home governments. The "winners" from stronger IP laws were firms based in the industrialized countries, and the "losers" were firms and consumers in the developing world. Accordingly, a tripartite coalition of business interests from the US, Europe, and Japan emerged that lobbied for IP to be included in the Uruguay Round talks and then made sure their respective governments steadfastly worked to strengthen IP laws worldwide. Any chance of overcoming the predictable opposition from developing countries hinged on the industrialized countries working in unison. That, in turn, hinged on MNCs from the Triad nations being able to reach agreement among themselves on what to aim for in the Uruguay Round talks.

Within the United States, Pfizer teamed up first with IBM and then with eleven other firms to form the Intellectual Property Committee (IPC). The thirteen US firms were leading producers of intellectual property, including firms in pharmaceuticals (Pfizer, Merck, Bristol-Myers, and Johnson and Johnson), computer/software (IBM), office products (Hewlett-Packard), entertainment (Warner Communications), chemicals (Du Pont, Monsanto), and manufacturing (General Electric, General Motors, and Rockwell International). The IPC added breadth and depth to Pfizer's efforts, as member firms added staff and money, and patent-oriented companies teamed up with copyright- and trademark-oriented companies.

The IPC's other great contribution was finding allies on the IP issue in Europe and Japan, and then evolving a common position on issues with those partners. The resulting Tripartite Coalition consisted of the IPC, the *Keidanren* in Japan, and the European Union of Industrial and Employers' Confederations (UNICE). In the first instance, this coalition persuaded the governments of industrialized countries that IP was an important issue to include in the Uruguay Round agenda. The Tripartite Coalition's other major achievement was to hammer out an agreement among the companies involved on the essential elements of any IP agreement resulting from the global negotiations. These principles were enshrined in 1988 in a 100-page document, *The Basic Framework of GATT Provisions on IP Protection: Statement of Views of the European, Japanese and United States Business Communities*. A senior Monsanto executive is reported to have said:

> ... our 'Trilateral Group' was able to distill from the laws of the more advanced countries the fundamental principles for protecting all forms of intellectual property ... Industry identified a major problem in international

trade. It crafted a solution, reduced it to a concrete proposal, and sold it to our own and other governments. The industries and traders of world commerce have played simultaneously the role of patients, the diagnosticians and the prescribing physicians. (*The Guardian*, 2000, quoting writer Vandana Shiva)

But holding the Tripartite Coalition together was apparently not easy. There were fault lines within the IPC, for instance, between firms concerned about strengthening patent rights (e.g., pharmaceutical firms) and those concerned about strengthening copyrights (entertainment and media firms). Likewise, on trade secrets, US and European firms shared common views, because both regions protected trade secrets strongly, but Japan did not. As part of the Tripartite Coalition's negotiations, Japan modified its position and passed a new law on trade secrets. UNICE and IPC were similarly united on treating software as literary works protected by copyright, whereas Japan wanted it treated as a special category and wanted the rules to allow decompilation of programs. On the other hand, Europe and Japan were united against the US that the "priority date" for a patent should be based on "first to file" a patent application rather than "first to invent" a product or process. UNICE and *Keidanren* also objected to the United States' aggressive use of bilateral trade negotiations to extract IP concessions from trading partners.

The interesting point is that these fault lines within the Tripartite Coalition did not rupture into major conflicts that tore apart the coalition. This was either the result of astute management of the coalition by Pfizer, IPC, and others, or, more likely, testimony to the strength of the common interest binding together MNCs from the three regions on the IP issue. Without strong common interests, it may be hard to hold together global coalitions of MNCs, no matter how able the leaders of the coalition. The other interesting point is that the Tripartite Coalition internalized public policy debates that would otherwise have occurred among government officials from the Triad regions. By negotiating a deal among themselves, MNCs from the Triad regions made it easier for their respective governments to arrive at a common position.

Another interesting aspect of the strategy pursued by Pfizer and other US MNCs is that they helped create new roles and institutions to further the IP cause rather than rely solely on existing institutions and forums.

Besides the IPC and the Tripartite Coalition, a very important example of this was using the Advisory Committee on Trade and Policy Negotiations to push for a new position in the USTR's office – that of Assistant USTR for International Investment and Intellectual Property. In one stroke, a powerful voice was created within the US administration that focused exclusively on the issues that Pratt, Pfizer, and other IP-intensive MNCs were purusing.

There was in the longer run a backlash against the success of Pfizer and other MNCs in promoting their interests through the public policy process. It may have added to the fears of consumers, workers, and other interest groups that MNCs were dominating public policymaking, and may have contributed to the mushrooming of non-governmental organizations that claimed to represent disenfranchised groups and countries.

Exploiting US trade leverage

Pratt and Pfizer may have done an outstanding job of advancing their IP agenda, but that alone may not have yielded the results it did if, after 1984, the US had not been willing to use trade leverage to force trading partners to strengthen their domestic laws on intellectual property. In 1984, for the first time, the Trade and Tariff Act gave the US government special powers to retaliate against countries that did not provide adequate IP protection for US companies (Section 301). Using this new threat, Korea was induced in 1986 to sign a bilateral agreement on intellectual property. In 1988, the Omnibus Trade and Competitiveness Act created the Special 301 provisions under which the intellectual property laws of US trading partners were scrutinized annually and the worst offenders identified for possible retaliatory action. These new provisions were used to change IP laws in Mexico, Thailand, Philippines, Brazil, and China, to name a few countries. Without the demonstrated willingness of the US to use these provisions to shut out of the American market trading partners who had weak IP laws, it is unlikely that developing countries would have agreed to include intellectual property in the Uruguay Round talks (Croome, 1999). The Hobson's choice they faced was to either negotiate IP issues with the US in the GATT forum or to do so one-on-one as part of a Section 301 proceeding.

Pratt and Pfizer recognized the enormous leverage that Section 301 provisions gave them in their negotiations with developing countries.

That was one reason the *Basic Framework* document produced by the Tripartite Coalition in 1988 laid out high minimum standards for any deal reached through GATT. The authors of that document preferred no deal to enshrining in GATT a weak IP regime, because, at least for US firms, it would have set a bad precedent for other agreements that were under negotiation, such as preferential trade deals (e.g., NAFTA) or bilateral deals that might be negotiated under the threat of Section 301. Interestingly, US ability to go it alone on IP issues, using the Section 301 provisions, also gave US firms an edge in their negotiations within the Tripartite Coalition, because neither European nor Japanese MNCs could expect their governments to be as effective in extracting concessions from developing countries.

Forum-switching: from WIPO to GATT

A final point about how the IP regime changed worldwide is that the global institution specifically meant for IP, namely the WIPO, proved an ineffective forum for negotiating regulatory changes. When industrialized countries tried to strengthen IP laws through WIPO, they found themselves out-voted by developing countries, which were quite content with the existing system that gave countries regulatory autonomy and only demanded national treatment. Multinational firms like Pfizer and their home governments then engaged in "forum switching," that is, shifting the arena in which global IP negotiations were conducted, from WIPO to GATT. Although in GATT, as in WIPO, decisions were made by consensus, and every country had one vote, and developing countries outnumbered industrialized countries, GATT had the advantage that IP issues could be linked to other issues of interest to developing countries, such as agriculture, textiles, and the dispute-settlement processes.

An important implication for MNCs is that they must select carefully the international institution in which to engage in policy bargaining. Where the gains from regulatory convergence are likely to be shared by all countries, a specialized forum can work; this seems to be true, for example, in the case of international accounting standards, where much of the work has been done through the International Accounting Standards Board (Gornik-Tomaszewski and McCarthy, 2003). But, if as in the case of IP the gains are lop-sided, with unequal benefits going to industrialized and developing countries, a multi-issue forum may be more appropriate. Hence the eagerness of industrialized countries to expand the World Trade Organization's agenda to include environmental and labor standards, rather than working through specialized agencies like the International Labor Organization, and the unwillingness of developing countries to allow it.

Conclusions/hypotheses

1. As global players, MNCs are natural leaders for promoting global convergence of regulations. However, the impetus for harmonizing regulations worldwide in any given area is likely to come from MNCs in those industries and from those countries that would benefit the most from it and that *ex ante* have the greatest likelihood of succeeding in the effort. In the case of IP, in the 1980s, American pharmaceutical firms were prime candidates to strengthen laws to protect IP.

2. MNCs must (and do) work through home and host governments to bring about global convergence of regulations, using international institutions as forums in which the global rules, and a transition plan for getting to them worldwide, are hammered out.

3. The United States plays a pivotal role in the convergence process because it is home to many multinationals and its government has more leverage than any other to push forward proposals for global convergence. Its leverage comes, among other things, from its ability and willingness to deny access to the US market for countries that do not cooperate with US efforts to change global regulations (e.g., using Section 301 provisions of US trade law). For the same reason, the US may have a veto over the process, because regulatory convergence that does not include the United States may not be worth seeking to the rest of the world. It follows that global regulations, when they do emerge, are likely to mirror US regulations and standards to a substantial degree.

4. To succeed in changing global regulations, MNCs must form broad coalitions of like-minded firms in their home country as well as across the Triad markets of North America, Europe, and Japan, which, in 2000, were home to 430 of the world's 500 largest multinational firms (Rugman and Verbeke, 2004). Achieving agreement among the leading firms in the Triad markets makes it more likely that governments in the Triad will reach agreement among

themselves. Any proposal for global convergence has a higher likelihood of moving forward if the US and the EU see eye to eye on the matter.

5. After the United States, the EU is probably the most important bloc that can promote or block global convergence. The EU's strength lies in its economic role in the global economy, if and when it can speak with one voice. Its accumulated experience in negotiating regulatory convergence within the EU bloc, starting with the Single European Act of 1985, is also a major strength. EU-wide standards, where they do exist, should be formidable alternatives to US standards. This was not the case with IP, but appears to be the case with respect to, say, accounting standards, where the EU will be switching to international accounting standards in 2005 (Quinn, 2003).

6. The tools available to MNCs to influence public policy in their own countries include industry associations that advocate their points of view (lobbying) and representation in important government committees or advisory boards that shape home-government strategy and policy. MNCs can also influence public policy in foreign markets by motivating subsidiary managers to pursue public affairs goals through the planning and budgeting systems, and by measuring and rewarding achievements in this area. Specific avenues for influencing host countries include taking a leadership role in local industry associations, in business councils (that link, say, US firms with local firms through a US–Host Country Business Council), and in associations of multinational firms from the same country (US Chamber of Commerce in Host Country X), or the association of MNCs from all countries operating in that host country. Umbrella forums, such as the Transatlantic Business Dialog, hold great promise as venues in which new opportunities for regulatory convergence can be discussed among firms from the US and the EU (Stern, 1997).

7. An important lesson from the IP case study is that managers of multinationals must also be prepared to create new institutions, forums, and coalitions to further their agendas, and not rely solely on existing institutions and forums.

8. Another lesson from the IP case study is that only when all countries stand to gain from regulatory convergence in a particular area can a specialized international institution be used to achieve convergence. Where the gains of convergence are lop-sided, as they were in IP,

regulatory convergence may have to be attempted through a multi-issue institution in which bargaining across several issues can be used to even out costs and benefits for all countries. This was one of GATT's advantages over WIPO, along with its stronger enforcement measures available via the WTO's dispute settlement mechanism.

9. If the IP example is typical, global convergence can take twenty or more years of negotiation, followed by ten or more years in transition time after a deal has been struck. The jury is still out on how committed developing countries are to the new IP regime. As illustrated by the example of drugs, especially in the context of the AIDS epidemic, developing countries have wanted to dilute the TRIPS deal, even as multinationals have sought to promote TRIPS-Plus regimes. Once again, US multinationals are using US trade leverage to advance TRIPS-Plus regimes in new bilateral agreements with small countries like Singapore, Chile, and Australia.

10. Another lesson from Europe's experience with convergence of drug testing rules (Vogel, 1999), the WTO's success in promoting agreements on e-commerce, or WIPO's work in copyrighting digital works (Cheek, 2001), is that global convergence may be easier in emerging fields, where no standards as yet exist, than in pre-existing fields (such as IP). Therefore, industries and businesses that emerge in today's globalized economy may see their regulations converging faster than historical experience would suggest.

11. The growing ability of MNCs to set the policy and reform agenda for home and host governments has produced a predictable backlash among consumers, workers, and other stakeholders that feel disenfranchised in comparison. The NGO movement is therefore partly of the MNCs' own making. It would be interesting to see if there are parallels between the global policy influence of MNCs today and the notion of "regulatory capture" that was advanced in the 1970s and 1980s to describe the power of regulated firms in the US over their regulatory masters.

15 | Regional multinationals and government policy: the end of global strategy and multilateralism

ALAN M. RUGMAN

Introduction

The interaction between multinational enterprises (MNEs) and the governments of nation-states has been studied for over thirty years, going back to the classic analysis of Vernon (1971). The interaction between MNEs and home and host governments has been further developed by Stopford and Strange (1991) in a model of triangular economic diplomacy. The entire development of a scholarly field known as international political economy takes as its focus the interactions between MNEs and States. What can be added to this literature?

The answer is new evidence that MNEs operate predominately on a regional basis, rather than on a global basis as many earlier studies have assumed. Yet, rather than MNEs operating across borders around the world, the evidence, e.g., in Rugman (2000), is that the vast majority of MNEs have as much as 80 percent of their sales within their home region. Further, these "Triad" regions of the EU, North America, and Asia account for well over 90 percent of all MNE activity (as revealed by sales, or assets, or employees). Thus a focus on regionalization is now required to analyze states and firms.

The issues to be explored in this chapter are the following:

1. Given the new evidence on the economic interdependence within each region of the Triad, is this being facilitated by regional or multilateral trade agreements? The EU is much more of an integrated common market than the looser free trade agreements of the North American Free Trade Association (NAFTA), the Free Trade Association of the Americas (FTAA), and the Asian Agreement of November 2002. Do international agreements really matter when 56 percent of all Asian trade was already intra-regional in 2001, before a formal trade agreement was announced?

2. With the trend toward increasing regionalism, is the WTO doomed? The United States is now negotiating many bilateral trade agreements, and it is not as focused on the WTO. The EU and United States still disagree over agricultural subsidies; China still has difficulty in respecting intellectual property; the dispute settlement system at the WTO is being challenged not only by governments, but also by NGOs, especially environmentalists (Rugman, Kirton, and Soloway, 1999; Kobrin, 1998). Brazil, India, China, and other mid-range economies, on behalf of the "poorer" countries, largely destroyed the current WTO round at Cancún in October 2003. The agenda of the civil society has targeted the WTO but largely neglected regional trade agreements, except for Mexico's role in NAFTA. Can the small staff of 300 people at the WTO deliver on multilateralism when they are vastly outnumbered by the EU bureaucracy and a growing NAFTA-based set of environmental and labor/human rights institutions?

3. How do MNEs and states actually interact today on a regional and multilateral basis? Are MNEs beginning to develop "regional" strategies instead of "global" ones? Do states understand this new emphasis?

Regional, not global, business

This chapter investigates the current interaction between states and firms within the institutional context of international trade and investment agreements. The basic logic of the chapter is that, today, MNEs largely operate within their home–Triad markets, or, at best, are bi-regional (competing only across two of the Triads of the EU, NAFTA, and Asia). Few MNEs are "global," and thus few MNEs are really interested in multinational trade and investment agreements. Instead, today, most of the largest 500 MNEs are interested in the deepening of regional agreements in Europe, the Americas, and Asia.

The data to support the regional nature of MNE activity are now becoming better understood. At an aggregate level they show that the majority of trade of the Triad is intra-regional (62 percent in the EU; 56.7 percent in NAFTA, and 56 percent in Asia) (Rugmans, 2000). The trend toward intra-regional trade has been increasing over the last twenty years. In addition, foreign direct investment (FDI) is mainly undertaken between the EU and NAFTA, or is intra-regional within each region of the Triad. There is relatively little FDI on a multilateral basis. The economic picture is one of increasing regionalization and decreasing "globalization" (Rugman, 2000; Rugman and Verbeke, 2004). This indicates that there is increasing economic interdependence both within each region of the Triad, and also between the regions of the Triad.

At the micro-firm level the evidence of regionalism is even stronger. Briefly, of the largest 500 corporations in the world, 320 of the 380 for which geographic sales data are available have, on average, 80 percent of their sales in their home region of the Triad. For example, the world's largest company, Wal-Mart, has 94 percent of its sales in NAFTA. Of the other top thirty companies, General Motors has 81 percent in NAFTA; Mitsubishi has 87 percent in Asia; Mitsui has 79 percent in Asia; TotalFinaElf has 56 percent in Europe; Allianz has 78 percent in Europe; VW has 68 percent in Europe; Deutsche Bank has 63 percent in Europe; and Crédit Suisse has 61 percent in Europe. Of the 380 companies for which data are available, only nine are "global" in the sense of having at least 20 percent of their sales in each region of the Triad and less than 50 percent in their home region. These are mainly MNEs in electronics such as IBM, Sony, Philips, Nokia, Intel, Canon, and Flextronics. The others are Coca-Cola and LVMH. There are also twenty-five of the "bi-regional" MNEs with at least 20 percent of sales in two of these regions of the Triad. These include: Toyota, Nissan, DaimlerChrysler, Honda, AstraZeneca, GlaxoSmithKline, Ericsson, Diageo, Michelin, etc. Overall, there are incredibly few truly global firms, and most MNEs operate mainly in the home region of the Triad (Rugman and Verbeke, 2003, 2004). These data are discussed in more detail in a section below.

Regional trade agreements

From the viewpoint of the state, we observe a greater emphasis by trade experts and trade negotiators to facilitate regional agreements than to complete the Doha Round of the World Trade Organization. Recently the following examples of events leading to regional integration occurred:

a. The EU agreed to a list of ten accession countries in Central and Eastern Europe, to join the EU in mid-2004. In Brussels, a vast bureaucracy of many thousands labors to deepen the economic, social, cultural, political, and financial integration of the EU. Over 2003, a new Constitution for the EU was developed.

b. In November 2002, in Quito, Ecuador, trade ministers for thirty-four countries agreed to continue to negotiate the terms and conditions for a Free Trade Agreement of the Americas (FTAA), first accepted by them, in principle, at the Quebec City Summit of April 2001. These meetings continued in Miami in November 2003 although no agreement occurred in Trinidad in October 2003. The FTAA is due to start in early 2005, and the implementing committee is co-chaired by the United States and Brazil. The FTAA builds on the twin principles of tariff reduction and national treatment of foreign direct investment established in NAFTA (Rugman, 1994).

c. On November 4, 2002, the ten members of ASEAN economies agreed to a new trade and investment agreement with China. This may well be expanded to include Japan and South Korea. Throughout 2003, a set of bilateral trade agreements were negotiated by Asian countries.

One of the arguments in Rugman (2000) was the prediction that economic multilateralism, especially in the form of the WTO, would be challenged by the logic of regional integration. Obviously, in the last three years this prediction has been confirmed. Between Seattle in 1999 and Cancún in 2003, the WTO has failed to develop a consensus for further trade liberalization, and the future success of the WTO is now in doubt. In contrast, over this period, the EU has moved toward greater political and social integration, and it has even developed a draft Constitution. Ten new members entered in 2004. In Asia, many bilateral and other intra-regional trade agreements have been signed and implemented. The FTAA meeting in Miami in November 2003 kept the Americas moving toward implementation of the full FTAA in 2005.

The evidence from economic diplomacy shows that regional agreements are still being developed whereas multilateralism has slowed down. It is important that managers be realistic about these developments and focus strategic decisions more at regional than global level. We are now seeing a greater congruence between the economic reality of regionalization and the political nature of regional rather than global agreements.

In Spring 2003, the war in Iraq illustrated the military power of the US hegemon, operating in a world where most European countries (except for the UK) were not supportive of the war and Asian countries (with the primary exceptions of Japan and Australia) were also critical of the US military power. The result of the war will likely be to reinforce regional economic policies, at the expense of multilateral institutions, (especially the United Nations and the WTO). The United States already exports 37 percent of its goods and services to its NAFTA partners and its trade with Canada alone exceeds US exports to all fifteen member states of the EU. In terms of energy, the United States already obtains the majority of its oil and gas from the Americas, and this regional self-sufficiency is likely to increase as security concerns remain. This issue is also discussed in a section below in more detail.

Regional economic determinism in the Triad

The importance of economic-based regionalization in the Triad, and the lack of globalization, is now reflected in political alignments. Following the definitive change to US political attitudes toward national security after the September 11, 2001 terrorist attacks, a new world political system is emerging. This is based on the Triad reality of regionalization.

The United States already has a significant degree of economic security on a regional basis. This was affirmed by the NAFTA agreement of 1994 (Rugman, 1994). Now Canada and Mexico supply energy and other natural resources to the United States in exchange for the enhanced business access to the world's single largest and richest market. NAFTA does not provide the depth of economic integration of the EU, and it has none of its political and currency integration. Yet it ties together these three economies in a gigantic and highly successful free trade area to the mutual economic benefit of all three partners.

So successful is NAFTA in terms of increased intra-regional trade that it is in the process of being expanded to the FTAA in 2005. This will bring all thirty-four countries of the Americas into an extension of NAFTA. The US economy will serve as the regional regime for growth and renewed prosperity for the states of Latin America and the Caribbean, just as NAFTA has done for Mexico.

The economic data on NAFTA show ever increasing interdependence in trade and FDI. Table 15.1 shows that intra-regional trade has increased from 49 percent to 56 percent between 1997 and 2000. Today the United States has 22.6 percent of its exports going to Canada

Table 15.1 Intra-regional trade in the Triad, 1980–2000

	Intra-regional exports (%)		
YEAR	EU	NAFTA	ASIA
2000	62.1	55.7	55.7
1997	60.6	49.1	53.1
1980	52.1	33.6	35.3

Source: IMF, 2002 and OECD, 2002.

and 14.1 percent to Mexico, for a total of 36.7 percent. It only has 21.3 percent to all fifteen member states of the EU. The United States is now a regional player in terms of trade. Similar data exist for FDI. In addition, at firm level, the 169 US firms in the list of the world's largest 500 firms have an average of 77.3 percent of all their sales within NAFTA. Of course, Canada and Mexico are more than pulling their weight on intra-regional trade. Canada has 87 percent of its exports to the United States; Mexico has 88.7 percent.

Table 15.1 also demonstrates that Europe and Asia are becoming increasingly regionalized. Intra-regional trade in the EU increased from 60.6 percent to 62 percent over the 1997–2001 period. In Asia, even without a formal trade agreement across the region, the intra-regional trade increased from 53.1 percent to 55.7 percent. Intra-regional FDI increases from 36 percent in 1986 to 46 percent in 1999 in the EU. In Asia intra-regional FDI increased from 20.5 percent in 1986 to 26.2 percent in 1999.

Regionalism is now the dominant economic force. As a direct corollary to this trend, there is even less trade between the Triad blocks. Elsewhere I have shown that the blocks are closing and becoming more inward looking and less global over time (Rugman, 2000). Indeed, there has been increasing regionalization over the last twenty to thirty years, not increasing globalization, as shown by trade and FDI data (Rugman, 2000). This economic reality is now being reflected in politics.

Analysis of the failure of the UN Security Council, in February 2003, to endorse a second resolution to authorize US-led military action in Iraq shows that the trans-Atlantic political relationships now reflect the broken economic one. Only the UK actually has any significant economic interest in North America. This is now through FDI (not trade) since the UK now has a majority of its trade with its EU partners. As shown in Rugman and Kudina (2002), the UK now has about 40 percent of its outward stock of FDI in North America. This is matched by a similar inward stock. In contrast, Germany and France have most of their FDI within the EU, not across the Atlantic.

Today the economic lenses of France and Germany are inward looking. Only the UK still needs a political alliance with the United States to match its economic interest. The political support of Spain and Italy for the United States in Iraq reflects more on internal EU politics than on any long-term economic affiliation of these states with the United States. Basically the EU now represents, as a block, an economic alternative to North America. The European-based MNEs have 80 percent of their sales within Europe. European business does not really need America, just as America does not need Europe, as there is relatively little inter-block trade.

All of this economic analysis also works for Asia. This region is becoming more interdependent, and it has almost identical intra-regional growth in trade and FDI to match its major Triad partners of North America and Europe. Again, most of the sales of Asian-based MNEs are within the Asian region (see table 15.1). This trend is increasing.

The world political picture is also one of expanding regionalism. The EU admitted ten new members in 2004 and will admit ten in a few years' time. NAFTA will extend from three nations to thirty-four in the FTAA by 2005. Asia, China, Japan, and South Korea will develop stronger ties with the ASEAN countries. The basic strategy of any business outside the triad is that it needs to become affiliated to a triad region to grow and succeed. Firms inside a triad region will continue to grow intra-regionally.

The Iraq war of 2003 simply reflects the economic reality of the Triad. The United States, as a hegemon, does not need support from the leading countries in Europe or Asia. It does not even need it from its NAFTA partners, both of whom made the mistake of not supporting the United States in its political hour of need. This was not smart policy when they are both totally dependent on the United States for economic success. This serious political mistake is unlikely to be repeated by the new Canadian Prime Minister, Paul Martin, or tolerated again by business interests in Mexico.

What is the role of France, Germany, Italy, the UK, Russia, and Japan after the Iraq war? Except for the UK all have demonstrated their military irrelevancy in world politics. Only the United States matters. Perhaps Canada will seek to re-align itself to US policy leadership as soon as possible. The UK–US relationship is strong, and it provides the UK with independent leverage across the EU and all of Europe. France has largely destroyed its ability to influence US policy. It now ranks below Russia as a political US ally. Germany ranks below Italy. The United States is unlikely to look to the G8 for any military or political alliance in the near future. It does not need the G8 as much as the G8 needs the United States.

The regional multinationals

The regional nature of multinational business is demonstrated in table 15.2. It reports the intra-regional sale of the twenty-five largest home-region based MNEs. The world's largest company is Wal-Mart. It has 94.1 percent of its sales in North America; it is not a global company. General Motors has 81 percent of its sales in North America; it is not global either. Ford has 66.7 percent in North America and 21.9 percent in Europe. It would be classified as bi-regional if it did not still have the majority of its sales in its home region. The rest of the table is interesting reading; the world's largest companies are not global, but home-region based.

   Table 15.3 only reported the largest twenty-five of a set of 320 firms with a majority of the sales in their home region. These 320 firms have an average of 80 percent of sales in their home region, whether this is North American, European, or Asian. Of the world's largest 500 firms, there are no geographic sales data for 134, leaving 366 with data. Of these, 320 form this group of home-region firms. A set of twenty-five are bi-regional, with 20 percent of sales in two regions of the Triad, and less than 50 percent in their home region. Only nine firms out of the top 500 are global, with at least 20 percent of their sales in each region of the Triad. These data are reported in table 15.3.

   The largest service companies appear even less global than manufacturing companies. Of the 500 largest firms, 280 are in services. In retail, only one of the forty-nine retail firms in the top 500 is global (Louis Vuitton Moët Hennessy), and only five are bi-regional (Rugman and Girod, 2003). In banking, all the 500 companies have the vast majority of their assets in the home region, e.g., Citigroup has 80 percent of its assets in North America. Insurance is even more local.

Table 15.2 The top twenty-five home region-based companies

	500 Rank	Company	Region	Revenues in bn US$	Foreign/ total sales	North America % of total sales	Europe % of total sales	Asia Pacific % of total sales
1	1	Wal-Mart Stores (q)	North America	219.8	16.3	94.1	4.8	0.4
2	3	General Motors	North America	177.3	25.5	81.1	14.6	na
3	5	Ford Motor	North America	162.4	33.3	66.7	21.9	na
4	9	General Electric	North America	125.9	40.9	59.1	19.0	9.1
5	12	Mitsubishi	Asia Pacific	105.8	13.2	5.4	1.7	86.8
6	13	Mitsui	Asia Pacific	101.2	34.0	7.4	11.1	78.9
7	15	TotalFinaElf	Europe	94.3	na	8.4	55.6	na
8	17	Itochu	Asia Pacific	91.2	19.1	5.5	1.7	91.2
9	18	Allianz	Europe	85.9	69.4	17.6	78.0	4.4
10	21	Volkswagen	Europe	79.3	72.3	20.1	68.2	5.3
11	22	Siemens	Europe	77.4	78.0	30.0	52.0	13.0
12	23	Sumitomo	Asia Pacific	77.1	12.7	4.8	na	87.3
13	24	Philip Morris	North America	72.9	42.1	57.9	25.8	na

Table 15.2 *The top twenty-five home region-based companies* (continued)

500 Rank	Company	Region	Revenues in bn US$	Foreign/ total sales	North America % of total sales	Europe % of total sales	Asia Pacific % of total sales
14	25	Marubeni	Asia Pacific	71.8	28.2	11.6	na	74.5
15	26	Verizon Communications	North America	67.2	3.8	96.2	na	na
16	27	Deutsche Bank	Europe	66.8	69.0	29.3	63.1	6.5
17	28	E.ON	Europe	66.5	43.4	9.4	80.1	na
18	29	US Postal Service	North America	65.8	3.0	97.0	na	na
19	30	AXA (q)	Europe	65.6	77.3	24.1	51.2	19.9
20	31	Crédit Suisse	Europe	64.2	73.3	34.9	60.9	4.1
21	32	Hitachi	Asia Pacific	63.9	31.0	11.0	7.0	80.0
22	34	American International Group	North America	62.4	na	59.0	na	na
23	35	Carrefour	Europe	62.2	50.8	na	81.3	6.6
24	36	American Electric Power	North America	61.3	12.3	87.7	11.8	na
25	39	Duke Energy	North America	59.5	13.1	96.5	na	na

Table 15.3 Classification of the top 500 MNEs

Type of MNE	No. of MNEs	% of 500	% of 380	Average % of intra-regional sales
Global	9	2.0	2.6	38.3
Bi-regional	25	5.0	6.6	42.0
Host region oriented	11	2.2	2.9	30.9
Home region oriented	320	64.0	84.2	80.3
Insufficient data	15	2.8	3.7	40.9
No data	120	24.0		NA
TOTAL	500	100.0	100.0	

Source: Calculations by the author from Annual Reports and websites of the world's largest 500 companies, ranked by revenues for 2001.

Even knowledge-intensive service industries are largely local. For example, professional service firms – such as law firms, consultants, accountants, etc., are usually embedded in local clusters, with partners being largely immobile and their loose networks being, at best, regionally based.

Basic theory suggests that the potential for scope economies resulting from the transfer of non-location-bound FSAs is usually lower in service firms. This is due to the impossibility of separating the upstream and downstream segments of the value chain (inseparability of production and delivery). This implies that regional-market responsiveness at the downstream end is only possible if innovation at the upstream end is also decentralized. In other words, decentralization of decision-making power to the regional level may require that large sets of decisions be delegated to that level, and this is usually associated with high, location-specific adaptation investments.

In the future, due to this regional business integration, the United States and US MNEs will be better placed to achieve their goals of economic and national security by a regional focus on NAFTA and the FTAA. It is apparent that most European nations and European MNEs still fail to understand the long-run political implications of September 11, 2001. Now the United States places national security first. The Iraq war was not for oil, or even for energy security, but to reduce future terrorist threats such as another September 11th, possibly involving weapons of mass destruction. The United States is at war with terrorism, and it will continue to attack governments that help to foster terrorism when this threatens US national security interests. The United States has no interest in multilateralism, given this overarching domestic security objective. The G8 members need to understand the new US concern over its own security and work with it to enhance US security.

Ultimately, the United States does not need to use multilateral agencies such as the United Nations or even the WTO. The huge US economy, now complemented by NAFTA and with the likely prospect of a FTAA, provides the United States with economic security, including energy security. But it still needs national security. Future policies will lead to tighter border inspections, more difficult landing and visiting requirements for immigrants, and a growing fortress North America. The internal market of NAFTA may then deepen, driven by MNEs and business interests, partly along the lines of the old EC, with a common immigration policy and border inspections across NAFTA. Canada has already signaled its support for such integrated border measures, and it will thereby become further integrated with the United States. The rest of the G8 will become outsiders; regional interests will dominate multilateral ones.

Security and regional US energy supply

The importance of NAFTA, and a potential FTAA, is highly relevant to the United States in terms of energy security. Despite the widespread popular feeling that the US-led military action in Iraq in March 2003 was due to Iraq's oil, there is no economic logic to support this belief.

The United States has 57.2 percent of all its oil produced within NAFTA. It produces 41 percent of its own consumption internally and imports another 16.3 percent from its two NAFTA partners. Another 9.2 percent comes from Venezuela and Colombia, so about two-thirds of all US oil consumption is from the Americas. The United States does not need oil from Iraq. Indeed, it only consumes 13.9 percent of all of its oil from all the states in the Persian Gulf, i.e., Bahrain, Iraq, Kuwait, Qatar, Saudi Arabia, and the UAE. Even though this area has large oil reserves, there are similarly large oil reserves in Canada (in the Athabaska tar sands but at a higher cost of development), so this position of oil security is not likely to be threatened for many years.

Table 15.4 US consumption of petroleum, by country of origin, 2001

	2001 thousand barrels per day	% of total
United States	8,031	40.9
Canada	1,786	9.1
Mexico	1,423	7.2
North America	11,240	57.2
Venezuela	1,538	7.8
Colombia	280	1.4
Persian Gulf	2,731	13.9
Others	3,861	19.6
TOTAL	19,650	100.0

While the Persian Gulf states, through control of OPEC, can influence the world price of oil, the United States can move to ensure safe supplies of oil on a long-range basis through regional sourcing.

In strictly economic terms Iraq and the rest of the Middle East is of minimal importance to the United States. Although the United States has free trade agreements with Israel and Jordan, total trade to these areas is under 1 percent of its trade. In contrast, the United States has 37 percent of its trade with its NAFTA partners. In short, Iraq does not matter to North America. It may matter to Europe and Asia, but that is a different issue.

In terms of consumption of oil the United States produces 41 percent of its total needs. Another 9.1 percent comes from Canada and 7.2 percent from Mexico as can be seen in table 15.4. Thus, the NAFTA region supplies 57.2 percent of all the oil required by the United States. A further 7.8 percent comes from Venezuela and 1.4 percent from Colombia, so as much as 66.4 percent of all the oil consumed in the United States is from the Americas. The Persian Gulf as a whole only supplies 13.9 percent of all US oil. These data are reported in table 15.4.

In terms of imports of oil in 2001 by the United States (remembering that it produces 41 percent of its consumption itself) the Persian Gulf supplies 23.5 percent of all US imports. Yet this is lower than the NAFTA partners of the United States, as Canada supplies 15.4 percent and Mexico 12.2 percent of all US oil imports (a total of 27.6 percent from

Table 15.5 US petroleum imports

	2001 thousand barrels per day	% of total
Canada	1,786	15.4
Mexico	1,423	12.2
North America	3,209	27.6
Venezuela	1,538	13.2
Colombia	280	2.4
Persian Gulf	2,731	23.5
Others	3,861	33.2
TOTAL	**11,619**	100.0

Note: Persian Gulf = Bahrain, Iran, Iraq, Kuwait, Qatar, Saudi Arabia, and United Arab Emirates.
Source: 1981–2000 – EIA, Petroleum Supply Annual, annual reports.
2001 – EIA, Petroleum Supply Monthly (February 2002).

these two neighbors). In addition, Venezuela supplies 13.2 percent and Colombia 2.4 percent, so a total of 43.2 percent of all US oil imports are from the Americas. These data are reported in table 15.5.

Looking at US oil import data for 2002 confirms this picture of regional dependence. Between 2001 and 2002, oil imports from Canada increased from 15.4 percent to 17.1 percent and those from Mexico from 12.2 percent to 13.4 percent, i.e., NAFTA imports increased from 27.6 percent to 30.5 percent. Another 14.4 percent come from Venezuela and Colombia (down from 15.6 percent in 2001). By 2002, US oil imports from all of the Persian Gulf had fallen to 22.0 percent (from 23.5 percent in 2001).

Implications of regionalization for business–government relations

The implications of MNE activity for societal welfare and public policy have been the subject of a particularly large and varied literature in economics and political science (Rugman and Verbeke, 1998). Regional trade and investment agreements have also been studied extensively, especially in the context of North American and European integration processes, as discussed earlier in this chapter. Much of the relevant literature has focused on two issues. First, the gains from regional free trade – the issue of trade creation versus trade diversion, whereby insiders and outsiders may be affected differently by a regional integration program. Second, the relative merits of regionalization versus multilateralism, such as through the General Agreement on Tariffs and Trade (GATT) and the WTO.

Rugman and Verbeke (2004) show that regionalism is an efficient substitute for ill-functioning multilateral institutions in terms of economic outcomes. Regional integration (with only a limited number of participants that are geographically close) is working better than the multilateral integration process requiring concession of all the 144 countries in the WTO. Regional clusters now drive regional integration. It reflects bottom-up efforts by a multitude of economic actors, who wish to expand their geographical business horizon, guided by immediate opportunities that are geographically close and associated with low transaction costs, as well as a high potential for agglomeration economies. This has been confirmed in NAFTA for autos and chemicals (Rugman, Kirton, and Soloway, 1999). In the long run, such agglomeration, in the sense of improved "regional diamond conditions" may improve the MNEs' capabilities to penetrate other Triad markets (Rugman and Verbeke, 2004).

Future research now needs to pay attention to the MNE as the appropriate unit of analysis in regional integration. Each firm's regional integration preferences and role will depend upon its FSA configuration, much in line with its preferences regarding trade and investment protection at the national level. These preferences may even vary from business to business in a single firm (Rugman and Verbeke, 2004). As implied by earlier sections of this chapter, the main question for the MNE is to assess how regional integration may reduce the need for location-specific adaptation investments in the various national markets, when expanding the geographic scope of activities.

Rather than merely analyzing macroeconomic or sectoral data, there is a rich avenue of work to be pursued on firm-level adaptation processes to regional integration, with a focus on the region-specific adaptation investments needed to link the MNEs' existing FSAs (non-location-bound and location-bound ones) with the regional-location advantages, and on the nature of these investments (internal development versus external acquisition) (Rugman and Verbeke, 2004). An analysis of such new knowledge development in MNEs may be critical to understand fully the societal effects of increased regionalization.

The impacts of regional trading agreements have often been interpreted in terms of changes in entry barriers facing insiders and outsiders, at the macro, industry, and strategic-group levels. From a resource-based perspective, however, there is a real need to understand how regional integration processes affect the creation or elimination of isolating mechanisms, and thereby economic performance, at the level of individual MNEs and subunits within MNEs.

Regional integration also has implications for knowledge exchange, as it is likely to increase the geographic reach of MNE networks in terms of backward and forward linkages, and even the MNEs' broader flagship networks (Rugman and D'Cruz, 2000). To the extent that such linkages and networks are associated with knowledge diffusion spillovers, these should also be taken into account in any analysis of the regional integration welfare effects.

Finally, regional integration can have an impact on the MNE's internal distribution of resources and FSAs; more specifically, firm-level investments in regional adaptation often imply the relocation of specific production facilities to the most efficient subunits, in order to capture regional scale economies and a reassessment of subsidiary charters. This implies to some extent a zero sum game with "winning" and "losing" subsidiaries.

Interestingly, it has also been observed that regional integration may energize subsidiaries to start new initiatives and to develop new capabilities (Rugman and Verbeke, 2001). This really implies a non-zero sum game, again with macro-level welfare improvements as an outcome. Will the deepening of a regional trading block, even if it has positive net welfare effects inside the region and at the world level, strengthen the affected insider MNEs in other legs of the Triad? Or will it, on the contrary, act as an incentive to focus these MNEs' resource allocation processes and market expansion plans even more on intra-regional growth opportunities? The empirical data presented in this chapter appear to indicate that regional integration during the past decade has had little effect on the abilities of MNEs to increase their globalization capabilities.

Conclusions

The evidence is that the world economy is now a Triad one; the economic regions of North America, the EU, and Asia dominate international business. Both aggregated data, and disaggregated data, on the sales of the world's largest multinational enterprises, show the regional pattern of economic activity. What does this mean for business–government relations?

The lack of globalization means a lack of multilateralism for governments and a lack of global strategy for firms. As economic power is regional, so is political power. The United States can achieve all of its post-September 11th national security desires within NAFTA. The United States does not need Europe or Asia for support in the Iraq war. This is just another example of the end of multilateralism. The United States calls the military tune. Other nations either need to dance to it or further deepen their own intra-regional economic relations. Canada and Mexico, in general, experience the strong economic benefits of NAFTA and have learned to live with US political power, with the Iraq war being a notable exception. Indeed, the Canadians in 2003 seemed to be operating on the old-fashioned model of multilateralism rather than the new reality of regionalism. As Canada was the first major country to negotiate its joining a Triad power (in the 1987 Canadian–US Free Trade Agreement) it is likely in the future to return to being a regional player as with Mexico.

Transaction cost economics reasoning largely explains this phenomenon of regionalization. Market-seeking expansion in host regions is often associated with high, location-specific adaptation investments to link the MNE's existing knowledge base with host-region location advantages. The firm's FSAs and CSAs do not simply meld together without managerial intervention. As the required investments to meld FSAs and CSAs become larger, driven by the cultural, administrative, geographic, and economic distance between home country/region and host regions, the attractiveness of foreign markets declines. Then regional, rather than global, strategies are needed to reflect the differential need for "linking" investments in each region. Only in a few sectors, such as consumer electronics, can a balanced, global distribution of sales be achieved.

It is likely that the upstream end of the value chain can be globalized more easily than the customer end, where sales data have been the focus of this chapter. Upstream location-specific investments are not one-sided (in the sense of lacking reciprocal commitments from the other economic actors involved, which is a critical problem at the customer end). Upstream globalization obviously need not be expressed in a balanced geographic distribution of R&D, manufacturing, etc., but rather in the

MNE's ability to choose and access locations around the globe where the firm's upstream FSAs can easily be melded with foreign CSAs and location advantages, without the need for major, location-specific adaptation investments. Yet, the available data on production also suggest the importance of home-region based production clusters and networks, as in the automobile sector. This indicates that the hazards of cultural, administrative, geographic, and economic distance between the home country/region and host regions are often also present at the upstream side.

For firms, this dominance of intra-regional activity means that their managers need to pay much more attention to regional trade agreements like NAFTA, regional political integration agreements like the EU, and a potential regional agreement in Asia. These managers already know how to achieve their FSAs on a regional basis and that outsourcing of the supply chain to Asia (as with Nike and Wal-Mart) is to take advantage of locational CSAs (in cheap labor), rather than to reconfigure their basic business model. Overall, business–government relations need to move toward a regional level of analysis, building upon the old-fashioned national sovereignty framework of states and markets. There is no evidence that globalization, global strategy, or multilateralism are of much relevance to either policymakers or managers.

16 How will third world countries welcome foreign direct investment in the twenty-first century?

STEFAN H. ROBOCK

I NTERNATIONAL business (IB) and government relations involve the interaction of at least four major groups of players, namely, multinational business enterprises, their home governments, host governments, and domestic business firms in the host countries. And the players in each of these groups have their own goals and behavior patterns that have been changing over recent decades.

In this chapter, I have chosen to focus on the host country policies of the developing countries toward inbound foreign direct investment (FDI) for two reasons. One reason is that my entry into the IB education field some forty years ago was from a background of working for the United Nations on economic development advisory missions in Brazil, India, and Bolivia. And because of this background and continued assignments in the Philippines, Mainland China, and other developing countries, I have been sensitive to the need for managers and multinational enterprises to enlarge their understanding of the thinking and the motivations underlying the host country policies toward inbound FDI of the less developed countries.

A second reason is that I expect the developing countries to have a much greater business attraction for multinational enterprises during the twenty-first century than they have had in the recent past. The developing countries have most of the world's population, and many have been achieving relatively high growth rates. As incomes rise, effective demand rises even faster for the kinds of advanced products that can be supplied by international firms. Furthermore, the former Soviet Bloc countries of Eastern Europe have recently become a significant area of interest for multinational enterprises.

And from this background, I will try to offer suggestions on how these host countries will receive inbound foreign direct investment in the twenty-first century.

Host country patterns

As the importance of multinational enterprises with global horizons has expanded in recent decades, nations have responded with new national policies to deal with this phenomenon. And slowly, but inevitably, most nations moved from piecemeal measures toward a general and coordinated national policy. However, the responses of host and dominant home countries have not been uniform, either in timing or in substance. Furthermore, even where levels of sensitivity to multinational enterprises are similar, responses have differed depending upon country characteristics and national goals.

In general, a major difference exists between the national policies of nations that are the home country of many multinational enterprises and the developing countries. In the home countries national policies are certain to be constrained by the possibility of retaliation. For example, if the United States establishes strong restrictions on domestic operations of non-US companies, other dominant home countries are likely to create similar or more burdensome restrictions on the foreign operations of US companies. In contrast, most developing countries do not have this constraint, at least, until they give birth to their own multinationals, which has been occurring.

Some historical perspective

For several decades after the Second World War, multinational enterprises directed only a minor share of total foreign direct investment to the developing countries. And much of this FDI went to a small number of countries, largely in the form of investments in exploitable raw materials, mainly oil and minerals, and agricultural products such as tea, cane sugar, and bananas. As market seekers, international enterprises showed only modest interest in most developing countries because of their small markets, low income levels, and perceived political risk.

The high concern for political risk peaked in the 1960s and 1970s when a number of developing countries nationalized foreign petroleum and mining investments. Political risk also peaked in some developing countries during this period for political reasons, such as the case of the 1964 military takeover in Brazil and a reversal of a previous "FDI welcome" policy (Robock, 1977). Yet some FDI flows to the developing countries continued by multinational production-efficiency seekers who established foreign plants to produce textiles, apparel, and electronic components for export to the advanced countries.

Also during the late 1960s and early 1970s, international business enterprises and their home governments, all of whom embraced the view that multinational enterprises are engines of development that provided developing countries with needed capital, technology, and know-how essential for the modernization of their economies, were shocked to discover that many government officials, political leaders, and academic scholars in the developing countries were expressing serious misgivings about the economic, political, and cultural impact of the multinationals on the developing countries. Equally disturbing was the emergence of antagonistic views by groups in the home countries toward outbound multinational enterprise expansions. In fact, the anti-multinational enterprise expansion had many of the same features as the anti-globalization movement of the 1990s.

Two American authors, Richard J. Barnet and Ronald E. Muller, in their book *Global Reach: The Power of the Multinational Corporation* (1974), nurtured this wave of antagonism. The book was translated into many languages and became a best seller throughout the world. The underlying theme of *Global Reach* as stated by the authors was as follows: "The confrontation between the multinational corporation and its enemies promises to influence the shape of human society in the last third of the century more than any other political drama of our time." The authors then ask a rhetorical question: "By what right do a selected group of druggists, biscuit makers, and computer designers become the architects of the new world?"

A few of the many indictments of multinational enterprises made in this study give a flavor of the prevailing MNC antagonism that existed in much of the third world. According to Barnet and Muller, the multinationals were:
Expanding to protect their monopolistic advantages;
De-nationalizing local managers;
Deteriorating living standards, employment rates, and economic justice in the underdeveloped countries;
Transferring the types of technology poor countries need least;
Compounding the world hunger problem.

The skillful writing and ninety pages of "Notes for Text and Tables" in the book combine to give the reader an overwhelming impression of scholarly support for these assertions. But *Global Reach* is more of a propaganda piece than a work of scholarship. As discussed elsewhere, the book uses many questionable techniques of guilt by association by comparing the "executive employment" charts of multinationals to "military operations" and using collections of data "much as the CIA amasses similar sorts of data" (Robock, 1975, pp. 20–21)

During the 1980s, however, as the United Nations reports, the relationship between developing countries and MNEs underwent a radical and significant change. In contrast to their past restrictive host country policies, most developing countries became receptive to FDI. A brief summary by the UN of the external factors that brought about this change is as follows:

Among them are the sluggish economic growth and the low levels of capital accumulation in most developing countries; the declining attractiveness of those countries as locations for new FDI; the continuing expansion of the techno-logical gap between developed and developing countries; and the foreign-debt burden affecting many developing countries. The influence of Governments of developed market economies, of international institutions and of foreign banks also accounts for the change in developing countries policy.[1]

The new relationship has been a real change of perception affecting both governments and companies. Governments of host countries increas-ingly accept that they can achieve a relationship with foreign investors that safeguards their national interests. Companies, on their side, no longer see political risk as a major factor inhibiting the flow of invest-ment funds. And this relationship has continued up to the present.

The socialist countries

The socialist countries, most of whom were in the developing country category, are a special case. After the end of the Second World War and during the Cold War, the socialist (or communist) countries of the Soviet Union, its Eastern European satellites, and China were ideo-logically out of the international business and government relations picture. If the socialist countries had strictly adhered to their ideology of government ownership and autarky, business relations with Western

---

[1] For a more detailed discussion of the liberalization trend by developing countries of policies on FDI see United Nations Centre on Transnational Companies (1988), chapter 17, pp. 260–298.

firms would have been restricted to traditional importing and exporting. Yet most socialist countries placed pragmatism ahead of ideology because of their desire to secure advanced technology, financial assistance, managerial know-how, greater access to Western markets, and other benefits available from Western multinationals.

To achieve these benefits, the Eastern European countries encouraged Western firms to participate in their economies through nonequity cooperation agreements – the most numerous forms of arrangement – and in many cases allowed foreign direct investment in the form of equity joint ventures.[2] China, however, beginning in the late 1970s, expanded its relations with multinational investors while still retaining as a sort of mythology that it still is a socialist country in its political system. And since the dissolution of the USSR, the former socialist countries of Eastern Europe have given up almost completely this ideological restraint.

Some interesting details of Mainland China's decision to encourage foreign direct investment are revealed in the memoirs of Lee Kuan Yew (Yew, 2000, p. 637) who tells of the great influence Singapore had on Mainland China during the 1980s after Deng adopted a policy of opening China to a market economy.

Singapore's greater development success attracted the attention of China because the Singapore leaders were Chinese.

In 1980, Jiang Zemin, who was later to become General Secretary of China, visited Singapore to study its development program. Toward the end of two weeks, after being briefed by Ng Pock Too, a director of Singapore's Economic Development Board, Jiang looked Ng in the eye and said, "You have not told me everything. You must have a secret. China has cheaper land, cheaper water, cheaper power, (and) cheaper labour. Yet you get so many investments and we don't. What is the secret formula?"

Nonplussed, Ng explained the key importance of political confidence and economic productivity. He pulled out his copy of the Business Environment Index (BERI) report, and pointed out Singapore's rating as 1A on a scale of 1A down to 3C. China was not even included in the rating. (p. 637).

And after learning what Singapore had done to make a safe area for foreign investments, Mainland China went ahead to become during the 1990s and 2000 the most successful country in the world in attracting FDI.

---

[2] For greater detail see chapter 14 of Robock and Simmonds (1989).

Major elements that shape host country policies

Thus, as the twenty-first century begins, both the developing countries and the former socialist countries have become receptive to FDI. Yet the specifics of each host country's policies vary significantly and must be analyzed by the MNE before making an investment. And on the basis of my personal experience in working with developing countries the major elements in the host country policies of the developing countries that I have chosen for comment are ideologies and nationalism, development strategies, national security, negotiation muscle and experience, incentives, controls, and degrees of pragmatism.

Ideologies

Although the end of the Cold War almost completely eliminated the anti-private-industry ideology as a dominant element in host government policies, some significant remnants of this ideology still remain in some countries. India, for example, when it achieved its independence in 1949, was influenced by the example of the Soviet Union in adopting its economic policies. One of these Indian policies followed for decades was to require that only public enterprises be permitted in a long list of important industries. In recent years, this industry policy has lost much of its force but a number of important officials are still biased against private enterprises and especially foreign private ownership of industries. China also has lingering government enterprise defenders, but mainly as a result of vested interests rather than ideology.

Fortunately, however, the private versus public enterprise issue has largely moved into the empirical rather than ideological arena. Many privatization case studies have been made in recent years which suggest that the preference for either public or private industry should depend upon the specific situation. Some industries, like telephone systems or steel plants, can operate more efficiently by becoming private enterprises and subject to market competition.

Likewise, as the once chief economist of the Tennessee Valley Authority, I can testify that the public enterprises power operations of the TVA can operate efficiently when subject to competition in attracting industries, in addition to making other unique contributions in the public interest. As a public enterprise, TVA was able to take the risk of demonstrating the price elasticity of electric energy by cutting prevailing rates by 50 percent, which was matched by its neighboring private utilities, and that resulted in greater profits to both public and private enterprises.

Nationalism should probably be included in the ideology category although it is an emotional belief rather than part of a socialist ideology. For example, the field of petroleum exploration has frequently been closed to foreign investment because of a belief that the benefits from this national resource belong completely to the nation. For example, in Brazil, for many decades foreign investment in petroleum exploration was opposed by popular demonstrations with banners, *petróleo e nosso* (petroleum is ours), but foreign investment in this area eventually became necessary to secure needed capital and technology.

Development strategies

Whether FDI and MNEs are welcome in a developing country will generally depend upon how a project fits into the country's adopted development strategy. For two decades until the end of the Second World War, the dominant economic policy issue for most nations was business cycles and avoiding depressions. But by the late 1940s, both economic redevelopment of the war-torn countries and economic development of the newly decolonized and other less developed countries became the highest priority economic goal. And several different growth strategies emerged and became popular. One strategy emphasized import substitution. Another emphasized export expansion as the dynamo for growth. And still another was the venerable infant industry protection strategy.

The import substitution strategy focused on encouraging domestic production that substituted for imports and improved the country's foreign exchange position. The limitation of this strategy, however, turned out to be that many of the large foreign exchange consuming industries in which FDI was welcomed, such as substituting local production of automobiles for imports, did not have the potential of becoming internationally competitive. For example, the automobile assembly plants established by FDI in a number of countries produced cars at such high costs because of their small scale that they required continued high levels of tariff protection, and they were eventually abandoned (Robock, 1970).

The infant industry strategy, in contrast, welcomed FDI in a different set of industries that were considered to have the potential for becoming internationally competitive. Such industries would be given a limited period of protection for the time-consuming learning process and for expansion to an efficient scale of production. And after the infants mature, the protection measures are gradually eliminated. Brazil adopted the infant industry strategy to develop its automobile industry from zero production to current annual production levels of more than a million cars, some of which are being exported. Japan also used the infant industry strategy with great success. And it is interesting to note that Alexander Hamilton in his 1971 *Report on Manufactures* submitted to the US House of Representatives elaborated the infant industry argument persuasively enough to encourage the United States to follow such a strategy with great success.

The export-oriented strategy welcomed FDI that would produce products that could be exported to foreign markets, making use of available natural resources such as minerals and timber and/or low skilled manpower. This strategy was used successfully by a number of Asian countries such as Singapore, Korea, and China.

National security

National security elements have long been shaping host country FDI policies, both in the advanced and developing countries. But although national security continues to be important, the specific sectors that are considered national security issues keep changing. Industries such as electric power, transportation, and communication are examples of national security areas in which nations have frequently barred foreign ownership.

As an example, as of January 2002, Brazil has the following FDI restrictions:

Participation of foreign capital is prohibited in the following activities:
• Development of atomic power;
• Business on international borders;
• Fishing industry;
• Post office and telegraph services;
• Airlines with domestic flight concessions;
• Aircraft and space industry;

- Foreign capital in financial institutions, as well as in newspapers, magazines, and other media, is limited to minority holdings with voting capital. But this rule can be changed in accordance with the national interest.
(Marcondes Advogados Associados, 2003, p. 12)

The Brazil example illustrates how the choice of specific national security restraints on inbound FDI can vary with unique host country characteristics. The Brazilian prohibition of FDI on international borders results from a traditional concern for protecting a hollow interior of the country. The prohibition of FDI in the aircraft industry is explained by the coveted existence of the successful Embraer Company in Brazil, now the fourth largest aircraft company in the world.

Transfers of technology

Most developing countries have given a high priority in their development strategies to achieving technology transfers from the advanced countries. However, the specific programs adopted to achieve this goal have varied greatly among the countries, depending largely on the country's absorptive capacity, namely the availability of trained scientists and engineers, and the nation's bargaining power. Japan, for example, was in the less developed category after the Second World War but was able to import technology without relying on inbound FDI because of the country's sizable cadre of trained scientists and engineers. This cadre was put to work studying professional journals and visiting industrial plants in the United States and Europe to identify available and desired technology. Then through licensing and technical assistance, Japan secured the desired technology from foreign interests holding the patents and know-how without FDI.

In countries where the absorptive capacity was limited – including most of the developing countries – FDI has been heavily relied upon for technology transfers. And the policies governing inbound FDI generally require that the most advanced technology be imported, that nationals be trained to use these technologies, and that royalty payments to the parent companies for technology be limited. As an example, China has achieved significant transfers of technology, such as getting foreign aircraft firms to transfer technology by doing some of the manufacturing and assembly in China, because of China's tremendous bargaining power through access to its vast domestic market.

Furthermore, a number of developing countries like China, India, and Korea have increased their technology capacity by attracting trained and experienced nationals to return to their home countries. In many cases, the return of experienced personnel was voluntary because of expanding opportunities at home, and in other cases the home countries used attractive incentives to stimulate the return of technicians.

FDI incentives

Nations and their governmental units (provinces, states, cities, etc.) have long used special incentives to attract both domestic and foreign direct investment. Most developing countries provide a variety of incentives for foreign investors. Such incentives seek to either increase the rate of return for FDI or decrease the non-commercial risks associated with investing in developing countries. The former type of incentives cover tax and customs exemptions, subsidies, access to local financial institutions so as to reduce foreign exchange risk, etc.; the latter include guarantees against expropriation, settlement of disputes arrangements, etc.

The host countries have become more sophisticated by tying incentives to certain criteria. In some cases, incentives are tied to the extent of local participation in the enterprise, such as creating a joint venture, or future performance rather than the initial characteristics of the investment. In other situations, the granting of incentives may be limited to certain sectors or locations in specific areas such as an underdeveloped region. Brazil, for example, has long had highly attractive special incentives available for direct investments in the poorer regions of the Amazon and the Nordeste (northeast).[3]

From the standpoint of the foreign investor, such incentives as offered may greatly improve the attractiveness of the investment. But most experienced companies feel that their projects must be profitable without incentives because new political leaders may have them cancelled at a later date.

---

[3] In fact, I undertook an assignment for a major American paper company to review a potential project located in northeast Brazil that could have had such a fabulous return that the internationally inexperienced company was afraid to undertake it.

Controls on remittances of profits, royalties and capital

In the past, many nations have established controls on profit remittances, usually in the form of maximum limits calculated as a percent of the investment, and repatriation of capital. The reason for controls on profit remittances may be a concern about the nation's balance of payments or a feeling about what is "fair." But a reduction in profit remittance controls has been occurring as an indication of a favorable attitude toward foreign investment. Repatriation of capital controls, however, still exists in some countries, and control over royalty remittances for technology may also exist because many host countries feel that profit remittances already include technology payments.

Outlook for the twenty-first century

On the whole, the outlook for host government policies and behavior of the developing countries toward inbound foreign direct investment during the early twenty-first century is favorable. One must remember, however, that the goals of international business enterprises are different from those of a developing nation and that nations have sovereign power over activities within their borders. Yet, though the goals of a private enterprise and a nation are different and may be in conflict in some areas, international business enterprises have the great attraction that they can help a nation reach its goals and at the same time help the enterprise reach its own.

The greater welcome that MNEs are facing in international relations is a result of a learning process over recent decades on the part of enterprises and governments. Enterprises have become more flexible in their behavior, such as becoming more open to joint ventures rather than insisting on complete ownership and being more open to admitting foreign nationals into the higher bureaucracy of the firm. Also, after the past experience of many expropriations of petroleum and mineral projects, political risk has been greatly reduced.

At the same time, most developing nations have also gone through a learning process and acquired much greater confidence in their own ability to negotiate with foreign enterprises. Many government officials have learned a great deal about multinational enterprises through business school training and employment with business enterprises as well as through information about the experience of other countries.

Also, several international agencies and private consultants have become available to assist governments in developing their host country policies.

Probably the major uncertainty in international and host country relations is the anti-globalization movement and the international disagreements in the area of international trade. The key issue in the globalization area has been the failure of national benefits from foreign investment and foreign trade to be widely distributed within the host countries. And although this shortcoming is basically a deficiency of internal policies and programs within the host countries, it is usually easier for some groups in the country to blame this failure on outside forces.

In the international trade area, however, the policy in many advanced countries of giving large subsidies to agricultural producers and making it difficult for farmers in the poor countries to compete with imports or in foreign markets has become a serious problem for host countries, a problem that spills over into international business as well as international trade.

As a final note, the development of the field of international business education over the last half of the last century and academic research has undoubtedly played a significant positive role in helping both international business firms and host nations improve their international relations to the benefit of both parties.

17 Assessing government policies for business competitiveness in emerging market economies: an institutional approach

DENNIS A. RONDINELLI

Introduction

As transnational corporations expand in emerging market economies, they find not only new opportunities for trade and investment, but also new challenges, uncertainties, and risks in countries still undergoing the long process of economic, political, and social transition. The success of transnational corporations (TNCs) depends not only on their ability to assess specific business opportunities and the viability of potential partners, suppliers, distributors, and other components of their value chains in emerging market economies, but also on their capacity to determine how effectively governments support market-oriented policies that allow domestic and foreign corporations to compete fairly, expand their market share, and increase profits.

The uncertainties facing TNCs in emerging market countries vary among nations and regions of the world. Many countries that had government-controlled economies in Latin America, Asia, Central and Eastern Europe, and Africa have undergone fundamental changes in their political and economic systems and in their societies and cultures over the past decade (UNDP, 2000). Yet, TNCs entering emerging markets face complex uncertainties that can lead to economic, transfer, regulatory, exchange rate, operational, sovereign debt, and political risks (Meldrum, 2000). Not the least of their problems is the difficulty of calculating risks associated with potential political and economic instability and adverse government policies toward business (Rondinelli, 1994a; Iankova and Katz, 2003).

Country business climate affects all aspects of TNCs' international expansion. US firms entering Eastern European countries have selected different entry modes depending on their perceptions of host country market potential and national competitiveness (Shama, 2000). Country risks determine how strongly TNCs invest, the types and amounts of resources they commit, and the means by which they hedge against uncertainty (Iankova and Katz, 2003). Economic and political risks not only affect TNCs' decisions about where and how to enter foreign markets but they also strongly influence capital flight (Lensink, Hermes, and Murinde, 2000).

TNCs expanding into emerging markets often turn to commercial risk ratings and rankings that tend to be incomplete or selective in the indicators they use and, as a result, can be misleading or inaccurate in their forecasts (Oetzel, Bettis, and Zenner, 2001; deMortanges and Allers, 1996). As international business conditions become more complex, however, TNCs are analyzing the opportunities and risks in transitional economies more carefully. In a survey of more than thirty-seven large TNCs that make foreign direct investments in emerging market countries, the World Bank (2003, p. 21) found "a marked shift toward integrated management of FDI related risks." The report (p. 16) pointed out that in addition to " . . . a sound macroeconomic environment for FDI, the TNCs take into account two other sets of factors. First, those that directly underpin their economic and commercial interests – such as market size and growth prospects, cost of local labor, availability of infrastructure, and the tax regime; and second, institutional and regulatory factors and policies such as the licensing system, legal framework and quality of bureaucracy that, among other things, facilitate FDI."

Given the crucial role that country business climate plays in shaping conditions for trade and investment, a thorough analysis of the institutional foundations of an emerging market economy and of the implied risks should be an important component of TNCs' due diligence and international expansion strategies (Root, 1994). How can TNCs and domestic firms seeking to expand their businesses in emerging market economies assess the opportunities and risks arising from economic and political uncertainty? How can corporations evaluate government's commitment to supporting market-oriented economies and to creating the conditions for competitiveness in transition countries?

In this chapter I argue that an institutional framework for analyzing the business climate and national competitiveness in transition countries can provide a useful context for or a supplement to conventional financial, political, or issue-based models of risk analysis. An institutional perspective can help TNCs evaluate both the short-run willingness of governments to create competitive conditions and the long-run strength and stability of emerging market economies (Rondinelli,

2003a). In the following sections I outline the argument for using an institutional analysis framework to assess the strength and competitiveness of emerging market countries, describe the relationship between institutions and market economies, and identify the roles of government in strengthening institutions that create conditions for competitiveness.

Both theory and the lessons of business experience in emerging market countries indicate that governments must strengthen economic and political institutions so that domestic and international firms can compete fairly and equitably (Behrman and Grosse, 1990; Rondinelli, 1994b, 2003a). In the early 1970s, Behrman (1971) made a strong case for why TNCs must recognize the importance of policies and institutions in shaping the business environment for trade and investment. The role of institutions was largely ignored by TNCs and international financial and development assistance organizations, however, until recently. It is now more widely recognized that the effective operation of markets depends on institutions that are inextricably embedded in each other and in society. Studies by the International Monetary Fund (2003) show, for example, the close correlation between income differences among countries and indicators of institutional quality.

Why are institutions important?

One of the reasons that international financial organizations and TNCs have generally ignored institutions is the difficulty of defining and analyzing them. Williamson's (2000) review of the institutional economics literature identifies four concepts:
1. informal institutions, customs, traditions, and norms;
2. formal "rules of the game" set by the polity, judiciary and bureaucracy;
3. governance institutions or "the play of the game" affected by aligning governance structures with transactions; and
4. resource allocation and employment institutions affecting incentives alignment.

North (1990) argued that institutions are preconditions for economic systems based on impersonal exchange. He defined institutions as "rules, enforcement characteristics of rules, and norms of behavior that structure repeated human interaction" (North, 1989, p. 1321).

The recent recognition of the importance of institutions in emerging market countries came with the discovery that differences in the pace and level of economic development can be explained largely by differences in the strength and quality of countries' institutions (North, 1990). Examining experience with economic growth and social development in 140 countries over the past century, Rodrik, Subramanian, and Trebbi (2002) contend that the primacy of institutions becomes clear in distinguishing those that progressed economically and those that did not. They conclude that strong institutions can overcome geographical disadvantages, promote integration into the world economy, enhance the capacity to trade, and increase income levels of the population. Behrman (1986) argued earlier that institutions also influence the distribution of benefits domestically and internationally.

The roles of government in market- and institution-building

North argues (1989, 1990) that although rules and policies are important, it is their institutionalization as norms of behavior structuring repeated interaction that creates the conditions for effectively operating market systems. Assessing current government policies or rules alone, without evaluating the norms of behavior and the culture in which they are embedded, could mislead TNCs attempting to determine whether or not and how to enter emerging markets. Simply examining single-issue risk factors or specific government policies or regulations is insufficient because, as North (1989) and others have pointed out, regulatory enforcement is always imperfect when measurement is costly and the interests of principals and agents are not consistent (Rondinelli, 1995).

Although recent studies emphasize the pivotal role that institutions play in the economic and social development of emerging market countries, they also recognize that government has a vital role in creating or strengthening them (Rondinelli and Behrman, 2000). Numerous studies have uncovered interactions between institutions and government policies affecting economic growth (IMF, 2003). Weak or inappropriate government polices can constrain institutions, and weak institutions can undermine the implementation of government policies (World Bank, 2002). In an empirical analysis of the impact of governance infrastructure on foreign direct investment flows in a large sample of developed and developing countries, Globerman and Shapiro (2002, p. 1899) found that political, institutional, and legal environments are strong determinants of both FDI inflows and outflows; they conclude that "investments in governance infrastructure not only attract capital, but also create the conditions under which domestic multinational corporations emerge and invest abroad." Thus, a thorough examination of government policies in an institutional context can be the foundation for a more comprehensive approach to country business climate analysis and risk assessment.

Institutions and emerging market economies

If efficient market systems require strong institutional underpinnings and supportive government policies, then TNCs seeking business opportunities in emerging market economies should, as part of their due diligence and international expansion strategies, assess the strength of the institutional foundation for policies that shape the country business climate. In order to assess which institutions governments should be creating, strengthening, or maintaining it is important to understand the institutional requirements of market systems and the roles of government in institutional development.

   Behrman and Rondinelli (1999) contend that governments in emerging market countries seeking to foster domestic exchange and facilitate international trade and investment must create and sustain policies and institutions that promote or strengthen seven underlying attributes of market systems. Building on earlier work by Rondinelli and Behrman (2000), I argue here that these attributes imply the need for strengthening norm-setting and -enforcing policies that are inextricably interrelated and mutually reinforcing in creating an effectively operating market system, and that this institutional framework provides a sound basis for assessing the business climate in emerging market countries (see figure 17.1).

Institutions of economic adjustment

First, TNCs should carefully assess the institutions and policies for economic adjustment. Macroeconomic changes in transition countries have strong impacts on the financial condition of corporations, and, in turn, the financial practices of corporations – if they are overleveraged, squeeze credit from the private sector, or decline into insolvency – can negatively affect macroeconomic conditions (Gray and Stone, 1999).

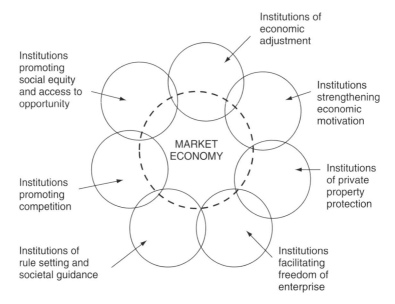

Figure 17.1 Institutional attributes of market economies

The most important roles of government in creating or strengthening macroeconomic institutions are adopting and enforcing:

1. economic adjustment policies;
2. price reform policies;
3. policies for privatizing state-owned enterprises and reforming public corporations;
4. tax reforms;
5. economic stabilization policies.

Efficient markets depend on institutions that can make adjustments when the economy is adversely affected by internal or external shocks, while at the same time promoting sufficient stability to facilitate orderly and effective exchange. Acemoglu et al. (2003) found that countries that did not adjust macroeconomic policies that led to high inflation, excessive budget deficits, and fluctuating exchange rates suffered greater economic volatility and lower levels of economic growth over the past fifty years.

Institutions of macroeconomic adjustment are important because in order to maximize profits, individuals and businesses must continually adjust their own production and distribution decisions through market signals in order to respond to consumer demands. Even in advanced economies, however, market mechanisms do not always operate in reality as they should in theory. As they participate more heavily in international trade and investment, emerging market countries can become more financially vulnerable to potential downturns in foreign net investment, increasing external debt servicing burdens, the possibilities of capital flight, and deterioration in the terms of trade, all of which constrain the ability of firms to adjust to changing conditions. Changes in the composition of trade and in patterns of imports and exports can also have serious adverse effects. National industries can suffer shocks when decline in external demand or supply reverberates throughout the system and begins to squeeze domestic input suppliers and customers, as it did in Latin America during the 1980s and in Asia during the late 1990s. In studies based on large panel estimations from twenty-seven African countries from the early 1960s to the late 1990s, Berthélemy and Söderling (2001) found that macroeconomic adjustment and structural change strongly influenced total factor productivity and economic growth in that region as well.

Policies and institutions of macroeconomic adjustment encourage the development of market mechanisms that promote capital accumulation, efficiently and effectively allocate scarce economic resources, and free up price-setting for production inputs and consumer goods. This requires financial liberalization and the reduction (and eventual elimination) of price controls. In order to achieve these objectives, governments in countries with emerging markets must strengthen policies and institutions that reduce or eliminate inefficient state-owned monopolies, transfer ownership of productive activities from the state to the private sector, enact laws and regulations allowing private sector development and bankruptcy, and adopt business laws that promote competition and discourage monopoly practices (Rondinelli and Iacono, 1996).

The fiscal aspects of structural adjustment seek to broaden the tax base and promote tax efficiency by reducing a country's reliance on international trade taxes and by increasing revenues from domestic sources. In many emerging market countries, tax reforms are crucial for creating a strong business climate and for strengthening tax administration, improving equity, and simplifying the tax system.

Macroeconomic adjustment policies often pursue price reforms to reduce or eliminate government controls on prices of producer goods, final products, and capital, to increase price flexibility, and to rid the economy of price distortions. Policies aim at linking producer prices to world market prices, eliminating subsidies on production, and taking other measures that allow domestic markets to clear. Price reform policies can create real competition in product and factor markets, encourage relatively free entry of new firms into the market, and impose financial discipline by making firms sensitive to costs and subject to "hard budget" constraints (Sokil and King, 1993).

TNCs must carefully assess institutions and policies promoting economic stability because emerging market countries in every region of the world have experienced some degree of chronic inflation or hyperinflation before, during, or after the transition period (Reinhart and Savastano, 2003). Those countries that face serious problems of inflation and decline in national output must be able to enact economic stabilization policies aimed at reducing balance-of-payments deficits, rescheduling debt, controlling the money supply, reducing subsidies, and restraining wage increases. A strong emerging market economy depends on government's ability to control inflation and restore macroeconomic stability by increasing savings and investment and by making the economy less vulnerable to internal and external economic shocks (Easterly, Loayza, and Montiel, 1997). Macroeconomic instability also often leads to exchange rate instability (Coeure and Pisani-Ferry, 1999). Stabilization policies must frequently be put into place quickly to stem political backlash against the social impacts of structural reforms.

Institutions strengthening economic motivation

A second set of institutions that TNCs considering trade or investment in emerging markets should assess is those strengthening economic motivation. World Bank (2002) analysts point out that transition country governments face the challenges of both imposing market discipline on existing enterprises and encouraging the creation of new enterprises willing to compete without state subsidies. Economic motivation is essential because market systems depend on society's acceptance of material gain and on businesses' ability to make profits as primary motives for individual production and investment. A market economy is a process through which individuals, households, and businesses – acting in their own interests – exchange money, factors of production, goods, and services. To help markets operate effectively, governments in transition countries should have strong policies promoting: entrepreneurship; marketing of goods and services; distribution; efficient labor allocation; and foreign direct investment.

Among the most difficult institutions to develop in emerging market countries, and perhaps the most difficult for TNCs to gauge, are the social values that strengthen the economic motivation on which markets thrive. All economic systems are based on social values, and market systems have their own underlying principles that must be recognized and accepted if they are to function effectively (Behrman, 1987). Much of the growth that has taken place in emerging markets has been driven by small- and medium-sized enterprises and entrepreneurial activities in countries where market-supporting institutions were strengthened or created (Kolodko, 2000; World Bank, 2002). New entrepreneurial enterprises often performed better and increased their output faster than privatized state enterprises and public enterprises, for example, during the transitions in Poland, the Czech Republic, and Hungary (Winiecki, 2003).

Entrepreneurs and markets thrive on social values that encourage and reward individualism, risk-taking, innovation, responsiveness to change, and the belief that those who take entrepreneurial risks should be amply rewarded for success and allowed to suffer the penalties for failure. These are not values that were promulgated in socialist or centrally planned economies and, indeed, communist regimes tried to eradicate them in favor of a form of egalitarianism that stifled initiative and discouraged entrepreneurial activity for profit. As a result, entrepreneurs and business owners in many transition countries continued to face widespread public ambivalence about the values and assumptions underlying market systems after central-planning regimes collapsed (Kornai, 1992). Both government and civil society institutions have important roles in instilling the values of democratic governance because market systems depend on the same values of autonomy, freedom to innovate, ability to experiment, and willingness to change that have historically fueled economic growth in Western societies (Lindblom, 1977).

Economic motivation depends in part on entrepreneurs' ability to market and distribute goods and services effectively. Market institutions include the organizations, processes, and rules of behavior for getting raw materials to producers and products to consumers. Within enterprises the market system encompasses research, product development, design, and testing in order to meet customer needs. Marketing institutions allow firms not only to tailor products to consumer demands, but also to price products competitively, promote their sale through advertising, distribute products efficiently and effectively through wholesalers and retailers, and service products after they are sold.

In the early stages of transition, governments must often take a strong role in arranging for the provision of market infrastructure, including marketplaces, roads, ports, and storage and transfer facilities as well as adequate communications and transportation services. They must also sometimes strengthen distribution infrastructure including collecting-wholesale, distributing-wholesale, and retail outlets, and organizations that provide marketing information and advertising. Financial and credit institutions and marketing education and training organizations also facilitate the exchange of goods and services. Consumer education and protection associations and organizations that develop new technology and products and that facilitate their transformation to commercial use are essential for marketing and distribution. Finally, a system of commercial regulations that provides guidelines and parameters for marketing goods and services helps prevent fraud and consumer abuse.

An effectively operating labor market motivates people to provide their labor, and businesses of all sizes to expand. Many transition countries face serious labor market problems, including high levels of employment in the public sector and of both open and hidden unemployment. Enterprises in some emerging market countries are unprofitable because of overstaffing, politically required pay egalitarianism, and distorted inter-industry wage structures. Many distortions in the labor market were created and sustained by deficient labor market legislation in former regimes (World Bank, 1993). Factor markets in China, for example, remained underdeveloped despite policy reforms aimed at strengthening market systems because of the inefficient operation of labor market institutions (Bowlus and Sicular, 2003). Studies of the problems of achieving long-term efficiency gains and sustainable economic development in Poland concluded that improvements were conditioned on reducing structural constraints in labor markets (Dries and Swinnen, 2002).

Efficient labor market institutions distribute workers among sources of productive employment through mechanisms of supply and demand. The task of governments in countries in which the state largely controlled or restricted the conditions of employment is to create a freely operating labor market, to assure that private employers are free to decide on the size of their workforces based on efficiency criteria and that workers are free to allocate themselves with little or no restriction between the public and private sectors, between large and small enterprises, between corporations and self-employment, and among industries and sectors of the economy.

Governments seeking to motivate economic activity have a strong role to play in establishing policies and institutions that attract inbound foreign direct investment, especially in sectors requiring external capital, technology, or know-how. The United Nations Conference on Trade and Development (UNCTAD, 2002) emphasizes the importance of creating a favorable investment climate in emerging markets to attract and support FDI. This includes liberalizing foreign direct investment policies by reducing market distortions and improving standards of treatment, enacting FDI promotion policies, creating a general legal framework for facilitating inbound and outbound FDI, and liberalizing other international economic transactions. Governments can reduce market distortions by easing restrictions on entry and establishment, ownership and control, operations, and authorization and reporting, and by abolishing unfair trade incentives such as tax advantages, other financial incentives, and non-financial measures that inhibit or restrict FDI. They can improve standards of treatment by granting foreign investors "national treatment" or "fair and equitable treatment," recourse to international means of settling investment disputes and the ability to transfer funds, and by making government-regulated FDI procedures transparent.

Institutions of private property protection

A third set of criteria that TNCs can use to assess the business climate in emerging market countries is the degree to which governments have created institutions and policies for protecting private property ownership and intellectual property rights. Protection of private property ownership is necessary in market systems so that those who produce goods and services are adequately rewarded. How effectively governments enforce intellectual property rights affects TNCs' decisions about whether or not to enter, and how they operate in, emerging markets. Javorcik's (2003) study of firm-level decisions in countries in Eastern Europe and the former Soviet Union shows that weak intellectual property rights discouraged foreign investors in technology-intensive sectors and encouraged investments in projects that focused on distribution rather than local production. Strong enforcement of intellectual property rights may induce TNCs to switch from exporting to local production (Markusen, 2001).

Without effective property rights institutions, a country's resources can be allocated inefficiently, private agents can bribe officials to grant them preferential use of property, bureaucrats may engage in rent-seeking behavior, intellectual property developed through innovation can be difficult to protect by those who invested in its creation, and common property may be depleted. Property rights institutions are an array of laws and rules that clearly define the rights of organizations and individuals to own, control, and use property for economic purposes and transfer it freely by transparent administrative and legal means that are enforced in an efficient and neutral manner (Orr and Ulen, 1993). Without an institutionalized system of property ownership and property rights it is difficult to convince domestic or foreign investors to participate in privatization or economic investment.

Institutions facilitating freedom of enterprise

Freedom of enterprise is a hallmark of market economies that TNCs should assess carefully in transition countries. Panel data analyses of eighteen Latin American countries found that economic freedom in host countries was positively correlated with FDI flows and with economic growth; countries with high degrees of economic freedom, adequate human capital, economic stability, and liberalized markets continued to attract capital flows over long periods of time (Bengoa and Sanchez-Robles, 2003).

These findings should not be surprising. To employ private property effectively, owners must be permitted to mobilize the resources needed to make it more productive. TNCs can assess the potential of emerging market countries by how strongly government strengthens institutions and policies facilitating private sector development, entrepreneurship, and freedom of individuals and organizations to participate in economic activities. In market systems, economic and business decisions must be made by market signals, that is, primarily through consumer decisions affecting supply and demand. TNCs should be especially attuned to two types of policies and institutions in emerging markets that directly affect the ability of enterprises to operate freely: political liberalization and good governance; and financial institutions. Political liberalization and good governance are foundations for freedom of enterprise. Financial institutions provide the resources for enterprises to enter and operate in the market.

Freedom of enterprise requires a political system that allows individuals and organizations to make economic choices without undue restrictions by the state. Although studies of the relationships between democracy and market-based economic growth yield mixed results, economic freedom is often restricted by totalitarian or authoritarian governments in ways that undermine the efficient operation of markets and limit economic growth (Fidrmuc, 2003). Gwartney and Larson (2003) developed an index of economic freedom that includes indicators of the degree of personal choice, voluntary exchange, freedom to compete, and protection of person and property, all of which imply the necessity of a liberalized political system. Political structures in emerging market countries fundamentally affect the types of policies that governments adopt and their ability to make macroeconomic adjustments, stabilize the economy, and react to external shocks (Zhang, 2003). Political instability or unrest can have significant impacts on currency returns and on investment in emerging market countries (Crowley and Loviscek, 2002).

For enterprises to operate freely and for economies to grow, emerging market countries must also have institutions promoting good governance. Kaufmann, Kraay, and Zoido-Lobatón (1999), in a series of studies for the World Bank, found that governance strongly affects the level and pace of economic growth in transition countries. They define governance as the ways in which governments are chosen, held accountable and replaced, their capacity to manage resources efficiently, their ability to enact and implement sound policies and regulations, and their legitimacy and acceptability among citizens. Good governance is associated with a variety of attributes that N'Diaye (2001) argues include transparency, simplicity of procedures, responsibility and accountability of public officials, anti-corruption measures, protection of individual freedom and collective expression, and independence of the legal system.

In a digital age of electronic commerce and communications technology, good governance is also seen increasingly as government that is facilitating, participatory, and responsive. In more and more countries government is expected to provide the infrastructure and services that facilitate e-commerce and e-government. E-government should be transparent and open, providing easy access for citizens to services and information, and facilitating processes for fulfilling regulatory, tax, licensing, and other requirements (Tapscott and Agnew, 1999).

For individuals and enterprises to operate freely they must also be able to obtain the financial resources they need to enter the market and carry out business transactions. Banks and non-bank financial intermediaries, stock exchanges, investment funds, insurance companies, and other financial service institutions are essential to create capital markets and to allow enterprises to operate freely and effectively. Stock markets, brokerage institutions, and rating services that assess the soundness of debt instruments are crucial to the development of an effective capital market (Hermes and Lensink, 2000). The development of stock markets and other financial institutions in transition countries can promote the inflow of foreign direct investment by encouraging portfolio equity investments.

Both ineffective macroeconomic adjustment and stabilization policies and weak financial institutions have led to financial crises in emerging market countries that TNCs must not only monitor but also develop strategies for coping with (Mudd, Grosse, and Mathis, 2002). Weak banking and financial institutions contributed heavily to the financial crises in Asian countries in the late 1990s, and earlier to the slow pace of economic transformation in many countries in Eastern and Central Europe (Nord, 2000). Strong financial clearing-houses such as central bank institutions can help promote stability and prevent or moderate the effects of financial crises (Kroszner, 2000). Efficient capital markets can help governments to transfer ownership of enterprises from the public to the private sector by establishing organized and regulated trading mechanisms providing non-bank sources of capital to privatize or restructure enterprises and equity to private sector businesses. Capital markets facilitate the inflow of foreign investment.

Institutions of rule setting and societal guidance

Among the most important indicators of the strength of emerging markets are policies and institutions of rule-setting and societal guidance. Although many institutions in society – religious, educational, and media organizations, for example – have strong roles in setting and enforcing rules of social interaction, two institutions should be of particular concern to TNCs: the legal system, and policies for combating corruption.

In all emerging market countries legal institutions are critical in determining how businesses are organized and operate (Webb, 1999). Business law influences how corporations are structured and organized, the types of activities in which they may engage, and the nature and characteristics of business practices. Parker (1999) points out that effective regulatory institutions balance accountability, transparency, and consistency, the lack of which raises suspicions about the fairness of the system and increases uncertainty for investors.

An institutionalized system of business law usually includes the requirements for organizing and structuring industrial and com-mercial enterprises and their rights, responsibilities, and obligations. It should also define eligibility standards for national treatment of foreign-owned or multinational corporations, conditions of business entry and exit, business registration, liquidation and bankruptcy, and import and export requirements. A strong institutional structure for business support includes regulations affecting product and pricing standards, access to credit and capital, and ownership requirements. Securities and exchange regulations, anti-trust laws and regulations of competition, and contract laws and regulations concerning commercial litigation and dispute settlement are important legal institutions, along with a judicial system that assures enterprises and citizens equal access to the courts and reasonable and timely resolution of disputes. Judicial institutions enforce business and civil laws, offering adequate remedies for wrongs determined through litigation (Sherwood, Shepherd, and De Souza, 1994).

One of the most damaging risks that TNCs must consider in entering emerging market economies is the threat of corruption, which under-mines economic reform and, ultimately, national economic stability. In many countries transnational corporations are the targets and victims of corruption far more frequently than domestic companies (Habib and Zurawicki, 2001). Corruption weakens public confidence in market systems, has a corrosive effect on political institutions, and destroys public trust (Seligson, 2002). Corruption raises the cost of doing business, distorts the allocation of resources and the price of goods and services for consumers, and discourages foreign direct investment

(Zhao, Kim, and Du, 2003). Where corruption restricts freedom of enterprise, it prevents businesses from entering and leaving the market, leads to operational inefficiencies, and inhibits the introduction of new products and services and of new technologies (OECD, 2000). Surveys of private firms in Latin America found that corruption negatively affects sales, investment, and employment growth, thereby reducing firm competitiveness without producing any positive effects (Gaviria, 2002). Studies in China indicate that political corruption in state-owned enterprises contributed strongly to growing economic inequality (Chen, 2002).

Effective legal institutions and strong enforcement of national anti-corruption laws are among the strongest deterrents in emerging market countries, although legal restrictions alone are unlikely to eliminate persistent corruption (Herzfeld and Weiss, 2003). In a wide-ranging study of corruption in emerging market countries, Broadman and Racanatini (2001, p. 359) concluded that a "well-established system of market institutions – one characterized by clear and transparent rules, fully functioning checks and balances, including strong enforcement mechanisms, and a robust competitive environment – reduces rent-seeking opportunities and, in turn, the incentives for corruption." Other social and civic institutions such as a free press that can uncover and make public corruption in political and business transactions can also exert powerful controls (Brunetti and Weder, 2003).

Institutions promoting competition

If TNCs expect to succeed in emerging market countries they must closely evaluate government policies and institutions that promote competition. Competition is a basic attribute of market economies and the primary motivator for individuals and producers to divide labor, specialize, develop comparative advantages, improve quality, cut costs, and innovate. Competition among producers requires them to gain comparative advantage through innovation: that is, finding new methods of production, new products, new raw materials and inputs, or new ways of organizing to make better products at lower cost. Competition raises the quality of goods and services and lowers prices over time by rewarding participants who act on market signals, and by punishing with bankruptcy those who do not. Competition generates jobs, providing workers with higher incomes and more resources to consume and save. Among the policies and institutions that promote international competition in emerging market countries are: liberalization of trade and investment; exchange rate policies; and technology transfer and development policies.

How governments liberalize trade and investment policies directly affects the ability of TNCs to enter and compete in emerging market countries. Governments in countries with former communist or central planning regimes have had to adjust their trade and investment policies in order to become or remain competitive (Stotsky, Suss, and Takarick, 2000). The combination of trade liberalization and macroeconomic adjustment and stabilization had profound impacts on economic growth in Central American countries that were in transition to market systems during the 1990s (Cardemil, DiTata, and Fantischek, 2000). Liberalization of trade laws and regulations and the enactment of more favorable investment policies have become crucial aspects of market reforms in both advanced- and emerging-market countries. The International Labor Organization (1994, p. 6) emphasizes that "in the long run, it is freer trade and investment flows which will provide the enabling conditions for high and sustained growth in output and employment in the world."

Trade liberalization policies reduce barriers to exporting, importing, and marketplace interaction. Studies of twenty-two developing and emerging market countries found that reduction of tariff and non-tariff barriers improved import growth (Santos-Paulino, 2002). The reduction of export barriers usually involves easing export restrictions on domestic and foreign companies operating within the country, foreign exchange controls and taxation on remittances of funds, and controls on remission of capital, royalties, and profits. Such policies also reduce controls on the transfers of people and technology involved in exporting. Easing import barriers also involves reducing export barriers by lowering tariffs, import quotas, and restrictions on property transfer. Such policies protect intellectual property rights, create transparent and uniform trade regulations, eliminate import deposits and local content requirements, and ease technology transfer restrictions. Lowering marketplace barriers that impede both exporting and importing is achieved by shortening customs delays and accelerating bureaucratic licensing and approval procedures. These policies attempt to increase access to marketing, supply and distribution channels, eliminate price controls, and assure that safety, health and environmental regulations are reasonable, necessary, and fairly applied to both domestic and foreign companies. National trade policies are influenced increasingly by international, regional, and bilateral trade agreements and institutions. These trade agreements are the international "rules of the game" by which nations and industries must play in order to build competitive advantage. The types of international trade agreements to which emerging market countries are signatories can either facilitate or constrain trade and investment for TNCs.

Promoting competition also requires governments in many emerging markets to reform their exchange rate regimes. Hutchinson (2003) found that currency stability gives emerging market countries greater flexibility in using monetary and fiscal policy to stabilize the economy. Exchange rate policies should contribute to making currency convertible where it is not yet so, by pegging its value to a strong international currency or to a "basket" of strong currencies. Fischer (2001) argues that governments in emerging market countries must not only stabilize their exchange rates by choosing among a range of alternatives from free floating exchange, to crawling pegs, to hard pegs. Governments in emerging market countries must often devalue currencies distorted by inflation, allow the market to determine exchange rates, reduce or eliminate exchange controls, and make foreign exchange available to firms involved in investment and trade (Frankel, Goldstein, and Masson, 1991). The reforms should create, as Williamson (1994, p. 27) argued, a "unified (at least for trade transactions) exchange rate set at a level sufficiently competitive to induce a rapid growth in non-traditional exports and managed so as to assure exporters that this competitiveness will be maintained in the future."

Technology transfer and development institutions help promote competition in emerging market countries by opening new opportunities for entrepreneurship and business expansion. Technology shocks have led to increased productivity in both advanced and emerging market economies (Pakko, 2002). New technologies enhance factor mobility, create new varieties of products, and change the relative costs of production and distribution. Carlaw and Lipsey (2003) found that a driving force for economic growth is continuous creation of opportunities for further technological development. Technologically driven growth requires governments to expand transport and communications infrastructure as speed and agility become more crucial factors in competition, but also to provide educational opportunities that allow their citizens to work in technology-driven and transnational companies (Rondinelli, 2003b).

Policies and institutions for technology transfer should be of special interest to TNCs that expand into new markets with technologies transferred from home- or third-country operations. Examining the experience in Central and Eastern European countries, Tihanyi and Roath (2002, p. 196) concluded that "assessment of a country's institutional development is critical for successful technology transfer. Specifically, the macro issues that affect the technology transfer in both the short- and long-term should be examined with respect to the company's goals." Even those countries that choose a strategy of simply transferring and adapting technologies developed elsewhere must build the institutional capacities to select appropriate technologies, adapt them to local needs and conditions, and integrate them with existing machinery and equipment (UNESCAP, 1990). Moreover, successful technology adaptation requires new skills and work behaviors in the receiving country, new infrastructure to absorb technology effectively, and organizational changes to use the technology efficiently.

Institutions promoting social equity and access to opportunity

TNCs should also assess the strength of institutions and policies in emerging market countries that promote social equity and access to opportunity. Equality of opportunity allows all individuals and groups to engage in economic activity through property ownership and enterprise formation or by fair sale of their labor for income. Adjustments in market economies can, of course, produce cycles of economic decline, financial crises, and recessions or depressions that cast some groups of people into poverty or temporary economic hardship. Growing inequalities in the distribution of income can put some groups of people at an economic disadvantage, preventing them from participating in or benefiting from market processes. Some groups of people – the unskilled, the physically or mentally disabled, the aged, and those suffering from serious health problems, for example – may not be able to earn sufficient amounts of income to participate at all. TNCs should assess the strength of three sets of policies and institutions affecting social equity and access to opportunity: civil society; human capital development; and social safety nets.

Governments in transition countries must often help to rebuild institutions of civil society that were weakened or abolished during totalitarian or authoritarian regimes (Bernhard, 1996). Civil society – social organizations, business associations, chambers of commerce and industry, labor unions, religious groups, charitable organizations, public interest groups, the media, and others – can provide functions and services that the market cannot or will not offer, facilitate social transactions, and protect vulnerable groups from adverse economic impacts. Institutions of civil society have especially strong impacts on economic, political, and social development when they work in cooperation with each other, the government, and the private sector (Malik and Wagle, 2003). They help to create conditions for entrepreneurship, mitigate the potentially adverse effects of market weaknesses and market failures, develop human resources, protect the economically weak segments of the population from the potentially adverse effects of economic transformation, and help alleviate poverty.

Developing the stock of human capital is crucial to restructuring the economy and sustaining growth in emerging market economies (Benhabib and Spiegel, 1994; Tamura, 2002). Human capital contributes to an efficient market system by making people more suitable for productive employment, developing skills and talents, and expanding managerial capacity (Xiao and Lo, 2003). Literacy and numeric and vocational skills developed through primary and secondary education increase labor productivity and people's willingness and capacity to learn, and can have a positive effect on economic growth in many emerging market countries, especially in the early stages of transition (Lin, 2003). As economies mature, continued growth depends more heavily on the quality of institutions of higher education for improving technological and managerial capabilities.

Health and social services programs also have strong impacts on human capital development, economic productivity, and growth (Ranis, Stewart, and Ramirez, 2000). Improvements in health and nutrition reduce worker absenteeism due to illness and lethargy, increase people's energy levels and stamina, and improve mental processes. Economic and social benefits come as well from the favorable impacts of better health and nutrition on the abilities of children and adults to learn and through prolonging the duration of working lives.

Because the poor usually are the most vulnerable and suffer the most during economic transitions and cyclical economic downturns, public and private institutions that offer social safety nets are essential to prevent political instability and to create greater social equity (Green and Bauer, 1998). In many emerging market countries governments have had to reform their social sector institutions to protect the poor and promote economic growth. Among the social policies that governments in Eastern and Central Europe and in Latin America are addressing are health and medical insurance systems, pension programs, disability benefits, subsidies for basic utilities and social services, and unemployment compensation (Heller and Keller, 2001). In countries with large numbers of rural poor, the safety net may include food-for-education programs to keep children in school, rural public works and regional development programs, food subsidies, or subsidized credit for small businesses (Ravallion, 2002). In addition, governments have a strong role in maintaining social assistance programs for the disabled, disadvantaged, or the poor who are adversely affected by economic reforms or who are unable to participate in market transactions.

Conclusion

An institutional framework for assessing the role of government in creating conditions for business competitiveness can give TNCs seeking to expand their trade or investment in emerging market economies a sound basis for analyzing country business climate and potential opportunities and risks. The factors identified in table 17.1 can be used as a checklist for determining if and how well government policies contribute to strengthening institutional attributes of market economies. By adding indicators for each institutional category, rating their strength, and weighting them by their importance or priority to the company, TNCs can obtain an overall ranking of the institutional strength of an emerging market country and compare and contrast emerging markets with each other.

The potential advantage of an institutional framework is that it focuses attention not only on the impacts of current government policies but also on the institutional foundation on which those policies are based and through which they are implemented. It can supplement less comprehensive financial or political risk analyses or be combined with other versions of national competitiveness rankings – such as IMD's *World Competitiveness Yearbook* or the World Economic Forum's *Global Competitiveness Report* – that do not focus on the same

Table 17.1 Institutional framework for assessing country business climate

Institutions and policies	Rating 1 (weak) to 5 (strong)	Weight (importance to TNC)	Score = rating × weight
Institutions of economic adjustment and stabilization			
• Macroeconomic adjustment policies			
• Fiscal reform policies			
• Price reform policies			
• Economic stabilization policies			
Institutions strengthening economic motivation			
• Entrepreneurship development institutions			
• Marketing and distribution systems			
• Labor market institutions			
• Foreign direct investment policies			
Institutions of private property protection			
Institutions promoting freedom of enterprise			
• Political liberalization and good governance institutions			
• Financial institutions			
Institutions of rule setting and societal guidance			
• Legal institutions			
• Policies for controlling corruption			
Institutions promoting competition			
• Trade and investment facilitation policies			
• Exchange rate stabilization policies			
• Technology transfer and development policies			
Institutions promoting social equity and access to opportunity			
• Institutions of civil society			
• Human capital development institutions			
• Institutions providing social safety nets			

Table 17.2 TNC country selection matrix

		Institutional foundation of market economy		
		Strong	*Moderate*	*Weak*
	Strong	Country A	Country B	Country E
		Country M	Country F	Country H
		Country L		Country S
Business opportunities	Moderate	Country C	Country G	Country D
		Country N		Country I
				Country T
	Weak	Country R	Country O	Country P
			Country J	

institutional attributes. Indicators can be selected from these reports and commercial political risk analyses and recombined in the institutional framework. Or, TNCs can develop their own indicators of these institutional attributes of market economies from World Bank, United Nations, International Monetary Fund, regional development bank, and host country government databases.

Understanding the institutional foundations of transition countries can help TNCs choose which countries to select for trade and investment based on a comparison of business opportunities and the institutional strength of the market economy, as shown in table 17.2. Or they can use the same type of matrix to select methods of entry suggested by Root (1994) – indirect export, direct export, contractual arrangements, or foreign direct investment – that best fit current business opportunities and institutional characteristics of emerging market countries. TNCs with a better understanding of the institutional context of government policies and competitive business conditions in emerging markets can also develop more sophisticated and effective international expansion strategies suggested by Haley (2003), based on avoidance, control, cooperation, imitation or flexibility, and modify them as the strength of market-oriented policies and institutions changes over time.

18 | Protecting foreign investors in the developing world: a shift in US policy in the 1990s?

LOUIS T. WELLS

O VER the years, US investors in developing countries have frequently faced demands from host governments that they renegotiate the deals under which they made their original investment decisions. In some cases, the demands have amounted simply to expropriation. Few developing countries offer much security to foreign investors. Since sovereign governments can easily break promises, it is difficult for them to make commitments that investors find credible. The history of broken promises makes investors wary of new commitments. The blatant expropriations that were characteristic of the 1960s and early 1970s may have passed, but today's fights over electricity projects, water systems, and telecommunications in the developing world show that investors' property rights are still quite insecure. Outright takings may have evolved into what investors call "creeping expropriation," but whatever the mechanism, the original promises given investors when they enter a country have often fallen by the wayside.

Facing uncertain property rights systems in developing countries, US multinationals have turned to their home government for support to counter threats by developing countries. At times help has been forthcoming. At other times, a few comforting words from the US government have been backed by little action. Responses have not been random.

The early 1990s witnessed a substantial shift in what the US government was willing to do to support and protect its investors in the developing countries. The extent of the change has hardly been noted in the literature on international business. The decade saw both the creation of new institutions in government for the purpose of promoting and protecting US business interests and revision of stances taken by old ones. This chapter contrasts what I claim to be substantially new policies of the 1990s and early twenty-first century with those of the 1960s through the 1980s; offers an explanation as to why the purported changes might have occurred; raises questions about the impact of new policies on US foreign relations; and addresses the possibility that the new policies may fall victim to the war on terrorism. The 1990s may prove to have been a very special decade. Unfortunately, the evidence is anecdotal, and may have to remain so. In documenting change, I draw heavily on personal experiences and current case research, especially in Indonesia.

Policies until 1990

Since the end of the Second World War, the US government has rather consistently supported the opening of foreign markets to US exporters and investors. The Marshall Plan and subsequent aid bills called for some markets to be reserved for US suppliers, for example. In the GATT, the US pushed for lower tariffs abroad, and it pressed individual countries to loosen their restrictions on foreign direct investment. Most notably, it convinced the Japanese to relax their tight controls on incoming investment. But, when it came to intervening on behalf of an individual firm, the US government has been much more circumspect and seemingly less predictable, especially when the American firm was an investor involved in a serious dispute with the government of a host developing country.

Weapons

By the Second World War, the days of sending in the marines to defend American property or to collect foreign debts had passed. But, even in the late nineteenth and early twentieth centuries, US policy shifted somewhat from administration to administration.[1] Not only did the US government discontinue use of the military to defend investors,

---

[1] For an excellent account of one such intervention, and of earlier changes in US policies, see Veeser (2002). This book tells the story of US intervention in the Dominican Republic on behalf the New York-based San Domingo Improvement Company around 1900, and then changing attitudes as the administration of Theodore Roosevelt began to give priority to broader foreign policy interests of the United States. Policies seem to have taken another turn when William Howard Taft became president in 1909. A substantial section of his first "Annual Message" (December 7, 1909) was concerned with defense of American investors abroad. The speech mentions explicitly US intervention to support the claim of the Emery

but other aggressive tools also were used infrequently. Applying prohibitive tariffs to allegedly "stolen" goods, for example, became difficult under the GATT commitments to bound tariffs and most-favored nation rules.[2] Nevertheless, during the 1960s, 1970s, and 1980s, the US government had at its disposal a number of weapons that it could use to protect US investors abroad. Perhaps the first post-Second World War provision to protect US-owned property overseas was contained in the Sugar Act of 1948, which called for the suspension of import quotas on sugar from countries that had expropriated US property. Much more significant were the later Hickenlooper Amendment (or the First Hickenlooper Amendment, as it was eventually called) and the Gonzalez Amendment.

The Hickenlooper Amendment, in its various versions, came out of the US Congress as a supplement to the 1961 foreign aid bill.[3] The goal of the Amendment's sponsors was to provide an effective way of enforcing what the United States considered to be international law. The principle was referred to as the Hull Rule: "under every rule of law and equity, no government is entitled to expropriate private property, for whatever purpose, without provision for prompt, adequate, and effective payment therefor"(ibid.).[4] Even if all countries accepted the Hull Rule as international law, there was no international body to enforce it. With the Hickenlooper Amendment, the United States acquired legislation that would, at least in theory, allow it to enforce the rule unilaterally with respect to American investors abroad.

The Amendment authorized the US president to end foreign aid to a country that took American property without prompt compensation at full value and in convertible currency. Under the Amendment, the definition of a "taking" was broad, and included moves that:

Company against Nicaragua and the Alsop and Company claim against Chile. See also his further work in Veeser (forthcoming).

[2] In the late nineteenth or early twentieth century, threats of tariffs shutting Mexican ores and metals out of the US market served to protect the property rights of US investors in Mexican mines, according to Noel Maurer (2004).

[3] Amendment to the Foreign Assistance Act of 1961, Pub. L. No. 87–195, 77 Stat. 386 (1963) (codified as amended at 22 USC. § 2370(e)(1)(1994)).

[4] For an elaboration of the rule, see part III of Andrew T. Gusman, "Explaining the popularity of bilateral investment treaties: why LDCs sign treaties that hurt them," August 26, 1997, available at http://www.jeanmonnetprogram.org/papers/97/97–12.html (viewed 11/03).

- nationalized or expropriated the property of any United States person;
- repudiated or nullified any contract with any United States person;
- took any other action (such as the imposition of discriminatory taxes or other exactions) which had the effect of seizing ownership or control of the property of any United States person.

At the outset, the actions called for by the Amendment were mandatory. In early 1969, however, the State Department faced the prospect that the Amendment would be applied to Peru, which had expropriated assets of the US International Petroleum Corporation. Reluctant to cut off aid to Peru, a State Department memo to the new Nixon administration said, in part:

What has made the situation so tragic is the mandatory requirement of the US law. Were it not for that, the US would have more flexibility, more options, and greater time to handle the problem, and without the need to appear to 'punish' which makes the confrontation more serious ... Aside from the expectable consequences already noted, application of US sanctions will surely precipitate widespread and vehement criticism of the US throughout Latin America. The larger Latin American countries especially would view such action as 'intervention,' and would see the power to sanction in this way as threatening to themselves. In short, it would almost surely provide impetus toward unifying the now fractionated anti-US sentiment that exists in the region. (Duncombe, 2001)

The preference of the State Department seemed to be no Hickenlooper Amendment. A September 1970 meeting closed with the conclusion:

With respect to protection policy, there may be some difference of emphasis, but there seems to be agreement that we do not need the Hickenlooper Amendment.[5]

Recognizing, however, that the Amendment was not going to disappear, the Deputy Under Secretary for Economic Affairs in the State Department said:

At the first opportunity, the Hickenlooper Amendment should be revised to afford the President greater flexibility. The Administration AID bill to be submitted to the 92nd Congress may be the best opportunity. (Ibid.)

The Peruvian crisis did eventually lead to a new provision that provided for the flexibility that the State Department wanted. As the

---

[5] "Memorandum of Conversation," Washington, September 8, 1970, in Foreign Relations ... Vol. IV, op. cit., page 4. Duncombe (2001).

matter ended up, the executive branch could waive the application of the penalties under the Hickenlooper Amendment under either of two conditions. First, US aid could continue to the offending government if it returned the property, provided adequate and effective compensation in convertible foreign exchange or other mutually acceptable compensation, offered a domestic procedure providing prompt, adequate, and effective compensation, or submitted the dispute to arbitration. Second, and most important, "the President may waive the prohibitions … for a country, on an annual basis, if the President determines and so notifies Congress that it is in the national interest to do so" (ibid.).[6] In other words, the president did not have to cut off aid if doing so was contrary to US foreign policy interests.

The so-called Gonzalez Amendment[7] of 1972 provided an additional means for enforcing what the United States considered to be the rights of its investors abroad. In response to actions by foreign governments that were similar to those considered as a "taking" under the Hickenlooper Amendment, the Gonzalez Amendment required that:

The President shall instruct the United States Executive Directors of each multilateral development bank and international financial institution to vote against any loan or other utilization of the funds of such bank or institution for the benefit of any country … [imposing the same conditions as the Hickenlooper Amendment] unless such assistance is directed specifically to programs which serve the basic human needs of the citizens of that country.[8]

The US president had authority to waive this punishment very much like what he or she was granted for the Hickenlooper Amendment. The president did so soon, in 1972 for the Chilean nationalization of copper companies and a subsidiary of ITT.

---

[6] This is the version adopted in 1973.
[7] Section 21 of the Inter-American Development Bank Act, P.L. 92–246; Section 12 of the International Development Association Act, P.L. 92–247; and Section 18 of the Asian Development Bank Act, P.L. 92–245.
[8] The provisions were long known under the names Hickenlooper and Gonzalez Amendments. Eventually, the provisions were consolidated into the so-called Helms Amendment to the 1961 Foreign Aid Act. The quotations are from the most recent version. The amendment is available at: http://www.classactioncenter.net/HELMS_ AMENDMENT_TO_THE_1961_ FOREIGN_ AID_ACT.htm (viewed 11/03).

Although these two amendments were the principal legal weapons of the time, others were eventually added. The various extensions of the Trade Law of 1974 authorizing the Generalized System of Preferences (GSP) have included similar provisions. A developing country can become ineligible for preferential treatment if the country faces outstanding expropriation claims by US investors.[9] Further, Overseas Private Investment Corporation (OPIC) insurance is not available to future investors in countries that have taken over insured property and not reimbursed OPIC for claims it has paid.

The cumulative punishment against an offending country could be large: it could lose US foreign aid; US authorities could be instructed to vote against loans to the country in multilateral institutions such as the World Bank, the Asian Development Bank, and the Inter-American Development Bank; it could lose its duty-free access to the US market through the withdrawal of GSP privileges; and US investors in the country would not be able to obtain political risk insurance sponsored by the US government.

Use of weapons

The striking thing is not that the US armory was so full, but that the United States almost never used its weapons to defend its investors when trouble struck. The Hickenlooper Amendment, for example, was used extremely sparingly from its passage until 1990: in fact, only twice, against Ceylon in 1963 and against Ethiopia in 1979 (Gusman, 1997).[10]

To be sure, US officials commonly pronounced a few words of warning to countries that engaged in acts against US companies that might be called "creeping expropriation," or even outright nationalization. US embassies spoke up on behalf of US investors, and senators and congressmen were wont to write letters to foreign governments on behalf of their constituents, sometimes warning that aid was threatened. (See

---

[9] See, for example, "Foreign Relations Series Released: Foreign Assistance, International Development, Trade 1969–1972," from the Office of the Historian, Bureau of Public Affairs. United States Department of State. Available at: http://www.unc.edu/depts/diplomat/archives_roll/2003_01–03/frus_200301/frus_200301.html (viewed 11/03).

[10] The infrequency of use led to a nice article title: "Requiem for Hickenlooper" (Lillich, 1975).

Behrmann, Boddewyn, and Kapoor, 1975, p. 100 for a few examples.) But, in the overwhelming majority of instances, the words were not backed by concrete actions.

One might argue that the existence of the weapons was itself sufficient deterrent. Brandishing them might have been adequate to cause countries to back away from actions that might harm the interests of US firms. But, that appears not to have been the case. US property was frequently taken, and often without what the investor, at least, might consider adequate compensation. Moreover, the US president granted explicit waivers; they would not have been necessary if the threat alone had worked as a sufficiently strong deterrent.

Bureaucratic politics

The decision whether the weapons should be used in a particular case often generated tension within the US government, as various departments saw their interests differently. One set of events in which I was involved illustrates what I believe was a common pattern. In this case, in the early 1980s, the owner of an allegedly US company, Sea Oil & General Corporation, complained to the Indonesian government that its assets had been expropriated under the previous regime of Sukarno, and that it had never received compensation. It sought some $35 million. The owner of the company induced Senator Inouye, of Hawaii, to support his case. Inouye began to agitate in Congress for the application of the Hickenlooper Amendment against Indonesia.[11] As a consultant to the Indonesian minister of finance, I grew suspicious of the claim and asked the minister for permission to make an unofficial visit to the US embassy in Jakarta to try to learn more, especially about how embassy personnel stood on the matter. The ensuing discussions at the embassy made it clear that embassy officials did not know details about the company itself, but they did know of the claims and Senator Inouye's involvement. They were primarily interested in ensuring that the dispute did not disrupt US–Indonesian relations. Given their priorities, good bilateral relations were more important than purely commercial interests. Consequently, embassy officials had not pressed

---

[11] See Cong. Rec. S13631 (November 17, 1981); H.R. Rep. No. 97–245, 97th Cong., 1st Session, p. 45; Sen. Rep. No. 97–266, 97th Cong., 1st Session, p. 23.

the Indonesians to pay the claim, although they had passed on communications about the matter. They proved willing quietly to help the
Indonesians through an unofficial intermediary.

In this case, the claim turned out to be fraudulent, or at least seemed
to be so when US counsel engaged by the Indonesians submitted its
findings.[12] On counsel's recommendation, Indonesians offered to submit the claim to international arbitration in London. By doing so,
Indonesia disarmed the threats to aid. The State Department argued
that the Indonesians had met the requirements of the Hickenlooper
Amendment by offering to arbitrate. In the end, apparently the high
costs of arbitration and the likely unfavorable outcome ended the
claims. It is, however, doubtful that the threats to Indonesia would
have ever been enacted, given the strong opposition from the US
embassy in Jakarta.

The alignments within the US government were typical of the times.
The US Congress, or at least some senators or representatives, sided
with what they saw as constituents. They expressed little concern about
the effects that support for an investor might have on possibly conflicting foreign policy interests of the United States. In many cases, the
Treasury, and later the Department of Commerce, also sided with
investors. The Department of Commerce generally saw itself as the
friend of business.[13] But, even Commerce faced conflicts. US firms that
were not in trouble in the controversial country sometimes resisted the
application of US pressure, fearing that ill will created by strong US
support for one investor would spill over onto their activities.[14] The
Treasury's eagerness to protect US investors sometimes arose from the

---

[12] The story is rather long, but interesting, since the alleged American
appeared to be a Yugoslav with questionable claim to US nationality,
and the company a shell Dutch company he had acquired. Dutch claims
had long been settled by an Indonesian–Dutch accord on expropriations
under Sukarno.

[13] It was the Commerce Department that sent a "diplomatic note," on behalf
of the Reagan administration, to the European Community to discourage
their pursuit of an anti-trust case against IBM (Tagliabue 1982, Section 2,
p. 31).

[14] This opposition was sufficiently frequent that one writer saw it as evidence that US multinationals do dominate policy, leading to the lack of
use of the Hickenlooper Amendment. This interpretation of causality is
inconsistent with the changes of the 1990s, which will be described later.
See Lipson (1976), pp. 396–421.

potential financial obligations the US government might incur. Disputes might lead to claims against OPIC insurance or default on loans to overseas investments made by OPIC or the Export–Import Bank. One must suspect, as well, that Treasury's position was occasionally influenced by the fact that several Treasury secretaries came from business. Under Nixon, for example, Treasury Secretary Simon, who had come from Wall Street, seems to have been especially supportive of US investment abroad. As an advisor in Egypt in 1974, I encountered his eagerness to support the entry of US banks, in spite of the fact that his approach directly to President Sadat on their behalf disrupted the new decision-making processes that the Egyptians were attempting to build to handle future foreign investment applications. For the Treasury secretary, short-term help for the banks seemed to outweigh any long-term foreign policy interests, or even encouragement for the steps Egyptians were taking that might help in opening the country to other investors.[15]

Although they were silent in the Egypt case where there was no outright dispute involved, the local US embassy and the US State Department usually stood on the other side from Congress, Treasury, and Commerce when tensions rose. From the end of the Second World War until 1990 or so, embassies and the State Department were overwhelmingly concerned about foreign relations, as opposed to private commercial interests. As we have noted, the State Department had fought the Hickenlooper Amendment from the outset, seeing its application as potentially undermining its foreign policy objectives (Vernon and Spar, 1989, p. 157). Here lay the principal constraint on using what appeared to be overwhelming weapons. In the bulk of the cases of US firms' seeking US help, the State Department in the end prevailed. It could convince the president that US foreign policy interests would be damaged if powerful tools, such as the Hickenlooper Amendment, were actually applied. To be sure, senators

---

[15] There is some slight evidence that business origins matter in the behavior of former Wall Street executive Robert Rubin and former academic Larry Summers, both under Clinton. Rubin is said to have helped Mission Energy and GE in their negotiations for Paiton I, although the facts are not perfectly clear and Rubin has not responded to a request for clarification. When the 1997 Asian crisis hit Indonesia, Larry Summers – still Rubin's deputy – responded to Mission's request for help by saying he had "bigger fish to fry." Later as secretary, Summers, the former academic, seems not to have intervened in the ensuing disputes.

and representatives continued to send their letters, and officials sometimes put in a word for their constituents. But little real action took place.

In sum, Treasury officials, and eventually Commerce officials, typically saw disputes over foreign investment as big issues, when State viewed them as being minor in the scheme of things. As examples of the contrasting positions, consider first an excerpt from one of a series of memos from the Secretary of the Treasury to President Nixon, in 1971:

> We are facing a situation of snowballing expropriations of the property of American investors in Latin America and the Caribbean. We are facing a serious situation in Bolivia, Chile, Guyana and Jamaica. If we allow these actions to go forward without showing our serious concern by imposing financial penalties, we can expect other countries to take similar expropriatory action .... We must act to ... protect American business overseas ... (Duncombe, 2001, p. 7)

The memo went on to emphasize the exposure of OPIC. It recommended the application of the Hickenlooper Amendment and advocated votes against loans from multilateral financial institutions to offending countries.

A State Department memo, from the Acting Assistant Secretary of State for Inter-American Affairs, August 4, 1971, forcefully took the other side on the issue:

> ... having read the final (and to my mind retrograde) version of the response to .... Having been told that Treasury intends to pursue its so-called 'hard line' vigorously in the SRG meeting this afternoon, and having much in mind my responsibilities in the execution of our policy toward the countries of Latin America, I am obliged to ask you to consider the following observations in your approach to that meeting: ... 2. The basic judgment in 1969, reconfirmed earlier this year, was that our interests were endangered by the 'hegemonic' posture of the past and that the realities required that we seek an easier, more flexible, less directive association with the countries of Latin America ... 5. There is still, apparently, some attractiveness for some in the thesis that "if you get tough with the Latins, they may not like you but, by God, they respect you and shape up." I should have thought that this thesis, always of the most doubtful validity, would have been destroyed by the Dominican intervention, the most direct application of US authority in the recent history of our relations with Latin America, the most superficially successful exercise of that authority, and one of the most destructive in terms of our broad interests .... 8. Does anyone with even the most superficial knowledge of the psychological drives and the economic and political

imperatives of the developing countries seriously believe that the invocation of Hickenlooper in Peru would have produced compensation for IPC or have prevented Velasco from taking any other restrictive measures or deterred Allende from expropriating copper or kept the OPEC countries from moving against the oil companies? (Duncombe, 2001, p. 20)

The memo finished even more stridently:

In sum, I believe it essential that we turn back the onslaught of Treasury and its allies which is directed not only against the basics of the President's policy toward Latin America but also against the primacy of the [State] Department in the formulation and execution of foreign policy. Our objective should be to preserve the maximum flexibility in handling expropriation cases so that all our national interests can be assessed and so that we can consider, as we must if we are to be responsible, not only the short-term but also the middle and long-term play of those interests. (Duncombe, 2001, p. 20)

The State Department usually ended up the victor, as the changes in the Hickenlooper Amendment and its rare application indicate. In the end, investors in disputes often got little backing from home. It would be up to them to defend their property rights without strong support from the US government.

Indeed, from time to time the US government even stood on the opposite side from its overseas investors, when it saw its foreign policy interests as requiring an action that might be viewed as counter to the interests of its investors. These cases are very difficult to document. One fascinating example, however, is the story of ITT in Indonesia. In 1967, ITT was negotiating with the Indonesian government to establish a subsidiary (Indosat) that would operate the link between the country's domestic telephone system and the international satellite system. A middleman of Czech origin, Vladimir Gold, served as something of an agent for ITT. A part of his task was to deliver the required bribe to an Indonesian official (this was before the passage of the US Foreign Corrupt Practices Act). An ITT manager reports that the company gave Gold the money (something between $1 million and $5 million) to deliver to the important official. Soon thereafter, the Hong Kong office of ITT received a visitor, from the Central Intelligence Agency (CIA). The agent reported to ITT managers that the Indonesian official in question was a "friend" of the United States, and he had complained to the CIA that the promised money had not been paid. In the absence of signed receipts, the ITT management was unable to determine whether the middleman had kept the money or the "friend" of the United States had simply wanted to be paid twice. In response to US government pressure, ITT paid again.[16]

When ITT's same investment in Indonesia became the subject of a serious dispute in 1980, the US government was of no help. ITT attracted government attention when it refused to have its subsidiary construct an underwater cable to Penang, which Indonesia's President Suharto wanted for political reasons. The result was a challenge to the monopoly over international telecommunications that had been granted to ITT. Having determined that its nationals had mastered the technology and could operate the facility without foreign help, the Indonesian government set out to nationalize the project. It offered to pay compensation, but nothing close to ITT's requested net present value of projected earnings. The government argued that those projections included unwarranted monopoly returns. Although some of the loans to the project were covered by political risk insurance with OPIC, the US embassy remained completely aloof from the "renegotiation." No pressure from the US official community in support of ITT was at any time evident.[17] Negotiations were concluded and the Indonesians bought the facility for more or less 40 percent of the company's net present value calculations.

For the US embassy and the State Department, when the investment was originally negotiated US foreign policy interests lay unambiguously in supporting the new anti-communist government in Indonesia, not in assisting a specific US investor. After all, the regime of the left-leaning Sukarno had been toppled only two years earlier and the new Indonesian government had moved quickly to "eradicate" the communist movement. The recipient of the original bribe had been very cooperative with the United States in the process. Keeping him

---

[16] The events described here were related by a retired ITT executive in the 1980s and then confirmed again in 2002. Requests, under the Freedom of Information Act, to the CIA for relevant documentation were turned down, with the response that the Agency neither denies nor confirms the existence of such documents.

[17] The author was an advisor to the Indonesian negotiating team. The stories of the ITT/Indosat negotiations and renegotiations and the subsequent electric power conflicts of the 1990s will be related in a forthcoming book by this author and Rafiq Ahmed, tentatively titled *Wired for Conflict: Foreign Investment, Property Rights, and Development*.

happy was more important to US foreign policy than was supporting ITT. Thirteen years later, when it came time for renegotiation, US foreign policy interests with respect to Indonesia seem not to have changed.

Occasional support

There were, of course, occasions when the US government did much more for investors than simply supplying some supportive words from cabinet secretaries or members of Congress. Where no direct disputes were involved, the US government could be quite helpful to US business. Arthur Schlesinger, Jr., described one such case:

So long as no one paid much attention to that controversy, the American Embassy in Lima functioned almost as a branch office of Standard Oil of New Jersey. But once the Peruvian government nationalized the company and the controversy became a question of acute hemisphere concern, the United States, instead of applying the Hickenlooper amendment ... postponed the application of the amendment for the time being and is earnestly seeking ways to avoid applying it at all. (1970)

Other interventions occurred when the issue involved the interests of a number of US firms, but no serious dispute. The embassy might, for example, take at least a mild stance against new legislation that would harm the interests of investors.[18]

On occasion, the US government did align itself with investors who were engaged in major disputes. Perhaps in most of these cases, however, government support for US business abroad was forthcoming because the interests of the investors were seen as being congruent with other US foreign policy goals. The aim of the United States was not primarily the protection of US business, but rather the protection of some greater US interest. Thus, when access to oil was at issue, and could likely be best served by a continuing US private presence, the US government rather unabashedly supported US oil companies (Yergin, 1991). Even in oil cases, however, when supply did not appear to be threatened or where support of US business might involve pushing a government dangerously far, the US government tended to back off,

---

[18] For examples of this and other positions taken by US embassies, see Behrman, Boddewyn, and Kapoor (1975), pp. 84–89.

and even to support change sought by host countries. US oil companies had been encouraged to renegotiate their arrangements with Mossadegh in Iran, and the United States had even encouraged the British to strike a new deal, as well, under Truman.[19] Later, after Mossadegh's overthrow, the State Department was at most lukewarm in its support of US oil interests in Iran in 1976, as the Department was engaged in holding back Soviet influence in the region.[20] Similarly, it did not invoke harsh punishments against other oil-producing countries that took over US companies' concessions in the 1970s. Aramco became Saudi, for example, without strong US reaction.

Another kind of exception occurred when the offending country was already in what was perceived as the enemy camp. In those cases, cutting off US aid and voting against multilateral loans were acceptable but toothless tools, since such countries generally received no US aid or international loans anyway. Although Castro's actions were a proximate cause for Congress's original enthusiasm for the Hickenlooper Amendment, it had no bite in that case. Sugar quotas were withdrawn from Cuba; this was costly to Cuba. But they would have been withdrawn even if no US property had been involved. In another case, when Iran eventually fell into unfriendly hands, Iranian assets overseas were seized and were held against compensation for US assets that the Iranian government had taken. But with little effect. Like in Cuba and Iran, the conventional tools were ineffective against Allende's Chile, when his government took over US copper companies. In these extreme cases, the United States had no hesitancy to pass additional legislation and take other steps that would harm a country after an unfriendly government had taken power.

And there were the odd cases that might be described as "renegade." One example: When I and a colleague were advisors to the Liberian government on mining arrangements in the 1960s, the US ambassador to the country circulated a memo to US government employees in the embassy and USAID station telling them not to cooperate with us. When Liberian officials discovered the existence of the memo, their ambassador to the United States took up the matter with the US State

[19] *Business Week*, 2003, p. 28. Truman is quoted as saying: "We tried to get the blockheaded British to have their oil company make a fair deal with Iran."

[20] For this and other examples, see Vernon and Spar (1989), pp. 184–185.

Department, which had the embassy rescind the instruction. The State Department claimed that the ambassador was acting on his own, against US policy, because he was a close friend of the manager of a US mining firm the interests of which were being threatened by our efforts to see that the Liberians received their due from mining operations. In this case, the State Department quickly brought the ambassador in line with US foreign policy concerns. Liberia was not only anti-communist, but an occasional site for US military training and a major site for US diplomatic and CIA telecommunications facilities. From the State Department's viewpoint, these interests were much more important than the tax payments of some US mining firms.

Pre-1990 policies

In fact, US policy was complex. When no US strategic interests were involved, or when business and US strategic interests coincided, the US government could be quite helpful to American business abroad. When strategic interests and business interests conflicted, as was most often the case, the US government tended to back off from policies that might cause deterioration in important foreign policy relationships. Fear that a host government might move to the Left, or otherwise away from what the United States desired, was the greatest brake on help to business.[21] The State Department typically represented this interest.

Although the US government occasionally intervened on behalf of its investors in the 1960s, '70s, and '80s, an individual investor could not rely on government help when it got into trouble. As a result, investors abroad were left largely to their own devices and perhaps a little jawboning from Congressional supporters to mount their defenses in disputes with host governments. Not surprisingly, the period's most notable academic article (Moran, 1973) on protecting investments abroad recommended a set of defenses that was based on the explicit recognition that direct help from the US government was unlikely to be forthcoming.

---

[21] "Going communist" was not always the worry. Arthur Schlesinger, Jr., described Soviet objectives as including simply moving states away from close ties to the United States. See Schlesinger (1970).

End of the Cold War

The decade of the '90s saw sharp change in the US government's stance toward its investors abroad. I believe that the change resulted largely from the end of the Cold War. Two implications of the "peace" led the move toward new policies.

First, US foreign policy was no longer dominated by a fear that communism would spread in the Third World. One result was that the State Department could not credibly invoke the need to check the spread of communist influence to restrain other government agencies – in particular, the US Treasury and the Department of Commerce – in their zeal to support US business interests abroad. In response to constraints, the Commerce Department undertook new initiatives to help American business as the resistance of State declined.

Second, the State Department had to shift its policies in response to the challenges to its budget mounted in the US Congress, especially by the Senate Foreign Relations Committee. Budget pressure was, of course, closely connected to the end of the Cold War. With the demise of State's argument that it should be supported for its efforts to halt communism, the Department's ability to obtain funding started to erode. The Senate Foreign Relations Committee began to squeeze budgets and even to try to rearrange the structures of the organizations involved in foreign relations. Especially when Jesse Helms ascended to chairmanship of the Committee in 1995, the Committee grew very aggressive with respect to foreign relations appropriations and organization. In 1996, the Committee held up eighteen nominations to ambassador posts in an effort to force the merger of the US Information Agency, the Arms Control and Disarmament Agency, and the State Department. The president refused the merger, but the Committee released the nominations only when the White House accepted a cut of $1.7 billion in spending on foreign affairs over the next five years. As foreign-affairs budgets eroded, embassies abroad implemented sharp cost-cutting measures. In the mid-1990s, the US embassy in Jakarta, for example, reported that it had gone so far as to cancel subscriptions to local magazines that had served as important sources of information for officials and American visitors.

With the disappearance of its principal argument for substantial budget support, the State Department needed a new *raison d'être*. To fill the gap, it turned to supporting US business as a goal. Interviews in early 2003 with a foreign service official posted in Indonesia provided evidence for one of the mechanisms for implementing this turn. He said that his training (in the '90s) as a new foreign-service officer included explicit lessons in the need to support US business in order to defend the Department's budget. He viewed advocacy of business interests as an essential part of his job.

New institutions and new missions

With the brakes released by the State Department, the US Department of Commerce stepped in to build new institutions to support US investors. In 1993, for example, it created the Advocacy Center, with the explicit task of providing help to US business. Long a supporter of US exports, the Department increased assistance to US investors abroad, as well. Although the Center falls administratively under the parts of Commerce devoted to trade development, its web-posted "success stories" include help to a number of US investors abroad.

The Center's website says:

Assistance can include a visit to a key foreign official by a high-ranking US government official; direct support by US officials (including Commerce and State Department officers) stationed at US embassies; and coordinated action by US government agencies to provide maximum assistance. (http://www. export.gov/advocacyassistance.html [viewed 11/03])

An applicant for the Center's help is asked to fill out a questionnaire. The questions are aimed at determining whether the international transaction to be supported is in the US national interest. The questions suggest that US interest is measured largely by the US content in the transaction. Thus, an American investor that plans to use US equipment for its foreign subsidiary is likely to satisfy the criteria for the Center's assistance.

The US company requesting help must also certify that it and its affiliates:

- have not engaged and will not engage in the bribery of foreign officials in connection with the matter for which advocacy assistance is being sought; and
- maintain and enforce a policy that prohibits the bribery of foreign officials.

The firm must further acknowledge that failure to comply with the terms of the agreement may result in the denial of advocacy assistance (website of the Advocacy Center: http://www.ita.doc.gov/td/advocacy/ guidline2.htm [viewed 11/03]).

The application offers no definition of bribery. Presumably, however, the implied meaning is the same as that in the US Foreign Corrupt Practices Act, with its substantial loopholes. If so, it is not clear why a firm should have to certify that it is obeying a law that it is required to honor anyway. Beyond this, a question about environmental impact, and the instruction to the firm to "highlight the competitiveness of your bid in terms of technology and price," the Center seems to pay little attention to whether the transaction for which a business is seeking support is in the interest of the foreign country.

Amusingly, in late 2001 the Center's website listed among its success stories its interventions on behalf of Enron in India, Nicaragua, and Turkey. These "successes" no longer appeared in the list in September 2002! This even though some of the success stories still posted appear to have been contemporaneous with those that had been erased.

The Advocacy Center promised broad help to applicants:

[T]he Advocacy Center acts as a unique, central coordinating point to marshall [sic] the resources of 19 US government agencies in the Trade Promotion Coordinating Committee (TPCC). (http://www.ita.doc.gov/td/ advocacy/ [viewed 10/03])[22]

Within the Commerce Department a second organization also became increasingly involved in supporting US investors. This was the Foreign and US Commercial Services in the US Department of Commerce (eventually named simply US Commercial Service). This organization incorporates the commercial officers in US embassies abroad. The organization's website gives its purpose:

For over 20 years the US Commercial Service of the US Department of Commerce has successfully brought together exporters and importers of US goods and services around the world. Our team of more than 1,800 trade professionals in 105 US cities and 151 US Embassies, Consulates and Trade Centers around the world is here to help companies navigate the complex

---

[22] For a description of the TPCC, see: http://www.exportmichigan.com/ tpcc.htm#sectB (viewed 11/03). The TPCC fell under the Department of Commerce's jurisdiction.

international trade process. How can we help you? (http://www.buyusa.gov/home/ [viewed 11/03])

Its officers are charged with:

- trade counseling
- trade contact services
- product and service promotion
- essential market research
- customized market research
- trade leads
- advocacy on behalf of US business interests
- trade finance information and support
- promotion and management of trade shows
- organization of international trade missions
- credit checks on potential overseas business partners
- certification of established trade events.

(http://www.usemb-ashgabat.usia.co.at/commerce.html [viewed 11/03])

This organization grew out of the transfer, in 1979 by President Carter, of overseas commercial programs from the Department of State to the Department of Commerce. In 1980, the Foreign Commercial Service was created, which became the US and Foreign Commercial Service. Commercial officers in embassies abroad reported to Commerce, rather than to State. Thus, the organization considerably predates the end of the Cold War. It was long associated primarily with promoting US exports. And, its literature suggests, it was charged with focusing on small- and medium-size enterprises. But, it has gradually taken on the role of the field operative for the Advocacy Center, and it has clearly not limited itself to advocacy for small American firms. Presumably the item "advocacy on behalf of US business interests" reflects its increasingly important role of defending US investors overseas. The Indonesian office lists its functions in a way that seems to make it clear that it is interested in more than US exports:

Our Mission
- To promote the export of goods and services from the United States.
- To help US businesses find qualified international partners.
- To represent US business interests internationally.

(http://www.buyusa.gov/indonesia/en/ [viewed 11/03])

The mission statement makes no claim that the service operates in the interest of any broader US foreign policy, or in the interest of development in its country of location.

A number of websites accuse the Commerce Department, especially when it was under Ron Brown's administration, of choosing its candidates for support by their contributions to Clinton's political funds. One might even hypothesize that increased competition for campaign finance was also a factor leading to new US support for business. But this hypothesis is difficult to prove or disprove without access to the Department's internal records. It may be the case that any applicant was served equally. It may not be.

New laws

The 1990s saw not only change in the interests of the State Department, the creation of new institutions to support US business abroad, and shifting roles for long-existing ones, but during the period US laws were also strengthened to protect US property overseas and even to extend the definition of US property.

Like earlier foreign aid and trade bills, the May 2000 African Growth and Opportunity Act (AGOA)[23] withheld its benefits from countries facing outstanding expropriation claims. The mechanism for implementing the constraint was to make GSP eligibility a condition for AGOA benefits. To be eligible for GSP, the reader will remember, a country had to be free of expropriation claims.

Perhaps the strangest 1990s extension of law affecting foreign investment was the granting of retroactive rights to Latin Americans whose property had been taken before they became US citizens. This occurred with the passage of the Helms–Gonzalez Amendment to the 1994 Foreign Assistance Act. Aimed at dealing with properties taken in Nicaragua by the Sandinista government in the previous decade, it applied a range of sanctions to countries guilty of taking properties from current US citizens of Latin American origin, even though they may not have been US citizens at the time of the expropriation. In the end, the new law would support primarily the interests of former Cubans and Nicaraguans.

At first the State Department objected to Jesse Helms' effort to pass this amendment that would dramatically extend the impact of the old Hickenlooper Amendment. It would, State believed, make cooperation with the new Chamorro government in Nicaragua exceedingly

[23] H.R. 1432.

difficult. After all, this government had replaced the previous Marxist Sandinista regime and should be supported. Eager to help this non-communist government, State resisted making property claims of US citizens the central issue in determining US aid to, and cooperation with, the new regime. In 1994, however, the State Department backed off from its opposition; eventually, the US embassy in Nicaragua even ran advertisements in Miami inviting Nicaraguans to file claims under the amendment (Kaufman and Zimmerman, 1997). Helms, remember, chaired the committee that determined the budget for the foreign service.

Administration pressure

US support for American investors went further. The White House itself exerted increasing pressure on foreign governments on behalf of American investors. Some degree of verbal support for US business had always been a feature of presidential and secretarial visits to countries. And business executives hitchhiked on the back of those visits. In the 1990s, however, White House entourages abroad grew to be loaded with business executives seeking investment and other business opportunities. This was true whether the president was Republican or Democratic.

Just to illustrate, when Ron Brown's plane crashed in 1996 in Croatia, the following executives were on-board:

Barry Conrad, Barrington Corp.
Paul Cushman, Riggs National Bank
Robert Donovan, ABB, Inc.
Claudio Elia, Air and Water Technologies Corp.
Leonard Pieroni, The Parsons Corp.
John Scoville, Harza Engineering Corp.
Donald Terner, Bridge Housing Corp.
Stuart Tholan, Bechtel Corp.
David Ford, Interguard Corp.
Frank Maier, Ensearch International Corp.
Walter Murphy, AT&T Submarine Systems, Inc.
Robert Whittaker, Foster Wheeler Energy International, Inc. (PBS Online Newshour, 1996)

Similarly, when Secretary of Commerce Evans and other members of the Bush Administration traveled to Asia in April 2002, they took along fifteen senior executives, representing medical products, information technology, telecommunications, and clean energy and environmental technology. (http://www.technology.gov/PRel/p_ma020426.htm [viewed 11/03])

White House support of US business abroad began in the 1990s to extend beyond this kind of general help, which was probably growing in scale during the decade. Direct pressure was applied to countries reluctant to give investment opportunities to particular firms.

One tool used by the US government was the bilateral investment treaty (BIT). Before the 1990s, BITs seemed to have mattered little to investors. In fact, in my experience most foreign investors in the 1980s did not even know whether their host countries had signed a BIT with the investors' home countries. That began to change in the 1990s. First, the number of BITs grew rapidly. The rapid spread of BITs probably had little to do with the change in US policy toward investors; rather, it was more likely the result of the increasing enthusiasm for foreign investment in the developing world. BITs appeared to address a need on the part of developing countries to add credibility to commitments these countries made to investors.[24] Since a sovereign government finds it difficult to make convincing credible commitments, and even more so when the legal system and political processes might be weak or discriminate against foreigners, governments negotiated bilateral investment treaties that allowed enforcement of their commitments outside their borders, usually by international arbitration. Thus, when a dispute arose, the home country party to the treaty could press, under the treaty, for disputes to go to arbitration. Since they incorporated essentially the Hull Rule, and required prompt and adequate compensation in the case of nationalization, BITs almost to a case supported investors' interests. Often the critical question that arbitrators resolved was whether government acts amounted to expropriation and what the financial awards ought to be.

BITs not only protected investors, but their new popularity on the part of developing countries was used by the US White House in extralegal ways to support American firms' interests. Eager for a BIT with the United States as a tool to encourage US investment, a host country could be pressed to support American investors as an informal condition of the US agreeing to a BIT. One example occurred in

---

[24] For a well-argued explanation of the spread of BITs, see Guzman (1997).

Mozambique.[25] In 1995 and 1996, US officials intervened on behalf of Enron, which was seeking a contract for a gas line to a proposed steel plant, for which Enron would also be responsible. CNSNews.com reports that the Mozambican Minister of Mineral Resources complained of "outright threats to withhold development funds if we didn't sign." The US government (according to the minister, through the US Embassy Deputy Chief of Mission) pushed for the agreement. The deputy chief, the minister said, "pressured me to sign a deal that was not good for Mozambique. He was not a neutral diplomat,"[26] the *Houston Chronicle* said. My interviews in Maputo at the time confirmed that the US embassy threatened to cut off US aid if Enron did not get the deal, a substantial threat to desperately poor Mozambique (Morano, 2002). These threats were reinforced when Clinton visited to sign a BIT. He is reported to have asked the Mozambican president why he should sign the BIT if a US company did not receive the gas pipeline contract.[27]

The old kinds of pressures continued, of course. With no dispute involved, in 1991 Bush I's Vice President Quayle pushed Indonesians to give the $2.5 billion Paiton I power project to a small New England power company, Intercontinental Energy, which had no experience in building any power plants abroad, much less a plant of this size. Intercontinental's project was pushed by Quayle, who issued a "personal appeal" to the Indonesians in May.[28] Some supplemental help

---

[25] Parts of the story are reported in Morano, (2002). I had learned of the events in Mozambique at the time, from interviews at the US embassy and with Mozambican officials.

[26] *Newsmax* (Morano, 2002) credits the *Houston Chronicle* for this quote.

[27] The pressure was mentioned by an Enron employee and confirmed by US embassy officials. It worked. Enron received the contract. On the other hand, lower-level bureaucrats had become so outraged at Enron's behavior that it is, in my view, unlikely that Enron could have ever actually undertaken the project. This was never tested, since it had not been begun by the time of Enron's collapse.

[28] See Solomon and Waldman (1998). The contents suggest that authors might almost have well used a different subtitle: "Critics Accuse Companies of Using Links with US Government to Win Contracts." Perhaps Intercontinental's contributions had helped it a bit. I know only those made in New Jersey; according to the web, they amounted to $10,200 from 1993 to 1997 for the Republicans, with $1,000 for Democrats. See http://www.opensecrets.org/

for Intercontinental was also forthcoming from others in the US government. In July of the same year, US Senator Brock Adams (Democrat from Washington State) added his support in a letter to the Indonesian ambassador to the United States, in which he stated that US–Indonesian trade relations would improve if BNIE were awarded the project. He made the then-inaccurate claim that Intercontinental was the only US firm interested in the project. The second firm (a consortium including Mission Energy and General Electric affiliates) later received help from the US executive branch and from the US embassy in Jakarta in negotiating the power purchase agreement for Paiton I, which was signed in February 1994. One illustration of US intervention: late in the negotiations, in January 1994, three US official government delegations pressed the deal with Indonesians; one group was led by the then US Treasury Secretary, Lloyd Bentsen (Mills, 2002, p. 128). The US embassy in Jakarta found no reason to try to counter this pressure. Still, perhaps up to this point, US support differed only somewhat from the Simon intervention in Egypt. No dispute was involved, just pressure for a business deal. That was to change.

Stronger intervention

After the Cold War, embassy support went much further than before when disputes arose between investors and host governments. The extent of the shift in attitudes of US embassies toward investors was again reflected in the activities of Enron, a company that learned early how to use the newly emerging support that was becoming available from both the Bush I and the Clinton administrations. When Frank Wisner was ambassador to the Philippines in 1991–1992, Enron was negotiating two Subic Bay power plants. When he moved on to become ambassador to India, in the words of a critical report: "he fought long and hard to secure various deals for Enron. He went so far as to boycott the 'India Power '96 – Beyond Dabhol' summit, despite being scheduled to give an address (this was part of a US advisory to companies to avoid

capi/report/cgi-win/rpt_single.exe?404 (viewed 5/03). The lead entrepreneur behind this family-controlled company did not respond to a request for an interview in connection with a book that I am writing on infrastructure agreements in Indonesia.

India for six-months, a pressure tactic on India during the winter of 1995–1996)" (Prashad, 1997). In October 1997, within a few months after his leaving the ambassadorial post in India, Wisner was appointed to the board of an Enron affiliate, Enron Oil and Gas. Some critics have viewed this as his reward for helping the company in these two difficult negotiations. Wisner's lack of a business background that might qualify him for the board offers some plausibility to the claim. The Enron story turned out to illustrate a very different attitude of the State Department from the story cited earlier, about a "renegade" ambassador in Liberia at a time when the Cold War was still raging. There seemed to have been no effort from Washington to rein in Wisner's help to Enron.

There is considerable evidence that the Department of Commerce became the principal instrument within the US government for bringing other agencies into line with the new policies of supporting American investors abroad. When it came to assembling finance for the Paiton I project in Indonesia, Secretary of Commerce Ron Brown is said to have played a personal role in making sure that US government finance would be available. The Asian Development Bank had declined to put up money, supposedly because of the involvement of President Suharto's family. With this source not available, Commerce pressed for $1.8 billion in limited recourse project financing from US Export–Import Bank and OPIC (and eventually from the Japanese Export–Import Bank, as well).[29] Commerce Department support continued even as some Indonesians expressed their lack of enthusiasm about the project. One report says: "When the representative of the US EXIM Bank visited Indonesia, several experts of the government and PLN pointed out to her that the country did not need Paiton I" (Bossard, 2000). Yet, some $500 million in "US content" (that is, US business) was purportedly to result from the deal (White House, 1994). The US Export–Import Bank stepped in and offered a construction loan and $540 million of political-risk guarantee (ExIm, n.d.).

---

[29] Meetings of Mission managers with Department of Commerce officials, the reluctance of the Asian Development Bank to support the project, and subsequent efforts by the Commerce Department to involve other US agencies in providing finance are documented in material released under the Freedom of Information Act and posted on the web at: http://www.softwar.net/paiton2.html (viewed 11/03).

OPIC also put up money and political-risk insurance for GE.[30] President Clinton and his entourage (including probably Warren Christopher, as Secretary of State, but formerly on the board of Mission, the principal investor) arrived in Indonesia for an APEC meeting and witnessed the signing of the preliminary financial package on November 16, 1994.[31]

Although these interventions in support of Mission and General Electric were possibly greater than what would have been provided prior to 1990, they did not occur in an open dispute between investor and host country. That was, however, soon to come. The Asian Currency Crisis of 1997 slowed the growth in demand for electricity in Indonesia. And the decline in the value of the Indonesian currency meant that the state-owned power company did not have the income to pay the largely dollar-denominated prices for all the electricity the contracts required them to buy, much of which was unneeded. Indonesians sought to postpone projects and to lower prices of electricity. Paiton I was one of the projects the Indonesians sought to renegotiate. In the ensuing disputes, the US government showed little hesitancy to intervene on behalf of US investors.

Early on in the conflict, US support was much like that of the pre-Cold War days. Two US senators, Trent Lott (Republican, Mississippi) and Newt Gingrich (Republican, Georgia), spoke up in support of US investors in power generating, for example. When Mission managers sought support from then-Deputy Secretary of the US Treasury Larry Summers, who visited Indonesia during the early stage of the crisis, they were rebuffed, with the response that he "had bigger fish to fry."[32] In other words, dealing with an economic crisis that seemed contagious was more important than defending the interest of a few US firms. This was a traditional kind of US position.

But new attitudes on the part of the US government would soon emerge. Mission managers again sought help from the US Department

---

[30] See documents concerning Paiton I obtained under the Freedom of Information Act and posted on the web at: http://www.softwar.net/paiton2.html (viewed 11/03).

[31] When I contacted him, Christopher declined to confirm or deny his presence at the meeting or to comment on his role in Mission's entry to Indonesia.

[32] Reported to me by a foreign manager involved in the effort to enlist support.

of Commerce. On August 6, 1998, Edward Muller, CEO of Mission's parent company, met with US Secretary of Commerce Daley. At the time, Daley, who had taken over Brown's job after Brown's 1996 death in a Bosnian airplane crash, seemed cautious. He would commit only to generic calls for the Indonesians to honor their contracts. In limiting his support, he seemed to be responding to the risk that other investors might resist US intervention, not to any principled reluctance to defend an investor.[33]

The hesitancy of the new Secretary of Commerce did not constrain the new head (James Harmon) of the Export–Import Bank, which had made loans to Paiton I. Soon Summers' concerns about broad US interests in the region and Commerce's temporary worry about other investors no longer held back the US government. Since Indonesia was not about to go communist, the State Department had no credible basis to resist the new moves, if it had desired to do so. The Export–Import Bank stepped in aggressively to defend the projects to which it had made loans. *The Wall Street Journal* was soon to say of Harmon, the bank's head: "[he] has played the hero in Asia's economic crisis and he has played the bully." Indonesians we interviewed would say he earned the "bully" appellation. One step on the part of the bank was the construction of a coalition of the usually competing official creditors to enforce their claims. After gathering creditors in Tokyo, Harmon reported: "the US Exim Bank and 18 other credit agencies committed themselves in Tokyo to 'greater cooperation on maintaining and increasing trade finance, resolving workouts, and other issues.'" (Wall Street Journal, 1999). Export–Import Bank officials visited Indonesia from October 14 to 17, 1998, to "reinforce the message that a speedy and transparent handling of these issues is in both countries' interest."[34] US pressure was beginning, but would grow.

---

[33] See documents obtained from the Freedom of Information Act referred to earlier. There are numerous examples of other American investors fearing that US support of a particular investor might backfire and harm their interests in the same host country. For an example at the beginning of the twentieth century, see Veeser (forthcoming), p. 133. He describes the concerns of US planters in the Dominican Republic over intervention on behalf of the San Domingo Improvement Company.

[34] A State Department memo reporting from the meetings is reproduced at: talking_points.tripod.com/enron/id4.html (viewed 7/03).

Soon the US government's OPIC, which had loans and political risk insurance at stake, became involved in the disputes over Paiton I and other electricity generating projects. It sent "Advocacy Missions" to Indonesia (Martin, 2001, p. 66) in July, September, and November of 1998. By December, OPIC's head, George Munoz, was quoted as saying: "Contracts must be honored" (Solomon and Waldman, 1998).[35] This and other stronger support from Munoz were considered by a number of Indonesians as hard-line and ill mannered.[36] One advisor to the Indonesian government described the style of his intervention in terms that are not suitable for print.

US pressure continued to grow. The US delegation to the Paris Club discussions of rescheduling Indonesia's debt brought up the controversy over Indonesia's failure to honor the power purchasing agreements. In the same month, US support for its companies turned from visits, admonition, and threats to real action. It attempted (but failed) to block a $400 million loan from the Asian Development Bank to Indonesia, even though no formal charges of expropriation had been made against Indonesia and the successor to the Gonzalez Amendment had not been invoked.

The US soon issued a formal threat: it would apply the Helms–Gonzalez Amendment (as the latest version was known) and vote against loans by multilateral agencies to Indonesia. The implied next steps were the ending of US aid and the withdrawal of Indonesia's duty-free access to the US market under the Generalized System of Preferences. Indonesia's textile quotas might also be threatened. To make sure that the point was clear, on December 9, 1999, the export credit agencies wrote the coordinating minister for the economy, the finance minister, the new minister for state-owned enterprises, the head of BAPPENAS, and the minister of energy and mines that "the private power problem ... should be settled as among first priority and as soon as possible (*Suara Pembaruan*, 1999)."

---

[35] The statement may have been made when Munoz visited Indonesia September 11–13, 1998, to advocate on behalf of projects in which OPIC had an interest.

[36] Especially damaging to OPIC's reputation was a meeting in Washington between a team of Indonesians and their advisors and Munoz. I plan to report on that meeting in a forthcoming book. Unfortunately, Munoz refused to be interviewed in connection with the research for that book.

US pressure came from other sources, as well. The Indonesian press reported on parliament's complaints about interference, saying that US Senators Dianne Feinstein (Democrat, California), Chuck Hagel (Republican, Nebraska), Paul Coverdell (Republican, Georgia), Chuck Robb (Democrat, Virginia), Daniel Inouye (Democrat, Hawaii), and John Breaux (Democrat, Louisiana) had written a letter to President Habibie warning him to take care of the power sector problems, and in particular Paiton I.[37]

Under President Habibie, the Indonesians had filed a case in local courts against Paiton I, charging that the contract was illegal. The plaintiffs alleged corruption, violation of the authorizing decrees, and overbilling of investment by the company.

But, Indonesia soon gained a new president, Abdurrahman Wahid (Gus Dur). The US ambassador to Indonesia, Gelbard, sought to stop the case. He promised that the US company would in exchange, the day after the case was withdrawn, drop the arbitration request that it had initiated. In fact, in late 1999 or early 2000, Gus Dur had ordered the case dropped, but there was some delay in (and resistance to) implementing the order. When the case was withdrawn, the company behaved as the ambassador had promised.

Many Indonesians we spoke with believe that the Indonesian president had dropped the case as a result of pressure from the United States government. A number said that the US government pressed the new president hard when he visited the United States, in November 1999, for treatment at the Moran Eye Center in Salt Lake City, Utah. Gus Dur did talk with President Clinton on the trip, but what transpired is not a part of the public record. One version of the story is that the US government threatened to have the IMF withdraw support for Indonesia if he remained committed to the legal route. In June 2003, I asked Gus Dur himself why he had dropped the Paiton I court case.[38] I pointed out that many in Indonesia thought the decision to be the result of US pressure. The former president said: "No, Clinton and I saw eye-to-eye on everything, with the exception of Monica

---

[37] Tekak No. 10, year 11, January 3–9, 2000, cited in presentation by Situmeang (2001). Hardiv was the head of the Indonesian negotiating team.

[38] Gus Dur was visiting Harvard to attend the graduation of a daughter from Harvard's Kennedy School of Government.

Lewinsky." The meaning of this from a blind Javanese politician is something the reader will have to puzzle out. It is, however, likely that US pressure played at least some role in the decision.

As the Paiton renegotiations proceeded, US intervention became more strident. In January 2000 OPIC again sent representatives to various ministers in Jakarta to press for a settlement with Paiton I; OPIC even threatened to seize Indonesian assets abroad if the government did not meet its payment obligations to US power companies.

Paiton I was, of course, not the only electric power facility under renegotiation. The US government intervened in others, as well. Two CalEnergy geothermal projects became the subject of arbitration, and CalEnergy eventually collected from OPIC under its political risk insurance. OPIC then turned to the Indonesians for compensation. The resulting negotiations turned quite sour. In July 2000, the US ambassador, Gelbard, who was already noted for his brusque behavior and small reserve of patience, said he was "running out of patience" with Indonesia's tardy payment to OPIC. The threat: "There is always the possibility of declaring expropriation .... If we were to do this, it would result in a dramatic deterioration of the rupiah and would hurt Indonesia very much" (Billington, 2001). In other words, Gelbard was warning of the application of the principles of the Hickenlooper Amendment, which would have cut off aid to Indonesia. The ambassador's comments generated a sharp response from the Coordinating Minister for the Economy, Kwik Kian Gie, who "slammed" the ambassador for his threatening statements. The Minister of Finance, Bambang Sudibyo, was equally annoyed and rejected the ambassador's threat: "Go ahead and threaten us. You will not deal with me, but with the state" (Lawrence et al., 2000). A legislator, Priyo Budi Santoso, answered that he would block government payment to OPIC because of the corruption, cronyism, and nepotism in the deal, and pointed out that local contractors still had not been paid for their work on the project. He boasted: "If the US government seizes our assets, then we will seize their assets here." OPIC went ahead and removed Indonesia from the list of countries eligible for political risk insurance. OPIC and the US embassy were not making friends for the United States, but at the time this did not seem to be high priority.

The US stance on behalf of its investors in Indonesia was not unique. Turkey had faced similar problems with generating projects. The problems of power companies in Turkey had their origins, like those in Indonesia, in forecasts of rapidly growing demand for electricity in the second half of the 1990s. The government seemed to be willing to offer sovereign guarantees for the sales contracts that would underlie the power generating investments. But, in late 2000 Turkey faced its own economic crisis. As a part of the response, it decided not to guarantee new power deals and to reduce guarantee offers on projects under discussion from twenty to ten years. The new policy was implemented, Turkish officials claim, at the urging of the IMF. Some investors, however, had at least some signatures (but perhaps not all that were required) on contracts. Simultaneously, the Turkish courts began to challenge the legality of the underlying "build, operate, and transfer" contracts, claiming that they were concessions subject to legal review (US Department of Energy, 2003). Absent the supposedly promised guarantees and with some of the contracts facing legal challenges, investors were unwilling to proceed. They wanted the guarantees or they wanted their investment thus far returned, and perhaps more. When I visited Turkey in 2002, the commercial officer in the US embassy seemed all consumed by his drive to press the Turkish government to provide compensation to US companies for electric power contracts that had been "cancelled." The intensity of the conversation on this subject would have suggested that this was the only foreign relations issue with Turkey that interested the United States.

Extending the reach

In another odd case, in the 1990s both the Bush I and the Clinton administrations extended helping hands to Chiquita Brands. This was an American firm that was not exporting from the United States, but which was facing trade barriers in Europe for products from its investments in third countries.

The US government had built a history before the Second World War of defending its plantation investors in Central America. The United Fruit Company had been viewed by some nationalists as little more than an extension of the US government in the "banana republics." But, the Cold War saw the US withdraw from aggressively defending the interests of US plantation companies abroad. That is, until the 1990s. And when it returned to the defense of Chiquita Brands, the descendent of United Fruit, the US government did so in an interesting way.

The new challenge to this US foreign investor did not come from host country threats. Rather, in 1993 the European Union took steps that would limit Chiquita's sales in Europe. As a part of the 1992 effort to create a single market, the Europeans had agreed on a common policy toward banana imports. Up to this point, bananas were one of a few products that were not subject to a common import regime. The new policy hurt exports from Colombia, Costa Rica, Ecuador, Guatemala, Nicaragua, Panama, and Venezuela, and it allocated quotas for the European market by firm. This was a direct challenge to Chiquita, whose principal sources were in the region affected by the restrictions, and whose quotas would have limited its sales more than would the old policies.

Chiquita first supported the countries in which it produced bananas, as those that were members of the GATT filed cases against Europe. The GATT ruled in favor of the complaining countries, but the organization had no teeth to enforce its decision. Chiquita, a substantial contributor to both the Republicans and the Democrats, then turned to the US government for support.

Of course, the United States had a long history of aiding US exports. But the United States was hardly likely to be a major supplier of bananas to the European Union. Bananas were not US exports. Rather, it was the interests of a US foreign investor that were under attack. Helping it could, of course, have been seen by potential exporting developing countries as helping their interests as well. Thus, no cost to US foreign policy in those locations. On the other hand, US intervention would harm the interests of the developing countries that benefited from the new European Union rules. US intervention was sure to anger some subset of developing countries. Moreover, the solidarity of the countries facing new restrictions had been broken somewhat as the European Union offered separate deals to Costa Rica and Colombia. In spite of the foreign policy risks, the United States took up the case on behalf of Chiquita in the World Trade Organization, when that institution replaced GATT. In addition, Chiquita induced Senator Bob Dole (no relation to Chiquita's competitor Dole) to threaten to withdraw aid from Colombia (drug-fighting money) and to eliminate Costa Rica's preferential access to the US market. These were penalties for breaking ranks with other Latin American banana producers. Senator Dole backed off only when his run for the presidency was coming up and Common Cause challenged him on his support for Chiquita.

If these events had occurred before the end of the Cold War, the State Department would probably have tried to apply the brakes before US intervention threatened relations with several countries. But, those brakes were slipping in the 1990s.[39]

In a twist to the banana story, the US government became involved next in the battle between Chiquita and Dole (the fruit company, this time) over the European market. The Europeans first proposed a solution that would have allocated quotas in a way that might have helped Dole more than Chiquita. Under US pressure, the Europeans turned to an alternative allocation method that satisfied Chiquita.

The new willingness of the US government to intervene on behalf of its investors seems well understood by firms in other countries. So well understood that one firm, Chile's Endesa, has tried to capture US identity and the resulting protection by entering joint ventures with US partners when it went to third markets. According to Patricio Del Sol and Joe Kogan, "The American partner was essential. It was believed, for example, that the American partner, if supported by the American Embassy, might help to prevent arbitrary changes in the rules of the local government" (Del Sol and Kogan, 2003).

Another kind of extension of US government power has occurred with political risk insurance. Insurance companies, including Lloyd's, have recently started to attach their private political risk insurance policies to the US government's OPIC insurance. With a "claims cooperation agreement," OPIC will use the full power of the US government to collect from a host country what is supposedly private, and even British, insurance. The first instance of actual operation of such a compact took place in the CalEnergy (MidAmerican) case for the Dieng and Patuha geothermal power projects in Indonesia.[40] The US government forced Indonesia not only to reimburse OPIC for its payments to CalEnergy for what OPIC considered to be an expropriation, but also to reimburse private

---

[39] The Chiquita story is told in two teaching cases written by Debora Spar: Chiquita Brands International (A) and (B), Harvard Business School, 1996 (case numbers 9–797–015 and 9–701–106). They are the source for this account.

[40] "Memorandum of Determinations: Expropriation Claim of MidAmerican Energy Holdings Company (formerly CalEnergy Company, Inc.), Contracts of Insurance Nos. E374, E453, E527, and E759," November 1999.

insurers.[41] The result, of course, is to raise the cost to a host country of what the United States considers to be a taking of US property. And irritation on the part of a host government over the resulting US pressure.

Documenting the change and the debate

It is difficult to assemble statistical evidence to support the hypothesis that US policy has undergone a sharp shift since the collapse of the Soviet Union and the end of the Cold War. The evidence probably has to remain anecdotal. Fortunately, however, the Advocacy Center provides its own statement that supports the hypothesis:

USG [US government] officials, particularly in our Embassies abroad, are increasingly approaching foreign governments on behalf of US commercial interests. (Advocacy Center, n.d.)

Documents released from earlier administrations provide rather strong evidence of sides taken by the various departments over the debate within the US government about protection of US assets abroad. Those cited earlier comprise only a small sample of what is easily available.

Reactions to new policies

Developing countries' reactions

There can be little doubt that strong support for US investors engaged in investment disputes comes at a cost to other US foreign policy objectives. In the Indonesian electric power cases of the 1990s, anger with the United States, and especially with OPIC, ran deep in the Indonesian officials who were directly involved in the struggle over revising electric power contracts. The annoyance spilled over at least on occasion to the newly influential parliament, as we have pointed out.

Indonesian anger is understandable. US intervention was aimed at keeping the contracts between American firms and Indonesian state-owned enterprises fixed, at a time when those enterprises probably did

---

[41] For OPIC's side of the story, see Martin (2001). See also "Memorandum of Determinations" referenced in previous note.

not have the ability to honor them, regardless of their wishes. In fact, from an economic point of view, honoring them would have made no sense when the Asian Currency Crisis hit. The optimistic forecasts of electricity demand had to be revised sharply downwards. The power company did not need the power that it had agreed to buy. Further, it could not pay from its rupiah revenues for power priced largely in dollars, after the exchange rate deteriorated from Rp 2,400/$ to a range of Rp 9,000/$ to Rp 11,000/$. In Richard Posner's words, the need to revise the contracts was "involuntary" or "efficient" (1986, pp. 106–107).

One could also argue that the contracts were obtained under at least questionable circumstances. In several of the power deals, relatives of the Indonesian president received shares with no payment, or against loans that were to be repaid only out of a portion of future dividends. These conditions shed some suspicion on the legality of the contracts.[42] It is quite possible that US influence would have been greater if it had explicitly recognized the need to revise the deals, because of their questionable origins or because of the economic crisis that had rendered them inefficient or virtually impossible to honor. But, the dominant US position remained that contracts were sacred. The most publicized quote from a US official on the subject was that of George Munoz, cited above: "Contracts must be honored" (Solomon and Waldman, 1998).

The increased intervention by the US government on behalf of its foreign investors may generate a reaction from the developing countries. Developing countries – especially Latin American ones – had decades ago attempted to stop intervention by investors' home countries in support of their overseas subsidiaries. Home country intervention led to the increased popularity of the so-called "Calvo Doctrine."[43] According to this doctrine, an investor's home country should not intervene to support its investor abroad. The exchange

---

[42] Indonesian officials were never willing to provide convincing evidence to support their claims of corruption. Many of the Indonesians accused of corruption retained a great deal of influence, even after the fall of Suharto. As a result, there is no way of knowing what evidence might have existed.

[43] The Doctrine was put forward by Carlos Calvo, an Argentine diplomat. The most famous exposition was in his *Derecho Internacional Teórico y Práctico de Europa y América*. There were many editions of this book that was first published in Paris in 1868.

offered, when the doctrine was pushed in negotiations, has sometimes been that the foreign investor would be assured "national treatment" in the country in which it invested. Various versions of this kind of exchange were included in the proposals for a global agreement to cover foreign investment that had been the subject of negotiation under the United Nations. These negotiations, of course, failed.

BITs have typically supported only one side of this trade-off. They have guaranteed national treatment to foreign investors, but they have contradicted the Calvo Doctrine by specifying dispute settlement outside a host country's boundaries and they have not constrained home country intervention on behalf of its investors. As a result of the dispute settlement provisions, foreign firms have, at least on paper, been offered better treatment than local firms, which remain subject to local courts. This may not be a stable outcome. In the past, political pressures have generally evolved to assure that foreigners are not better treated than domestic business people. The rigidity with which international arbitrators of investment disputes have seen their role – generally defending investors' agreements regardless of their perceived fairness, Posner's efficiency, or even one side's ability to honor the agreements – may further encourage movements to reverse what appears to be favoritism for foreign investors over domestic investors. The Calvo Doctrine is not dead, and could re-emerge as the World Trade Organization begins to consider incorporating more rules on foreign direct investment. Discussions of new agreements on foreign direct investment would probably include attempts to obtain promises by host countries to give national treatment to foreign investors. But, developing countries, in turn, might insist on restraining home-country intervention on behalf of investors.

US values

US government intervention on behalf of individual American firms has begun to run up against a long-held US value. As reported by Vernon:

Americans have usually demanded as a matter of right that all enterprises similarly situated should be entitled to the same treatment under the law. Provisions of law that seemed to empower the bureaucracy to distinguish among cases, therefore, have been suspect in the US setting... (Vernon, 1998, p. 126)

Under this principle, pressing a country to open its markets for US exports or for US investment was acceptable. Supporting the interests of an individual firm, as would be required in most cases when a firm seeks help in negotiations to enter a market or in disputes over existing investments, was much more suspect.

Of course, as Vernon admitted, this value had often been violated. The 1990s, however, saw a rather sharp increase in the frequency with which such firm-specific intervention took place, at home and in the international sphere. At home, beginning before the 1990s, but growing during the period, there appeared to be an expansion of amendments to various pieces of legislation that were designed to benefit particular firms, as opposed to classes of firms. This seemed especially so with respect to special tax rules. Although such benefits had been conferred in the past, there was a time when most Americans probably viewed such blatant support of certain chosen firms as inappropriate. In the 1990s, intervention at the firm level became common practice with respect to measures taken by the US government to support its investors abroad, whether those investors were negotiating deals or involved in disputes.[44] Whether old values would reassert themselves was unclear.

End of new policies?

Any discussion of long-term reactions to the new US policies could very soon become moot. The US support for American business abroad that emerged in the 1990s could weaken just as suddenly as it strengthened, without the need for any new international accords that would bind US hands. Remember, the hesitancy to support US firms in the past was not the result of any deeply held belief that such support was inconsistent with market principles or international law. Sure, American beliefs that general policies were better than policies that favored particular firms may have imposed some constraints. But, earlier support for American investors abroad was largely a victim of foreign policy objectives that

---

[44] If two American firms were competing for the same investment contract, embassy pressure tried not to distinguish between the two. This happened when Mission Energy and GE joined the fray with Intercontinental Energy for Indonesia's Paiton I project.

were of greater importance, rather than any deep beliefs. When the Cold War ended, the constraint ended as well.

We may be re-entering a world in which new and clear goals other than commercial ones will again dominate US foreign policy. With the emerging war on terrorism, US interest in lining up countries on its side may become the equivalent of the old Cold War interests. Although in 2003 the US administration was still acting as if it could run the new war alone, or with only a bit of foreign financial help, the odds seemed high that US attitudes would again change, and soon. A casualty of a new foreign policy might well be active and reliable defense of the business interests of American firms abroad.

Both Indonesia and Turkey might provide test cases.

In the case of Turkey, at least, US ardor in pressing the cases of US power investors may have begun to cool, but only slightly. A 2002 joint press conference of the US Under Secretary of State for Economic, Business, and Agricultural Affairs and the Turkish Under Secretary to the Ministry of Foreign Affairs suggests a more conciliatory tone than early statements.[45] Interest in access to Iraq through Turkey may have played a role in establishing the new tone. The need for Turkish cooperation in access was followed, in 2003, by an eagerness for Turkish troops in Iraq. And with the Istanbul bombings of November 2003, enlisting further Turkish help in the battle against terrorism may well sideline US defense of the interests of American investors in Turkey. Still, a colleague who visited Turkey in the fall of 2003 reported receiving comments from the new US commercial officer there on the power disputes that differed little from those I encountered earlier. One could, however, imagine a change in the future.

With the Bali bombing and the attack on an international hotel in Jakarta, Indonesia also became a front-line state in the struggle against terrorism. No impact on US government support for its companies was evident in the fall of 2003, however. The electric power disputes had, by the summer of 2003, all been settled, with one exception. The one remaining conflict was between the Karaha Bodas Company

---

[45] "Joint Press Conference by Under Secretary of State for Economic, Business and Agricultural Affairs Alan Larson and Ambassador Ugur Ziyal, Under Secretary to the Ministry of Foreign Affairs," Ankara, Turkey. February 27, 2002. Available at: http://turkey.usembassy.gov/PRESS/PRJ0227.htm.

(KBC)[46] and the Indonesian government, or more accurately two state-owned enterprises. KBC was trying to collect an arbitration award by seizing assets of Pertamina, the national oil company, in the United States, Canada, Hong Kong, and Singapore. The Indonesian government had asked the US government to intervene in the case to block collection efforts. Any intervention would require that the United States declare a national interest to be involved in the dispute. It is not clear whether the Indonesians had linked the interests of a US investor to Indonesia's responsiveness to US requests for assistance in pursuing terrorists. In any event, at the time of writing of this chapter, the US government had not stepped in on the Indonesian side.

At the end of 2003, one could only speculate about the possibilities that the United States might again change its policies toward investors, in response to the war on terrorism. It seemed quite possible, however, if the United States abandoned its neo-conservative go-it-alone foreign policy.

---

[46] The US partners in the Cayman Island company were Caithness Energy and Florida Power and Light.

Conclusions

ROBERT GROSSE

T H E study of international business–government relations has evolved extensively since the early analyses after the Second World War. As Boddewyn captured in his chapter, the intellectual leaders of that era established a number of bases for further exploration. These included: Vernon's idea of the obsolescing bargain; Robinson's argument that MNEs create conflicts with national governments because of conflicting goals – and that MNE managers would thus have to try to defuse these clashes; Behrman's emphasis on the need for firms to pursue strategies that would give them *legitimacy* in the eyes of government stakeholders; and Fayerweather's conceptual model of the international firm which showed that the firms produced gains from global efficiency, while governments had to pursue more fragmented, national goals that often conflicted with those of the firms. Altogether, this was a very conflictive view of international business–government relations, which reflected the reality of those times.

Evolution of thinking about this subject has moved in tandem with analyses of companies in general, and also with changes in the international environment. In the first instance, a wide range of social science disciplines have turned their analytical efforts to explaining company behavior, which was previously a focus mainly of economists and management theorists. In the second case, the dramatic change in world politics with the fall of the Soviet Union, together with the enormous technological shift marked by the arrival of the internet, has left the US as the dominant global political power, with a wide range of governments and pressure groups seeking to gain advantage from their new roles in the internet economy.

With respect to the analysis of companies, traditional disciplines have advanced thinking about the firm in a number of directions. Following these leads, analyses of international companies and their dealings with governments have likewise advanced. For example, as research developed in the economic analysis of transactions costs, a number of studies have focused on the governments as imposing transactions costs on the firms, and the ways in which firms could or should react. As research developed into organizations, the MNE–government relationship was viewed as multi-level and multifaceted, depending on the context and the issue (Brewer, 1992). As corporate governance research developed in exploring the relations of firms with various stakeholders, the MNE–government relationship has been seen as part of a tripartite context (Stopford and Strange, 1992), and as a multi-party interaction (Post, Preston, and Sauter-Sachs, 2002). And as other research on institutions develops (e.g., Hall and Soskice, 2001), looking at historical development of national institutions that have led to particular patterns of government–company relations in different countries, this research also may be extended to consider international firms in addition to the application to domestic firms.

As the international environment has changed, particularly since the end of Soviet communism, the relations between companies and governments have become broadly less confrontational. While conflicts still exist and will continue to exist, the basic premise that (international) companies offer something of value to governments has been accepted, and now the broad thrust of government–company relations tends to focus on governments' effort to obtain the maximum benefits from company activities. And concomitantly, from the company side, the focus is on dealing with governments to obtain the best regulatory/subsidy treatment possible. As described by several authors in this volume, government policies toward multinational firms now tend to use subsidies to entice companies into desired behaviors, rather than taxes or restrictions to force company compliance. The policy of restrictiveness has become more counterproductive in the globalized world, since companies often find that if one country does not offer attractive conditions, another can be used to produce products/services or to sell them, without the burdens of restrictive policies. (This activity is called regulatory arbitrage or jurisdiction arbitrage.)

Despite the generally more positive relations that exist today between governments and multinational firms, the idea of the *obsolescing bargain* still offers value in understanding policies and motivations of each actor. As described by Wint in his essay about investment disputes in general and the Jamaican case in particular, disputes between foreign direct investors and host (emerging market) governments continue into the twenty-first century as before. While the industries most frequently found in disputes now tend to be infrastructure ones (e.g., telecommunications and electric power), rather than mining and oil, the issues remain the same. And Jamaica's government has learned from its dealings with foreign aluminum countries in the past to inform its (still sometimes conflictive) dealings with foreign telephone and power companies in the present.

Eden, Lenway, and Schuler in their chapter suggest that the obsolescing bargain may better be seen today as one case of a broader political bargaining model, in which government and company negotiate and renegotiate their positions over time. They emphasize the great differences in the bargaining positions of government and company depending on whether the business activity in question is extractive, market-seeking, offshore assembly, or aimed at obtaining strategic assets such as technology. They also emphasize the key differences between bargaining situations in emerging markets versus those in more-developed countries. By dividing the turf in this way, they point out that the obsolescing bargain is a useful model in situations such as those examined by Wint, but not as helpful in high-tech sectors or in Triad countries. Even this conclusion can be debated, because the bargaining power situation between government and company will shift over time in any industry and country as conditions change – but their key point is to emphasize the more cooperative bargaining relations that tend to exist today.

Grosse and Luo in their chapters do not directly use the obsolescing bargain, but their findings in other emerging markets do illustrate the continuing value in considering the government–business relationship as a bargaining context. The relative bargaining power of each side depends on the bargaining resources that they hold and what is at stake for each side, and so the overall outcome of company–government dealings can still be understood in this perhaps conflictive style of reasoning. The bargaining conditions may well lead to cooperative outcomes, but the fundamental context pits two actors with somewhat different constituencies and goals in an interaction that will always have some degree of conflict involved. The obsolescing bargain does, in fact, live on.

As the debate on *globalization* continues in the literature and in society, the role of the multinational firm and its relation to governments will certainly be a central point in the arguments. From apologies for the price that needs to be paid in order to benefit from global access to products, ideas, etc., to protests and anti-foreign rules and rhetoric in response to those costs, multinational firms figure centrally as carriers of the process.

Globalization may be seen as the threat of loss of national sovereignty and even national identity. The homogenization of lifestyles around the world is a growing fact; the opposition of French culture defenders to US music and television (as sold by multinational media and entertainment companies) is a classic symptom of this phenomenon. What does this imply for a country's effort to be different or independent? Certainly, independence is alien to the globalization trend, in the sense that some parts of national difference must be sacrificed in order to share the benefits of, for example, computers and advanced telecommunications.

On a parallel dimension, globalization is also often seen as a threat to national sovereignty. This occurs as a result of the ability of multinational firms to circumvent the powers of uni-national governments. Firms can make decisions about where to locate production, how to distribute their products, and even what information and funds to transfer across national borders – almost without regard to national government concerns. The loss of national sovereignty also occurs as a result of amazon.com selling products and services around the world without regard to national borders. And separate from companies, national sovereignty is reduced by the ability of individual citizens to move their wealth overseas, to buy what they want from overseas sources, and even to move themselves overseas out of the reach of the home government. Even currencies are reducing the independence of national governments to set their policies – witness the coming of the euro, which has replaced a dozen currencies in Europe and now is managed by a supra-national central bank.

Perhaps the most striking aspect of globalization today is its decentralized nature. It is not just multinational firms acting at the trans-national level, but millions of consumers acting individually to internationalize their purchases, styles, and other lifestyle aspects. For governments to rein in multinational firms in some way would not confront the problem that individual citizens are the ones carrying out the globalization[1]

---

[1] While Rugman may debate the use of this term, the globalization discussed here is really the 'internationalization' of our lives. Whether firms are oriented toward serving markets in one or two regions of the world, or

process. The internet is clearly the main culprit in enabling individuals to internationalize their lives.

The problems of globalization tend to obscure another feature of company–government relations that has become a focus of academic research in recent years. The idea of *trust* between partners in business activities – usually focusing on strategic alliance partners, but also relevant in the government–business context – is receiving great attention in the literature (Das and Teng, 1998; Gulati and Singh, 1998). In the initial studies, trust was viewed as a key component of relations between partner firms in strategic alliances such as joint ventures (Blomqvist, 1997; Inkpen and Currall, 1998). The broad goal was to identify means through which partners could be compelled to commit resources and effort to joint projects without shirking or otherwise undermining such shared activities. A range of mechanisms (e.g., non-compliance penalties, hostages, etc.) were identified as contributing to the creation of trust between the parties.

Trust equally comes into the government–business relationship, once that relationship is identified as a context in which both participants can gain, and the problem is to optimize the gains received by each from the relationship. How can a company gain trust in a government, when the government has the sovereign right to raise taxes, impose other constraints on the company – or offer incentives? From the other point of view, how can a government gain trust in a (foreign) multinational company, when that company may shift its production and employment overseas, transfer funds abroad and thus cause problems for the balance of payments, and otherwise serve the firm's own interest to the potential detriment of the government's constituencies? Once again, the literature has developed a number of potential mechanisms – from joint ownership of companies, to performance requirements, to simple subsidies – that can produce greater trust in this relationship. What remains is for the international business

---

even just one country, they still face the same pressures from foreign (and internet-based) competition, foreign styles, and the generalized individualization of consumption in the twenty-first century. Whether governments like it or not, they face incursions into their jurisdictions by foreign firms (even just in forms such as amazon.com) and by foreign governments trying to extend their power. Thus relations between international firms and national governments have to adjust to reflect this reality.

literature to move this analysis further in the study of multinational firms and their relations with national governments.

Another phenomenon that has taken on greater significance as a result of the globalization process is *offshore sourcing of production.* This activity, in which a company either moves its own manufacturing or service production overseas to a lower-cost location, or contracts out with a third party overseas to perform that work, has gained quite negative visibility in recent years. Of course, the reason is that labor groups and governments tend to see direct job losses when business is moved overseas, failing to recognize the possibilities of job gains through specialization in other activities (e.g., R&D and marketing). As a result of the very negative publicity earned by this "offshoring," relations between governments and the foot-loose multinational firms have worsened.[2]

Offshore sourcing of production, and offshore assembly of products, are not new phenomena at the turn of the twenty-first century. The subject has been discussed in the international business literature for decades – Vernon described it as part of the international product cycle back in 1966. The Mexican economic boom has been aided very substantially by the "maquila" business of electronics, clothing, auto, and other assembly activity of products subsequently sold in the US market – since the late 1960s.

Offshore sourcing has become more of a concern as activities such as call centers and software development are moved from the US and Europe to emerging markets such as India (Agrawal, Farrell, and Remes 2003). These service-sector activities were seen as immune to the traditional manufacturing pressures, due to their higher skill content. Now, as it becomes clear that many functions can be moved abroad to take advantage of lower wages or other costs, more people are afraid for their own jobs. And of course governments are paying

---

[2] This is partly a misplaced criticism by the governments. If the multinational firms did not move production to low-cost locations when that made them more competitive, then they would lose out to firms from other countries that did take advantage of this opportunity. So, the offshore sourcing can be seen as a defensive strategy that protects the firm from an even worse alternative – losing out to foreign competitors and potentially ceasing to exist.

greater attention to the issue now that more and more constituents are worried about it.

The resolution to this issue is still to be seen. Judging from the results of offshore sourcing of manufacturing, it appears that some production of services is likely to move offshore, some will remain in the industrial countries, and new jobs will develop to incorporate the distributed production process into the global economy. That is, new jobs will be created in different activities in the industrial countries, just as they have despite the move of large amounts of auto, steel, computer chip, and other production to emerging markets in the past.

It might appear that one of the limitations of the approaches used in much of this volume is the fact that some of the authors have focused on *emerging markets*, rather than the Triad countries. This, of course, is to emphasize the contexts in which international business–government relations have been most visible and perhaps most complicated. Nevertheless, the fact remains that the vast majority of MNE activity is in the developed markets of North America, the European Union, and Japan. Rugman decidedly emphasizes this point in his chapter here, as well as his recent writing elsewhere (Rugman, 2004). And in fact, most of the authors here, from Boddewyn to Stopford, consider issues that either emphasize governments in the Triad regions or that cover all parts of the world. Still, the detailed country examples in the book often do focus on emerging markets, as in the analyses of Wint, Luo, and Meyer and Jensen.

As a counterpoint it should be noted that in addition to the broad analyses of Boddewyn, Preston, Stopford, and Brewer, which cover issues that appear in both emerging and developed countries, several other authors take their examples from both types of country. Kobrin's analysis of an oil company in Sudan clearly focuses on government–MNE relations in Canada and the US. Grosse's bargaining framework may be more often applied in emerging markets, but the chapter also explores examples of Monsanto dealing with European Union governments, and the Japanese car companies dealing with the US government, among other examples in the Triad. Ramamurti's analysis of Pfizer's dealings with intellectual property rights certainly discusses the issue in emerging markets, but his focus is more on US and European Union policies toward pharmaceuticals. In sum, over half of the conceptual frameworks presented in our analyses are considered in both emerging and developed countries;

but there is no doubt that the interest of several of our authors is more in the emerging markets.

Perhaps the main lesson from the analyses in this volume is that the international business–government relationship is part of a broader context in which multinational firms seek *legitimacy* in international, national, and local environments. The relations between any national government and a foreign or domestic multinational firm must contemplate not just the interests of company shareholders and government policymakers, but also those of other stakeholders such as workers, consumers affected by the company's activities, competitor firms – and the list could go on and on.

Consider Kobrin's analysis of the problems faced by the Talisman oil company. This Canadian multinational firm encountered a lawsuit in the United States accusing the company of violating human rights in Sudan, where its subsidiary had been exploring for and producing oil. The Muslim government of Sudan was believed to be systematically killing non-Muslim citizens of the country (ethnic cleansing), and Talisman was accused of complicity in this activity. This case dramatically emphasizes the broader context of government–MNE relations. The company's relations with the host government may have been excellent, and its relations with the home country government probably were good as well. But the US government, using international treaties in which the United States and Canada were both signatories, agreed to hear the case which involved only activities in Sudan. And the plaintiffs in the case were led by the Sudanese Presbyterian Church! Clearly, the international business–government relationship operates in a broader context, and the relations between a government and a company must reflect, to one degree or another, the interests of a wider group of stakeholders. The legitimacy of the firm in this context is the ultimate question that must be answered.

The essays in this volume do not pretend to answer the question of legitimacy of the multinational firm, but they do offer insights into the kinds of stakeholders and interests that must be taken into account by both firms and governments. These concerns are just as relevant in Triad countries as in emerging markets. For example, one can readily expect that multinational oil and auto companies will be pursued by pressure groups for their contribution to global warming, whether or not the Triad country governments initiate the action. This follows the example encountered by the multinational tobacco companies that have been successfully sued in several Triad countries for their contribution to lung cancer and other smoking-caused illnesses.

One might argue that an encompassing concept to be applied here is the economic one of "externalities." That is, when multinational firms and their activities of production, distribution, and then consumption of products/services by their customers cause social costs such as diseases, human rights violations, cultural imperialism, etc., these costs are subject to efforts to force the companies to pay them, rather than the societies. Given the global fishbowl in which we live, it appears that people everywhere will be able to see events and conditions anywhere – so that the externalities produced by multinational firms will have to be identified and measured much more carefully to avoid the kinds of costly prosecutions and public relations problems that appear in newspapers around the world.

Whether the externality perspective is used, or some other framework is applied, it is interesting that the chapters here have frequently taken the issue of MNE legitimacy in home and host countries explicitly into account. This kind of response demonstrates that the authors have helped to advance thinking on this theme that was raised by Behrman (1965, 1969) and others in the early years of international business analysis.

References

1999. The human factor. *Petroleum Economist*: 48.

2002. Exploration hums as Sudan's output reaches pipeline capacity. *Oil and Gas Journal*.

2002. Sudan. *Oil and Gas Journal*.

2002. Talisman to sell Sudan assets for C$1.2 billion. Calgary: Talisman Energy – Press Release.

2003. Talisman closes sale of Sudan oil stake. *Ottawa Citizen*. Ottawa.

Acemoglu, D., S. Johnson, J. Robinson, and Y. Thaicharoen 2003. Institutional causes, macroeconomic symptoms: volatility, crises and growth. *Journal of Monetary Economics*, 50(1): 49–123.

Adorno, Theodor W. and Max Horkheimer. 1944. *Dialektik der Aufklarung: philosophische Fragmente*. Frankfurt am Main: Suhrkamp.

Advocacy Center. n.d. US government guidelines. See http://www.ita.doc.-gov/td/advocacy/guideline 2.htm (viewed 11/03).

Agrawal, Vivek, Diana Farrell, and Jaana Remes. 2003. Offshoring and beyond. *The McKinsey Quarterly* (Special Edition Issue 4, December): 24–33.

Aguilera, R. V. and G. Jackson 2003. The cross-national diversity of corporate governance: dimensions and determinants. In Daily, Dalton, and Canella, pp. 447–465.

Alden, Edward. 1998. Talisman in $196m purchase of Arakis. *The Financial Times*. London.

Amon, Elizabeth. 2000. Coming to America. *National Law Journal*.

Andreff, Wladimir. 2003. The newly emerging transnational corporations from transition economies – comparison with Third World outward foreign direct investment. *Transnational Corporations*.

Antal-Mokos, Z. 1998. *Privatisation, Politics, and Economic Performance in Hungary*. Cambridge: Cambridge University Press.

Aoki, M. and H.-K. Kim. 1995. *Corporate Governance in Transitional Economies*. Washington, DC: World Bank.

Arakis Energy Corporation. 1998. Notice of special meeting of security-holders. Calgary.

Argyres, Nicholas and Julia Porter Liebeskind. 1999. Contractual commitments, bargaining power, and governance inseparability: incorporating history into transaction cost theory. *Academy of Management Review* 24: 49–63.

Arris, L. (Ed.). 1997. *Global Warming Yearbook*. Arlington, MA: Cutter Information.

1998. *Global Warming Yearbook*. Arlington, MA: Cutter Information.

2000. *Global Warming Yearbook*. Arlington, MA: Cutter Information.

Averyt, William F. and K. Ramagopal. 1999. Strategic disruption and transaction cost economics: the case of the American auto industry and Japanese competition. *International Business Review* 8: 39–53.

Balling, M., E. Hennessy, and R. O'Brien (Eds.). 1998. *Corporate Governance, Financial Markets and Global Convergence*. Dordrecht: Kluwer.

Barnet, Richard J. and Roland E. Muller 1974. *Global Reach: The Power of the Multinational Corporation*. New York: Simon and Schuster.

Barney, Jay. 1991. Firm resources and sustained competitive advantage. *Journal of Management* 17: 99–120.

Beattie, Alan. 2003. Private sector steps up global AIDS battle. *Financial Times*. US edn. London.

Behrman, Jack N. 1960. Promoting free world economic development through direct investment. *American Economic Review* 1(2) (May): 271–281.

(with Raymond F. Mikesell) (Ed.). 1962. *US Private and Government Investment Abroad*. Eugene: University of Oregon Press, Part II – Direct Private Foreign Investment pp. 177–230.

1965. Foreign investment muddle. *Columbia Journal of World Business*, Inaugural Issue: 51–60.

1969. Multinational corporations, transnational interests, and national sovereignty. *Columbia Journal of World Business* (March–April), pp. 15–22.

1970. *National Interests and the Multinational Enterprise: Tensions among the North Atlantic Countries*, Englewood Cliffs, NJ: Prentice Hall.

1971. *U.S. International Business and Governments*, New York, NY: McGraw-Hill.

1971. Is there a better way for Latin America? *Columbia Journal of World Business* 6(6): 61–68.

1974. *Decision Criteria for Foreign Direct Investment in Latin America*, New York, NY: Council of the Americas.

1986. The future of international business and the distribution of benefits. *Columbia Journal of World Business* 20(4): 15–22.

1987. *Essays on Ethics in Business and the Professions*, Englewood Cliffs, NJ: Prentice-Hall.

Behrman, J. N. and Grosse, R. E. 1990. *International Business and Government: Issues and Institutions.* Columbia, SC: University of South Carolina Press.

Behrman, J. N. and D. A. Rondinelli. 1999. The transition to market oriented economies in Central and Eastern Europe: lessons for private enterprise development. *Global Focus – Journal of International Business, Economics and Social Policy* 11(4): 1–13.

Behrman, J. N., J. J. Boddewyn, and A. Kapoor. 1975. *International Business–Government Communications.* Lexington, MA: Heath–Lexington Books.

Bengoa, M. and B. Sanchez-Robles. 2003. Foreign direct investment, economic freedom and growth: new evidence from Latin America. *European Journal of Political Economy* 19(3): 529–545.

Benhabib, J. and M. M. Spiegel. 1994. The role of human capital in economic development: evidence from aggregate cross-country data. *Journal of Monetary Economics* 34(2): 143–173.

Bennett, Douglas C. and Kenneth E. Sharpe. 1979. Agenda setting and bargaining power: the Mexican state versus transnational automobile companies. *World Politics* 32(1): 57–89.

Berglof, E. and E.-L. von Thadden. 2000. The changing corporate governance paradigm: implications for developing and transition economies. In Cohen and Boyd, pp. 275–306.

Bernhard, M. 1996. Civil society after the first transition: dilemmas of post-communist democratization in Poland and beyond. *Communist and Post-Communist Studies* 29(3): 309–330.

Berthelemy, J. C. and L. Söderling 2001. The role of capital accumulation, adjustment and structural change for economic take-off: empirical evidence from African growth episodes. *World Development* 29(2): 323–343.

Bevan, A. and S. Estrin. 2000. The determinants of foreign direct investment in transition economies. London, CEPR Discussion Paper No. 2638.

Bevan, A., S. Estrin and K. Meyer 2000. Institution building and the integration of Eastern Europe in international production. London Centre for New and Emerging Markets. Discussion Paper Series No. 11.

2004. Foreign investment location and institutional development in transition economies. *International Business Review* 13(1): 43–64.

Beyer, J. 2002. Please invest in our country – how successful were the tax incentives for foreign investment in transition countries? *Communist and Post-Communist Studies* 35: 191–211.

Biermann, F. and R. Brohm. 2004. Implementing the Kyoto Protocol without the United States: the strategic role of energy tax adjustments at the border. *Climate Policy* 4(1).

Billington, Michael. 2001. Looting Indonesia: the energy brokers "warm up" for California. Larouche Society, March 28; available at http://www.odiousdebts.org/odiousdebts/index.cfm? DSP=Content & Content ID =2746 (viewed 11/03).

Birkinshaw, J. M. and N. Hood (Eds.). 1998. *Multinational Corporate Evolution and Subsidiary Development.* London: Macmillan.

Blair, M. M. 2001. Corporate governance. In *International Encyclopedia of the Social and Behavioral Sciences*, ed. Neil J. Smelser and Paul B. Baltes. Burlington, MA: Elsevier, Vol. IV, pp. 2797–2803.

Blomqvist, Kirsimarja. 1997. The many faces of trust. *Scandinavian Journal of Management* 13(3): 271–286.

Blomstrom, Magnus, Irving B. Kravis, and Robert E. Lipsey. 1988. Multinational firms and manufactured exports from developing countries. Working Paper No. 2493, National Bureau of Economic Research.

Blumberg, Phillip I. 2002. Asserting human rights against multinational corporations under United States law: conceptual and procedural problems. *American Journal of Comparative Law* 50 (Fall): 493–529.

Boddewyn, Jean. 1981. Motivations, precipitating conditions. *Weltwirtschaftliches Archiv (1981).*

   1988. Political aspects of MNE theory. *Journal of International Business Studies* 19: 341–363.

Boddewyn, J. and T. L. Brewer. 1994. International–business political behavior: new theoretical directions. *Academy of Management Review* 19: 119–144.

Bossard, Peter. 2000. Publicly guaranteed corruption: corrupt power projects and the responsibility of export credit agencies in Indonesia. November. (available at www.gnginitiative.net Documentazione %5C ISSUES %5 Cerviroment %5 CECAS %5 Callegato 31.doc (viewed 6/00).

Bowley, Graham. 1999. World news: Talisman may not find good fortune from Sudan oil. *Financial Times.* London.

Bowlus, A. J. and T. Sicular. 2003. Moving toward markets? Labor allocation in rural China. *Journal of Development Economics* 71(2): 561–583.

Bratton, W. W. and J. A. McCahery. 2002. Comparative corporate governance and barriers to global cross reference. In McCahery et al., pp. 23–55.

Brenton, P., F. Di Mauro and M. Lücke. 1999. Economic integration and FDI: an empirical analysis of foreign investment in the EU and in Central and Eastern Europe. *Empirica* 26(2): 95–121.

Brewer, T. L. 1992. An issue-area approach to the analysis of MNE–government relations. *Journal of International Business Studies* 23(2): 295–309.

Brewer, T. L. 1993. Government policies, market imperfections, and foreign direct investment. *Journal of International Business Studies* 24(1): 101–120.

Brewer, T. L. 2003a. The trade regime and the climate regime: institutional evolution and adaptation. *Climate Policy* 3(4): 329–341.

Brewer, T. L. 2003b. The Kyoto Protocol and the WTO: institutional evolution and adaptation. Centre for European Policy Studies (CEPS), Policy Paper. See www.ceps.be.

Brewer, T. L. 2003c. Seeds of change in the US. *New Economy* 10(3): 150–154.

Brewer, T. L. 2004. WTO–Kyoto Protocol interactions: interaction issues. *Climate Policy* 4(1).

Brewer, T. L. 2005. Business perspectives on the EU emission trading scheme. *Climate Policy* 5(1): 139–147.

Brewer, T. L. In-progress-a. Political-economy models of strategic behavior: explaining firms' responses to global warming issues.

Bridgeford, Tawny Aine. 2003. Imputing human rights obligations on multinational corporations: the Ninth Circuit strikes again in judicial activism. *American University International Law Review* 18: 1009–1057.

Broad, Robin and John Cavanagh. 1998. *The Corporate Accountability Movement: Lessons and Opportunities*. World Wildlife Fund.

Broadman, H. G. 1999. *Russian Enterprise Reform: Policies to Further the Transition*. Washington, DC: World Bank.

Broadman, H. G. and F. Racanatini. 2001. Seeds of corruption: do market institutions matter? *Economic Policy in Transitional Economies* 11(4): 359–392.

Brooke, M. and L. Remmers. 1971. *The Strategy of Multinational Enterprise*. London: Longmans.

Brunetti, A. and B. Weder. 2003. A free press is bad news for corruption. *Journal of Public Economics* 87(7/8): 1801–1824.

Burke, Pamela L. 1999. Embedded private authority: multinational enterprises and the Amazonian Indigenous Peoples Movement in Ecuador. In A. Claire Cutler, Virginia Haufler, and Tony Porter (eds.), *Private Authority and International Affairs*. Albany: State University of New York Press.

Business Roundtable. 2002. Principles of Corporate Governance. Washington, DC: Business Roundtable.

Business Week. 2003. Review of Stepen Kinzer, *All the Shah's Men: An American Coup and the Roots of Middle East Terror*. August 25: 28.

Carbon Disclosure Project. 2003. *Carbon Finance and the Global Equity Markets*. New York: Innovest Strategic Value Advisors.

Cardemil, L., J. C. DiTata and F. Frantischek. 2000. Central America: adjustment reforms in the 1990s. *Finance & Development* 37(1): 34–37.

Carlisle, Tamsin. 2000. For Canadian firm, an African albatross – oil driller Talisman Energy pays a painful price for its Sudan investment. *The Wall Street Journal*. New York.

Carlow, K. I. and R. G. Lipsey. 2003. Productivity, technology and economic growth: what is the relationship? *Journal of Economic Surveys* 17(3): 457–495.

Cattaneo, Claudia. 1998. Talisman has resources, experience to tackle Sudan. *The Financial Post*. Toronto.

CERES (Coalition for Environmentally Responsible Economics). 2003. *Corporate Governance and Climate Change: Making the Connection*. Boston: CERES.

Charkham, Jonathan P. 1994. *Keeping Good Company: A Study of Corporate Governance in Five Countries*. Oxford: Clarendon Press.

Charney, Jonathan I. 1983. Transnational corporations and developing public international law. *Duke Law Journal* 767.

Cheek, Marney L. 2001. The limits of informal regulatory cooperation in international affairs: a review of the global intellectual property regime. *The George Washington International Law Review* 33(2): 277–324.

Chen, A. 2002. Socio-economic polarization and political corruption in China: a study of the correlation. *The Journal of Communist Studies and Transition Politics* 18(2): 53–74.

China Securities Regulatory Commission. 2001. Code of corporate governance for listed companies in China. http://www.csrc.gov.cn/CSRCSite/eng/edeplt/rule/frzl02042901.htm

Cho, Dong-Sung. 1984. Incentives and restraints: goverment regulation of direct investments between Korea and the United States. In Karl Mostowitz (ed.), *From Patron to Partner: The US–Korean Economic and Business Relationship*. New York: Lexington Books.

    1992. From subsidizer to regulator: the changing role of Korean government. *Long Range Planning* 25(6): 48–55.

Chung, Wilbur. 2001. Identifying technology transfer in foreign direct investment: influence of industry conditions and investing firm motives. *Journal of International Business Studies* 32(3) (2nd Quarter): 211–229.

Chuta, Enyinna and Carl Liedholm. 1985. *Employment and Growth in Small-Scale Industry*. London: Macmillan.

Coeure, B. and J. Pisani-Ferry. 1999. The case against benign neglect of exchange rate stability. *Finance & Development* 36(3): 6–8.

Coffee, J. C. 2002. Convergence and its critics: what are the preconditions to the separation of ownership and control? In McCahery et al., pp. 83–112.

Cohen, S. S. and G. Boyd (Eds.). 2000. *Corporate Governance and Globalization*. Cheltenham: Edward Elgar.

Commission for the EU. 2003. Report on the results of the negotiations on the accession of Cyprus, Malta, Hungary, Poland, the Slovak Republic, Latvia, Estonia, Lithuania, the Czech Republic and Slovenia to the European Union. Paper prepared by the Commission's departments, The Commission for the European Union, Brussels.

Confederation of Danish Industries. 2003. En slagkraftig og barrierefri Østersøregion? –Spræng murbrokkerne Væk! Confederation of Danish Industries, June 2003, Copenhagen.

Corporate Social Responsibility Group. 2001. *Corporate Social Responsibility 2001*. Calgary: Talisman Energy Incorporated.

Croome, John. 1999. *Reshaping the World Trading System: A History of the Uruguay Round*. The Hague; Boston: Kluwer Law International.

Crowley, F. and A. Loviscek. 2002 Assessing the impact of political unrest on currency returns: a look at Latin America. *Quarterly Review of Economics and Finance* 42(1): 143–153.

Cutler, A. Claire. 1999. Locating authority in the global political economy. *International Studies Quarterly* 43: 59–81.

2001. Critical reflections on the Westphalian assumptions of international law and organization: a crisis of legitimacy. *Review of International Studies* 27: 133–150.

Cutler, A. Claire, Virginia Haufler, and Tony Porter. 1999. *Private Authority and International Affairs*. Albany: State University of New York Press.

Dabrowski, Wojtek. 2002. Out of Sudan: Talisman's shares climb after reported oil-stake sale. *Montreal Gazette*. Montreal.

Daily, C. M., D. R. Dalton, and A. A. Canella. 2003. Special Topic Forum on Corporate Governance. *Academy of Management Review* 28(3).

Das, T. K and Bing-Sheng Teng. 1998. Between trust and control: developing confidence in partner cooperation in alliances. *Academy of Management Review* 23(3): 491–512.

D'Avino, Cary R. 2002. Talisman law suit: business and human rights.

Davis, Carlton E. 1995. *Jamaica in the World Aluminium Industry, Volume 11 1974–1988: Bauxite Levy Negotiations*. Kingston, Jamaica: Jamaica Bauxite Institute.

Del Sol, Patricio and Joe Kogan. 2003. Global competitive advantage based on pioneering economic reforms: the case of Chilean FDI. Draft paper September 16, p. 7 fn2.

deMortanges, C. P. and V. Allers. 1996. Political risk assessment: theory and the experience of Dutch firms. *International Business Review* 5(3): 303–318.

Department of Economic and Social Affairs and United Nations Conference on Trade and Development. 2003. *World Economic Situation and Prospects 2003*. New York: United Nations.

de Soto, Hernando. 1989a. *The Other Path: The Invisible Revolution in the Third World*. New York: Harper and Row.

1989b. An interview with Hernando de Soto. *Health and Development* 1(1) (March/April).

Development Bank of Japan. 2003. Promoting corporate measure to combat global warming: an analysis of innovative activities in the field. Research Report No. 42.

Developments in the Law. 2001. International criminal law: V. corporate liability for violations of human rights law. *Harvard Law Review* 114: 2025–2048.

Dijkstra, B. R. 1999. *The Political Economy of Environmental Policy: A Public Choice Approach to Market Instruments*. Cheltenham; Northampton, MA: Elgar.

DiMasi, Joseph A. 1991. *Rising Research and Development Costs for New Drugs in a Cost Coutainment Environment*. Boston, MA: Center for the Study of Drug Development, Tufts University.

DiPaola, M. and L. Arris (Eds.). 2001. *Global Warming Yearbook: 2001*. Arlington, MA: Cutter Information.

Djankov, S., R. L. Porta, F. Lopez-de-Silanes, and A. Shleifer. 2002. The regulation of entry. *Quarterly Journal of Economics* 117(1): 1.

Donaldson, T. and L. E. Preston. 1995. The stakeholder theory of the corporation: concepts, evidence, and implications. *Academy of Management Review* 20: 65–91.

Doyle, A. 2003. Scientists report global warning kills 160,000 annually. Reuters, October 1.

Doz, Yves, José Santos, and Peter J. Williamson. 2001. *From Global to Metanational: How Companies Win in the Knowledge Economy*. Cambridge, MA: Harvard Business School Press Books.

Dresdner Bank. 2003. *Investing in Central and Eastern Europe*. Frankfurt am Main: Dresdner Bank AG, Group Economics.

Dries, L. and J. F. M. Swinnen. 2002. Institutional reform and labor reallocation during transition: theory evidence from Polish agriculture. *World Development* 30(3): 457–474.

Drohan, Madelaine. 1999. Sudan play bad timing for Talisman. *Globe and Mail*. Toronto.

2003. *Making a Killing: How and Why Corporations Use Armed Force to do Business*. Toronto: Random House, Canada.

Duncombe, Bruce F. (Ed.). 2001. *Foreign Relations, 1969–1976*. Vol. IV: *Foreign Assistance, International Development, Trade Policies, 1969–1972*. General editor: David S. Patterson. Washington, DC: United States Government Printing Office.

Dunn, S. 2002. Down to business on climate change: an overview of corporate strategies. *Greener Management International* 39: 27–41.

Dunning, J. (ed.). 1971. *The Multinational Enterprise.* London: Allen and Unwin.

1993a. Governments and multinational enterprises: from confrontation to cooperation? In Lorraine Eden and Evan Potter (eds.), *Multinationals in the Global Political Economy.* London: Macmillan, 59–83.

1993b. *Multinational Enterprises and the Global Economy.* Wokingham, UK: Addison-Wesley.

1995. *Multinational Enterprises and the Global Economy.* New York: Addison-Wesley.

1997. *Governments, Globalization, and International Business.* New York: Oxford University Press.

1998a. An overview of relations with national governments. *New Political Economy* 3(2): 280–284.

1998b. Location and the multinational enterprise: a neglected factor. *Journal of International Business Studies* 29(1), 45–66.

2000. *Regions, Globalization and the Knowledge-Based Economy.* Oxford: Oxford University Press (see especially chapters 1, 13, 14, 15, and 16).

(Ed.). 2003. *Making Globalization Good: The Moral Challenges of Global Capitalism.* Oxford; New York: Oxford University Press.

2004. Determinants of foreign direct investment: globalization induced changes in the role of FDI policies. In World Bank, *Towards Pro Poor Policies: Aid, Institutions and Globalization.* Washington, DC: World Bank.

Dunning, J. H. and R. Narula (Eds.). 1996. *Foreign Direct Investment and Governments.* London and New York: Routledge.

Dunning, J. H. and C. Wymbs. 2001. The challenge of electronic markets for international business theory. *International Journal of the Economics of Business* 8(2): 273–302.

Dunning, J. H., Kim Chang-Su, and Jyh-Der Lin. 2001. Incorporating trade into the investment development path: a case study of Korea and Taiwan. *Oxford Development Studies* 29(2) 45–54.

Easterly, W., N. Loayza, and P. Montiel. 1997. Has Latin America's postreform growth been disappointing? *Journal of International Economics* 43(3–4): 287–311.

EBRD. 1999, 2001, 2002. *Transition Report.* London: European Bank for Reconstruction and Development.

Economist. 2001. War, famine and oil in Sudan. *Economist*: 41.

Economist Intelligence Unit (EIU). 2001. *East European Investment Prospects.* London: EIU.

2002. *World Investment Prospects.* (2002 edition.) London: EIU.

2003. *World Investment Prospects.* (2003 edition.) London: EIU.

Eden, Lorraine. 1996. The emerging North American investment regime. *Transnational Corporations* 5(3): 61–98.

Eden, Lorraine and Stefanie Lenway. 2001. Multinationals: the Janus face of globalization. *Journal of International Business Studies* 32(3): 383–400.

Eden, Lorraine and Stewart Miller. 2004. Distance matters: liability of foreignness, institutional distance and ownership strategy. In M. A. Hitt and J. L. C. Cheng (eds.), *The Evolving Theory of the Multinational Firm. Advances in International Management.* Vol. XVI. Amsterdam: Elsevier.

Eden, Lorraine and Maureen Appel Molot. 2002. Insiders, outsiders and host country bargains. *Journal of International Management.*

Elkins, A. and D. W. Callaghan. 1975. *A Managerial Odyssey.* New York: Addison-Wesley.

Emmons. W. R., and F. Schmidt. 2000. Corporate governance and corporate performance. In Cohen and Boyd, pp. 59–94.

Energy Information Administration. 2003. *Sudan Country Analysis Brief.* Washington, DC: Department of Energy.

Enright, M. J. 2002. Geographics and international business: a three dimensional approach. Paper presented at Academy of International Business Annual Meeting at San Juan, Puerto Rico, July.

Esty, Daniel C. and Damien Geradin. 2001. *Regulatory Competition and Economic Integration: Comparative Perspectives.* Oxford: Oxford University Press.

Eurelectric. 2002. *Experiences in the Electric Industry with Potential Joint Implementation (JI) and Clean Development Mechanism (CDM) Projects.* Brussels: Eurelectric.

    2003. Electricity industry: a key actor in the development of JI and CDM projects. In *Responding to Climate Change 2003.*

European Bank for Reconstruction and Development (EBRD). 2000. *Transition Report.* Paris: EBRD.

European Commission. 2002. *Comparative Study of Corporate Governance Codes, Final Report.* Study Contract ETD/2000/B5–3001/F/53.

EXIM. n.d. Press Release, available at http://www.exim.gov/press/dec 1699a.html (viewed 6/00).

Fagre, Nathan and Louis T. Wells, Jr. 1982. Bargaining power of multinationals and host governments *Journal of International Business Studies* 13(2) (Fall): 9–24.

Farmer, R. N. and B. M. Richman. 1966. *International Business: An Operational Theory.* Homewood, IL: Irwin.

Fayerweather, J. 1960. *Management of International Operations: Text and Cases.* New York: McGraw-Hill.

1969. *International Business Management: A Conceptual Framework.* New York: McGraw Hill.

1973. *International Business–Government Affairs: Toward an Era of Accommodation.* Cambridge, MA: Praeger.

Fidrmuc, J. 2003. Economic reform, democracy and growth during post-communist transition. *European Journal of Political Economy* 19(3): 583–604.

Fischer, S. 2001. Exchange rate regimes: is the bipolar view correct? *Journal of Economic Perspectives* 15(2): 3–25.

Foster, Peter. 1999. Talisman in ethical no man's land. *National Post.* Toronto.

Frank, Steven. 1999. Crude pressures: a Canadian oil company operating in Sudan gets targeted by rebels, the US State Department and its own Foreign Affairs Ministry. *Time Canada.*

Frankel, J. A., M. Goldstein, and P. R. Masson. 1991. Characteristics of a successful exchange rate system. Occasional Paper 82, Washington, DC: International Monetary Fund.

Friedman, Milton, 1962. *Capitalism and Freedom.* Chicago, IL: University of Chicago Press.

Friedman, Thomas. 1999. *The Lexus and the Olive Tree.* New York: Farrar, Strauss, and Giroux.

Gagnon, Georgette and John Ryle. 2001. *Report of an Investigation into Oil Development, Conflict and Displacement in Western Upper Nile.* Sudan: Canadian Auto Workers Union, Steelworkers Humanities Fund, The Simons Foundation, United Church of Canada, World Vision of Canada.

Gagnon, Georgette, Audrey Macklin, and Penelope Simons. 2003. *Deconstructing Engagment: Corporate Self-Regulation in Conflict Zones – Implications for Human Rights and Canadian Policy.* Toronto: Social Sciences and Humanities Research Council and Law Commission of Canada.

Gaviria, A. 2002. Assessing the effects of corruption and crime on firm performance: evidence from Latin America. *Emerging Markets Review* 2(2): 245–268.

Geertz, Clifford. 1969. Myrdal's mythology. *Encounter* (July).

Gillis, Charles. 1999. US pension fund dumps its stake in Talisman. *Financial Post.* December 9 edn.

Gladwin, Thomas N. and Ingo Walter. 1980. *Multinationals under Fire: Lessons in the Management of Conflict.* New York: John Wiley and Sons.

Global Compact. 2003a. *The Global Compact: A Report on Progress and Activities: July 2002–July 2003.* New York: United Nations.

Global Compact. 2003b. *The Nine Principles.* New York: United Nations.

Global Environmental Change Report. 2001a. Auto giant positions for fuel cell market. June 22: 7–8.

Global Environmental Change Report. 2001b. Shell enters US wind market. August 10: 6–7.

Globerman, Steven and Daniel Shapiro. 2002. Global foreign direct investment flows: the role of governance infrastructure. *World Development* 30(11): 1899–1919.

Goldsmith, Arthur. 1985. The private sector and rural development: can agribusiness help the small farmer? *World Development* 10/11 (October–November).

Gomes-Casseres, Benjamin. 1990. Firm ownership preferences and host government restrictions: an integrated approach. *Journal of International Business Studies* 21(1): 1–22.

Gordon, R. A. and J. E. Howell. 1969. *Higher Education for Business*. New York: Columbia University Press.

Gorer, David J. 1984. Contract farming and smallholder outgrower schemes in less developed countries. *World Development* 12(11–12) (November–December).

    1987. Increasing the benefits to smallholders from contract farming: problem for farmers' organizations and policy makers. *World Development*, 15(4).

Gornik-Tomaszewski, Sylwia and Irene N. McCarthy. 2003. Cooperation between FASB and IASB to achieve convergence of accounting standards. *Review of Business* 24(2) (Spring): 52–59.

Gray, D. F. and M. R. Stone. 1999. Corporate balance sheets and macroeconomic policy. *Finance & Development* 36(3): 56–59.

Green, D. J. and A. Bauer. 1998. The costs of transition in Central Asia. *Journal of Asian Economics* 9(2): 345–364.

Grosse, Robert. 1996. The bargaining relationship between foreign MNEs and host governments in Latin America. *The International Trade Journal* 10: 467–99.

Grosse, Robert and Jack N. Behrman. 1992. Theory in international business. *Transnational Corporations* 1: 93–126.

Grosse, R. and L. J. Trevino 2003. New institutional economics and FDI location in Central and Eastern Europe. American Graduate School of International Management, Phoenix, AZ. (Mimeo.)

Grubb, M., T. Brewer, B. Müller, J. Drexage, K. Hamilton, T. Sugiyama, and T. Aiba. 2003. A strategic assessment of the Kyoto–Marrakech system. Royal Institute of International Affairs; www.riia.org.

Guisinger, Stephen E. 1986. Host country policies to attract and control foreign investment. In Theodore H. Mann and contributors, *Investing in Development: New Roles for Private Capital*. New

Brunswick and Oxford: Overseas Development Council, Transaction Books.

Gulati, Ranjay and Harbir Singh. 1998. The architecture of cooperation: managing coordination costs and appropriation concerns in strategic alliances. *Administrative Science Quarterly* 43.

Guzman, Andrew T. 1997. Explaining the popularity of bilateral investment treaties: why LDCs sign treaties that hurt them. August 26. Available at http://www.jeanmonnet program. org/papers/97/97/97-12.html (viewed 11/03).

Gwartney, J. and R. Lawson. 2003. The concept and measurement of economic freedom. *European Journal of Political Economy* 19(3): 405–430.

Habib, M. and L. Zurawicki. 2001. Country-level investments and the effect of corruption – some empirical evidence. *International Business Review* 10(6): 687–700.

Haley, U. C. V. 2003. Assessing and controlling business risks in China. *Journal of International Management.*

Hall, P. and D. Soskice. 2001. *Varieties of Capitalism.* New York: Oxford University Press.

Halpern, P. J. N. 2000. Systemic perspectives on corporate governance systems. In Cohen and Boyd, pp. 1–58.

Haner, F. T 1973. *Multinational Management.* Columbus, OH: Merrill.

Hansmann, Henry and Reinier Kraakman. 2002. Toward a single model of corporate law? In McCahery et al., pp. 56–82.

Hansted, Morten. 2003. *Rubler og Skrupler – danske erhvervsfolks fantastiske.*

Harker, John. 2000. *Human Security in Sudan: The Report of a Canadian Assessment Mission.* Ottawa: Department of Foreign Affairs and International Trade.

Harvey, Michael G. and Laurie A. Lucas. 1996. Intellectual property rights protection: what MNC managers should know about GATT. *Multinational Business Review* 4(1): 77–93.

Haufler, Virginia. 2001. *A Public Role for the Private Sector: Industry Self-Regulation in a Global Economy.* Washington, DC: Carnegie Endowment for International Peace.

Heller, P. S. and C. Keller. 2001. Social sector reforms in transition countries. IMF Working Paper No. 01–35, International Monetary Fund, Washington, DC.

Henisz, W. J. 2000. The institutional environment for multinational investment. *Journal of Law, Economics and Organization* 16(2): 334–364.

Hennart, J.-F. 1982. *A Theory of Multinational Enterprise.* Ann Arbor: University of Michigan Press.

Hermes, N. and R. Lensink. 2000. Financial system development in transition economies. *Journal of Banking and Finance* 24(4): 507–524.

Herzfeld, T. and C. Weiss. 2003. Corruption and legal (in)effectiveness: an empirical investigation. *European Journal of Political Economy* 19(3): 621–632.

Holden, N., C. Cooper, and J. Carr. 1998. *Dealing with the New Russia: Management Cultures in Collision*. Chichester: Wiley.

Holland, David and Jeffrey Owens. 1996. Taxation and foreign direct investment: the experience of the economies in transition. *Bulletin for International Fiscal Documentation* 50(2).

Holland, D., M. Sass, V. Benacek, and M. Gronicki. 2000. The determinants and impact of FDI in Central and Eastern Europe: a comparison of survey and econometric evidence. *Transnational Corporations* 9(3): 162–212.

Hopkins, Michael. 1989. Comments on Professor S. Kannappan. In Bernard Salome (ed.), *Fighting Urban Unemployment*. Paris: Development Centre of the OECD.

Human Rights Watch. 2003. *Sudan, Oil and Human Rights*. New York: Human Rights Watch.

Hutchinson, M. M. 2003. Intervention and exchange rate stabilization policy in developing countries. *International Finance* 6(1): 109–127.

Hymer, Stephen H. 1960(1976). *The International Operations of National Firms: A Study of Direct Foreign Investment* (PhD. thesis, MIT). Cambridge, MA: MIT Press.

Iankova, E. and J. Katz. 2003. Strategies for political risk mediation by international firms in transition economies: the case of Bulgaria. *Journal of World Business* 38(3): 182–203.

Idahosa, Pablo. 2002. Business ethics and development in conflict (zones): the case of Talisman Oil. *Journal of Business Ethics* 39: 227–246.

IETA (International Emissions Trading Association). 2003. *Greenhouse Gas Market 2003*. Geneva: IETA.

Inkpen, Andrew and Steven Currall. 1998. The nature, antecedents, and consequences of joint venture trust. *Journal of International Management* 4(1): 1–20.

International Crisis Group. 2002. *God, Oil and Country: Changing the Logic of War in Sudan*. Brussels: International Crisis Group Press.

International Labour Office. 1972. *Employment, Incomes and Equality: A Strategy for Increasing Productive Employment in Kenya*. Geneva: International Labour Office.

International Labour Organization. 1994. *Toward Full Employment*. Geneva: ILO.

International Monetary Fund (IMF). 2002. *Directory of Trade Statistics Yearbook, 1983–2001*. Washington, DC: IMF.

2003. *World Economic Outlook*. Washington, DC: IMF.

IPCC [International Panel on Climate Change], 2001. Climate Change 2001. Figure 2–3.

Javorcik, B. S. 2003. The composition of foreign direct investment and protection of intellectual property rights: evidence from transition economies. *European Economic Review*.

Jenkins, Barbara. 1986. Re–examining the 'obsolescing bargain': a study of Canada's National Energy Program. *International Organization* 40: 139–165.

Jensen, C. and T. J. S. Mallya. 2003. Foreign direct investment and regional growth in transition economies – a comparative study of the Czech Republic and Poland. Unpublished working paper.

2004. Are FDI incentive programs a good investment for the host country? An empirical evaluation of the Czech National Incentive Scheme. *Transnational Corporations* 13(1).

Jensen, Michael C. 2000. *A Theory of the Firm: Governance, Residual Claims, and Organizational Forms*. Cambridge, MA: Harvard.

John, K. and Lamma Senbet. 1998. Corporate governance and board effectiveness. *Journal of Banking and Finance* 22: 230–247.

Johnson, Simon and Daniel Kaufmann. 2001. Institutions and the underground economy. In O. Havrylyshyn and S. M. Nsouli (eds.), *A Decade of Transition: Achievements and Challenges*. Washington, DC: International Monetary Fund.

Jones, Jeffrey. 1998a. Cash crunch may force sale of Canada's Arakis Energy. *Journal of Commerce* (July 9).

1998b. Talisman gets quick lessons in the risks of Sudan. *Journal of Commerce* (August 26).

Jones, Leroy P. and Il Sakong. 1981. *Economic Development and the Role of Government and Businessmen*. Korea Development Institute.

Kashap, S. P. 1988. Growth of small-size enterprises in India: its nature and content. *World Development* 16(6) (June).

Kaufmann, Chuck and Lisa Zimmerman. 1997. US policy threatens Nicaragua property settlement. Nicaragua Network Education Fund, World History Archives, Hartford Web Publishing, February 21. Available at http://www.hartford-hwp.com/archives/47/305, html (viewed 11/03).

Kaufmann, D., A. Kraay, and P. Zoido-Lobaton. 1999. Governance matters. World Bank Research Working Paper No. 2196, Washington, DC.

Keillor, Bruce D., Gregory W. Boller, and O. C. Ferrell. 1997. Firm-level political behavior in the global market place. *Journal of Business Research* 40: 113–126.

Kekic, L. 2002. Foreign direct investment and the East European transition. In EIU (ed.), *World Investment Report* (2002 edition). London: EIU, pp. 76–92.

Kindleberger, C. 1969. *American Business Abroad*. New Heaven, CT: Yale University Press.

Kline, J. M. 2003. Political activities by transnational corporations: bright lines versus grey boundaries. *Transnational Corporations* 12(1) (April): 1–26.

Kobrin, S. J. 1982. *Managing Political Risk Assessment: Strategic Responses to Environmental Changes*. Berkeley, CA: University of California Press.

   1987. Testing the bargaining hypothesis in the manufacturing sector in developing countries. *International Organization* 41(4): 609–638.

   1997. The architecture of globalization: state sovereignty in a networked global economy. In John H. Dunning (ed.), *Governments, Globalization and International Business*. Oxford: Oxford University Press.

   1998. The MAI and the clash of globalization. *Foreign Policy* 112: 97–109.

   2003. *Oil and Politics: Talisman Energy in Sudan*. Philadelphia: Wharton School, University of Pennsylvania.

Kolodko, G. W. 2000. Transition to a market and entrepreneurship: the systemic factors and policy options. *Communist and Post-Communist Studies* 33(2): 271–293.

Kopp, R. J. and M. A. Toman. 2000. International emissions trading: a primer. In R. Kopp and J. B. Thatcher (eds.), *The Weathervane Guide to Climate Policy: An RFF Reader*. Washington, DC: Resources for the Future.

Korean Ministry of Culture and Tourism. 2000. *The Vision of Cultural Industry in the Twenty-first Century*. Seoul: Korean Ministry of Culture and Tourism.

   1959–2002. Annual estimated expenditures on culture and art.

Korean Ministry of Government Legislation. 1959–2002. The Copyright Act and its amendments.

   1959–2002. The Film Act and its amendments.

   1959–2002. The Performance Act and its amendments.

   1959–2002. The Recording, Video, and Game Act and its amendments.

Kornai, J. 1992. *The Socialist System: The Political Economy of Socialism*. Princeton: Princeton University Press.

Kostova, Tatiana. 1996. Success of the transnational transfer of organizational practices within multinational companies. Unpublished doctoral dissertation, University of Minnesota.

Kostova, Tatiana and Srilata Zaheer. 1999. Organizational legitimacy under conditions of complexity: the case of the multinational enterprise. *Academy of Management Review* 24: 64–81.

Kraar, L. 1992. Korea's tigers keep roaring. *Fortune,* 4, May.

Kroszner, R. S. 2000. Lessons from financial crises: the role of clearing-houses. *Journal of Financial Services Research*, 18(2/3): 157–171.

Lall, Sanjaya. 1985. A study of multinational and local firm linkages in India. In *Multinationals, Technology, and Exports*. London: Macmillan.

Lansbury, M., N. Pain, and K. Smidkova. 1996. Foreign direct investment in Central Europe since 1990: an econometric study. *National Institute Economic Review* 156: 104–124.

Lawrence, Bob and associates. 2000. Opic faces long wait for $290-million claim for Indonesian geothermal plants, 800 Mwe. In *Green Green: Financing News for the US Geothermal Industry*. September 30; available at http://www.bl-a.com/ECB/Green%20Green/093000.htm (viewed 11/03).

LBS (London Business School). 2001. The transformation of BP. London Business School casestudy.

Learmount, S. 2002. *Corporate Governance: What Can Be Learned from Japan?* Oxford: Oxford University Press.

Leblanc, Richard W. 1999. Are global corporate governance practices converging? *Global Focus* 11: 151–161.

Lecraw, Donald J. 1984. Bargaining power, ownership, and profitability of transnational corporations in developing countries. *Journal of International Business Studies* 15(1) (Spring/Summer): 27–43.

Lensink, R., N. Hermes, and V. Murinde. 2000. Capital flight and political risk. *Journal of International Money and Finance* 19(1): 73–92.

Levy, D. L. and Kolk, A. 2001. Strategic responses to climate change in the oil industry: home-country effects or global convergence? Paper prepared for presentation at the annual meeting of the International Studies Association, Chicago.

Li, Z. 2002. *Corporate Governance in China: Model Selection and Mechanism Improvement. International Business Overview*. Beijing: CEIBS, pp. 5–17.

Liedholm, Carl and Donald Mead. 1987. *International Development Paper No.9*. East Lansing, MI: Department of Agriculture, Michigan State University.

Lillich, R. 1975. Requiem for Hickenlooper. *American Journal of International Law* 69 (January).

Lin, T. C. 2003. Education, technical progress and growth: the case of Taiwan. *Economics of Education Review* 22(2): 213–220.

Lindblom, C. E. 1977. *Politics and Markets: The World's Political-Economic Systems*. New York: Basic Books.

Lipson, C. H. 1976. Corporate preferences and public policies. Foreign aid sanctions and investment protection. *World Politics* 28(3) (April): 396–421.

Littlejohns, Michael and David Buchan. 1999. Annan backs rights beyond borders. *Financial Times*. US edn. London.

Luo, Yadong. 2001. Toward a cooperative view of MNC–host government relations: building blocks and performance implications. *Journal of International Business Studies* 32: 383–419.

Maher, M. and T. Andersson. 2002. *Corporate governance: effects on firm performance and economic growth*. In McCahery et al., pp. 386–418.

Mahini, Amir. 1988. *Making Decisions in Multinational Corporations: Managing Relations with Sovereign Governments*. New York: John Wiley and Sons.

Malik, K. and S. Wagle. 2003. Building social capital through civic engagement. In D. A. Rondinelli and G. S. Cheema, eds., *Reinventing Government of the Twenty-first Century: State Capacity in a Globalizing Society*. Bloomfield, CT: Kumarian Press, pp. 145–163.

Mallya, Thaddeus J. S., Zderek Kukulka, and Camila Jensen. 2004. Are incentives a good investment for the host country? An empirical evaluation of the Czech National Incentive Scheme. *Transnational Corporations* 13(1): 109–148.

March, J. and J. Olsen. 1984. The new institutionalism: organizational factors in political life. *American Political Science Review* 78: 734–749.

Marcondes Advogados Associados. 2003. *Foreign Investments in Brazil: Guidelines*. São Paulo: Marcondes Advogados Associados.

Markusen, J. R. 2001. Contracts, intellectual property rights and multinational investment in developing countries. *Journal of International Economics* 53(1): 189–204.

Martin, Julie. 2001. OPIC modified expropriation coverage study: Mid American's projects in Indonesia. In Theodore H. Moran (ed.), *International Political Risk Management: Exploring New Frontiers*. Washington, DC: World Bank.

Martin, Randolph. 2002. Sudan's perfect war. *Foreign Affairs* 81(2): 111–127.

Maurer, Noel. 2004. Natural resources, institutions, and civil war: evidence from Mexico. Author's draft paper.

McCahery, Joseph A., Piet Moerland, Theo Raaijmakers, and Luc Renneboog (Eds.). 2002. *Corporate Governance Regimes: Convergence and Diversity*. Oxford: Oxford University Press.

Medical Advertising News. 1990. Top fifty companies. *Medical Advertising News*. September.

Meldrum, D. H. 2000. Country risk and foreign direct investment. *Business Economics*, 35(1): 33–40.

Merton, R. K. 1967. *On Theoretical Sociology*. New York: Free Press.

Meyer, K. E. 2001a. Institutions, transaction costs and entry mode choice in Eastern Europe. *Journal of International Business Studies*, 32(2): 357–368.

2001b. International business research in transition economies. In A. Rugman and T. Brewer (eds.), *Oxford Handbook on International Business*. Oxford: Oxford University Press, pp. 716–759.

2002. Management challenges in privatization acquisitions in transition economies. *Journal of World Business* 37: 266–276.

Meyer, K. and S. Estrin. 2001. Brownfield entry in emerging markets. *Journal of International Business Studies* 31(3): 575–584.

Meyer, K. and H. V. Nguyen. 2003. Foreign investor's entry strategy and sub-national institutions in Vietnam. SMS Mini-conference, Hong Kong, December 2003.

Meyer, K. and M. W. Peng. 2005. Probing theoretically into Central and Eastern Europe: transactions, resources, and institutions. *Journal of International Business*.

Miller, Danny and Jamal Shamsie. 1996. The resource-based view of the firm in two environments: the Hollywood film studios from 1936 to 1965. *Academy of Management Journal* 39: 519–543.

Mills, Karen. 2002. Corruption and other illegality in the formation and performance of contracts and in the conduct of arbitration relating thereto. *International Arbitration Law Review* 5(4) (October): 128.

Minor, M. S. 1994. Demise of expropriation as an instrument of LDC policy, 1980–1992. *Journal of International Business Studies* 25(1): 177–188.

Monks, Robert A. G. and Nell Minow. 2000. *Corporate Governance*. 2nd edn. Oxford: Blackwell.

Moran, Theodore. 1973. Transnational strategies of protection and defense by multinational corporations: spreading the risk and raising the cost for nationalization in natural resources. *International Organization* 27(2) (Spring): 273–287.

1977. *Multinational Corporations and the Politics of Dependence: Copper in Chile*. Princeton, NJ: Princeton University Press.

(Ed.). 1985. *Multinational Corporations: The Political Economy of Foreign Direct Investment*. Lexington, MA: Lexington Books.

Morano, Marc. 2002. Enron and the Clinton Administration: ties that bind. CNS News. com. March 18. Available at http://www.newsmax.com/archives/articles/2002/3/18/83918/shtml (viewed 11/03).

Morisset, Jacques and Neda Pirnia. 2000. How tax policy and incentives affect foreign direct investment – a review. *Policy Research Working Paper*, 2509, The World Bank, Washington DC.

Muchlinski, Peter T. 2001. Human rights and multinationals: is there a problem? *International Affairs* 77(1): 31–47.

Mudambi, R. and P. Navarra. 2002. Institutions and international business: a theoretical overview. *International Business Review* 2(6), 635–646.

Mudd, S., R. Grosse, and J. Mathis. 2002. Dealing with financial crisis in emerging markets. *Thunderbird International Business Review* 44(3): 399–430.

Munich Reinsurance. 2003. Annual review: natural catastrophes 2002. (See also www.munichre.com, August 21.)

Murtha, T. and S. Lenway. 1994. Country capabilities and strategic state: how national political institutions affect MNCs' strategies. *Strategic Management Journal* 15 (Summer): 113–129.

Murtha, Thomas P., Stefanie Ann Lenway, and Jeffrey A. Hart. 2001. *Managing New Industry Creation: Global Knowledge Formation and Entrepreneurship in High Technology*. Stanford: Stanford University Press.

N'Diaye, S. 2001. The role of institutional reforms. *Finance & Development* 38(4): 18–21.

Neumeister, Larry. 2003. Talisman can be held liable for genocide. *The Gazette*. Montreal.

Newman, Peter (Ed.). 1998. *The New Palgrave Dictionary of Economics and the Law*. London: Macmillan.

New York Times. 2003. Funds focus on polluters. *International Herald Tribune* November 24: 12.

Nikifouruk, Andrew. 1999. Oil patch pariah. *Canadian Business Magazine*.

Nord, R. 2000. Central and Eastern Europe and the new financial architecture. *Finance & Development* 37(3): 32–35.

North, D. C. 1989. Institutions and economic growth: an historical introduction. *World Development* 17(9): 1319–1332.

　　1990. *Institutions, Institutional Change and Economic Performance*. New York: Cambridge University Press.

Oetzel, J. M., R. A. Bettis, and M. Zenner. 2001. Country risk measures: how risky are they? *Journal of World Business* 36(2): 128–145.

Ohmae, Kenichi. 1995. *The End of the Nation State: The Rise of Regional Economies*. New York: HarperCollins.

Okimoto, Daniel I. 1989. *Between MITI and the Market*. Stanford: Stanford University Press.

Olive, David. 2002. Sudan's misery sure to outlast Talisman. *Toronto Star*. Toronto.

Oliver, C. 1991. Strategic responses of institutional processes. *Academy of Management Review* 16(1): 145–179.

Olsen, Janeen. 2002. Global ethics and the Alien Tort Claims Act: a summary of three cases within the oil and gas industry. *Management Decision* 40(7): 720–724.

Oman, Charles. 2000. *Policy Competition for Foreign Direct Investment – a Study of Competition among Governments to Attract FDI*. Paris: Development Center Studies, Organisation for Economic Co-operation and Development.

O'Neill, K. and F. Reinhardt. 2000. What every executive needs to know about global warming. *Harvard Business Review* 78: 128–135.

Organization for Economic Cooperation and Development (OECD). 1999. *Principles of Corporate Governance*. Paris: OECD.

2000. *No Longer Business as Usual: Fighting Bribery and Corruption*. Paris: OECD.

2002. *International Direct Investment Statistics Yearbook, 2001*. Paris: OECD.

Orr, D. and T. S. Ulen. 1993. The role of trust and the law in privatization. *The Quarterly Journal of Economics and Finance* 33 Special Issue: 135–155.

Oxfam. 2001. *Oxfam Company Briefing Paper: Pfizer*. UK: Oxfam (July).

Oxley, J. E. 1999. Institutional environment and the mechanisms of governance: the impact of intellectual property protection on the structure of inter-firm alliances. *Journal of Economic Behavior and Organization* 38(3): 283–310.

PA Cambridge Economic Consultants. 1995. The effects of foreign direct investment in UK manufacturing. PA Cambridge Economic Consultants, London (mimeo).

Pakko, M. R. 2002. What happens when the technology growth trend changes? *Review of Economic Dynamics* 5(2): 376–407.

Parker, D. 1999. Regulation of privatized public utilities in the UK: performance and governance. *International Journal of Public Sector Management* 12(3): 213–235.

Parsons, Talcott and Jan Loubser. 1976. *Explorations in General Theory in Social Science*. New York: Free Press.

PBS Online Newshour. 1996. Unfinished mission. April 4. Transcript available at http://www.pbs.org/newshour/bb/remember/brown_4–04.html (viewed 11/03).

Pearce, R. D. 1999. The evolution of technology in multinational enterprises: the role of creative subsidiaries. *International Business Review* 8: 125–148.

Peattie, Lisa. 1987. An idea in good currency and how it grew: the informal sector. *World Development* 15(7) (July).

Pederson, Torben and J. Myles Shaver. 2003. Internationalization revisited: the big step hypotheses. Working Paper.

Peng, M. W. and P. Heath. 1996. The growth of the firm in planned economies in transition: institutions, organization, and strategic choices. *Academy of Management Review* 21(2): 492–528.

Perlez, Jane. 2002. US backs oil giant on lawsuit in Indonesia. *New York Times*. New York.

Pfeffer Jeffrey and Gerald R. Salancik. 1978. *The External Control of Organizations: A Resource Dependence Perspective*. New York: Harper and Row.

Porter, M. E. 1990. *The Competitive Advantage of Nations*. New York: Free Press.

1998. *On Competiton*. Boston: Harvard Business School Press.

Posner, Richard. 1986. *Economic Analysis of Law*. Boston: Little Brown and Co. 3rd edn., pp. 106–107.

Powell, W. and P. DiMaggio (Eds.). 1991. *The New Institutionalism in Organizational Analysis*. Chicago: University of Chicago Press.

Poynter, T. A. 1985. *Multinational Enterprises and Government Intervention*. New York: Saint Martin's Press.

Prashad, Vijay. 1997. The power elite: Enron and Frank Wisner. *People's Democracy*. November 16; available at http://www.apfn.org/enron/wisner.html (viewed 11/03).

Preston, L. E. 2003. The truth about corporate governance. In Thomas A. Kochan and David B. Lipsky (eds.), *Negotiations and Change, from the Workplace to Society*. Cornell: ILR Press, pp. 205–222.

Prowse, S. 1995. Corporate governance in international perspective: a survey of corporate control mechanisms among large firms in the US, UK, Japan and Germany. In Ingo Walter (ed.), *Financial Markets, Institutions and Instruments*. New York: NYU Salomon Center, vol. 4, pp. 1–63.

Puffer Sheila M. et al. 1996. *Business and Management in Russia*. Cheltenham: Edward Elgar (see also http://web.cba.new.edu/~spuffer/Bus&MgmtInRus.html).

Quinn, Lawrence Richter. 2003. Closing the GAAP. *Camagazine* (August): 16–22.

Ramamurti, Ravi. 2001. The obsolescing bargaining model? MNC–host developing country relations revisited. *Journal of International Business Studies* 32(1) (First Quarter): 23–39.

Ranis, G., F. Stewart, and A. Ramirez. 2000. Economic growth and human development. *World Development* 28(2): 197–219.

Ravallion, M. 2002. An automatic safety net? *Finance &Development* 39(2): 21–23.

Reinhart, C. M. and M. A. Savastano. 2003. The realities of modern hyper-inflation. *Finance & Development* 40(2): 20–24.

Resmini, L. 2000. The determinants of foreign direct investment in the CEECs. *Economics of Transition* 8(3): 665–689.

Rice, David. 2002. Human rights strategies for corporations. *Business Ethics: a European Review* 11(2) (April): 134.

Riding, Alan. 1988. Peruvians combating red tape. *New York Times*, July 24.

Rivoli, P. and T. L. Brewer. 1991. Country risk and country instability. *Global Finance Journal* 2(3): 197–208.

Robinson, Richard. 1964. *International Business Policy*. New York: Holt, Rinehart and Winston.

Robock, Stefan H. 1970. Industrialization through import substitution or export industries: a false dichotomy. In Jesse W. Markham and Gustav F. Papanek (eds.), *Industrial Organization and Economic Development*. Boston, MA: Houghton Mifflin.

1971. Political risk: identification and assessment, *Columbia Journal of World Business* (July–August): 6–20.

1975. Their reach exceeds their grasp. *MBA*.

1977. Controlling multinational enterprises: the Brazilian experience, *Journal of Contemporary Business* (Autumn).

Robock, Stefan H. and Kenneth Simmonds. 1973. 4th edn. 1989. *International Business and Multinational Enterprises*. Homewood, IL: Irwin.

Rodriguez, Peter, Klaus Uhlenbruck, and Lorraine Eden. Forthcoming. Corrupt governments matter: how corruption affects the entry strategies of multinationals. *Academy of Management Review*.

Rodrik, D., A. Subramanian, and F. Trebbi. 2002. Institutions rule: the primacy of institutions over geography and integration in economic development. National Bureau of Economic Research Working Paper 9305, Cambridge, MA

Roe, M. 1998. Comparative corporate governance. In *The New Palgrave Dictionary of Economics and the Law*. Basingstoke: Macmillan, pp. 339–346.

Rondinelli, D. A. 1994a. Privatization and economic reform in Central Europe: lessons of international experience. In D. A. Rondinelli (ed.), *Privatization and Economic Reform in Central Europe: The Changing Business Climate*. Westport, CT: Quorum Books, pp. 1–40.

1994b. Capacity building in emerging market economies: the second wave of reform. *Business and the Contemporary World* 6(3): 153–167.

1995. Processes of strategic innovation: the dynamics of decision-making in the evolution of great policies. In J. D. Montgomery and D. A. Rondinelli (eds.), *Great Policies: Strategic Innovations in Asia and the Pacific Basin*. Westport, CT: Praeger Publishers, pp. 222–239.

2003a. Promoting national competitiveness in a global economy: the state's changing roles. In D. A. Rondinelli and G. S. Cheema (eds.), *Reinventing Government for the Twenty-first Century: State Capacity in a Globalizing Society*. Bloomfield, CT: Kumarian Press, pp. 33–60.

2003b. Metropolitan areas as global crossroads: moving people, goods and information in an international economy. In R. Hanley (ed.),

Moving People, Goods and Information: The Cutting-Edge Infrastructures of Networked Cities. London: Routledge/Spon Press, chapter 2.

Rondinelli, D. A. and J. N. Behrman. 2000. The institutional imperatives of globalization. *Global Focus – Journal of International Business, Economics and Social Policy* 12(1): 65–78.

Rondinell, D. A. and M. Iacono. 1996. *Policies and Institutions for Managing Privatization: International Experience*, Geneva: International Labor Office.

1994. *Entry Strategies for International Markets*, San Francisco: Jossey-Bass.

Root, F. R. 1968. US Business Abroad and the Political Risk. *MSU Business Topics*: 73–80.

1987. *Entry Strategies for International Markets*. Lexington, MA: Lexington Books.

Rosenau, James N. 1997. *Along the Domestic–Foreign Frontier: Exploring Governance in a Turbulent World*. Cambridge; New York, NY: Cambridge University Press.

Rosenzweig, P. M. and J. V. Singh. 1991. Organizational environments and multinational enterprises. *Academy of Management Review* 16: 340–361.

RTCC (*Responding to Climate Change*). 2003. *Responding to Climate Change 2003*. Cambridge: Entico.

Rugman, A. 1981. *Inside the Multinationals: The Economics of Internal Markets*. New York: Columbia University Press.

1994. *Foreign Investment and NAFTA*. Columbia, SC: University of South Carolina Press.

2000. *The End of Globalization*. London: Random House.

2001. Subsidiary-specific advantages in multinational enterprises. *Strategic Management Journal* 22(3): 237–250.

2005. *The Regional Multinationals: MNEs and Global Strategic Management*. New York: Cambridge University Press.

Rugman, A. M. and J. D'Cruz. 2000. *Multinationals as Flagship Firms*. Oxford: Oxford University Press.

Rugman, A. M. and S. Girod. 2003. Retail multinationals and globalization: the evidence is regional. *European Management Journal* 21(1): 24–37.

Rugman, A. M. and A. Kudina. 2002. Britain, Europe and North America. In M. Fratianni, P. Savona and J. Kirton (eds.), *Governing Global Finance*. Aldershot: Ashgate, pp. 185–195.

Rugman, A. M. and A. Verbeke. 1998. Multinational enterprises and public policy. *Journal of International Business Studies* 29(1): 115–136.

2001. Subsidiary-specific advantages in multinational enterprises. *Strategic Management Journal* 22(3): 237–250.

2003. Regional multinationals and triad strategy. In Alan M. Rugman (ed.), *Leadership in International Business Education and Research.* Oxford: Elsevier, pp. 253–268.

2004. A perspective on regional and global strategies of multinational corporations. *Journal of International Business Studies* 35(1): 3–18.

Rugman, A. M., J. Kirton, and J. Soloway. 1999. *Environmental Regulations and Corporate Strategy: A NAFTA Perspective.* Oxford: Oxford University Press.

Russo, Michael V. 1991. Regulatory restructuring and strategic evolution: lessons from the American experience. *Long Range Planning* 24(2): 37–43.

Sabel, Charles F. 1986. Changing models of economic efficiency and their implications for industrialization in the third world. In Alejandro Foxley, Michael S. McPherson, and Guillermo O'Donnell (eds.), *Development, Democracy, and the Art of Trespassing: Essays in Honor of Albert O. Hirschman.* Notre Dame: University of Notre Dame Press pp. 27–55.

Sandor, R. 2002–2003. Markets everywhere. *Environmental Finance* 4(3) (December–January): 13.

Santoro, Michael A. and Lynne Sharp Paine. 1992. *Pfizer: Protecting Intellectual Property in a Global Marketplace.* Boston: Harvard Business School Case, No. 9392073.

Santos-Paulino, A. U. 2002. The effects of trade liberalization on imports in selected developing countries. *World Development* 30(6): 959–974.

Schelling, Thomas. C. 1979. Command control. In *Ethical Theory and Business.* Prentice-Hall.

Scherer, Michael. 2001. Gas War. *Mother Jones.*

Schlesinger, Arthur, Jr. 1970. The lowering hemisphere. *The Atlantic Monthly* (January); available at http://the atlantic.com/issues/70jan/lowering.htm (viewed 12/03).

Schoonmaker, Sara. 2002. *High-Tech Trade Wars: US–Brazilian Conflicts in the Global Economy.* Pittsburgh, PA: University of Pittsburgh Press.

Seligson, M. A. 2002. The impact of corruption on regime legitimacy: a comparative study of four Latin American countries. *The Journal of Politics* 64(2): 408–433.

Sethi, D., S. Guisinger, D. L. Ford, and S. E. Phelan 2002. Seeking greener pastures: a theoretical and empirical investigation into the changing trend of foreign direct investment flows in response to institutional and strategic factors. *International Business Review* 2(6): 685–706.

Shama, A. 2000. Determinants of entry strategies of US companies into Russia, the Czech Republic, Hungary, Poland and Romania. *Thunderbird International Business Review* 42: 651–676.

Sherwood, R. M., G. Shepherd, and C. Marcos De Souza. 1994. Judicial systems and economic performance. *The Quarterly Review of Economics and Finance* 34 (Special Issue): 101–116.

Shleifer, A. and R. W. Vishny. 1997. A survey of corporate governance. *Journal of Finance* 52: 737–783.

Simpson, Seamus and Roden Wilkinson. 2001. Conceptualizing regulatory change: explaining shifts in telecommunications governance. Paper prepared for the twenty-ninth Telecommunications Policy Research Conference, Communication, Information, and Internet Policy, October, 27–29 2001, Alexandria, VA.

Singh, N. and S. Kundu. 2002. Explaining the growth of e-commerce corporations (ECCs). An extension and application of the eclectic paradigm. *Journal of International Business Studies* 33(4), 679–698.

Sinha, Radha, Peter Pearson, Gopal Kadekodi, and Mary Gregory. 1979. *Income Distribution, Growth and Basic Needs in India*. London: Croom Helm.

Situmeang, Hardiv H. 2001. Challenges facing IPP model in Asia: the experience of PLN in Indonesia. Presentation at the 10th World Economic Development Congress, Kuala Lumpur, June 27–29.

Sokil, S. and T. King. 1993. Financial reform in socialist economies. In C. Kessides, T. King, M. Nuti, and C. Sokil (eds.), *Financial Reform in Socialist Economies*. Washington, DC: World Bank, pp. 1–27.

Solomon, Jay and Peter Waldman. 1998. US power deals in Indonesia draw flak: Critics accuse companies of using links with Suharto to win contracts. *Asian Wall Street Journal* December 24.

South, S. G. (Ed.). 2000. *Corporate Leadership on Climate Change*. Arlington, MA: Cutter Information.

Stanwick, P. A. and S. D. Stanwick. 2002. The relationship between corporate governance and financial performance: an empirical study. *Journal of Corporate Citizenship* 8: 35–48.

Stark, D. 1992. Path dependence and privatization strategies in East Central Europe. *East European Politics and Society* 6: 17–54.

  1996. Recombinant property in East European capitalism. *American Journal of Sociology* 101: 993–1027.

Steiner, George A. 1975. *Business and Society*. Random House. New York.

Stern, Paula. 1997. New paradigm for trade expansion and regulatory harmonization: the Transatlantic Business dialogue. *European Business Journal* 9(3): 35–46.

Stigler, G. 1971. The theory of economic regulation. *Bell Journal of Economics and Management Science* 2: 3–21.

Stiglitz, J. 1999. Whither reform? Ten years of transition. Keynote address at the Annual Bank Conference on Development Economics, World Bank, Washington.

Stobaugh, R. 1969. How to analyze foreign investment climates. *Harvard Business Review* (September–October): 100–108.

Stopford, J. M. 1994. The growing interdependence between transnational corporations and governments. *Transnational Corporations* 3(1): 53–76.

Stopford, John and Susan Strange. 1991. *Rival States, Rival Firms: Competition for World Market Shares.* Cambridge: Cambridge University Press.

Stotksy, J., E. Suss, and S. Takarick. 2000. Trade liberalization in the Caribbean. *Finance & Development* 37(2): 22–25.

Strange, Susan. 1996. *The Retreat of the State: The Diffusion of Power in the World Economy.* Cambridge: Cambridge University Press.

Streeten, Paul. 1981. *Development Perspectives.* London: Macmillan.

Suara Pembaruan. 1999. Lembaga Kredit Païton Surati lima menteri. December 22.

Sudan Update. 1999. Raising the stakes: oil and conflict in Sudan. *Sudan Update.*

Sundaram, A. (with M. Bradley, C. Schipani, J. Walsh). 2000. Comparative corporate governance and corporate strategy. In *Thunderbird on Global Business Strategy.* New York: Wiley Publishers, April.

Svetličič, M. and C. Bellak. 2002. The investment development path of small countries: comparative evaluation of Slovenia and Austria. Paper prepared for the AIB 2002 Annual Meeting, in San Juan, Puerto Rico.

Svetličič, M. and M. Rojec (Eds.). 2002. *Facilitating Transition by Internationalization.* Aldershot and Burlington (USA): Ashgate.

Swaan, W. 1997. Knowledge, transaction costs and the creation of markets in post-socialist economies. In P. G. Hare and J. Davis (eds.), *Transition to the Market Economy.* London: Routledge, pp. 53–76.

Swedish National Board of Trade. 2004. Climate and trade rules – harmony or conflict? Available from www.kommers.se.

Tagliabue, John. 1982. Common Market says it will push IBM suit. *New York Times.* April 3. Cited in Julio J. Rotemberg. Competition Policy in the European Union and the Power of Microsoft. Harvard Business School case 9–701–043, revised June 26, 2001.

Talisman Energy. 1998. Sudan – the Greater Nile Oil Project: Background Paper. Calgary.

    2000. *Corporate Social Responsibility Report 2000.* Calgary: Talisman Energy Corporation.

    2001. *Corporate Social Responsibility Report 2001.* Calgary: Talisman Energy Corporation.

Tamura, R. 2002. Human capital and the switch from agriculture to industry. *Journal of Economic Dynamics and Control* 27(2): 207–242.

Tapscott, D. and D. Agnew. (1999). Governance in the digital economy. *Finance & Development* 36(4): 34–37.

Teece, D. 1981. The multinational enterprise: market failure and market power considerations. *Sloan Management Review* 22(3) (Spring): 3–17.

1993. Multinational enterprise, internal governance, and industrial organization. In B. Gomas–Casseres and D. B. Yoffie (eds.), *The International Political Economy of Direct Foreign Investment*. London: Edward Elgar Publishing, pp. 196–201.

Teece, David J., Gary Pisano, and Amy Shuen. 1997. Dynamic capabilities and strategic management. *Strategic Management Journal* 18: 509–533.

Tendler, Judith. 1987. The remarkable convergence of fashion on small enterprise and the informal sector: what are the implications for policy? Mimeo. MIT.

Tenev, S. and C. Zhang. 2002. *Corporate Governance and Enterprise Reform in China*. Washington: World Bank and International Finance Corporation.

The Guardian. 2000. TNCs: owners of intellect and life. Newspaper of the Socialist Party of Australia. See http://www.globalpolicy.org/socecon/tncs/proprght.htm.

Thornbecke, W. 2000. A public choice perspective on the globalizing of America. In T. L. Brewer and G. Boyd (eds.), *Globalizing America: The USA in World Integration*. Cheltenham, UK, and Northampton, MA: Elgar, pp. 83–97.

Tian, G. L. 2003. Corporate governance in China. PhD thesis, London Business School.

Tihanyi, L. and A. S. Roath. 2002. Technology transfer and institutional development in central and Eastern Europe. *Journal of World Business* 37(1): 188–198.

Toman, M. 2000. *Climate Change Risks and Policies: An Overview, Revised*. Climate Issues Brief No. 1. Washington, DC: Resources for the Future.

Trevino, L. J., J. D. Daniels, H. Arbelaez, and K. P. Upadhyaya. 2002. Market reform and foreign direct investment in Latin America: evidence from an error correction model. *The International Trade Journal* 26(4): 367–392.

Turner, Louis. 2003. The (a)political multinational: state rivalry revisited. In Julian Birkinshaw et al. (eds.), *The Future of the Multinational Company*. Chichester: Wiley.

Uhlenbruck, K. and J. De Castro. 1998. Privatization from the acquirer's perspective: a mergers and acquisitions model. *Journal of Management Studies* 35: 619–640.

2000. Foreign acquisitions in Central and Eastern Europe: outcomes of privatization in traditional economies. *Academy of Management Journal*.

UNCTAD. 1998. *World Investment Report: Trends and Determinants*. New York and Geneva: United Nations.

2001. *World Investment Report: Cross Border Mergers and Acquisition.* New York and Geneva: United Nations.

2002. *World Investment Report.* New York: UNCTAD.

2003a. *World Investment Directory – Volume VIII Central and Eastern Europe 2003.* New York and Geneva: United Nations Conference on Trade and Development.

2003b. *World Investment Report 2003: FDI Policies for Development: National and International Perspectives.* New York and Geneva: United Nations.

United Nations Center on Transnational Companies. 1988. *Transnational Corporations in World Development.* New York: United Nations.

United Nations. 1999. *World Investment Report 1999: Foreign Direct Investment and the Challenge of Development, Overview.* New York and Geneva: UNCTAD.

United Nations Economic and Social Commission for Asia and the Pacific (UNESCAP). 1990. *Restructuring the Developing Economies of Asia and the Pacific in the 1990s.* New York: United Nations.

United Nations Office for the Coordination of Humanitarian Efforts. 2000. *United Nations Consolidated Inter-Agency Appeal for Sudan.* New York: United Nations.

United Nations Social and Economic Council. 2003. *Norms on the Responsibilities of Transnational Corporations and Other Business Enterprises with Regard to Human Rights.* New York: United Nations.

US Department of Energy. 2003. An energy overview of the Republic of Turkey. *Fossil Energy International* (last updated October 20, 2003; available at http://www.fe.doe.gov/international/turnover html and viewed 11/03).

Useem, Micheal. 1998. Corporate leadership in a globalizing equity market. *Academy of Management Executive* 12: 43–59.

Vachani, Sushil. 1995. Enhancing the obsolescing bargain theory: a long-itudinal study of foreign ownership of US and European multinationals. *Journal of International Business Studies* 26(1): 159.

Van den Berghe, L. 2002. *Corporate Governance in a Globalizing World: Convergence or Divergence?* Dordrecht: Kluwer.

Van den Berghe, L. and Levrau, A. 2003. Measuring the quality of corporate governance: in search of a tailormade approach. *Journal of General Management* 28: 71–86.

Veeser, Cyrus. 2002. *A World Safe for Capitalism: Dollar Diplomacy and America's Rise to Global Power.* New York: Columbia University Press.

Forthcoming. *In Pursuit of Capital: Concessions as a Modernizing Strategy in the Dominican Republic, 1876–1916.*

Vernon, Raymond. 1968. Conflict and resolution between foreign direct investors and less developed countries. *Public Policy* 17.

1971. *Sovereignty at Bay: The Multinational Spread of US Enterprises.* New York: Basic Books.

1977. *Storm over the Multinationals: The Real Issues.* Cambridge, MA: Harvard University Press.

1980. The obsolescing bargain: a key factor in political risk. In M. B. Winchester (ed.), *The International Essays for Business Decision Makers,* Vol. IV. New York: AMACOM: 281–286.

1998. *In the Hurricane's Eye: The Troubled Prospects of Multinational Enterprises.* Cambridge, MA: Harvard University Press.

Vernon, Raymond and Debora Spar. 1989. *Beyond Globalism: Remaking American Foreign Economic Policy.* New York: Free Press, p. 157.

Vickers, John and George Yarrow. 1991. Economic perspectives on privatization. *Journal of Economic Perspectives* 5(2): 111–132

Vives, X. 2000. Corporate governance: does it matter? In X. Vives (ed.), *Corporate Governance: Theoretical and Empirical Perspectives.* Cambridge: Cambridge University Press, pp. 1–10.

Vogel, David. 1999. The dynamics of regulatory convergence. Paper presented at a conference on Regulation in Europe, sponsored by the London Business School and the Max Planck Institute, Bonn, in association with the Anglo-German Research Foundation, November 4–5, 1999.

Wall Street Journal. 1999. US Export–Import Bank's clout speeds Asia's restructuring. May 19.

2003. NYSE begins its huge overhaul. November 6: 1.

Webb, D. 1999. Legal and institutional reform strategy and implementation: a World Bank perspective. *Law and Policy in International Business* 30(1): 161–171.

Weidenbaum, Murray L. 1980. *Business, Government and the Public.* New York: Prentice-Hall.

Wells, Louis T., Jr. and Eric S. Gleason. 1995. Is foreign infrastructure investment still risky? *Harvard Business Review* (September–October): 45–55.

Werner, R. 2003. Location, cheap labor and government incentives: a case study of automotive investment in Central Europe since 1989. *Chazen Web Journal of International Business* (Spring) (www.gsp.columbia.edu/chazenjournal).

Wesson, T. 2003. *Foreign Direct Investment and Competitive Advantage.* Cheltenham: Edward Elgar.

Westney, E. 1993. *Organization Theory and the Multinational Corporation.* New York: St. Martin's Press.

White House. 1994. Press Release 11/17/94 available at http://clinton6. nara.gov/1994/11/1994–11–17-administration-secures-contracts-for-exports. html (viewed6/00).

Williamson, J. 1994. In search of a manual for technopols. In J. Williamson (ed.), *The Political Economy of Policy Reform.* Washington, DC: Institute for International Economics, pp. 11–28.

Williamson, O. E. 1975. *Markets and Hierarchies: Analysis and Antitrust Implications.* New York: Free Press.

   2000. The new institutional economics: taking stock, looking ahead. *Journal of Economic Literature* 38(3): 595–613.

Winiecki, J. 2003. The role of the new, entrepreneurial private sector in transition and economic performance in light of the successes in Poland, the Czech Republic, and Hungary. *Problems of Economic Transition* 45(11): 6–38.

Wint, Alvin G. 1996. Pioneering telephone privatization: Jamaica. In Ravi Ramamurti (ed.), *Privatizing Monopolies: Lessons from the Telecommunications and Transport Sectors in Latin America.* Baltimore: Johns Hopkins University Press.

Wood, D. J. 1991. Corporate social performance revisited. *Academy of Management Review* 16(4): 691–718.

World Bank 1993. *Kyrgyzstan: The Transition to a Market Economy.* Washington, DC: World Bank.

   2002. Far from home: do foreign investors import higher standards of governance in transition economies? WB Discussion Paper, The World Bank, Washington.

   2003. Foreign direct investment in emerging market countries. Report of the working group of the Capital Markets Consultative Group, World Bank, Washington, DC.

Wright, M., S. Thompson and K. Robbie. 1993. Finance and control in privatisation by management buy-out. *Financial Accountability and Management* 9(2): 75–99.

Wymeersch, E. 2002. Convergence or divergence and board effectiveness. In McCahery et al., pp. 230–247.

Xiao, J. and L. N. K. Lo. 2003. Human capital development in Shanghai: lessons and prospects. *International Journal of Educational Development* 23(4): 411–427.

Yeung, H. W. and K. Olds (Eds.). 2000. *Globalization of Chinese Business Firms.* London: Macmillan.

Yew, Lee Kuan. 2000. *From Third World to First: The Singapore Story, 1965–2000.* New York: Harper Collins.

Zhang, X. 2003. Political structures and financial liberalization in pre-crisis East Asia. *Studies in Comparative International Development* 38(1): 64–92.

Zhao, J. H., S. H. Kim, and J. Du. 2003. The impact of corruption and transparency on foreign direct investment: an empirical analysis. *Management International Review* 43(1): 41–63.

Zingales, Luigi. 1998. Corporate governance. In Newman, pp. 497–503.

Selected publications of Jack N. Behrman on international business–government relations

1955. Aid for economic development and the objectives of United States foreign economic policy. *Economic Development and Cultural Change* (November): 55–67.

1959. United States interest in overseas business. Proceedings of Wisconsin's Fifth Annual House – Counsel Institute on Corporate Law, pp. 83–112.

1960. Promoting Free World economic development through direct investment. *American Economic Review* 1(2): 271–281.

1962. (with Raymond F. Mikesell, eds.) *US Private and Government Investment Abroad*. Eugene: University of Oregon Press. Part II on "Direct Private Foreign Investment," pp. 77–230; reprinted in part, in R. N. Farmer, R. W. Stevens, and H. Schollhammer (eds.), *Readings in International Business*, California: Dickenson Pub. Co. 1972, pp. 354–378.

1965. Foreign investment muddle. *Columbia Journal of World Business*, Inaugural Issue: 51–60. (Reprinted in *Congressional Record-House*, July 26, 1967, pp. H9449–53; and in S. P. Sethi and J. N. Sheth (eds.), *Multinational Business Operations – Financial Management*, vol. IV, California: Goodyear Publishing Company, 1972.)

1966. Foreign private investment and the government's efforts to reduce the payments deficit. *The Journal of Finance* (May): 283–296.

1969. Multinational corporations, transnational interests, and national sovereignty. *Columbia Journal of World Business* (March–April): 15–22. (Reprinted in Courtney Brown (ed.), *World Business*, New York: Macmillan, 1970, pp. 114–126; and in James Baker, John Ryan, Jr., and Donald Howard (eds.), *International Business Classics*, Lexington, MA: Lexington Books, 1988, pp. 169–178.)

1969. Multinational enterprise: the way to economic internationalism? *Journal of Canadian Studies* (May): 12–18. (Reprinted in Etienne Cracco, *International Business – 1970*, MSU International Business & Economics Studies, pp. 39–46; and in S. P. Sethi and J. N. Sheth (eds.), *Multinational Business Operations – Environmental Aspects*, vol. I, California; Goodyear Publishing Company, 1973; and in *France Expansion* [Paris, 1974].)

1969. *Some Patterns in the Rise of the Multinational Enterprise*, UNC School of Business, Research Paper No. 18, 180 pages (Korean translation: Modern E & B Library, 1973).

1970. *National Interests and the Multinational Enterprise*. Englewood Cliffs, NJ: Prentice-Hall, 192 pages (Japanese edition: 1975. Korean translation: Modern E & B Library, 1973).

1971. Can governments slay the dragon of multinational enterprise? *European Business* 28 (Winter): 53–64. (Reprinted in *Problems Economiques*, La Documentation Française, May 13, 1971.)

1971. *US International Business and Governments*. New York: McGraw-Hill, 244 pages.

1972. The multinational enterprise: its initiatives and governmental reactions. *The Journal of International Law and Economics* (January): 215–233.

1974. Actors and factors in policy decisions on foreign direct investment. *World Development* (August): 1–14

1974. *Conflicting Constraints on the Multinational Enterprise*. New York: FMME, 109 pages, translated into Spanish.

1974. *Decision Criteria for Foreign Direct Investment in Latin America*. New York: Council of the Americas, 1974.

1974. (with Ashok Kapoor and J. J. Boddewyn) *Effects of US International Companies on Intergovernmental Relations* for US Department of State, Bureau of Intelligence and Research, Washington, DC, July, 445 pages. Published as *International Government–Business Communications*, Boston: Lexington Books, 1975, 205 pp.

1980. *Industry Ties to Science and Technology Policies in Developing Countries*. Cambridge, MA: Oelgeschlager, Gunn, and Hain, 200 pages.

1981. Transnational corporations in the new international economic order. *Journal of International Business Studies*, Anniversary Issue (Spring/Summer): 29–42. (Selected as one of top twenty articles in International Business over past twenty-five years by the Fellows of the Academy of International Business, and reprinted in W. A. Dymsza and R. G. Vambery (eds.), *International Business Knowledge*. New York: Praeger, 1987, pp. 44–57.)

1984. *Industrial Policies: International Restructuring and Transnationals*. Lexington, MA: Lexington Books 230 pages. (Translated by Ruy Jungmann, *Politics Industrial: A Reestruturação Internacional e as Multinacionais*, Rio de Janeiro, Brazil: Edition Record, 1988.)

1990. (with Robert E. Grosse) *International Business and Governments: Issues and Institutions*. Columbia, SC: University of South Carolina Press, 434 pages.

1993. The emerging world economic order and the criteria of acceptability. *Development & International Cooperation* 9(16) (June): 9–23. (Reprinted in Marjan Svetlicic and H. W. Singer (eds.), *The World Economy: Challenges of Globalization and Regionalization.* New York: St. Martin's Press, 1996, pp. 41–54.)

2001. Adequacy of international codes of behavior. *Journal of Business Ethics* 31: 51–64.

Index

accountability 47
    corporate governance and 5, 94, 98
    of governments 409
    and multinational firms 13, 98, 197,
        215, 221
Acemoglu, D. 402
acquisition 11, 122, 127, 128, 131–135,
    144
Adams, Brock 446
Adorno, T. W. 175
Advisory Committee on Trade and
    Policy Negotiations 355
Advocacy Center 439, 440, 441, 456
aggregation 240
Agnew, D. 410
Agrawal, Vivek 470
agro-business 230–231
Aguilera, R. V. 84, 92, 96
Aharoni, Yair 30, 43, 45
Aiba, T. 164
ALCOA 327
Alden, Edward 203
Alien Tort Claims Act 194–195, 216
Allers, V. 398
Amnesty International 112, 199
Amon, Elizabeth 194
Andersson, T. 94
Andreff, W. 123
Annan, Kofi 109, 199, 216
Antal-Mokos, Z. 132
anti-globalization movement 312, 394
anti-multinational firm attitudes 268,
    385
anti-trust law 181, 411
Aoki, M. 89
Arakis Energy 202, 203
arbitration, international 335, 407,
    430, 444, 458
Argentina 227, 349
Argyres, Nicholas 265

Arris, L. 157
ASEAN 19, 245, 366, 369
Asia, regionalization 369
Asian Development Bank 447, 450
Australia 359
automobile industry *137–138*, 142, 389
    Brazil 106, 240, 390
    China 299
    Czech Republic *138*, 143
    Japan 278
    Mexico 257
Averyt, William F. 267
Axworthy, Lloyd 211, 214, 214–215
Azberbaijan 70, 73

Bankers Trust *284*
banks 15, 64, 83, 90, 129, *283*, *284*
    in Germany and Japan 86, 97
bargaining 14–18, 41, 135–143
bargaining power
    of government 115, 276
    of investors 36, 144, 265, 307
    in the obsolescing bargaining model
        36, 255, 278
    in the political bargaining model 254,
        264–265, 266, 267, 467
    relative 15, 144, 467
bargaining relationship 6, 15, 15–16,
    17–18, 280, 336–338
    and triangular diplomacy 105, 276
Barnet, Richard J. 385–386
Barney, Jay 262, 263
Bartlett, Chris 33, 43
Bauer, A. 417
Baum, Gerhart 206
Beattie, Alan 199
Behrman, Jack 27, 36, 45, 46, 47,
    289, 405
    Behrman–Grosse model 276–280, *287*
    career 30, 32

Behrman, Jack (cont.)
  definition of multinational
    enterprises 32, 33
  foreign direct investment 275, 293
  institutions 59, 399, 400, 401
  legitimacy 33, 465, 473
  model for government–business
    relationship 276–280
  obsolescing bargain model 127, 253,
    255, 256
Belarus 123, 125
Bellak, C. 123
Benacek, V. 65
Bengoa, M. 408
Benhabib, J. 416
Bennett, Douglas C. 257, 276
Bennett, Peter 46
Bennike, Carsten *131*
Bentsen, Lloyd 446
Berglof, E. 90
Bernhard, M. 416
Berthélemy, J. C. 403
Bettis, R. A. 398
Bevan, Alan A. 127, 129
  institutions 64, 65, 128, 129, 130
Beyer, J. 142
Biermann, F. 165
bilateral investment treaties 66, 266,
    317, 321, 335
  US use of 356, 359, 444–445
Birkinshaw, Julian 60
Blair, M. M. 84
Blake, David H. 46
Blomqvist, Kirsimarja 469
Blomstrom, Magnus 241
Blumberg, Phillip I. 196
board, two-tiered 97
Boarman, P. M. 29
Boddewyn, Jean 8–9, 259, 275, 465,
    471
  multinational firm goals 258, 263,
    311
Boller, Gregory W. 267
Bowley, Graham 211, 214
Bowlus, A. J. 406
Bratton, W. W. 94
Brazil
  aerospace industry 106, 391
  automobile industry 106, 240, 390
  computer industry 106, 287

foreign direct investment 390–391,
    392
  intellectual property protection 355
  oil industry 389
  shoe industry 239
  and the WTO 364
Brenton, P. 128
Brewer, Thomas 11–12, 259, 466, 471
  cooperation 43, 258, 311
  foreign direct investment 293, 294
  obsolescing bargain model 253, 255
  bribery 433, 439–440; *see also*
    corruption
Bridgeford, Tawny Aine 194, 199
British Commonwealth Corporation
    221, 230
Broad, Robin 200
Broadman, H. G. 130, 412
Brohm, R. 165
Brooke, Michael 46
Brown, Ron 442, 443, 447
Browne, Lord 112
brownfield investment *137*
Brunetti, A. 412
Buchan, David 199
Buckee, Jim 204, 210, 214
Bulgaria 70, 123, 125, 138
bureaucracy 67, 73, 135, 223
Burke, Pamela L. 198
Bush, George H. 446–447, 453–455
Business Environment Index 46, 66, 67,
    70, 72, 73, 74, 75–76, 77, 387
business–government relations 10–14,
    29–32, 114–116, 179–183,
    275–289, 321
  Behrman–Grosse model 276–280,
    287
  implications of regionalization
    376–378
  theory of 29–32, 41–45, 47, 153, 180
business–government relations studies
    8–10, 27–47, 149–170

Cable & Wireless 328, 330, 331, 332,
    335
California, greenhouse gas emission
    legislation 162
Callaghan, D. W. 178
Calvo Doctrine 457, 458
Canada 213, 256, 379

North American Free Trade
    Agreement 367, 368, 379
and Talisman 204, 214–215
capital markets 96
capitalism 96, 108, 109, 177
carbon dioxide emissions 153, *160*
Carbon Disclosure Project 151, 157
carbon markets 150–151, 158, 166
Cardemil, L. 413
Carlaw, K. I. 414
Carlisle, Tamsin 204
Castro, Fidel 436
Cattaneo, Claudia 203
Cavanagh, John 200
CERES 157
Ceylon 428
Charkham, Jonathan 86, 93–94, 97
Charney, Jonathan I. 197
Chase, Rodney 113, 203
Chase Manhattan *284*
Cheek, Marney L. 345, 359
Cheffins, Brian R. 94
Chen, A, 412
Chevron 202, 211
Chicago Climate Exchange 151
Chile 359, 427, 455
    copper industry 256, 427, 436
China 73, 82, 90, 387
    automobile industry 299
    banking sector 299
    bargaining power 279, 391
    bureaucracy 296, 301, 313
    competition 301, 308
    corporate governance 89, 90–91, 97,
        99
    corruption 412
    Economic and Technological
        Development Zones 297, 305
    employee consultation 89
    environmental protection 302
    foreign direct investment, 16, 219,
        293–313
    foreign exchange control 299, 300
    ideology 388
    informal networks 134
    insurance industry 308
    intellectual property protection 306,
        307, 355, 364
    internet companies 301, 308
    joint ventures 303, 387

labor policy 299, 406
legal systems 300, 302
levels of governments 305, 306, 307,
    308
and multinational firms 309–313
ownership requirements 303, 308
policy on multinational firms 16
    convergence with domestic policy
        303–304, 310
    covert vs. overt control 300–303,
        310
    entry intervention vs. operational
        interference 296–300
    rigid vs. elastic 307–309
    shifts in 295–309;
    simplicity vs. complexity 304–307
regulation 303–304, 310
    legislation 296, 298, 304
Special Economic Zones 242, 305
transparency 300, 303, 306
and World Trade Organization 300,
    312, 364
Chinese National Petroleum Company
    202
Chiquita Brands 453–455
Cho, Dong-Sung 12–13, 173, 187
Chung, Wilbur 258
CIS 123, 125, 128
Citibank *283–284*
Cities for Climate Protection campaign
    162
Citigroup 370
civil society 107, 109–112, 416
climate change 11–12, 149–170
Clinton, Bill 446–447, 451–452,
    453–455
clusters of economic activities, sub-
    national 62, 113–114, *137*, 145, 239
code of conduct 98, 105, 110, 213
Coeure, B. 404
Coffee, J. C. 89, 94
Cold War, end of 106–108, 438–456
Colombia 233, 454
communications 62, 63, 67, 73, 467
community, international 199, 216
comparative advantage 59, 92, 242, 412
competition 39, 129–130, 282, 309,
    395–419
    among governments 67, 105
    support of 59, 412–415

competition policy 223, 411
  in emerging market economies 65,
    70, 129–130, 395–419
  and privatization 133
competitive advantage 59, 60, 106,
  262, 346
competitiveness, conditions for 57, 105,
  254, 260, 261, 282, 417
complementarity 220, 260, 264, 310
complicity 194, 200, 208–213, 216,
  472
  definitions of 205, 211, 212
computer industry 60, *286–287*
Confederation of Danish
  Industries 127
conflict 257, 294, 465, 466
conflict resolution 43–45
Congress of Vienna 108
consistency, in regulatory systems 411
constitutionalist model of government
  policy 180, 181, 187, 188
consumer education and protection 406
convergence, regulatory 266, 343–359
cooperation 6, 242, 268
  between host countries and
    multinational firms 3, 4, 19,
    261, 294, 309, 467
  between informal sector firms 226,
    239
  and competition 309, 310, 313
copyright 347; *see also* intellectual
  property protection
corporate citizenship 209, 313
corporate governance 9, 73, 81, *95*,
  466
  alternative systems of 87–92, *91*, 96
  aspects of 86, 100–101
  convergence among systems 83, 90,
    94–99, *95*, *97*, 98
  definitions of 84–86, 99–100
  hybrid systems 90, 98
  importance of 92–94
  market-based 87, 88, 91, 92
  monitoring-based 87, 88, 89, 90,
    91, 98
  structures 97
corporate performance 93, 134
corporations 81, 85, 86, 221, 465
  status of 82, 83, 85, 100, 196–197
Corrall, Steven 469

corruption 105, 127, 135, 142, 411
  anti-corruption policy 70, 409
  and attracting foreign direct
    investment 66, 73, 260
  bribery 433, 439–440
Costa Rica 279, 454
country-specific advantages 262, 263,
  264, 266, 379, 380
Cracco, E. F. 46
Croome, John 355
Crowley, F. 409
Cuba 436
cultural industries 12, 173, *187*
Cutler, A. Claire
  authority 195, 197, 198
  corporations 196–197, 198
Czech Republic 70, 138, 141, 142, 143,
  405
  automobile industry *138*, 143

Dabrowski, Wojtek 204
Daily, C. M. 84
Daley, William M. (US Secretary of
  Commerce) 449
Dandy company *130–131*
Das, T. K. 469
D'Avino, Cary R. 193
Davis, Carlton E. 324, 325, 326, 327,
  328, 337
D'Cruz, J. 378
de Buck, Philippe 164
De Castro, J. 129, 133
de Soto, Hernando 226
decentralization 60
Declaration of Human Rights 109, 113,
  213
Del Sol, Patricio 455
deMortangas, C. P. 398
Denmark 127, 151
Deutsche Bank *284*
developing countries 106, 242, 244,
  293, 391
  and foreign direct investment
    383–394, 421–461
  and intellectual property law 347,
    353, 356, 359
Development Bank of Japan 157
DiMaggio, P. 4
DiPaola, M. 157
disclosure 98, 150

dispute settlement 319–322, 392; *see also* investment disputes
distance 61, 264, 380
distribution, efficient 405
DiTata, J. C. 413
Djankov, S. 122
Dole, Bob 454
Donaldson, William 86
Doyle, A. 149
Doz, Yves 43, 258
Dresdner Bank 137
Drexage, J. 164
Dries, L. 406
Drohan, Madelaine 214, 215
Du, J. 412
Dunning, J. H. 5, 30, 43, 123
    cooperation 254, 261, 294, 310
    country-specific advantages 263
    foreign direct investment 9, 47,
        51–78, 123, 125, 258, 263
    morality 59–61, 109, 112

E-commerce 62
Easterly, W. 404–407
economic adjustment, institutions of
    401–404
economic cycles 282, 288
economic development 11, 39–41, 59,
    389–390, 404
    and institutions 399, 400
    role of government 82, 179, 275
    role of multinational firms 220, 385
economic freedom index 128
economies
    coordinated 6, 87
    liberal 6, 87, 125, 338
    market 121, 122
economies, transitional 8, 11, 51–78, 89
    Business Environment Index 67
    location-bound advantages 62, 75
    opportunities and challenges of 61–63
    policies 62, 67
    structural transformation 294
Economist Intelligence Unit 65, 66,
    68–69, 70
Ecuador 15, *285–286*
Eden, Lorraine 14–15, 16, 467
education 63, 236, 406
efficiency, economic 92, 169, 238,
    258–259, 261, 457, 458

Egypt 431, 446
electricity provision 17, 467
electronics revolution 244
Elkins, A. 178
Emmons, W. R. 92, 93, 96
employee consultation 89, 97
employment 150, 228, 244
    exploitation 234, 237
    in the informal sector 223–224, 227,
        228
    and wages 232, 234
enforcement procedures 55
Enron 440, 445, 446–447
entrepreneurial culture 63, 66, 405,
    408, 416
Environmental Defense 151
environmental protection 3, 113, 329,
equity 415–417
Estonia 123, 137
Estrin, S. 127, 129, 131
    institutions 64, 65, 128, 129, 130
Esty, Daniel C. 344
Ethiopia 428
Eurelectric 167
European Bank for Reconstruction and
    Development 63, 121, 125
European Union 3, 19, 108, 198, 245,
    266, 363
    accession to 65, 76, 143, 365
    bureaucracy 364
    competition 144, 279
    corporate governance 96
    Emissions Trading Scheme 11, 151,
        164, 165, 166
    enlargement of 98, 122, 143, 369
    intellectual property protection 347
    intra-regional trade and FDI 136,
        368
    regionalism 144, 366, 380
    role in world economy 358
European Union of Industrial and
    Employers' Confederations 353,
    354
exchange controls 129, 300, 411
    and foreign direct investment 73, 299
    rates 240, 246, 404, 414
export expansion 241, 389, 390
Export–Import Bank 431, 447, 449
export processing zones 242–246; *see
    also* Special Economic Zones

expropriation 29, 35, 36, 319, 392,
    423, 425
  creeping 423, 428
  and the obsolescing bargain model
    253, 336
externalities 156, 168, 473
extractive industries 321, 322, 334, 467

Fagre, Nathan 276, 294, 318
Fantischek, F. 413
Farmer, Richard 45
Fayerweather, John 8–9, 27, 28, 29,
    30–31, 36, 43–45, 46
  conceptual framework for IBGR
    41–45, 465
Ferrell, O. C. 267
Fidrmuc, J. 409
film industry, Korean 173–175
financial crises 410, 448, 457
financial institutions 406, 409, 410
financial sector 64, 67, 70, 392
firm-specific advantages 256, 266, 373,
    379, 380
  and regional integration 377
  as resources in bargaining 262, 263,
    264, 267
Fischer, S. 414
Flexible Specialization 238
Ford 370
Ford, D. L. 55
foreign direct investment 51–78, 105,
    121–140, 217–247, 258, 383–394
  by acquisition 11, 122, 127,
    131–135, 144
  costs and risks 245, 398
  crowding-in 142, 220, 222–239
  determinants of 53, 57, 64, 66, 75,
    128, 276
  greenfield entry 11, 135–143, 144
  incentive schemes 246, 255, 278, 392
  and institutions 63, 75, 129
  mode of entry 53, 122, 128, 144, 419
  opposition to 337, 385–386
  role of government 9, 51, 246–247
  Special Economic Zones 137–141
  using the judo trick 217–247, 229
  variables influencing 53–55
forum switching 356–357
Foster, Peter 211, 214
France 89, 97, 369

Franco, Leonardo 207
Frank, Steven 214
Frankel, J. A. 414
freedom 408–410
free economic zones 137
Free Trade Area of the Americas 3, 363,
    366, 374
  expansion of 19, 367, 369
Friedman, Milton 112, 179
Friedman, Thomas 107

Gagnon, Georgette
  civilian casualties 202, 207
  civil war in Sudan 201, 202, 206,
    207, 211
  complicity 208–209, 211, 215
  oil industry 202, 203, 206
GATS 266
GATT negotiations 82, 105, 353,
    356–357, 359, 377
Gaviria, A. 412
Gelbard, Robert S. (US Ambassador to
    Indonesia) 451, 452
General Motors 370
Geradin, Damien 344
Germany
  banking sector 86, 97
  corporate governance 94, 97, 98
  foreign direct investment 369
  two-tiered board system 89, 97–98
Ghoshal, Sumantra 33, 43
Gillis, Charles 204
Gingrich, Newt 448
Girod, S. 370
Gladwin, Thomas N. 41, 43, 45, 318
Gleason, Eric S. 317, 322, 336
global warming 11–12, 149–170,
    472
  climate regime and trading regime
    164–165
  costs and benefits 149, 154
  and economics 154–155, 156,
    168–169
  and externalities 156, 168
  impacts 149, 150, 154, 158–161,
  issues facing firms and governments
    152–153
  and politics 155–156, 169
  regulation 157, 158, 161–165, 169
  responses to 155–156, 157–158

research 153, 158, 167–169,
169–170
science of 153, 168
taxes and subsidies 156, 169
transaction risks 166, 170
trends and projections 158, 159, *161*
uncertainties 153, 163–165, 168, 170
globalization 33, 59, 98, 106–108, 379,
467
decentralized nature of 468, 469
governance gap 194, 215–216
and international organization and
politics 195, 198
lack of 365, 367, 379
problems of 468, 469
Globerman, Steven 400
Gold, Vladimir 433
Gomes-Casseres, B. 318
Gonzalez Amendment 425, 427
Gornik-Tomaszewski, Sylwia 356
governance, good 59, 216, 409
government 178, 179, 400–401; *see
also* host government
government, local and regional 3, 134
government policy 178, 232–233, 363
and the banking sector *284*
bargaining over 254, 267, 336
constitutional model of 180, 181, 187
and foreign direct investment 28, 73,
121–141, 388–393
and global warming 149–170
laissez-faire model of 180, 181, 187
mercantilist model of 180, 181
paternalistic model of 180, 181, 187
governments, national 4, 12, 18–21, 19,
20, 29, 44
Grameen Bank 222, 232, 235
Gray, D. F. 401–402
Greater Nile Petroleum Operating
Company 202
Greece 65
Green, D. J. 417
Green, Robert T. 46
greenfield entry 11, 122, 127, *137*, 144,
145
incentive 143, 145
greenhouse gas emissions *160*, 163,
165–167
reducing 150, 153, 156, 162
trading schemes 11, 150, 157

Gronicki, M. 65
Grosse, Robert 3–21, 31, 45, 65, 309,
399, 410, 467, 471
Behrman–Grosse model 276–280,
287
foreign direct investment 293, 294
obsolescing bargain model 255, 256,
257
Grubb, M. 164
Guisinger, S. 55
Gulati, Ranjay 469
Gwartney, J. 409

Habib, M. 411
Haley, U. C. V. 419
Hall, P. 6, 87, 96, 466
Halpern, P. J. N. 96
Hamilton, Alexander 390
Hamilton, K. 164
Haner, F. T. 35, 46
Hansmann, Henry 88, 92, 94
Hansted, Morten *131*
Harker, John 201, 202, 206
Harker Report 207, 211, 212, 214, 215
Harmon, James 449
harmonization 82, 343, 344, 346
harmonization, regulatory 19
Hart, Jeffrey A. 258
Harvey, Michael G. 347
Haufler, Virginia 198, 199
health services 236, 416
Heath, P. 134
Heller, P. S. 417
Helms, Jesse 438, 442
Henisz, W. J. 122
Hennart, J.-F. 5
Hermes, N. 398, 410
Herzfeld, T. 412
Hickenlooper Amendment 425–427,
428, 442
Holden, N. 134
holding companies 312
Holland, D. 65, 142
Hong Kong 60
Hood, Neil 60
Horkheimer, M. 175
host government 37, 255, 260, 319,
383, 384, 388–393
bargaining relationship 244,
263–264, 265–266, 288

host government (cont.)
  goals of 255, 259–260, 260–261, 288
  location-bound advantages 263
  perceptions of foreign investors 38,
    386
  stakes involved 278
Hull Rule 425, 444
human capital 63, 416
human rights 193–216, 199–200
  multinational firm responsibilities for
    13, 112–113, 205, 210, 212, 215
  responsibility for violations 194, 199,
    472
  Universal Declaration of Human
    Rights 109, 113, 213
Human Rights Watch 199, 206, 209, 214
  displacement of civilians 207, 208, 211
Hungary 70, 123, *138*, 405
  incentive schemes 138, 143
Hutchinson, M. M. 414
Hymer, Stephen 39, 275

Iankova, E. 397, 398
Ianoco, M. 403
Idahosa, Pablo 201
ideology 388–389
ILO 110, 225–227, 357, 413
IMD 417
import protection 141, 247, 413
import substitution 240, 241, 389
incentives 136–137, *140*, 141, 142,
    181, 236, 246, 278
  impact of 142–143
  policy 6, 55, 63, 392
income 236, 415
India 70, 73, 242, 279, 364, 392, 470
  industries 60, 230, 349
  and the US 446
Indonesia
  and ITT 433–435
  Paiton I power project 445, 447, 448,
    449
  and the US 446, 450, 451, 452, 455,
    456, 460–461
industrial parks 63, 137, 144
industrial policy 239, 240
infant industry encouragement 247,
    389, 390
informal sector 225–227, 228–229,
    235, 237

complementarity to formal sector
    firms 14, 229, 236–237
  cooperation 226
  employment in 223–224, 225, 227,
    228
  firms in 224, 225
  government and 231, 234, 235–236
  potential to help the poor 223, 229
  productivity of 228, 235
infrastructural industries 321, 322,
    327–332, 334, 336
infrastructure 237, 247, 406
Inkpen, Andrew 469
innovation 221, 236, 238
Inouye, Daniel 429
instability 397
institution-building 65, 66, 121,
    400–401
institutional development 122, *124*,
    127–*131*, 128, 144, 466
institutional infrastructure 51, 52–53,
    63–75, 121
  significance of 67, 75
institutional theory 4, 9, 20, 397–419
institutions 6, 51–78, 128, 266, 399,
    410–412, 411, 423
  and competition 412–415
  and economic adjustment 401–404
  and economic motivation 404
  and emerging market economies 401
  formal and informal 127, 134
  and freedom of enterprise 408–410
  importance of 9, 399–400
  and the informal sector 235, 236
  and intellectual property law 354
  location-bound 52
  of private property protection
    407–408
  promoting competition 412–415
  promoting social equity and equality
    of opportunity 415–417
  and promotion of private enterprise
    70
  quality of 55, 70, 400
  of rule-setting 52, 410–412
  supranational 266, 358
  weaknesses of 128
insurance industry 370, 410
integration, global 43, 294
Intel 114

Intellectual Property Committee 353, 354
intellectual property protection 18, 67, 122, 343–359, 407, 471
  global regime 347–348, 351–357
  and the TRIPS Agreement 261, 347, 348, 350
  weak 345, 347, 408
Inter-American Development Bank 235
Intercontinental Energy 445
interests, national and corporate 39, 47
Interfaith Center on Corporate Responsibility 112, 151
International Accounting Standards Board 356
International Center for the Settlement of Investment Disputes 318, 319, *320*, 322, 326, 327, 335
International Chamber of Commerce 112
International Code of Ethics for Canadian Business 213
International Crisis Group 200, 201, 206
International Emissions Trading Association 150, 157
International Finance Corporation 90
International Fund for Agricultural Development 235
International Monetary Fund 399, 400
internet 62, 107, 465, 469
investment 123, 125, 127, 220
  climate 47, 246, 317, 397, 398, 407, 417, *418*
  disputes 319, *320*, 321, *322*, 334, 335, 407, 458, 466
  multilateral agreements 317, 321
  policy 317
  rules and legislation related to *126*
    See also foreign direct investment
Investor Network on Climate Risk 151
Iran, and the US 436
Iraq, war in 366, 368, 369, 373, 375, 379
Italy 238
ITT 433–435

Jackson, G. 84, 92, 96
Jamaica 17, 318, 466
  bauxite and aluminum industries 17, 322, 323–327, 337
  Fair Trading Commission 329
  government policy 113, 329, 336
  internet companies 329
  Jamaica Public Service Company 332, 333
  National Bauxite Commission 325
  negotiations with multinational firms 322–323, 323–324, 326–327, 327–332, 332–334, 335
  obsolescence of bargains 324–327, 329–332, 334–335
  Office of Utilities Regulation 331, 333
  performance requirements 333, 336
  privatization 323, 328, 332, 336, 337
  tax incentives 323, 325
Japan 86, 179, 229, 391
  automobile industry 278
  banking sector 86, 97
  infant industry encouragment 390
  kanban system 231, 238
  Keidanren 353
Javorcik, B. S. 407
Jenkins, Barbara 256, 276
Jensen, Camilla 11, 84, 121–*140*, 471
Jiang Zemin 387
John, K. 84
joint ventures 131, 133, 221, 242, 246, 387, 392
Jones, Jeffrey 203
Jones, Leroy P. 179

Kaiser Aluminum 327
Kapoor, Ashok 31, 45, 46
Kashyap, S. P. 237
Katz, J. 397, 398
Kaufman, D. 409
Kazakhstan 70
Keillor, Bruce D. 267
Kekic, L. 65
Keller, C. 417
Kennecott 256
Kenya, tea industry 230
Kim, H.-K. 89
Kim, S. H. 412
Kindleberger, Charles 27, 28, 30, 39–41, 46
King, Peter 331
King, T. 404
Kirton, J. 364, 377

knowledge 107, 236, 263, 277
Kobrin, Stephen 13, 35, 256, 309, 471,
    472
  conflict resolution 43, 260, 364
  obsolescing bargain model 37, 253,
    255, 257, 276
Kogan, Joe 455
Kolodko, G. W. 405
Kopp, R. 157
Korea 12, 62, 173, 187, 229, 243, 392
  business–government relations 173,
    177–179, 188, 190
  constitutionalist model of
    government policy 180, 181,
    187, 188
  cultural industries 175–177
  Cultural Industry Bureau 184, 188
  film industry 173–175, 189
  government budget allocation to
    culture and the arts 183, 188
  industrial policy 176, 182, 188, 190
  laws regulating cultural industries
    183, 184, 188, 189, 190
  mercantilist model of government
    policy 180, 181
  Ministry of Culture and Tourism
    175, 188
  paternalist model of government
    policy 180, 181, 187, 189
  regulation and subsidization of
    cultural industries 184, 188
Kornai, J. 405
Kostova, Tatiana 259, 264
Kraakman, Reinier 88, 92, 94
Kraar, L. 173
Kraay, A. 409
Kravis, Irving B. 241
Kroszner, R. S. 410
Krugman, Paul 261
Kudina, A. 369
Kyoto Protocol 151, 152, 155, 157,
    161, 163–164, 165
  ratification of 163, 166

labor force 243, 244
labor policy 67, 113, 235–236, 405,
    406
laissez-faire model of government
    policy 180, 181, 187
Lall, S. 109

Lalor, Gerald 331
Lansbury, M. 65
Larson, R. 409
Latin America 412, 432
Latvia 123, 138
law, business 411
law, international 196, 197, 215, 327,
    425
Learmont, S. 97
Leblanc, Richard W. 96
Lecraw, Donald J. 293, 294, 318
Lee Kuan Yew 387
legal institutions 410–412
legal systems 65, 67, 93, 129, 300, 310
legitimacy 33, 47, 465
  of the multinational firm 9–10, 13,
    258–259, 266, 268, 472
Lensink, R. 398, 410
Lenway, Stefanie 14–15, 16, 253, 258,
    309, 311, 467
Levitt, Arthur 86
Levrau, A. 93
Levy, D. L. 157
Li, Zhaoxi 90
liability of foreignness 254, 259, 264,
    267
liberalization, political 409
Liberia 436
Liebeskind, Julia Porter 265
Lilienthal, David 29
Lin, T. C. 416
Lindblom, C. E. 405
Lipsey, R. G. 414
Lipsey, Robert E. 241
Lithuania 123, 137, 138
Littlejohns, Michael 199
Litvak, Alan 46
Lo, L. N. K. 416
Loayza, N. 404–407
Lott, Trent 448
Loubsser, Jan 289
Loviscek, A. 409
Lucas, Laurie A. 347
Luo, Yadong 16–17, 254, 264,
    467, 471

Macklin, Audrey 202, 203, 206, 207,
    208–209, 215
macroeconomic policy 235, 239–241,
    246, 288, 401, 403, 413

Maher, M. 94
Mahini, Amir 343, 351
Malaysia, palm oil industry 230
Malik, K. 416
Mallya, T. J. S. 122, 141, 142
managers 88, 97
Manley, Michael 324, 325, 326
Manley, Norman 324
manufacturing 10, 136, 142, 256
  modular 229, 231
March, J. 6
markets 35, 64, 121, 168, 404, 406
  efficient 169, 223, 258–259, 400,
    401, 402
  failure of 168, 169, 223
markets, emerging 278, 294, 295,
  395–419, 467, 471
  firms in 258, 293, 417
  foreign direct investment in 13–14,
    18–21
  institutions and 401
Marks and Spencer 234
Markusen, J. R. 408
Marshall Plan 424
Martin, Paul 369
Martin, Randolph 200, 201, 202, 206
Matalon, Mayer 326, 328
Mathis, J. 410
Mauritius 242
McCahery, J. A. 92, 94
McCarthy, Irene N. 356
McIntyre, Alister 326, 328
Meldrum, D. H. 397
mercantilist model of government
  policy 180, 181
Merton, Robert 27
metanational firm 114, 258
Mexico 239, 257, 355
  banking sector 15, *283–284*
  maquilas 238, 280, 470
  North American Free Trade
    Agreement 364, 367, 368, 379
  Tequila Crisis *283*
Meyer, Klaus 11, 63, 64, 65, 471
micro-enterprises 222–239
Miller, Danny 262
Miller, Stewart 264
Minor, M. S. 319
Minow, Nell 84, 86, 96
Moldova 123

Molot, Maureen Appel 266, 267
Monks, Robert A. G. 84, 86, 96
Montiel, P. 404–407
Moran, Theodore H. 46, 255, 256, 276
Morisset, J. 142
Moskowitz, K. 180
Mozambique 444–445
Muchlinski, Peter T. 197, 198, 199
Mudambi, R. 52, 122
Mudd, S. 410
Muller, B. 164
Muller, Edward 449
Muller, Ronald E. 385–386
multilateralism 363–376, 366, 377, 379
multinational firm 28, 32–34, 37,
  150–153, 193–216, 254, 363–376
  actors in international politics 196,
    197, 198, 199, 205, 208, 210
  arguments against 40, 46
  bargaining and 265, 307
  competitive pressures among 61
  decision making 55, 59–61
  and environmental NGOs 150
  goals of 33, 255, 258–259,
    267, 393
  and host countries 222, 243,
    260–261, 263–264, 280
  influence on public policy 358, 359
  power of 44, 234
  regional 18–19, 363
  regional activity 364–365, 370,
    372, 378
  and regional integration 311, *373*,
    377, 378
  and regulation 293, 343, 357
  resource-based view 262
  social engagement 113, 115, 259,
    311, 312, 313
  stakes involved 43–45, 279
  suspicion of 105, 110
Munich Reinsurance 149
Munoz, George 450, 457
Murinde, V. 398
Murrell, P. 122
Murtha, Thomas P. 258, 309, 311
mutual recognition 344, 346

Narula, R. 62, 123, 125
nation-state 41, 108–109, 115, 195,
  197, 198

national treatment 83, 266, 304, 310,
    346, 347, 356
  and foreign direct investment 407,
    411, 458
nationalism 46, 389
nationalization 36, 256, *285*, 384, 428
  and the obsolescing bargain model
    253, 255, 256
Navarra, P. 52, 122
N'Diaye, S. 409
Nehrt, Lee 45
New Institutional Economics 5
New York, greenhouse gas emission
    legislation 162
New York Stock Exchange 97
NGOs 109–112, 198, 266, 355, 359
  and human rights 112, 195, 199, 200
  and multinational firms 150, 151,
    169
  role of 115, 364
Ng Pock Too 387
  and Talisman 204, 211
Nguyen, H. V. 122, 141
Nicaragua 442
Nikifouruk, Andrew 214
Nord, R. 410
North, D. C. 9, 52, 121, 127, 399, 400
North American Free Trade Agreement
    266, 356, 363, 367, 374
  interdependence of trade and FDI 367

obsolescing bargain 7, 14–18, 36–37,
    47, 253, *271*, 334–335, 466
  and extractive industries 17
  in Jamaica 324–327, 329–332,
    334–335
  and negotiations 317–338
  Vernon on 334, 337, 465
obsolescing bargain model 254–257,
    267, *270–271*
  bargaining power 36, 255, 278
  Behrman on 127, 253, 255, 256
  Brewer on 253, 255
  expropriation and 253, 336
  Grosse on 255, 256, 257
  Kobrin on 37, 253, 255, 257, 276
  nationalization and 253, 255, 256
  and sovereignty 30, 37–39
  Vernon on 253, 254, 276, 317
OECD 63, 110

Oetzel, J. M. 398
offshore sourcing of production
    470–471
oil industry 15, 202–203, 204,
    284–288
  nationalizations *285*, *285*
Okimoto, Daniel I. 179
Olds, K. 91
Olive, David 204
Oliver, C. 5
Olsen, J. 6, 194
Oman, C. 142
O'Neill, K. 157
opportunity, equality of 59, 415–417
Orr, D. 408
outworkers 224, 234, 237
Overseas Private Investment
    Corporation 327, 337, 428, 431,
    432, 455
  and Indonesia 447, 448, 450, 452
Owens, J. 142
ownership 88, 254, 257, 469
  transfer to the host country 64, 221,
    222, 410
Oxfam 348
Oxley, J. E. 122

Pain, N. 65
Paine, Lynne Sharp 352
Pakko, M. R. 414
Park, Wijin 12–13
Parker, D. 411
Parsons, Talcott 289
patents 347
paternalist model of government policy
    180, 181, 187, 189
path dependencies 96, 121, 127
Paulwell, Phillip 329, 330, 331
Pearce, Bob 60
Pederson, Torben 264
Peng, M. W. 122, 134
performance requirements 137, 138,
    246–247, 333, 336, 469
Perlez, Jane 194
Perlmutter, Howard 31
personality, legal 196–197
Peru 227, 231, 435
  expropriation 426
Pew Center on Global Climate Change
    151, 157

Pfizer 18, 343, 344, 348–351, 355, 471
  strategies for strengthening IP laws
    350, 351–352, 352–355
pharmaceuticals industry 18, 345, 349
Phelan, S. E. 55
Philippines 241, 355
Pirnia, N. 142
Pisani-Ferry, J. 404
Pisano, Gary 262
Point Carbon 157
Poland 70, 127, *138*, 405, 406
  incentive schemes 138, 141, 143
policymaking, public 354, 355
political bargaining model 14–15,
    253–*271*, 467
  bargaining outcome 266–267
  constraints 265–266
  details of 257–268
  goals 257–262
  resources 262–265
  stakes 257–262
political economy, international 363
political science 6, 43
politicians 135
politics, international, private actors in
    196–200
Polk, A. 157
Porter, M. E. 177, 179, 261
Porter, Tony 198
Posner, Richard 457, 458
Post, James 466
poverty 154, 219, 229, 416
Powell, W. 4
power 44, 45, 107, 108, 114, 115, 379
Poynter, T. A. 293
Prahalad, C. K. 43
Pratt, Edmund 344, 348, 350, 351, 355
Prebisch, Raul *285*
prestige 40
Preston, Lee 9–10, 81, 466, 471
privatization 64, 83, 89, 121, 332, 388
  in central and eastern Europe 65,
    122, 128, 131–135, 134
  in Jamaica 17, 323, 328, 332, 336,
    337
property rights 59, 262, 407–408
protection 239, 240, 247, *287*
protests 115, 268, *286*
Prototype Carbon Fund 166
Prowse, S. 94

public authority 196, 197–198
public goods 109
public opinion 134
public–private partnerships 13
Puffer, Sheila M. 134
putting-out system 224, 234, 237

Quayle, Dan 445
Quinn, Lawrence Richter 345, 358

Racanatini, F. 412
Ramagopal, K. 267
Ramamurti, Ravi 18, 288, 471
  bilateral and multilateral agreements
    266, 276, 317, 321
Ramirez, A. 416
Ranis, G. 416
Ravaillion, M. 417
Reed, John 97
regional economic determinism
    367–370
regional integration 242, 377, 378
regionalization 364, 368, 369,
    376–378
regional organizations 3, 19, 108, 198
regional trade agreements 364,
    365–367, 376, 378, 380
regulation 152, 177, 178, 180, 182,
    288, 406
  enforcement procedures 400
  and global warming 150, 152,
    167–168
  heterogeneity of 344–345
  homogeneity of 345–346
  legislation 125, *126*, 293
regulatory policy 133, 293
Reinhardt, F. 157
Reinhart, C. M. 404
Reinhart, N. 157
Remmers, Lee 46
repatriation rules 66, 125, 393
reputational risk 10, 115
responsibility 110, 196
  of multinational firms 33, 47, 199, 208
  social 13, 94, 98, 111, 112, 135
Revere 327, 337
Reynolds Metals 327
Richman, Barry 45
risk, climate-driven 150
risk, commercial 398

risk, political 35–36, 122, 205, 384,
        393, 397
    insurance 455
    responses to 44, 398
    theory of 47, 170
risk, reputational 10, 115
Roath, A. S. 415
Robinson, Joan 223
Robinson, Richard D. 27, 30, 31, 36
    national interests 33, 38, 44, 47, 275,
        289, 465
    political vulnerability 34–35
Robock, Stefan 19–20, 35, 43
Rodriguez, Peter 260
Rodrik, D. 400
Roe, M. 94, 96
Romania 70, 123, 138
Rondinelli, Dennis 20, 47, 59
Root, Franklin 28, 30, 35, 44, 398, 419
Rosenau, James N. 195
Rosenzweig, P. M. 298
royalty remittances 393
Rugman, A. M. 5, 18–19, 43, 60, 363,
        376, 471
rule-setting 177, 410–412
Russia 70, 73, 125, 130, 166
    barriers to investment 127, *130–131*
    corruption 127, 135
    economic development 82, 123
    informal networks 128, 134
    ratification of the Kyoto Protocol 166
    state control of economic activity 82
Ryle, John 201, 206, 207, 211

safety nets 59, 223, 224, 236, 417
Sakong, Il 179
Sanchez-Robles, B. 408
Santoro, Michael A. 352
Santos, José 258
Santos-Paulino, A. U. 413
Sarbanes–Oxley Act 98
Sass, M. 65
Sauter-Sachs, Sybille 466
Savastano, M. A. 404
Schelling, Thomas C. 179
Scherer, Michael 204
Schlesinger, Arthur, Jr. 435
Schmid, F. 92, 93, 96
Schollhammer, Hans 29
Schoonmaker, Sara 287

Schuler, Doug 14–15, 16, *253–271*, 467
Seligson, M. A. 411
Senbet, Lamma 84
September 11, 2001 61, 367, 373, 379
service industries 370, 373, 470, 471
Sethi, D. 55
Shama, A. 397
Shamsie, Jamal 262
Shapiro, Daniel 400
shareholder activism 150, 151
shareowners 85, 88, 98, 100–101
Sharpe, Kenneth E. 257, 276
Shaver, J. Myles 264
Shell 113, 116
Sherwood, R. M. 411
Shirley, Gordon 332, 333
Shleifer, A. 84, 91
shocks, external 61, 325, 403, 404, 409,
        414
Shuen, Amy 262
Sicular, T. 406
Sierra Leone 238
Simmons, Kenneth 43
Simons, Penelope 202, 203, 206, 207,
        208–209, 215
Singapore 60, 62, 229, 241, 359, 387
Singh, Harbir 469
Singh, J. V. 298
Slovakia 70
Slovenia 123, 125
smallholder outgrower scheme
        230–231
Smidkova, K. 65
Smith, D. N. 45
social capital 63, 416
social responsibility 13, 94, 98, 112,
        135
social sciences 4–5, 289, 465
socialist countries, and foreign direct
        investment 386–387
Söderling, L. 403
Sokil, S. 404
Soloway, J. 364, 377
Soskice, D. 6, 87, 96, 466
South, S. G. 157
South Africa 110–111
Southern Electric 333
sovereignty 38, 107, 108–109, 110,
        115, 195, 197, 198, 199
    and commitments to investors 423

erosion of 107
and foreign direct investment 393
individual 109
and the obsolescing bargain model
30, 37–39
and regionalization 380
Special Economic Zones 137–141, 142,
144, 242–246
Spiegel, M. M. 416
stability
economic 178, 246, 404, 413
financial 97
political 73, 247, 417
regulatory 309
stakeholders 10, 92, 132, 254, 259, 472
multiple 132, 135, 254
rights and roles of 98
Stanwick, P. A. and S. D. Stanwick 93
Stark, D. 121, 128, 134
state control of economic activity 82,
133, 144
states, rivalry among 105–116
Steiner, George A. 178, 179
Stern, Paula 358
Stewart, F. 416
Stigler, G. 169
Stiglitz, J. 121
Stobaugh, Robert 45
stock exchanges 89
Stone, M. R. 401–402
Stopford, John 10, 30, 43, 45, 276, 294,
471
cooperation 254, 310
foreign direct investment 293
triangular diplomacy 7, 363, 466
Stotsky, J. 413
Strange, S. 7, 10, 105, 107, 198, 276,
363, 466
Streeten, Paul 13–14
Subramanian, A. 400
subsidies 135–143, 177, 180, 182, 392,
394, 404, 466
and global warming 156, 169
and trust 469
Sudan 13, 193–216
civil war in 200–202, 207, 210, 211,
212
human rights violations 203, 206–207
militias 202, 207
oil 201, 202–203, 205–206

Sugiyama, T. 164
Sullivan Principles 111
Summers, Larry 448, 449
Suss, E. 413
Svetličič, M. 123
Swaan, W. 128
Swedish National Board of Trade 165
Swill Reinsurance 149
Swinnen, J. F. M. 406

Taiwan 62
Takarick, S. 413
Talisman 13, 193–216
complicity 210–213
Corporate Social Responsibility
Group 210, 213
divestment campaign 204, 216
experience in Sudan 203–205
and human rights 205–208
response to criticism 213–214
responsibilities 208, 213, 216
Tamura, R. 416
Tapscott, D. 410
tax 6, 245, 404
policy 67, 245, 277
systems 73, 403
technology cycles 282
technology transfer 391–392, 414,
415
Teece, D. 5, 262
telecommunications 63, 67, 73, 129,
153, 467
Tendler, Judith 226, 239
Tenev, S. 90, 91
Teng, Bing-Sheng 469
Tennessee Valley Authority 388
terrorism 61, 203, 424, 460
Thadden, E.-L. von 90
Thailand, intellectual property
protection 355
Tian, G. L. 134
Tihanyi, L. 415
Toman, A. 157
trade policy 239, 240, 241, 413
training 236, 246, 406
transaction cost economics 5, 254, 265,
337, 379, 466
transactional relations 336–338, 337
transaction costs 63, 275, 310, 346
and institutions 52, 75, 128, 264

Transatlantic Business Dialog 358
transnational arrangements 152, 162
transnational companies 33, 114, 246;
    see also multinational firms
transparency 47, 67, 73, 321, 409
    and incentive schemes 136, 143
    in regulatory systems 300, 303, 411
Trebbi, F. 400
Trevino, L. J. 65
Triad of economic regions 367–370,
    368, 378
triangular diplomacy 107, 115, 363
Tripartite Coalition 353, 354
TRIPS agreement 261, 307, 344, 347
trust 469–470
Turkey 452–453, 460
two-tiered board system 89, 97–98

Uhlenbruck, K. 129, 133, 260
UK 151, 347
Ukraine 70, 73, 123, 125
    incentive schemes 141
Ulen, T. S. 408
umbrella companies 312, 313
uncertainties 153, 294, 310, 394, 397
unemployment 229
United Fruit Company 453
United Nations 63, 108, 109, *285*, 368
    code of conduct of multinational
        enterprises 105, 110, 213
    Global Compact 113, 209
    Norms on the Responsibilities of
        Transnational Corporations 210
    Office for the Coordination of
        Humanitarian Efforts 202
    Social and Economic Council 210
    Special Rapporteurs 206, 207, 211,
        212
    UNCTAD 142, 317, 321, 336, 407
    UNDP 397
    UNESCAP 415
US 39–41, 114, 152, 429–435, 456–458
    Advocacy Center 439, 440, 441, 456
    African Growth and Opportunity Act
        442
    Alien Tort Claims Act 194–195, 216
    banking sector 15, *284*
    bilateral agreements 152, 163, 364,
        444–445, 458
    and Brazil 106
    bureaucracy 429–435

campaign contributions 442, 454
and Chiquita Brands 453–455
Climate VISION program 163
Commercial Service 440
Congress 430, 438
Department of Commerce 430, 432,
    438, 439, 440, 447, 448, 449
Department of Energy 163
and Egypt 431, 446
embassy support for US business
    abroad 446–453
Environmental Protection Agency 163
Export–Import Bank 431, 447, 449
Foreign and US Commercial Services
    440–441
Foreign Corrupt Practices Act 440
foreign policy 431, 437, 438, 454, 456
foreign policy interests 430, 433, 434,
    435, 456, 459
Generalized System of Preferences
    428, 442, 450
Gonzalez Amendment 425, 427
and greenhouse gas emissions 152,
    162–163
Helms–Gonzalez Amendment 442,
    450
Hickenlooper Amendment 425–427,
    442
and Indonesia 452
Intellectual Property Committee 353,
    354
and intellectual property law 350
International Petroleum Corporation
    426
leverage over trading partners 350,
    355–356, 359
military strength 369
multinational firms 39–41
National Evnironmental Policy Acts
    162
oil 374–375, *375*, 376, *376*
Omnibus Trade and Competitiveness
    Act 355, 357
patent laws 347
policies on supporting US business
    abroad 421–461, 424–437,
    439–443, 456–459, 459–461
and regional integration 373
regional trade 366
role in regulatory convergence 357
role in world economy 350, 374

Savings and Loan crisis *284*
security 367, 374–376, 379
State Deparment 431, 432–433, 434, 437, 438
Sugar Act 425
and Talisman 204
Trade Law 428
Treasury 430, 431, 432, 438, 448
and Turkey 452–453
US Trade Representative 355
Voluntary Export Restraints 278
war on terrorism 424, 460, 461
White House support of US business abroad 443, 444
Useem, Michael 99

Vachani, Sushil 255, 256–257, 276
valuation 263–264, 266
values 405, 458–459
Van den Berghe, L. 93, 96
Verbeke, Alain 60, 357, 377
  regional integration 365, 376, 378
Vernon, Raymond 27, 28, 30, 268, 289, 321, 336, 470
  obsolescing bargain 7, 14, 36–37, 334, 337, 465
  obsolescing bargain model 253, 254, 276, 317
  values 458–459
Vickers, 129
Vietnam 141
Vishny, R. W. 84, 91
Vives, X. 89, 92
Vogel, David 344, 359
vulnerability, political 34–35

Wagle, S. 416
Wal-Mart 370
Walter, Ingo 41, 43, 45, 318
war on terrorism 460, 461
weather, extreme 150, 159–160
Webb, D. 411
Weder, B. 412
Weidenbaum, Murray L. 178
Weiss, C. 412
Wells, Louis 20–21, 37, 317, 322, 336
  bargaining relationship 45, 276, 294, 318
Werner, R. 136, 138, *138*, 141, 142
Wesson, T. 60
Westney, E. 5

Westphalia, Treaty of 195, 197, 198
Williams, Jody 107
Williamson, J. 414
Williamson, Oliver 5, 36, 337, 399
Williamson, Peter J. 258
Winiecki, J. 405
Wint, Alvin 17–18, 466, 471
Wisner, Frank 446–447
Wood, D. J. 259
World Bank 90, 115, 247, 398, 400, 404, 405, 406
  International Center for the Settlement of Investment Disputes 318, 319
  Prototype Carbon Fund 151, 166
World Business Council for Sustainable Development 157
World Development Movement 112
World Economic Forum 417
World Intellectual Property Organization 347, 356–357, 359
World Investment Report 295
World Resources Institute 151
World Trade Organization 82, 165, 198, 266, 357, 377
  Chiquita Brands 454
  Doha Round 365
  and foreign direct investment 458
  future of 364
  protests 109
  and regional integration 366
  rules and procedures 115, 164
  TRIPS agreement 18
World Wildlife Fund 151
Wright, M. S. 134
Wymeersch, E. 88

Xiao, J. 417

Yarrow, George 129
Yeung, H. W. 91

Zaheer, Srilata 259, 264
Zenner, M. 398
Zhang, C. 90, 91
Zhang, X. 409
Zhao, J. H. 412
Zimbabwe 240
Zingales, Luigi 84
Zoido-Lobaton, P. 409
Zurawicki, L. 411